NOTABLE
LATINO AMERICANS

NOTABLE
LATINO AMERICANS

A Biographical Dictionary

MATT S. MEIER
with Conchita Franco Serri and Richard A. Garcia

Greenwood Press
Westport, Connecticut • London

Library of Congress Cataloging-in-Publication Data

Meier, Matt S.
  Notable Latino Americans : a biographical dictionary / Matt S.
Meier ; with Conchita Franco Serri and Richard A. Garcia.
    p.   cm.
  Includes bibliographical references and index.
  ISBN 0–313–29105–5 (alk. paper)
    1. Hispanic Americans—Biography—Dictionaries. I. Franco Serri,
Conchita. II. Garcia, Richard A., 1941– . III. Title.
E184.S75M35   1997
920'.009268—dc20   96–27392

British Library Cataloguing in Publication Data is available.

Library of Congress Catalog Card Number: 96–27392
ISBN: 0–313–29105–5

First published in 1997

Greenwood Press, 88 Post Road West, Westport, CT 06881
An imprint of Greenwood Publishing Group, Inc.

Printed in the United States of America

The paper used in this book complies with the
Permanent Paper Standard issued by the National
Information Standards Organization (Z39.48–1984).

10 9 8 7 6 5 4 3 2 1

Cover photos courtesy of Lincoln Díaz-Balart, Henry B. González, and Vilma S.
Martínez.

Contents

Contents

Introduction

This book focuses on U.S. Latinos and Latinas, men and women who have made important contributions to American society who are citizens of the United States or who have spent appreciable portions of their lives in this country. The definition of these people is largely cultural, rather than strictly territorial or political. They are Americans with vigorous Latin cultural roots. In this work, in addition to being referred to by specific group names, they may be called U.S. Latinos and sometimes simply Latinos. However, elsewhere the reader may find authors referring to them as Hispanic Americans or Latin Americans, because those terms can refer to persons of Spanish cultural background in any country of the western hemisphere. For the sake of clarity we have reserved those two designations for the people of Mexico, Central America, and South America.

Between the 1980 and 1990 censuses the numbers of U.S. Latinos increased by more than 50 percent, and today they number more than 22 million persons. In a total U.S. population of approximately 250 million there are more than 13 million Mexican Americans, at least 2.5 million Puerto Ricans on the mainland, slightly more than 1 million Cuban Americans, and nearly 6 million other Latinos from Central America, South America, the Caribbean, and Spain. By the end of the 20th century Latinos may form the largest single minority group in the United States.

Now, as we prepare to enter the 21st century, U.S. Latinos continue to gain rapidly increasing cultural and political importance within our national ethnic mosaic. They live in all 50 states and are visible at every level of our society. They share many cultural commonalities, yet each subgroup is quite distinct. The special characteristics of each subgroup's members have been determined by their particular history, their numbers, and the length of time they have been in the United States. Moreover, within each group there exists a considerable range in race and class, in cultural background, in educational attainment, in occupational and professional achievement, and in Spanish language familiarity and use. Diversity is the norm. Each group, each person, is the product of a singular and complex history.

Largely because of their discrete histories each group has a distinct geographical clustering. Cuban Americans have the densest concentration. Three-fourths of them live on the East Coast and slightly more than half are located in the Florida Greater Miami metropolitan area, which for many has become the Havana of their memories. Puerto Ricans come next in degree of population density, with approximately half living in the state of New York—the overwhelming majority of them in the New York City metropolitan area. Mexican Americans, who form the largest subgroup, continue their 19th-century pattern of location in the underpopulated reaches of the Southwest. Today more than two-thirds of them are still located in the two states of California and Texas, with heavy concentrations in large urban centers such as El Paso and Los Angeles. However, since the 1920s and especially since World War II increasing numbers have settled in the Midwest and other parts of the United States. "Other" U.S. Latinos are the least concentrated geographically, because of their diverse origins and histories and possibly also because their immigration to the United States has been the most recent. Most reside in California, Florida, New York, and Texas—states currently receiving the bulk of immigration to the United States. As these people and their offspring make new lives in America, they will play ever larger and more important roles in all aspects of society.

For a variety of reasons, most deriving from their historical experiences, the peoples of these Latino cultures have long stressed individuality and heterogeneity. As with all peoples, each individual as well as each group has had a discrete personal and historical experience. Thus each Latino American is distinct, special, and unique. From these life stories the reader may become more aware of the considerable diversity within and between the various Latino communities and may appreciate more deeply their cultural singularities.

Broadly conceived as an academic, public library, and high school research tool, this biographical dictionary of Latinos in the United States has four principal goals: to provide student researchers with basic information about each biographee, to suggest bibliographic leads for further research, to foster deeper interest in all Latino cultures and the entire U.S. Latino experience, and to present students with a variety of role models. The authors hope that these biographies may also help overcome the sometimes subtle, often negative, stereotyping of Latinos in films, on the stage, in the daily press, and even (albeit unconsciously) at times in some textbooks.

This book describes the lives of 127 U.S. Latinos who have made important contributions to American society and to the world. The biographees range widely from distinguished scientists to champion tennis players, from actors to activists, from businesswomen to political personalities, from literary luminaries to labor leaders. They have distinguished themselves in various fields of endeavor and have been recognized for their outstanding accomplishments and important legacies to society. Many of them, probably a majority, have overcome extreme odds to reach eminence. Most of them succeeded, as their life stories indicate, because of deeply held goals, strong motivation to excel in their fields of endeavor, and great self-discipline. Their lives, the experiences of these immigrants and children of immigrants, demonstrate what individuals with the desire to achieve are able to accomplish despite formidable obstacles.

These biographies stress the individuals' goals, struggles, and commitment to their ethnic communities and to the common good. However, their accomplishments have not been the result solely of individual effort. The reader will note that many of those profiled here owe much to families, friends, and communities. Mothers often appear to be the catalysts in their attainments, and education often seems to be the vehicle of their success. Most of the biographees can be taken as positive role models; all of them have lessons to teach.

In choosing the biographees the authors made a selection from contemporary and recent historical Latino figures in all important fields of human endeavor: business, government, the performing arts, fine arts, literature, education, social service, sports, and the various professions. An effort was also made to choose persons from all sections of the country. Individuals were selected because of outstanding contributions in their chosen fields based on a significant level of recognition, typically expressed in honors, awards, and prizes. Consideration was also given to the biographees' likely appeal to high school students and to their potential as role models.

One of the authors' most difficult tasks was to decide whom to include and whom to leave out because of space limitations. Unfortunately, the roster could not include every person worthy of inclusion. No work of this scope could. Every inclusion raised the likelihood that somebody else would have to be omitted. Painful choices had to be made; they were made neither arbitrarily nor capriciously. Confronted with the impossibility of including all important U.S. Latinos within the limitations of this book, the authors finally recognized the hopelessness of the task, accepted it, and went ahead with their research and writing.

The names of many men and women included in the book will be recognized immediately; others may be less familiar to the reader. About one-third of the biographees have not appeared in any other published work. Recognizing that the roles of Latino women in the community and the larger society have often been unacknowledged and underrated, the authors made a conscious effort to seek out notable Latinas for inclusion in this volume. More than one-third of the biographees are women.

Not all the information on which these biographies are based is readily accessible. In the case of some biographees published materials were supplemented with personal oral and written interviews. However, the further reading section offered at the end of each biography lists sources that are most readily available and helpful to student researchers who wish to learn more about the individual. These sources, although not exhaustive, will enable students to become informed in greater detail about the profiled individuals and in turn may lead to further information on the biographee. They will also help students understand better how each individual fits historically into the overall Latino experience and into life in the United States.

A broad, agreed-on format for the biographies was developed for the book, but identical information for each entry was viewed as a broad goal rather than a straightjacket. A serious concern was that the individual biographies be detailed enough to be meaningful. The 127 biographies are arranged alphabetically and are followed by two appendices: one listing the biographees by ethnic subgroups, and one listing them by professional fields. The biographees are classified under those rubrics in which they have been most prominent; an individual may appear under more than one category. There is also a general subject index covering broader aspects of the Latino experience and leading to additional information on biographees who are referred to in entries other than their own. The index and the ethnic group and occupation appendices make it easy for the user to find an appropriate person. Cross-references to other biographees in this work are indicated in boldface.

This book has been both a group and an individual effort. The authors of the biographies are all specialists in Latino studies and therefore bring a lifetime of familiarity and experience to their work. Their expertise has made possible a solid, professional job in writing the biographies and has also enabled them to place the biographees within the context of their times.

Colleagues at our universities and at other institutions helped shape our work and deserve acknowledgement. We are also deeply indebted to librarians at our home institutions and elsewhere. For their various helpful contributions, Aimee Algier-Baxter, Carey Allen, Cindy Bradley,

Margo Gutiérrez, Julie Hurant, Francisco Jiménez, Linda Jocewicz, and Christine Marín merit special mention. Greenwood senior editor Barbara Rader is deserving of our sincere thanks for her strong backing, constant encouragement, and frequent help during the long period of gestation. Above all, our thanks to our families for their patience and support.

We dedicate this book to young Latinas and Latinos of the United States with the hope that some day they may see their biographies in a similar work.

Luis W. Alvarez

(1911–1988)

Spanish American Physicist, Inventor

Latino American physicist Luis W. Alvarez won the Nobel Prize in 1968. He was reared in the world of science where the central question is "Why?", not in a culture of ethnicity where the central question is "Who am I?" Alvarez always acknowledged his Spanish heritage, but because he was a third-generation American that recognition was distant and faint. It was not part of his everyday life nor of his world of science. However, he wrote, "People have sometimes been surprised that a tall, ruddy, blond should bear the name Luis Alvarez." Occasionally he encountered prejudice, even in the educated, sophisticated world of science. In 1938 when he was appointed to work on the atomic bomb in Los Alamos, New Mexico, he faced this bias. Some of his neighbors at Los Alamos, hearing that an "Alvarez" had been assigned to their apartment complex, made a complaint. After they met Luis the complaint was dropped.

Luis Alvarez was born in San Francisco on 13 June 1911 and died across the bay in Berkeley in 1988. His grandfather, who was born in northern Spain, had moved to Cuba in his youth and in the 1880s came to California. Here he obtained an education. Later he graduated from Cooper Medical College in San Francisco and married. His wife gave birth to a son, Walter (who later became Luis's father), just before they moved to Hawaii when Luis's grandfather became a government physician. In 1900, shortly after the American takeover of Hawaii, the Alvarez family returned to San Francisco, where Walter grew up, attended school, and later also graduated from Cooper Medical College.

In 1907 Walter married and subsequently took a position as a physician with a copper mining company at Cananea in the north Mexican border state of Sonora. After three years in Mexico the Alvarez family returned to San Francisco where Luis was born. Although his father's scientific world permeated his daily existence, in his early years Luis saw little of his workaholic father. Saturday was a special day for him because he accompanied his father to the Hooper Foundation and watched him conduct medical research. Although Luis's father was on his way to becoming a famous physician and medical researcher, Luis was more attracted to the scientific equipment used in the laboratory than to the research. Within a short time Luis could operate all the electrical equipment in his father's lab and even construct circuits.

This interest in scientific equipment and inventing had been evident even earlier when his father had taken him to the 1915 San Francisco Pan-American Exposition, where the young child was attracted to the Machinery Hall exhibits. At home his mother, who had a background in elementary school education, attended to the educational and intellectual development of Luis and his three siblings. His parents provided family closeness through church activities and Sunday drives, as well as camping in the California countryside. These family doings provided young Luis with a stable and nurturing environment secure in the company of both his mother and father. Because his home life provided an impetus to scientific curiosity as well as an atmosphere of love and a positive sense of identity, Luis was able to focus on his passion for technology and science.

Luis Alvarez combined two important occupational talents throughout his life: an attempt to push the limits of science by constant questioning, his intuitiveness, and a strong belief in himself; and a deep sense of obligation toward science and his colleagues. Essentially he believed in science not merely as employment but as a "calling," and he believed in teamwork just as much as in individual research. In addition, Alvarez had an amazing ability to recall any scientific article pertaining to his field that he had ever read and the name of its author as well. Consequently he seemed to be a veritable "walking card catalogue" to colleagues.

During his long career, Dr. Alvarez held more than 40 individual patents. However, his scientific prominence came largely from inventions developed as part of technical teams working for the government. During World War II he was a group leader in the atomic bomb project at Los Alamos, New Mexico, and was influential in developing ground-controlled approach radar, a radar anti-aircraft system, the radar bombsight named VIXEN, airborne radar for detecting enemy submarines, and many other important technological inventions and programs. After the war he played a vital part in conceptualizing and devising the linear accelerator. His outstanding contribution to science was the development of a range of technologies for the construction of a "bubble chamber" to detect elementary subatomic particles and compile data on them. Alvarez's discoveries in the "bubble chamber" led to a revolution in ideas about the ultimate nature of matter. For his work on the "bubble chamber" he received the Nobel Prize in physics in 1968.

If Alvarez found the public openness and clarity of science appealing, he also found confusion and fragmentation in daily living. There were private silences in his life. In 1957 he divorced his first wife after 21 years of marriage, a marriage held together largely by an agreement that they would not divorce until their two children (Walter and Jean) were grown. There was a silence about his passion for his new wife, former student Jan Landis, who was 26 years old when he was 46. He married her on 28 December 1958. There was also a virtual silence about his Latino background, although he did mention it in his autobiography, *Alvarez: Adventures of a Physicist* (1987).

Luis Alvarez preferred to live on the plane of science in a world of reason. In this world his new wife accompanied him, understood him, and cherished him. More than that, within this scientific world Alvarez, a plainspoken man devoid of pretensions and boasting a no-nonsense style but also a man of strongly idiosyncratic views about family, was able to demonstrate his love for the young sons from his two marriages.

At age 66 Luis and his older son, Walter, a geologist with a doctorate from Princeton University, began to explore new fields of scientific research. After recommending Walter for a teaching position at the University of California, Berkeley, where he taught, Luis Alvarez began an almost totally new scientific career by applying his expertise in nuclear physics to paleomagnetic and structural geology, his son's area of expertise. Studying an iridium layer in the earth's crust with a team of scientists, in 1980 Luis and Walter electrified the scientific community with their theory that dinosaurs disappeared 66 million years ago because an asteroid 10 kilometers wide had crashed into the earth and probably caused a "nuclear winter" effect at the end of the cretaceous period. Although this theory is still being debated today, many scientists accept its plausibility.

Engaging in scientific "detective work," Luis and his son used cosmic radiation from outer space to x-ray Chephren's pyramid in Egypt in a search for hidden chambers. In 1966 Luis Alvarez examined the Abraham Zapruder film that the Warren Commission believed to be of primary importance in the investigation of the 1963 assassination of President John Kennedy. Using principles of physics and Newtonian laws, Alvarez theorized that there had been three shots but only one gunman. The first shot, he argued, missed; the second hit Kennedy's throat; and the third hit the back of his head, snapping it backwards because (according to the law of conservation of momentum and energy) the force of the "incoming bullet," wrote Alvarez in his report to the *American Journal of Physics*, "in effect activates a small rocket engine . . . that ejects its high-speed fuel in the forward direction," thus driving Kennedy's head backwards because of the recoiling action. This recoil led to the belief that there was another gunman, but Alvarez argued that there was only one gunman and a "trick" of physics.

These experiments and scientific excursions were only "intellectual dessert" in a life devoted to exact science during which Alvarez won not only the Nobel Prize but also the U.S. Medal of Merit, the Collier Trophy of the National Aeronautical Association, and countless other awards. During his retirement years in the 1980s Luis Alvarez finally turned to introspection as he wrote his autobiography. In his self-contemplation, which focused basically on his public life, he remained skeptical about God, awed by the progress in scientific discoveries, fearful of nuclear war, and sure that communication was at the heart of a successful marriage. Still a believer in pure science, he was absolutely certain that in life there was nothing more rewarding than the never-ending adventure of asking and teaching about the scientific "whys" of life and nature.

Luis Alvarez died in September 1988, 10 years after his retirement from the University of California at Berkeley and 20 years after his Nobel award.

Further Reading

Alvarez, Luis W. *Alvarez: Adventures of a Physicist*. New York: Basic Books, 1987.
Barnes-Svamey, Patricia. "Luis and Walter Alvarez." *Ad Astra* 3:6 (July–August 1991): 53.
Byrne, G. "A Message from Alvarez." *Science* 240 (June 1988): 1411.
Codye, Cirinn. *Luis Alvarez*. New York: Raintree Publishers, 1990.
Galbraith, William. "A Legendary Physicist." *New Scientist* 118:1618 (June 1988): 80–81.
Greenstein, George. "Luie's Gadgets: A Profile of Luis Alvarez." *American Scholar* 61:1 (Winter 1992): 90–98.
Hecht, Jeff. "Evolving Theories for Old Extinctions." *New Scientist* 120:1638 (November 1988): 28–30.
Moritz, Charles, ed. *Current Biography Yearbook, 1988*. New York: H. W. Wilson Co., 1988.
Trower, W. Peter, ed. *Discovering Alvarez: Selected Works of Luis W. Alvarez with Commentary by His Students and Colleagues*. Chicago: University of Chicago Press, 1988.
20th Century Supplement, Encyclopedia of World Biography. Palatine, Ill.: Jack Heraty and Associates, 1992.

REINALDO ARENAS

(1943–1990)

Cuban American Novelist, Short Story Writer, Poet, Dramatist

Reinaldo Arenas belongs to a group of writers who developed their craft in the aftermath of the 1959 Cuban revolution. He is widely recognized as one of the most important members of that set and is perhaps the best known of all Cuban exile writers. Like a majority of the refugee writers, his many works reflect an obsession with the Cuba of his memories. His writings form an important segment in avant-garde Hispanic American literature and have been translated into more than ten languages. With their theme of opposition to oppression of all kinds at all levels of society, they have struck a chord all over Latin America and have brought him international recognition. His unspoken but unmistakable view that there is no complete escape from oppression, no absolute freedom, finds a congenial climate among fellow Hispanic American writers.

Reinaldo Arenas was born in rural Cuba near the town of Holguín in the northern part of Oriente province on 16 July 1943. His father, Antonio Arenas, abandoned wife and child soon after his birth, and his mother, Oneida Fuentes, then moved in with her parents' family. Reinaldo grew up in a poor rural home, a *bohío*, which housed his mother, 11 aunts, a religious fanatic grandmother, and an ineffectual and alcoholic grandfather who during his drunken rages often threatened suicide and occasionally threatened Reinaldo with an axe. His childhood was spent in this soul-searing, poverty-stricken rural environment far from people and civilized society—also far from schools. Reinaldo was taught to read and write by his mother. When he became a teenager he and his mother moved into Holguín, where he finally entered school. At this time he began to write imaginative, somewhat surrealistic fiction.

At age 15 Reinaldo joined Gibara Mountain guerrilla forces that were fighting under the leadership of Fidel Castro against the dictatorship of President Fulgencio Batista Zaldívar. After the Castro revolt succeeded, he completed his high school studies and was awarded a scholarship to study agricultural accounting in Havana. Upon the completion of his coursework he was sent to a poultry farm in the Sierra Maestra, but he soon became unhappy with his situation and managed to return to Havana in another government program. He began to study economic planning at the University of Havana but became bored with that and in 1963 got a job in the Biblioteca Nacional José Martí as an auxiliary librarian. By this time he had come to the conclusion that what he wanted to be for the rest of his life was a writer.

Arenas began writing during his teen years; in 1964 amid the early revolutionary enthusiasm he composed his first novel, *Celestina antes del alba*, which describes the sometimes grotesque, often brutal, but always fascinating poverty of rural life in Cuba as seen through the eyes of a mentally impaired child. It received first honorable mention from the Cuban Writers Union in a national Cirilo Valverde novel contest and was published in Havana in 1967, the only one of his works published in Cuba. Meanwhile, in 1965 Arenas studied philosophy and literature at the University of Havana and in the following year completed his second novel, *El mundo alucinante*, based on the life of the famous colonial Mexican preacher, Dominican Fray Servando Teresa de Mier. It also won first honorable mention from the Writers Union.

By this time Arenas's basic theme of resistance to oppression had antagonized the Castro government, which expelled him from the university in the course of a political purge and prohibited further publication of his writings. After one year as an editor at the Cuban Book Institute (1967–1968), he served for six years as a journalist and editor for the *Gaceta de Cuba*. Meanwhile he continued to write and managed to smuggle some of his works out of Cuba for publication. Although rejected in Cuba, his writings found great favor elsewhere in Latin America, Spain, and France. In 1969 he was named by the Paris newspaper *Le Monde* as the best foreign novelist published in France that year.

In 1973 Arenas was charged with being a homosexual and with various crimes against the state because of his writings and was jailed. He escaped from his detention cell before trial and went into hiding. Three months later he was recaptured, tried, and then spent about a year in El Morro prison in Havana's harbor. From El Morro he was sent to Reparto Flores, a Cuban rehabilitation center, a sugar *central* in western Cuba where he served six months of forced labor, suffering greatly under the extremely hard work and miserable conditions. He was released in 1976 and returned to Havana. There he began rewriting the fourth novel of his five-part quasi-autobiographical series. It was *re*writing because he had written it twice before, but his manuscripts had been destroyed or lost.

Between 1976 and 1980 Arenas continued writing while he worked at various grim menial jobs. To avoid trouble with the Castro government he developed a peripatetic and picaresque life-style, moving frequently from house to hovel. At the beginning of May 1980 he was one of some 130,000 "undesirables" forced or allowed to leave from the Cuban port of Mariel. He had only the clothes on his back and a clean shirt. Arenas stayed briefly in Miami after the Mariel exodus and then moved to New York, where, except for teaching jobs, he was to spend the rest of his life writing novels and short stories.

In the United States, Arenas seemed to have little difficulty in getting temporary positions as visiting professor of Cuban literature. He taught at Miami's Florida International University in 1981, at the Center for Inter-American Relations in 1982, and at Cornell University in 1985. He also was a visiting guest lecturer at a number of other first-rate schools including Princeton, Georgetown, and Stockholm universities and the universities of Puerto Rico and Miami. He enjoyed a Cintas Foundation fellowship in 1980, a Guggenheim in 1982, and in 1988 was a Wilson Center Foundation fellow. Nevertheless, the last decade of Arenas's life was spent in more or less genteel poverty. Always missing "his" Cuba, he was never recognized as a writer in his adopted country despite the cornucopia of excellent works he wrote there. His reputation suffered partly, perhaps, because of the strident anti-Castroism and anti-communism expressed in his works. In 1988 he wrote and widely circulated a letter demanding that Castro hold a plebiscite.

Among Arenas's most important works (in addition to those already mentioned) are *El palacio de las blanquísimas mofetas* (1975), a sequel to *Celestina* that describes Cuban social and political problems in the twilight of the Batista years; and *Otra vez el mar* (1982), a political novel of poetic realism in which Arenas reaffirms his opposition to Castro and the Cuban revolution. These, and his many novels, short stories, poems, essays, and plays, are all deeply rooted in Cuban history, thinly fictionalized. His numerous short stories and articles were published in a wide variety of journals. Of the long list of works that Arenas wrote during the last ten years of his life, only one novel has a U.S. locale. *El portero* (1987), the story of a New York doorman, was a finalist for the Medici Prize in Paris in 1988 and was published in translation as *The Doorman* two years later, shortly before the author's death.

On 7 December 1990 Arenas, who had been suffering from Acquired Immune Deficiency Syndrome (AIDS) for several years, died of what may have been a suicidal drug overdose. At the time of his death he left several works, which were published posthumously. Most important was his autobiographical *Antes que anochezca* (1992), translated into English and published in the following year as *Before Night Falls*.

Further Reading

Arenas, Reinaldo. *Before Night Falls*. New York: Viking Press, 1993.

Contemporary Authors, vol. 133. Detroit: Gale Research, 1991.

Flores, Angel. *Spanish American Authors: The Twentieth Century*. New York: H. W. Wilson Co., 1992.

González Echevarría, Roberto. "Before Night Falls." *New York Times Book Review* (24 October 1993): 1.

Lomelí, Francisco, and Carl R. Shirley, eds. *Dictionary of Literary Biography*, vol. 145. Detroit: Gale Research, 1989.

Magill, Frank N., ed., *Masterpieces of Latino Literature*. New York: HarperCollins, 1994.

Roca, Ana. "A Word with Reinaldo Arenas." *Américas* 33 (September 1981): 36–38.

Ryan, Bryan, ed. *Hispanic Writers*. Detroit: Gale Research, 1991.

DESI ARNAZ

(1917–1986)

Cuban American Musician, Actor, Television Producer, Businessman

One of the most widely known Cuban Americans because of the television show he created with his wife, Lucille Ball, Desi Arnaz was an energetic, multi-talented individual who in his lifetime was a vocalist, drummer, band leader, composer, stage and screen actor, television innovator, director, and producer. Long before the TV show *I Love Lucy*, Desi Arnaz was a band leader and musician widely known in the American entertainment field, but he let his wife take the principal role in the television series. As one critic remarked, his special ability was to recognize talent and to bring that talent to its maximum expression. He was always modest and proverbially in good humor; his life of continual struggle and great financial success provided a model for other Latinos.

Desiderio Alberto Arnaz y de Acha III was born on 2 March 1917 in Oriente province in Santiago, a large town on the southeastern coast of Cuba. He was the only child in a very wealthy landed family, which owned a palatial town house, several ranches, horses, cars, speedboats, and even a small island. His father, also Desiderio Alberto, was the mayor of Santiago and a friend and supporter of the Cuban political leader Gerardo Machado; his mother, Lolita de Acha, was a beauty known for her charitable interests. Desi grew up in this privileged atmosphere, enjoying the good life that his family's wealth and position afforded.

When Machado's dictatorship ended in August 1933 with his resignation from the presidency after resisting widespread opposition and violence for two years, Desi's father, then a member of the Cuban Congress, was put into prison for having been a supporter of the tyrant. Desi, who was then attending the Colegio de Dolores in Santiago, was forced to flee with his mother to the United States. In Miami he entered St. Patrick's High School and began a very different way of life because the new Cuban government had seized all the family's property and nearly all its wealth. As a youthful refugee he took on a variety of jobs: taxi and truck driver, retail clerk, and office worker. When he was 17 years old, after his father was able to rejoin the family in Miami, he found steady employment as a guitarist and drummer in a small four-member Cuban combo.

In 1936, while playing and singing in a larger rumba band, Desi came to the attention of the reigning king of rumba at that time, the bandleader Xavier Cugat. Desi's stage presence and winning personality got him a contract as vocalist with Cugat's large, sleek orchestra. He spent a year with Cugat and then left to organize his own Latin dance band, which, benefiting from the contemporary craze for Latin American music, developed a heavy schedule playing at various nightclubs throughout the United States. When roles in George Abbot's hit Broadway musical *Too Many Girls* were being cast, Desi Arnaz was selected for one of the lead parts, that of a Cuban football player. Later, when the play was made into a motion picture by RKO Productions, he was brought to Hollywood to recreate the role for the silver screen. On the set he became acquainted with fellow actor Lucille Ball, and they were married less than a year later in November 1940.

Despite their marriage and a five-acre ranch the couple purchased in the San Fernando Valley, north of Los Angeles, Desi continued to travel around the country with his band playing in theaters and nightclubs, and his wife continued to accept roles in numerous B movies. For the next decade both worked hard at building their careers in entertainment. In the course of World War II Desi Arnaz was drafted into the U.S. army in February 1943, but because of an accident suffered during basic training he was assigned to limited service in the Medical Corps. He spent most of his army time entertaining hospitalized servicemen and received his discharge in November 1945. Then it was back to traveling with his band again. During the second half of the 1940s he also did a stint as musical director of a popular radio show and had parts in a number of Hollywood films.

After a decade of marriage during which they estimated they spent less than three years together, Desi and Lucille decided that to remain together they would organize a corporation to handle their business affairs. This company, Desilu Productions (with Desi as president and Lucy as vice-president), was tremendously successful in enabling them to work together. Their first effort was a successful radio situation comedy series, *My Favorite Husband*; that was followed by an even more successful nationwide vaudeville tour. In 1951, when they were unable to convince the Columbia Broadcasting System of the viability and profitability of a similar battle-of-the-sexes situation comedy on television, they took a gamble.

Taking their savings and scraping together all the funds they could raise, they produced a pilot television film using techniques they felt were more suited to the new, less formal medium. Desi Arnaz is widely credited with developing the three-camera filming technique, today virtually standard in daytime television. *I Love Lucy*, as they named their effort, was an immediate and overwhelming success. It ran for 11 seasons, from 1951 to 1961, and the last episode was as popular as the first. Indeed, episodes are still being shown in syndication 45 years after the series was begun.

While they were producing and acting in *I Love Lucy* during the 1950s, Desi and Lucy were also expanding the activities of Desilu, Inc., a production company they had formed. By the latter 1950s it owned a music publishing company, a record company, real estate including a hotel, and RKO Studios. Desilu produced commercials, a number of pilot films for others, and several television hits: notably *The Untouchables, Our Miss Brooks, The Danny Thomas Show*, and *December Bride*. During this time Desi also had roles in a number of films.

By the late 1950s the couple's marriage was suffering severe strains, and in 1960 Desi and Lucy were divorced. Three years later Desi decided to bring his television career to an end. He sold his share in Desilu Productions to Lucy for $3 million and retired to his horse ranch in southern California. During the late 1960s and early 1970s he came back to television occasionally and was lured to Hollywood several times. In addition to *Too Many Girls* (1940), among Desi's better-known films were *Forever Darling* (1956), *Holiday in Havana* (1949), *Cuban Pete* (1946), and *Bataan* (1943).

Desi Arnaz died of lung cancer at his California ranch on 2 December 1986 at the age of 69.

Further Reading

Contemporary Newsmakers, 1987. Detroit: Gale Research, 1987.
Current Biography, 1952. New York: H. W. Wilson Co., 1952.
Current Biography Yearbook, 1987 [obit.]. New York: H. W. Wilson Co., 1987.
Olson, James S., and Judith E. Olson. *Cuban Americans: From Trauma to Triumph.* New York: Twayne Publishers, 1995.
Reyes, Luis, and Peter Rubie. *Hispanics in Hollywood*. New York: Garland Publishing, 1994.
Sinott, Susan. *Extraordinary Hispanic Americans*. Chicago: Children's Press, 1991.

Sullivan, Dita. "El exito del riesgo." *Mas* 3:6 (November–December 1991): 76.
Who's Who in America 1952–1953. Chicago: Marquis Who's Who, 1952.

ALFREDO ARREGUÍN

(1935–   )

Mexican American Painter, Teacher, Sculptor

Alfredo Arreguín has been described as an artist whose body is in the United States but whose soul still remains in Mexico. He is recognized worldwide as a pioneer in patterned and layered oil painting, often of exuberant jungle scenes, some of which form an intricate combination of landscape and portraiture. Arreguín derives his enchanting, delightfully evocative patterns from his childhood and youth in Mexico, from the recall (sometimes perhaps subconscious) of patterns from colonial Mexican tiles, indigenous textiles, baroque church façades, folk art motifs, and tropical plants and animals—as well as from Islamic, Oriental, and Amerindian influences. The untrammeled enthusiasm evident in his paintings is offset by his masterful and highly sophisticated technique. He says that many of the details in his works are unpremeditated and grow out of the painting as he adds layers.

Alfredo Mendoza Arreguín was born on 20 January 1935 in Morelia, the son of María Mendoza Martínez and Félix Arreguín Vélez. A reserved, somewhat solemn child, he was brought up in the beautiful old colonial capital of Michoacán, largely by his grandparents. As a child he was greatly influenced by his grandmother, but he credits his artistic mother for his early interest in drawing. His direct involvement in art began at age 8 when his grandfather bought him paint and brushes and enrolled him in the Morelia Bellas Artes academy, which he attended for two years.

At age 13 Alfredo went to Mexico City to enter the National Preparatory School and to live with his father, who had recently moved there. The next year, 1948, his father got him a vacation job on a dam being constructed in the wild mountains of Guerrero state. His experiences there in the rank vegetative jungle growth made a lasting artistic impact on the impressionable teenager, as is evident from many of his paintings. In Mexico City he studied engineering but then switched to architecture. In order to practice the English he studied at the university he formed

Alfredo Arreguín. Photo courtesy of Alfredo Arreguín.

the habit of striking up an acquaintance with tourists and guiding them to the architectural gems and many other cultural attractions of the Mexican capital.

In 1958 one of these contacts led to a lasting friendship with a family from Seattle, Washington; the Dams invited Arreguín to come visit them. He did; then he enrolled at the University of Washington as an architecture student; and six months later, because he had declared his intent to become a citizen, he was drafted into the U.S. army and spent over a year in Korea. Upon his discharge from the armed services he returned to Seattle and the university, switching his major from architecture to interior design. Later he settled on fine arts, obtaining his B.A. in 1967 at age 32. Two years later he was awarded his master's degree in fine arts (M.F.A.) and then taught briefly as an instructor in the university's art department. He has since been invited back to lecture on his painting technique and to make presentations of his artwork.

Even before he completed his M.F.A. studies, Arreguín had begun to develop the techniques that were to characterize his distinctive style— sometimes called pattern painting or deep painting. Abstract expressionism was the dominant mode in the art world in the late 1960s, and with his different approach to painting, success did not come quickly or easily. But he stuck to his convictions, working for several years as a waiter in a Mexican restaurant near the university to supplement the meager income from his painting. After a decade he became recognized as the pioneer in pattern painting and was acknowledged as an outstanding artist.

In the mid-1970s Arreguín blended and expanded his painting and drawing skills into the style that became characteristically his own. Typically he painted broad vistas, dense compositions with calligraphically detailed flora and fauna—often luxuriant tropical plants and animals, especially monkeys, colorful birds, and felines. By the beginning of the 1980s his paintings became somewhat more open than his earlier crowded works. Increasingly emphasizing luminosity, he incorporated another aspect of his rich Mexican legacy by adding pre-Columbian motifs, often in intricate designs.

With vibrant colors Arreguín's paintings celebrate the world of nature as viewed through his cultural heritage. He chooses his kaleidoscopic patterns to describe elements in nature rather than merely to fill space. He achieves the baroque effects of pattern painting by superimposing as many as eight to ten layers of paint, one on top of another. His scenes are mobile and fluid, and the patterns seem almost hypnotically to pull the viewer within their layered depths, often inducing a feeling of flowing serenity.

Arreguín's paintings have been exhibited in the United States and abroad. After being a two-time runner-up earlier in both the Grand Galleria National exhibitions and in the annual Pacific Northwest Arts and Crafts Fair, Alfredo Arreguín won the coveted and prestigious Palm of the People award at the 1979 International Festival of Painting at Cagnes-sur-Mer, France. During the 1980s he had two dozen solo exhibitions of his paintings and participated in twice that many thematic group exhibits. In the first half of the 1990s he has had five more solo exhibitions plus a particularly prestigious one at the National Academy of Sciences in Washington, D.C., from 16 January to 26 March 1996, and has participated in half a dozen group exhibits. In mid-1989, on the occasion of the 450th anniversary of the founding of the University of San Nicolás de Hidalgo in Morelia, he was honored by the university and the Museo Michoacano with a retrospective exhibition of 18 of his paintings and the publication of a book on his work, *Alfredo Arreguín: El Universo vegetal, animal y humano de un Pintor Moreliano.*

Arreguín has had over 30 solo showings of his paintings and has participated in 60 group shows, including the 1990–1994 CARA (Chicano Art: Resistance and Affirmation) exhibition. In all, he has won 19 national awards and prizes. He was twice the recipient of a fellowship from the National Endowment for the Arts (NEA), in 1980 and 1985. Among his other honors are the selection of one of his paintings for a UNICEF greeting card in 1985, the commission to do Washington state's Centennial Poster in 1989, and a Special Humanitarian Award from the Washington state legislature. His paintings have also been used as the cover design for 16 books of fiction, poetry, and history. Both his wife, Susan Lytle, and their young daughter Lesley are also painters.

Further Reading

Alcalá, Kathleen. "Deep Painting: An Interview with Alfredo Arreguín." *Raven Chronicles* 2:2 (Winter 1992): 34–36.

Alfredo Arreguín: El universo vegetal, animal y humano de un pintor moreliano. Morelia, Mexico: Universidad Michoacana de San Nicolás de Hidalgo, 1989.

Arteaga, David. "Alfredo Arreguín: An Artist and His Work." *La Voz* (March 1985).

Bates, Alansa. "UW-trained artist . . ." *University REPORT* 3:4 (June 1989): 5 [Seattle: University of Washington].

Chaplik, Dorothy. "Alfredo Arreguín." *Latin American Art* (Winter 1991): 40–41.

Cox, Charlene B. "Arreguín's Artistic Designs." *Américas* 37:1 (January–February 1985).

Gallagher, Tess. "Viva la vida." Tacoma, Wash.: Tacoma Art Museum exhibition catalogue, 1992.

ELFEGO BACA

(1865–1945)

Mexican American Folk Hero, Lawyer, Sheriff, Detective

The latter part of the 19th century saw the emergence of a number of Mexican American folk heroes—Santos Benavides, Juan Cortina, Catarino Garza, Gregorio Cortez, to name a few. But none was more colorful than Elfego Baca. Baca claimed acquaintance with Billy the Kid, and he certainly knew the bandit-revolutionary Pancho Villa and President Victoriano Huerta of Mexico. His folk reputation was made by a two-day shootout at the tiny settlement of San Francisco in New Mexico.

A gun-toting, cigar-chomping frontier figure with a reputation for headstrong behavior and reckless, almost foolhardy, courage, Baca is best known for a famous incident in 1884 when he stood off fourscore Texas

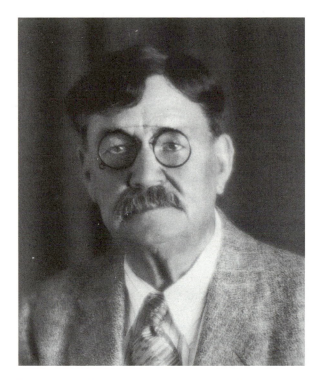

Elfego Baca. Photo courtesy of the Center for Southwest Research, General Library, University of New Mexico.

cowboys who allegedly fired an estimated 4,000 shots at him. In the siege Baca apparently caused the deaths of four cowmen and wounded eight more. On promise of a fair hearing he finally surrendered to a deputy whom he trusted.

As might be expected of a folk hero and legend in his own lifetime, many of the facts of Elfego Baca's life are in dispute. He was born of simple *nuevomexicano* parents, Juanita and Francisco Baca, on 27 February 1865, just a few weeks before the end of the Civil War, in a then much larger Socorro County, New Mexico. One story has Elfego, while still a baby, kidnapped by Indians but returned to his parents after a couple of days. Perhaps because of this occurrence the family moved to Topeka, Kansas, where Elfego grew up in the turmoil and violence of the post–Civil War western frontier. He received a limited primary education; he learned Anglo ways and his English was as fluent as his Spanish. His mother died when he was 15 years old, and the family returned to New Mexico. Soon, at a time of heavy movement into eastern New Mexico by midwestern Anglo farmers and Texas cattlemen, his father became marshall of Belen, an old "Mexican" town located on the Rio Grande River in the central part of the territory.

In the fall of 1884, while still in his teens, Elfego Baca had his infamous experience with the Texas cowboys. As a self-appointed deputy he rode into San Francisco Plaza, known as Frisco to the Anglos and today named Reserve, the county seat of Catron County. Here gangs of Anglo cowmen and gunslingers, stirred up by the recent Lincoln County War among cattlemen, had gotten into the habit of using local animals and occasionally their *mexicano* owners for drunken target practice. Baca's arrest and disarming of one of the miscreants, and his fighting off for two days of retaliatory attacks by the cowpoke's buddies, was the stuff folk heroes are made of. After an inquest and ultimately a jury trial in Albuquerque, Baca was acquitted of murder. And he was famous!

Baca's widespread reputation as a survivor served him in good stead in his subsequent long and generally successful career in law enforcement and politics. After he reached 21 years of age he ran for public office in virtually every election year and held the offices of county clerk, sheriff, mayor, district attorney for both Socorro and Sierra counties, deputy U.S. marshall, and superintendent of public schools for Socorro County. He was less successful later in party politics, in his effort as a Republican to be elected to the House of Representatives.

Elfego Baca had great ambitions and studied law in the Socorro law offices of a Judge Hamilton. In December 1894 he was admitted to the bar and early the following year organized the law firm of Freeman & Baca in Socorro. His partner, Judge A. A. Freeman, was an associate justice on the New Mexico Supreme Court. Two decades later Elfego was admitted to practice before the U.S. Supreme Court, but he never argued before that body. There is some evidence that he was not an eloquent trial lawyer; however, as an attorney he was also involved in corporate law. Here his bilingualism and territory-wide reputation and friendships greatly helped him, and he represented several large mining companies operating in the United States and Mexico.

The Mexican revolution of 1910 brought Elfego some new business. When General Victoriano Huerta arranged the death of President Francisco Madero and took over the presidency of Mexico, Elfego was hired as his government's representative in the United States. In connection with this employment he was indicted in 1914 for criminal conspiracy against the United States as a result of the escape from a federal prison of Mexican general José Inés Salazar. In his 1915 trial Baca was defended by the well-known New Mexican politician and lawyer Octaviano Larrazolo and was found not guilty. He emerged from the trial with his reputation as a vigorous, forceful politician enhanced.

Three years later Elfego was elected sheriff of Socorro County. The fact that he was a private detective and had also been working as head bouncer in a Ciudad Juárez gambling hall may have influenced some citizens to vote for him. From 1919 to 1929 he served intermittently as sheriff of Socorro County. He also continued his law practice in Albuquerque, where his occasionally flamboyant antics in defense of persons indicted for criminal behavior sometimes got him into difficulties.

Because of his activities in the legal profession and his years of political involvement, Baca was a well-known figure in New Mexico politics. He was active in the statehood movement, and in the 1920s he was mentioned occasionally in the press as a potential candidate for governor. Though he never was nominated, his vote-getting ability, as well as his extensive political friendships with local Hispanos, was put to good use. At age 45 he developed a political alliance with Bronson Cutting, New Mexico's powerful young liberal Republican senator, that persisted until Cutting's death in 1935. During this time Baca published and co-edited *La Opinión Pública*, a Spanish-language weekly that supported Cutting's political agenda. Baca also did some political detective work for him and after Cutting's death continued to work as a detective and lawyer out of the combination office, printing shop, and home he built in 1930.

After Cutting's death Elfego Baca continued to be politically active, but as a New Deal Democrat rather than as a Republican. In the early 1940s his health began to deteriorate. On 27 August 1945, just before the end of World War II, he died at the ripe age of 80 after having unsuccessfully sought nomination as the Democratic candidate for district attorney the year before. He was survived by one son, four daughters, and Francisquita Pohmer de Baca, his feisty wife of 60 years.

Further Reading

Beckett, V. B. *Baca's Battle*. Houston, Tex.: Stagecoach Press, 1962.

Bernard, Jacqueline. *Voices from the Southwest*. New York: Scholastic Book Services, 1972.

Castillo, Pedro, and Albert Camarillo, eds. *Furia y muerte: Los bandidos chicanos*. Los Angeles: Chicano Studies Center, University of California, 1973.

Crichton, Kyle S. *Law and Order, Limited: The Life of Elfego Baca*. Santa Fe: New Mexican Publishing Co., 1928; reprint, New York: Arno Press, 1974.

Fergusson, Harvey. *Rio Grande*. New York: Alfred A. Knopf, 1936.

Keleher, William A. *Memoirs: 1892–1969, A New Mexico Item*. Santa Fe: Rydal Press, 1969.

Perigo, Lynn I. *Hispanos: Historic Leaders in New Mexico*. Santa Fe: Sunstone Press, 1985.

HERMAN BADILLO

(1929–   )

Puerto Rican Politician, Attorney, Accountant

Herman Rivera Badillo did not have a comfortable, pleasant childhood. As an adult he reminisced that until he reached age 5 he had consumed no more than three gallons of milk and four dozen eggs. This comment was prompted by his being referred to as a "tall Puerto Rican," a characterization he considered disparaging. He argued that Puerto Ricans were short mainly because of poverty and its accompanying poor diet and inadequate food. Badillo, over 6 feet tall, claims that he grew 6 inches during the first summer he lived on the U.S. mainland, at age 12.

Badillo was born on 21 August 1929 in Caguas, Puerto Rico, a town neighboring on the San Juan metropolitan area. He was the only child of Francisco Badillo and Carmen Rivera, who belonged to the middle class. His father taught English in the public schools, and his mother was an educated woman who spent much time working for church and social causes. Badillo's mother, father, and one grandmother died in a tuberculosis epidemic that swept Puerto Rico in the mid-1930s, leaving him orphaned at age 5. This trauma came in the middle of the Great Depression, which affected Puerto Rico even more severely than it did the U.S. mainland.

After the death of his parents Herman lived with his aunt Aurelia Rivera, her two young sons, and Badillo's grandfather. No public welfare program existed then, and he recalls going to bed hungry nearly every night as a young child. In spite of his misery and a part-time job, Badillo was outstanding in school, always at the head of his class. While still in school he worked cleaning a theater to help the family finances.

During this time many Puerto Ricans migrated to the mainland to escape the tuberculosis epidemic and to search for a better life or just a new beginning. When Aurelia Rivera resolved to move to New York City, she decided that her elder son and Herman would accompany her. She had strong feelings that Badillo, being such a bright lad, could adjust readily to big city life in a foreign land. In April 1941, at age 12, Badillo arrived in New York.

Because his Aunt Aurelia was not doing well economically, Badillo soon left to join an uncle in Chicago. There Badillo became a paper boy, sold the *Saturday Evening Post* magazine, and continued his education in the Chicago schools. When his uncle was unable to continue supporting him Badillo was forced to leave Chicago, moving in with another uncle in Burbank, California. Here he began delivering the *Burbank News* on weekends and soon saved enough to buy a bicycle and a lawn mower, which enabled him to work part-time to support himself. In school his grades remained excellent, and his leadership skills resulted in his being elected president of his eighth grade class after only two years in Burbank. As a young adolescent he attended Sunday school at a Presbyterian church and was active in Boy Scouts.

At age 15 Badillo returned to New York City to resume living with his Aunt Aurelia, whose financial situation had improved. There he worked as a bus boy, pin boy in bowling alleys, dishwasher, and waiter. In high school Badillo was assigned to the vocational program despite his scholastic ability and achievements. Recognizing that his ethnic background caused this discriminatory action, he eventually managed to transfer to college-entry courses. In 1947 Badillo graduated with the highest marks in his high school class.

After high school Herman Badillo entered City College. He majored in business and continued to work odd jobs to support himself. In 1951 he graduated magna cum laude and secured a position as an accountant. At night he attended Brooklyn Law School, where he received the First Scholarship Prize and was class valedictorian and a member of the Law Review and Moot Court Team. He received his LL.B. degree cum laude in 1954. The following year he was admitted to the New York bar, and in 1956 he earned accreditation as a certified public accountant. Despite the many difficulties in his path, Badillo had become an accomplished and successful young man.

Between 1951 and 1961 Badillo was in private practice on Wall Street as a certified public accountant and later as a lawyer. His poise, his ability to communicate in public forums, and his skill in speaking two languages fluently made him widely known; and his readiness to assist the needy provided an opportunity to make the transition to public life. At the time he considered politics an avocation, not a career.

In 1958 Badillo joined the Caribe Democratic Club, where he perfected his political skills. Two years later he chaired the East Harlem Kennedy for President Committee and the following year set out to unite East Harlem Puerto Rican and African American voters, founding the John F. Kennedy Democratic Club. His club strongly supported Mayor Robert Wagner's successful bid for re-election, and Wagner named Badillo deputy real estate commissioner. Less than a year later Wagner named him commissioner of the Department of Relocation, a newly created office.

Badillo was now the highest Hispanic appointee in New York City history. During his tenure he moved to the Bronx, where there was a growing Puerto Rican population. In his capacity as housing commissioner he provided the homeless with single-room occupancy housing as well as social services, a new concept. He resigned as commissioner in 1965 to run for Bronx Borough president.

Badillo was successful in the election, becoming the first borough president of Hispanic origin. As president he focused on making himself available to his constituents and on acquainting himself with their problems. During his presidency more capital projects were initiated than ever before. These included a new Lincoln Hospital, a new North Central Hospital, and a new Hostos Community College. Sometimes a bit irreverent, Badillo was noted for his lack of interest in attending ceremonial functions because he felt they were a waste of his time. His many successes made headlines.

In 1969 Herman Badillo entered the race for mayor of New York City, but lost in the Democratic primary by a slim margin, perhaps because he aggressively expressed strong views about solutions to the city's problems. The following year he ran for Congress from the 21st Congressional District in the South Bronx and was elected overwhelmingly, becoming the first Hispanic congressman of Puerto Rican origin in history.

Notwithstanding his credentials and background, Badillo was treated as a rank novice and was appointed to the House committee on agriculture. A *New York Times* editorial sided with the indignant Badillo, calling the appointment an insulting waste of his talents and experience. After this furor he was appointed to the Education and Labor Committee and later served on the Banking, Finance, and Urban Affairs and the Judiciary committees as well. He was re-elected to Congress in 1972, 1974, and 1976. In 1978 he resigned from Congress in order to accept appointment from Mayor Edward Koch as deputy mayor of New York. However, soon his relationship with Koch soured and the following year he resigned, or was dismissed, returning to private law practice.

In 1984 Badillo was appointed chairman of the Board of Directors of the State of New York Mortgage Agency. During his tenure in that office the agency built Charlotte Street, a housing complex where mostly African Americans and Puerto Ricans owned units. In 1986 Badillo ran for state comptroller. He carried New York City by 61 percent of the vote, but lost statewide. After this defeat Badillo, a much weakened force in city politics, shunned elective office and in 1993 disavowed and halted an "unauthorized" campaign for mayor. Soon thereafter the 63-year-old Badillo found himself being aggressively courted as a potential candidate for city comptroller. Although backed by former mayor Koch, he lost the election in November by a vote of 41 to 56 percent. In April 1994 Badillo was appointed by Mayor Rudolph Giuliani as a mayoral counsel/fiscal monitor examining New York City school finances. His first report, rendered in October, led the school chancellor to cut the administrative staff by 2,500 persons by June 1995.

Presently Badillo is a full-time practicing attorney in the law firm of Fischbein-Badillo-Wagner-Itzler. He is a member of the Board of Trustees of the City University of New York and chairman of the Board of Directors of the Bronx Community Cable Programming Corporation. The author of *A Bill of No Rights: Attica and the American Prison System* (1972), he was the recipient of an honorary Doctor of Laws Degree from City College. Today Herman Rivera Badillo still refuses to become a political "has-been." He once quoted words the poet Tennyson ascribed to Ulysses: "how dull is it to pause . . . and . . . not to shine in use!"

Further Reading

"Courting Badillo: A Last Hurrah as Comptroller." *New York Times* (20 May 1993): B1 (L).
"Disputed Bronx Victor." *New York Times* (4 November 1965): B1 (L).
Moritz, Charles, ed. *Current Biography Yearbook, 1971*. New York: H. W. Wilson Co., 1972.
"Mr. Badillo's First Salvo." *New York Times* 144 (6 October 1994): A28.
Newlon, Clarke. *Famous Puerto Ricans*. New York: Dodd, Mead and Co., 1975.
Newman, Maria. "Urging Higher Standards . . ." *New York Times* 143 (11 April 1994): B7 (L).
Who's Who in American Politics, 13th ed., vol. 2. New York: R. R. Bowker, 1991.

JOAN BÁEZ

(1941–   )

Mexican American Peace Activist, Singer, Song Writer

Joan Báez is first and foremost a dedicated and tireless advocate for peace and civil rights who has used her gifted voice and her music to advance the causes she believes in so deeply. Her parents' strong religious beliefs (which led them to Quaker convictions) and the fact that both her grandfathers were clergymen may help explain her intense moral fervor, her undeniable integrity, and her passionate commitment to human rights.

Joan Báez. Photo by Matthew Rolston.

Joan Báez was born on Staten Island, New York, on 9 January 1941, the second of three daughters of Joan Bridge from Scotland and Mexico-born Alberto V. Báez, professor of physics at various American universities. As her father changed jobs, the Báez family moved around the country and abroad—including Paris and Baghdad, where Alberto, working for UNESCO, spent a year organizing a physics center at the university. Her childhood was relatively uneventful; she went to grade and high schools in the various cities in which her father taught and worked. She recalls occasionally experiencing prejudice and discrimination during her junior high school years in southern California because of her dark complexion. But apparently the episodes were not traumatic.

Joan's early public appearances included singing in church choirs and at her senior prom. While her father taught at nearby Stanford University, she attended and graduated from high school in Palo Alto, California, in 1958. In that same year her father received an appointment at the Massachusetts Institute of Technology, so Joan enrolled at Boston University but dropped out during her first semester. Meanwhile, her largely untrained but magnificent voice had begun to make her an attraction in Harvard Square coffeehouses, where she sang mostly folk ballads. In July of the following year she took part in the Newport Folk Festival, becoming an unanticipated instant celebrity. In 1960 she recorded her first solo album, "Joan Baez," made her concert debut at the 92nd Street YMCA in New York City, and also toured a number of colleges.

From the very beginning of her musical career Joan Báez was deeply involved in the civil rights protest movement in a very direct manner. In the summer of 1962 she toured small black colleges in the South. In the following year she participated in the civil rights march on Washington, D.C., and in 1965 joined Martin Luther King Jr. (whom she credits with crystallizing her ideas about discrimination) in his march from Selma to Montgomery, Alabama. In December she was an important participant in a free speech movement rally on the University of California Berkeley campus and then joined the students in occupying the administration building. She also began a long tax protest by refusing to pay the 60 percent of her 1964 income taxes she asserted went for armaments. The following year she sang at a Madison Square Garden rally against U.S. involvement in Vietnam and later took part in a large anti–Vietnam War demonstration in front of the White House. With the help of West Coast pacifist Ira Sandperl she also founded (and financed) the Institute for the Study of Nonviolence, which was to be active for the next decade.

In the mid-1960s Joan shared numerous concerts and some tours with Bob Dylan, including one to England in 1965. Early in 1967 she made her first solo concert tour abroad, in Japan; because her political remarks were misinterpreted, it was a disappointment to her. Having returned to the United States, in October she and her mother were among more than 100 protesters arrested for blocking the Oakland, California, induction center; they served ten-day jail sentences. Two months later Joan was again arrested for the same violation and received a 90-day sentence.

While in prison Joan was visited by David Harris, an anti-war activist whom she had met at the induction center, and they decided to tour colleges to promote draft resistance. In March 1968, in the middle of the tour, they were married; a few months later Harris was sentenced to three years in prison for draft resistance. While David served his sentence Joan, after giving birth to a son, Gabriel, continued touring the country to spread the doctrine of nonviolence. When Harris was paroled from jail in March 1971, together they wrote *Coming Out*, a book detailing their experiences. In the following year they separated and in 1973 were divorced.

Meanwhile, in the late 1960s and 1970s Joan Báez became a national symbol of nonviolence at popular music festivals such as Woodstock, Newport, Monterey, and Big Sur. She also visited North Vietnam at the time of the 1972 Christmas bombing by the United States and joined a peace march in Northern Ireland in 1976. She showed signs of maturing as a civil rights and pacifist leader. From an uncertain, sometimes quirky folk singer with simplistic views she became an articulate and self-confident, if sometimes preachy, idealist who argued for world pacifism and an end to destructive nationalism. In 1979 she founded Humanitas International, a human rights organization.

Toward the end of the 1970s Joan Báez toured the Soviet Union, visiting Russian dissidents Elena Bonner and Andrei Sakharov. In 1981 she made a trip to Latin America investigating human rights abuses and in the following year sang at a Washington, D.C., memorial service for the murdered Salvadorean rights leader, archbishop Oscar Romero. At mid-decade she was the opening performer for "Live Aid" in Philadelphia. She participated in Amnesty International's "Conspiracy of Hope" tour in 1986 and two years later joined its "Human Rights Now" tour. Throughout the 1980s her music—her tours, records, and albums—continued to be an extension of her nonviolent political beliefs. For Joan, her music was primarily the means to an end. Inevitably her music suffered. And so did her effectiveness as a one-woman human rights movement.

During the second half of the 1980s Joan Báez met with such disparate seekers after social justice as Polish Solidarity leader Lech Walesa and the Dalai Lama. She also published her second autobiographical work, *And a Voice to Sing With* (1987). At the end of the 1980s Joan decided on a musical "comeback." With a new manager, Mark Spector, she produced "Play Me Backwards," her 33rd album, released in October 1992. In addition to her usual concerts she again began touring the clubs that had made her the queen of folk music in the 1960s. In 1993 Vanguard Records released a boxed 60-song set of her music titled "Rare, Live and Classic."

In the process of reviving her singing career Joan Báez found it necessary to reduce her political involvement; that included closing down Humanitas International. She assured the press that it did not mean she was no longer concerned with human rights and peace. An illustration of her continuing concern was her April 1993 visit to war-devastated Yugoslavia, where she performed in a refugee camp in Zagreb and did two concerts in Sarajevo. In the mid-1990s she continues to be active both as a singer and as a citizen deeply involved in the issues of the day.

Joan Báez, the silver-voiced "Queen Mother" of folk music, is the proud possessor of eight gold albums and several gold singles. Among her most popular songs is "There But for Fortune" (1963), a sentimental social environmental ballad. Many of her successful songs have political themes or have arisen out of ecological concerns or political events. For example, her popular LP "Gracias a la vida," sung almost entirely in Spanish, arose out of Augusto Pinochet's coup in Chile in September 1973. Two years later she did "Diamonds and Rust," the title song of which reflected her romantic relationship with singer Bob Dylan. In 1977

A & M Records issued "The Best of Joan C. Báez," her last major-label album until 1992, when Joan released "Play Me Backwards." Meanwhile she did a number of albums with various record companies such as Gold Castle and Portrait, among them "Honest Lullaby" (1979) and "Speaking of Dreams" (1989). Her most recent release is "Ring Them Bells," a collection of old favorites recorded live at The Bottom Line in New York in April 1995 with the accompaniment of various fellow folk singers. The appearance showed a Báez resilient and still undiminished as well as nostalgic and romantic.

Further Reading

Báez, Joan. *And a Voice to Sing With*. New York: Summit Books, 1987.
Báez, Joan, and David Harris. *Coming Out*. New York: Pocket Books, 1971.
Bernikow, Louise. "The Ballad of Joan Báez." *Lear's* 6:2 (1 April 1993): 72.
Current Biography, 1963. New York: H. W. Wilson Co., 1963.
Draper, Hal. *The New Student Revolt*. New York: Grove Press, 1965.
Feito, Alvaro. *Joan Báez*. Madrid: Ediciones Júcar, 1975.
Holden, Stephen. "Joan Báez: Resilient, Romantic, Undiminished." *New York Times* (12 April 1995): C15.
New York Times (12 December 1989): C24.
Plotnikoff, David. "Voice of Her Generation." *Eye, San Jose Mercury News* (8 January 1993): 3, 20–21.
Rodnitzky, Jerome L. "Joan Baez: A Pacifist St. Joan." *Minstrels of the Dawn*. Chicago: Nelson-Hall, 1976.

ROMANA ACOSTA BAÑUELOS

(1925–   )

Mexican American Businesswoman, Civic Leader, Government Official

In late 1971 President Richard Milhous Nixon announced the appointment of Romana Acosta Bañuelos as treasurer of the United States. At the Senate Finance Committee hearings her appointment was opposed by union labor leaders—including **César Chávez**, who sent a telegram to the committee—because she hired undocumented workers in her food processing plant. She was confirmed in December by the U.S. Senate without opposition upon recommendation of the committee. When she took the oath of office on December 17 she became the 34th treasurer of the United States, the sixth woman and the first Mexican American to occupy that position. Her new appointment made her the top-ranking Mexican American in U.S. government service. She served as treasurer until February 1974.

Romana Acosta was born in the small copper-mining town of Miami, Arizona, on 20 March 1925, the daughter of Teresa Lugo and Juan Francisco Acosta, both undocumented Mexican immigrants. Although a U.S. citizen by birth, she was forced to leave the United States with her parents during the Great Depression when she was 8 years old. In a climate of repression and fear, her parents accepted the offer by authorities to pay their transportation back to the border. Her family resettled in the Mexican border state of Sonora on a small ranch belonging to relatives, and she grew up and received her education there.

As a young girl Romana helped out with the many family tasks. Not only did she help tend the crops that her hard-working father planted, but she also helped her mother who baked pastry goods and raised chickens for sale in the nearby town. The example of her energetic and resourceful mother and the work habits she learned as a youngster were undoubtedly of great importance to her as she grew into adulthood.

After a marriage while still a young teenager, two children, and a divorce, at age 19 Romana returned to the United States toward the end of World War II. Settling in Los Angeles with her two sons, she obtained work in a laundry and a clothing factory to support herself and her children. By 1949, when she was 24 years old, she had managed to put aside $400 from her meager earnings and those of her second husband. With these savings she began a tortilla "factory" in downtown Los Angeles, helped by an aunt. Romana later named their company Ramona's Mexican Food Products, Inc., after the heroine of Helen Hunt Jackson's romantic 19th-century novel, *Ramona*, the sentimental story of a young mestiza in early American California.

The tiny new business meant long hours and much hard work. Gradually Romana built up the market for her products, and by the mid-1960s sales and profits were booming. She also followed her mother's earlier example of diversifying. Sensing the mounting need for a financial institution that would cater especially to Latinos, in 1964 Romana was one of the instigators and founding directors of the Pan American National Bank in East Los Angeles. A few years later she was elected chairwoman of its board of directors. Later that same year, 1969, she was named Outstanding Businesswoman of the Year in Los Angeles in a ceremony presided over by Mayor Sam Yorty, who presented the award.

Romana Bañuelos proved to be just as effective in running a bank as she was in operating a food business. As chairperson she gave the Pan American Bank strong leadership, instituting a number of new policies that have been credited with much of the bank's considerable financial success. She was twice re-elected unanimously to the chairmanship of the board. Because of her business experience, in 1971 she was asked by local Republican political leaders to allow her name to be put on the list of possible appointees to become treasurer of the United States. She agreed although she had little expectation of anything coming of it. From the list President Nixon selected her as the candidate for appointment. While the U.S. Senate committee was holding hearings on her confirmation, the Romana plant in Gardena, California, was raided by Immigration and Naturalization Service (INS) agents, who rounded up 36 undocumented alien workers. At the Senate hearings Romana did not deny that she hired undocumented aliens (not at that time unlawful), and she suggested that the INS raid was politically motivated to embarrass President Nixon. Despite the adverse publicity, the Nixon administration continued to support her candidacy and she was confirmed. She served until February 1974, when she resigned in order to spend more time on her banking and manufacturing activities, her family, and her civic interests. While retaining a limited interest in politics, since her resignation she has devoted herself mostly to business interests.

Under Bañuelos's dynamic but careful leadership, Ramona's Mexican Food Products has achieved great commercial success. By 1980 her company employed some 400 workers and manufactured and distributed over 20 different food products with annual sales of about $12 million. Ten years later she was operating the largest independent Mexican food processing plant in California. At the same time Bañuelos supplied the Pan American Bank with her business acumen and outstanding skilled leadership, taking over as its president in the early 1990s. She also retains the presidency of Ramona's Mexican Food Products. Now in her early seventies, Romana no longer takes an active role in politics but in line with her convictions does continue to participate actively in social projects.

Romana Bañuelos believes that financial success brings with it social responsibility. As a result of this conviction she helped found and is a trustee of the Ramona Mexican Food Products Scholarship Foundation, which assists Mexican American high school students who want to go to college by annually awarding three full four-year scholarships for tuition, fees, and books. She also evidences a deep interest in the Los Angeles Mexican American community and its problems.

Romana Bañuelos has been the recipient of many honors in addition to having been appointed treasurer of the United States in 1971 and named Outstanding Businesswoman of the Year two years earlier. In 1969 she was also given a Commendation Award from the Los Angeles County Board of Supervisors, and in 1971 she received a Certificate of Merit from the Mexican American Agency Representatives of Los Angeles. Later in that same year she received from the County Board of Supervisors a plaque with the inscription: Citizen/Business Woman/ Civic Leader. In 1975 she was awarded an honorary doctorate in business administration by a Los Angeles university and two years later received the Woman Achievement Award from the East Los Angeles Community Union (TELACU), a Latino development agency.

Further Reading

Chacón, José. *Hispanic Notables in the U.S. of North America*. Albuquerque: Saguaro Publications, 1978.

Martínez, Al. *Rising Voices: Profiles of Hispano-American Lives*. New York: New American Library, 1974.

Martínez, Diana. " 'The Strength Is in Money,' Says Romana Bañuelos." *Nuestro* 3:5 (June/July 1979): 34.

Telgen, Diane, and Jim Kamp, eds. *Notable Hispanic American Women*. Detroit: Gale Research, 1993.

CASIMIRO BARELA

(1847–1920)

Mexican American Senator, Businessman

Widely known in his lifetime as "The Perpetual Senator," Casimiro Barela had a long, successful career as both a political leader and a businessman in the state of Colorado. For 40 years, from 1876 to 1916, he served in the state senate. In addition, he was an outstanding businessman with a vast empire of interests ranging from mercantile establishments, to sheep and cattle ranches, to mines in the Southwest and Mexico, and even a coffee plantation in Brazil. For nearly half a century he was, without question, the best-known Latino in Colorado.

Casimiro Barela was born in the middle of the war between the United States and Mexico on 4 March 1847 at Embudo, a small village on the Rio Grande River 35 miles north of Santa Fe, New Mexico. The son of José and María Barela, he was named after an ancestor who had helped Juan Bautista de Anza found San Francisco, California, 70 years earlier. Casimiro spent his early childhood in Embudo; when he reached school age the family moved east to Mora in the beautiful Sangre de Cristo mountains.

In Mora, Casimiro helped out in the family shop, the Barela Mercantile Store, and learned how to herd the family's sheep and cattle. An eager student, he attended two schools and also had several tutors. When he was 12 years old he came to the attention of the new parish priest of Mora (later bishop and archbishop), the Frenchman Jean Baptiste Salpointe. Greatly impressed with Casimiro's keen mind and eagerness to learn, Father Salpointe offered to take him into his home and give him the finest education available in Colorado. Casimiro's parents acceded. After studying with Salpointe for four years, Casimiro returned to work with his father and brothers in the family's expanding general store.

While traveling with Father Salpointe, Casimiro became acquainted with the potential of southern Colorado around Trinidad as a place for settlement. At his urging the family moved north from Mora to Las Animas County on Colorado's southern border with New Mexico when Casimiro was 20 years old. Leaving behind some of his brothers to take care of the store and merchandising business, the Barela family began raising sheep and cattle and opened another general store. To complete his personal dream, Casimiro returned briefly to New Mexico to wed Josefa Ortiz and brought her back to his new town, Barela, Colorado.

Two years later, in 1869, by winning election as justice of the peace Casimiro began what was to be a lifetime of public service in Colorado. In the next election he won the office of county assessor and was sent to the territorial legislature at Denver by the voters. At the end of his term he was easily re-elected and in 1874 won the race for sheriff of Las Animas County. The following year he was selected as one of the delegates to the convention being held to write a constitution for the new state.

In the Colorado constitutional convention of 1875 Barela took an important leadership role. One of a scant handful of Hispanos among 49 delegates, he fought for—and obtained—provisions in the constitution to protect the civil rights of Mexican Americans and secured publication of all legislation in Spanish and German as well as in English for 25 years. In the first state elections he won a seat in the Colorado senate and subsequently was regularly re-elected to that body. In a tribute to his skilled leadership he was twice elected president pro tem of the senate by his fellow senators. His transfer of allegiance from the Democratic to the Republican Party in 1900 did not stand in the way of his re-election, but it did reduce his electoral majorities. Finally in 1916 the perpetual senator was defeated in his senate bid. He was 69 years old.

In addition to his heavy commitment to government service, Casimiro Barela was extremely active as a businessman. Already by the early 1870s he was known as a successful entrepreneur and soon was considered one of the richest men in the state. He operated a vast network of businesses in the Southwest and Mexico. In addition to operating mercantile establishments in Mora, Barela, and Trinidad, he was a director in the Trinidad National Bank and in a local railroad and owned a cattle business in Kansas City. He owned a number of ranches in Colorado, New Mexico, and old Mexico that raised sheep and cattle he brought from Texas. He also raised thoroughbred horses and was an ardent race fan. He had two printing shops, one in Trinidad that published *El Progreso* and one in Denver that published *Las Dos Repúblicas*. He was appointed consul in Denver for a number of Latin American countries, including Mexico. A busy businessman!

After his wife, Josefa, died in 1883 Barela married a wealthy *nuevomexicana*, Damiana Rivera, and in time they adopted and raised nine children. After his defeat in 1916 he retired from politics to devote more time to his widespread business enterprises. He remained highly regarded for his 40 years of public service and relished his sobriquets of The Perpetual Senator and *El padre del senado del estado de Colorado*. On 18 December 1920 Casimiro Barela died of pneumonia contracted while on a trip to Mexico as a personal representative of Colorado governor Shoup at the inauguration of President Alvaro Obregón. In the rotunda of the Colorado capitol in Denver, Casimiro Barela's likeness is one of 16 stained glass portraits of Colorado pioneers.

Further Reading

Burrola, Ray. "Casimiro Barela: A Case Study . . ." *Perspectivas en Chicano Studies*. Los Angeles: National Association of Chicano Social Science, 1977.

Fernández, José. *Cuarenta años de legislador: Biografía del senador Casimiro Barela*. New York: Arno Press, reprint, 1976.

Hafen, Leroy. *Colorado and Its People*, 4 vols. New York: Lewis Historical Publishing, 1948.

Hunt, Inez. *The Barela Brand*. Colorado Springs: Colorado Springs Public Schools, 1971.

La Luz 1:3 (June 1972): 50–55; 1:4 (August 1972): 48–53.

López, Lino M. *Colorado Latin American Personalities*. Denver: A. M. Printing, 1959.

SAMUEL BETANCES

(1941–)

Puerto Rican Educator, Consultant

Samuel Betances has been recognized nationwide as an outstanding inspirational and motivational speaker. A one-time high school dropout, he is now a frequently sought-after Latino consultant to many U.S. educational and business establishments. Highly proficient in conceptualizing and teaching insights, the Harvard alumnus considers himself an "edutainer." Dr. Betances sometimes tells his audiences his family was so poor that "once somebody broke into our little apartment and didn't take anything!" His audiences roar with laughter. Betances explains that his objective is to educate and to promote critical thinking through the use of humor. He says, "I've learned to poke fun at myself about issues related to my body, social identity, gender relationship, absurd assumptions and fears, and [about] how I have grown and unlearned bad lessons while learning new good ones."

Betances was born in Harlem, New York City, on 17 May 1941, the son of an alcoholic father. He grew up on welfare, spending less of his youth in classroom learning than in neighborhood fights. The tough environment of the big city left him not only with knife scars but also with experiences that contributed to a negative image of himself, his culture, and his capabilities. Upon his parents' divorce after a rocky marital relationship, his mother sent the 4-year-old Samuel to Puerto Rico to be raised by his grandparents, with whom he then spent three years. Later, he lived with a well-to-do surrogate family for two years on a farm located in the western foothills near Mayagüez, the third largest city in Puerto Rico. While performing errands for this family he also attended a grammar school called "La Unidad" (Unity). His childhood memories are generally associated with feelings of rejection and abandonment.

Yet Betances fondly recalls an extremely positive incident that occurred in the fourth grade. His teacher had asked the children to share with their classmates what they wanted for Christmas. Whereas most of the children had lists of bicycles, balls, bats, dolls, and trains, Betances said he wished for everyone's happiness and for all his classmates' wishes to come true. His teacher was emotionally touched by this unselfish and mature gesture and pointed out to the class the selfless wisdom of his wish, the true spirit of Christmas. Betances was deeply impressed by the meaning of the word "wisdom" and has always treasured his recollection of this classroom event.

While in fourth grade, Betances often did translating for his teachers. His English skills gave him special status and enabled him to skip fifth grade. When he was 11 years old he returned to the mainland to live with his mother. After residing in the Bronx near Prospect Avenue and Kelly Street, they moved to New Jersey where he picked blueberries and worked on chicken farms. During his adolescent years Betances became more fully aware of family inadequacies and was disturbed by the neglect he had experienced as a child, the absence of role models, and his feelings of general unworthiness. Yet he held strict Christian values, instilled primarily by his mother. These values kept him from alcohol, drugs, and crime.

Frustrated by her ex-husband's irresponsible and undependable financial behavior and his unwillingness to provide child support, Betances's mother abandoned her son. He then moved to Chicago at age 15 to live with his father. Betances was deeply affected by his parents' impulsive and irresponsible actions, their parenting failures, lack of emotional and financial support, the family's economic instability, and the humiliation of growing up within the welfare system.

Scholastic stress and frustration drove Betances to drop out of school in 1956 at age 16; he started working in a hospital. There he met Mary Yamazaki, a second-generation Japanese American who as a child had spent several years in an American internment camp during World War II. They became friends. Yamazaki encouraged him to read books and to start saving his money and helped him return to school. She taught him how to make the best use of his time and urged him to prepare for college. Betances always marveled how she was able to empathize with him although they differed in gender, race, and class. Later, as an educator, Betances explained to his audiences how and why this strange and solid friendship developed. Betances tells them that Yamazaki took time to understand who he was, what he had gone through, and how he had survived. Next, he says, she developed a vision of what he could be if he was instilled with goals and the necessary passion to attain them.

Motivated by her counsel and support, Betances obtained a scholarship through his employer, Hillsdale Hospital. While attending school he met Ronald Lenhoff in a speech class. Impressed by the way Betances projected his voice and used gestures, Lenhoff proposed that he would teach Betances to say things "right" if Betances would teach him how to do "stuff like that." The deal was made, and Lenhoff encouraged Betances to memorize speeches of famous public figures. Soon Betances was studying great speakers and preachers. Learning about them helped him improve his stage presence and his speech delivery and, equally important, gave him new role models. This experience, says Betances, ultimately saved him.

Samuel Betances attributes much of his success to the people he has met along life's way. From them he learned how to become a productive individual and pay his own way in life. This was a departure from the welfare mentality he had been exposed to earlier. These lessons transformed his entire value system. Armed with experience, great faith, and abundant energy, Betances obtained his B.A. in history and religion from Columbia Union College in Maryland in 1965. Four years later he received his master's degree in education at Harvard University Graduate School of Education and then earned his doctorate in education from Harvard in 1972. Later he pursued postdoctoral studies at the University of Wisconsin in Milwaukee.

Betances is currently a professor of sociology in Chicago at Northeastern Illinois University. In addition to lecturing and publishing extensively, he serves as a consultant for various government agencies, community groups, and private corporations. His presentations are deeply informative and well documented, and also both challenging and entertaining. His consulting firm, Louder, Betances, and Associates, Inc., has developed video-based programs featuring Dr. Betances speaking on various aspects of diversity. He believes that the most significant contribution industry can make currently is to help employees understand and respect people from other cultures, to become more effective workers in a multicultural society.

He admits that speaking out on issues of diversity, racism, stereotyping, belittling of one group by another, and similar topics helped him come out of his own closet of insecurities. This lack of security came from rejection that, he explains, "sometimes causes me to reject myself even before people reject me!" His message stresses the importance of repudiating rejection instead of rejecting ourselves and one another.

Betances defines the role of diversity in education as the "opportunity to empower those who have experienced rejection to get their fair share of what has been denied them and ensure that folks that look like me, who have been denied access, are able to make a greater contribution than that which they were allowed to make in the past." He also stresses the importance of learning about the experiences of other ethnic groups so that those who feel they must respond to the effects of prejudice can form coalitions of interest.

As a media personality, Dr. Betances has hosted his own television show in Chicago and has appeared on various television talk shows. He also testified as a guest expert on a Peter Jennings special concerning prejudice and children. Betances tries to make people see diversity as a positive good. He would like to be remembered as a teacher and communicator who helped people find a common ground.

Betances was reunited with his mother in 1968, when she was 50 years old. They reestablished family bonds and he persuaded her to complete a book of her poems, which was published posthumously in 1992.

Further Reading

Betances, Samuel. "Using Humor to Promote Multicultural Understanding." In *Multicultural Education: Strategies for Implementation in College and Universities*, vol. 3, J. Q. Adams and Janice R. Welsch, eds. Macomb, Ill.: Western Illinois University, 1993.

Holt, Daniel. "An Interview with Samuel Betances." *Making Our Society Safe for Differences* [BE Outreach] (March 1993): 5–7.

"Meet Crusading Maverick Samuel Betances." *NEA Today* (October 1993): 9.

Press Kit. Chicago: Souder, Betances and Associates.

RUBÉN BLADES

(1948–   )

Panamanian American Actor, Composer, Singer, Attorney, Political Activist

Rubén Blades is a multi-talented, multi-faceted, and extremely creative individual—a serious composer, songwriter, singer, band leader, actor, and political activist. He even ran for the presidency of Panama and received 20 percent of the vote. In addition to the numerous songs and musical scores he has written, he is the composer of music for an opera, *Maestra Vida*, issued by Fania Records. His music and his singing have found great favor on the tour circuit, and he has performed in Europe and Latin America as well as in the United States. In late spring 1986 his solo debut appearance at Carnegie Hall sold out. His film career dates from *The Last Fight*, released in 1982, to the present.

Rubén Blades (he uses an Anglicized pronunciation, as in razor blades) was born in Panama City, Panama, on 16 July 1948. He was the second of five children born to Anoland Bellido, a Cuban-born pianist, singer, and actress, and her Panamanian police detective husband, Rubén Darío Blades, of West Indian descent. Young Rubén was raised mostly by his Colombian-born paternal grandmother, who was unusual for her day in that she was a vegetarian feminist with an active interest in literature and art. He was introduced to modern painters and writers by her and was taught by her to read by age 5.

Growing up in Panama, Rubén spent hours each day listening to music on the radio. Although he enjoyed Latino musical forms, like his young Panamanian peers he preferred the Beatles, the Platters, and American music, particularly rock and roll. Like his friends he learned to sing along in English with the radio songs. His first public appearance as a vocalist was singing with his older brother Laces's small band: he sang both rock and roll and ballads, as well as other kinds of popular American songs. In 1964 when U.S. troops clashed with Panamanian students in the Canal Zone over flying the Panamanian flag at Balboa High School and left nearly two dozen dead and several hundred wounded, Blades stopped singing in English and began reading history.

After his graduation from high school Blades enrolled at the University of Panama, where he followed his mother's wishes by studying law. While at the university he did some vocalist work with a local Afro-

Cuban band called Los Salvajes del Ritmo. A New York theatrical agent and producer, having heard him sing on an album Blades made in 1968, offered him a job with a fairly prominent Latino band in the United States. Blades turned down the offer in order to complete his law education. However, when student rioting closed down the university during the next year he left Panama for New York City. During his next few months in the United States he wrote lyrics, composed songs, and recorded an album titled "De Panamá a Nueva York." When the university resumed classes he returned to Panama and his law studies. After completing his degree in law he obtained employment as an attorney for the Bank of Panama. Two years later he resigned his position and returned to New York to pursue a career in music.

To support himself Blades took an office position with Fania Records, an important publisher of Latin music, especially salsa at this time. He also returned to singing with local bands and in 1976 was hired to write songs and sing with the well-known Willie Colón band. During his five years with Colón he pressed several albums, the most successful of which was "Siembra," issued in 1977; it included a take-off on "Mack the Knife," titled "Pedro Navaja" (literally, "Peter Razor"), which became a best-selling record and was nominated for a Grammy.

Deciding to move beyond salsa, in 1982 Blades left Willie Colón's orchestra to form his own six-man band, which he planned to use to develop and expand his musical offerings. With his new group he added elements of jazz, rock, soul, reggae, and other Caribbean and Latin American rhythms to the conventional salsa played by typical Latin bands of the day. His lyrics not infrequently contained social or political questioning and criticism. In 1984 he switched from Fania to the mainstream recording company Elektra/Asylum.

Blades titled his first album with Elektra "Buscando América" ("Seeking America"); among its powerful songs there was one lamenting the murder of Bishop Oscar Romero of El Salvador and another recalling the fates of the *desaparecidos*, the "disappeared ones," particularly the victims of the Argentine and Chilean military dictatorships. Other songs in the album had less serious topics. The album had excellent sales and made *Time* magazine's list of ten best rock albums of the year. Most of the songs in his second album for Elektra, "Escenas" ("Scenes"), issued in 1985, dealt with typical Latino personal difficulties, strongly emphasizing problems of personal relationships, heartbreak, and despondency. Although Blades received high praise from the critics for the album, sales were lower than those for "Buscando América."

After spending the summer of 1984 performing with his band at the Montreux International Jazz Festival in France and then touring Latin America, in the fall Blades entered a master's degree program in international law at Harvard University. Upon completing the course work and receiving his degree he returned to music and New York, where he performed in various clubs that specialized in Latin American music. In late 1985 with his band he performed concerts of his music, including songs of social and political commentary, at Carnegie Hall in New York and at the Capital Hilton hotel in Washington, D.C. He also began a film career by starring in the film *Crossover Dreams*, a story of the pitfalls and problems encountered by a Latino singer when he goes mainstream. Blades received praise both for his performance and for the music that he wrote for the picture.

Crossover Dreams was an independently produced 1984 English-language film for which Blades helped write the script as well as the music. It started the young singer-composer on his movie career and was followed by a number of successful Hollywood films: *Critical Condition* and *The Milagro Beanfield War* in 1986; *Fatal Beauty* in 1987; and *Predator II* and *The Super* in 1991. Blades also performed in several made-for-television films: *Dead Man Out*, 1990; *The Josephine Baker Story*, 1991; and *Miracle on I-880*, 1993.

At the beginning of the 1990s Blades turned his attention again to music, issuing his first CD, "Caminando," which had a huge commercial acceptance. Then, after running for the presidency of Panama and taking some time off, he joined his friend Willie Colón in producing an album symbolizing his comeback, "Tras la Tormenta" ("After the Storm"), issued by Sony in February 1995. A collection of salsa with sociopolitical overtones, it met with considerable success. In mid-1995 Blades had a couple of movies on the board and continued with his music.

Rubén Blades has been the recipient of a number of honors and awards. In addition to gold records presented by recording companies, he has received two Grammy Awards from the National Academy of Recording Arts and Sciences. In March 1986 he was a double winner in the first annual music awards sponsored and financed by the *New York Post*. Four years later he became the first Latino to receive the National Cable award, ACE, given him as best actor in *Dead Man Out*, and in 1991 he received an Emmy nomination for his role in *The Josephine Baker Story*.

Further Reading

Américas 39 (March–April 1985): 15.

Bamrud, Joaquim. "Performer Tries for Country's Top Seat." *Detroit News* (22 December 1991): 3A.

Current Biography Yearbook, 1986. New York: H. W. Wilson Co., 1986.

New York 18 (19 August 1985): 41.

Palmer, Robert. "The Pop Life: Rubén Blades Salsa." *New York Times* (4 April 1984): C21.

People 22 (13 August 1984): 75.

FERNANDO BUJONES

(1955–   )

Cuban American Ballet Dancer

Widely considered the best classical American dancer of his generation, Fernando Bujones was the youngest principal dancer in the history of the American Ballet Theatre (ABT) and the first American to win the coveted Varna gold medal. An electrifying principal dancer during the 1970s, he was given high accolades for the technical perfection of his dancing by all critics. Inevitably he has often been compared to the Russian Mikhail Baryshnikov, his senior by nearly a decade, and in the comparison he has occasionally been found somewhat wanting in dramatic presentation. Nevertheless, Bujones's mastery of technical precision, his lyric grace, and his overall spectacular performances have won him widespread praise. As one critic wrote of a presentation, his impeccable style and the zestful animation of his movements kept the audience on the edge of its seats, ready to stand up and cheer. The youngest ABT principal dancer in its history learned his skills and earned his outstanding reputation by long, hard work.

Fernando Bujones was born on 9 March 1955 in Miami, Florida. He was the son of Cuban emigré parents, María Calleiro and Fernando Bujones, who divorced when he was about 1 year old. At the end of the 1950s he and his mother moved from Miami to Havana, where they had Cuban relatives. Several years later, concerned about her son's health, his mother took him to see a doctor who suggested that the exercise of dance classes might help him overcome problems of listless appetite and general frailty. A former dancer herself, his mother enrolled him in beginning ballet classes when he was 8 years old.

The youngest student in his class at the Academia de Ballet Alicia Alonso in Havana, Fernando quickly proved to be an apt and eager pupil. He studied for nearly two years with the famous Cuban dancer Alicia Alonso and her husband, both well known in the Ballet de Cuba. He left the Academia in 1965 to return to the United States with his mother. In Miami he continued his ballet classes and also began private instruction from a cousin who had been a ballet dancer in Cuba. When the Ballet Spectacular performed in Miami in the mid-1960s Fernando's mother persuaded one of the principals to audition her son. Fernando's enthusiasm, talent, and potential impressed the man very much, and

Fernando was given a strong recommendation for a scholarship for further study and training.

In 1966 Fernando entered the summer classes at the School of American Ballet in New York; his mother and cousin moved to New York with him. In school he so impressed officials that he was recommended for and obtained various grants including a handsome Ford Foundation scholarship. During his six years at the school on full scholarships he also continued the private coaching from his dancer cousin. The word of his dancing skill spread so widely that he was invited by the choreographer George Balanchine to join the New York City Ballet when he was only 14 years old. After talking over the offer with his mother and cousin he turned Balanchine down, feeling that he needed much more experience to handle the City Ballet's extensive and varied repertory. Meanwhile he continued to gain in reputation and skill as he took part in school workshop productions.

In 1970, at age 15 Bujones made his professional debut at Carnegie Hall. On that occasion he danced the grand pas de deux from *Don Quixote* and later continued to dance lead roles in various workshops and other ballet productions. For his graduation performance from the School of American Ballet he danced the role of Prince Siegfried in *Swan Lake*. After graduating he signed up with the American Ballet Theatre, on the advice of his mother and cousin, rather than accepting a second invitation extended by Balanchine. He officially joined the ABT's corps de ballet in June 1972. He was immediately in great demand as a leading dancer, but the administration felt he needed more experience than his 17 years had provided. However, a scant year later he was being paired with some of the leading ballerinas of that time. In the late spring 1973 he danced the pas de deux from *Don Quixote* with the well-known ballerina Eleanor D'Antuono at the John F. Kennedy Center in Washington, D.C. His performance received high compliments from reviewers for its clean technique, forceful style, and Latino verve. In May he partnered Dame Margot Fonteyn in *Les Sylphides* as a guest artist with the André Eglevsky company and then rejoined the American Ballet Theatre with a promotion to soloist.

A year later in April, just turned 19, Bujones made his European debut in a charity program at the London Palladium, again dancing with D'Antuono. In a gala event studded with stars, their performance was the evening's outstanding presentation; it received exuberant praise from the usually undemonstrative British critics. Later in 1974 Bujones competed in the senior division at the International Ballet Competition at Varna, Bulgaria. On 24 July 1974 he became the first American to win at Varna, being awarded the gold medal by an international jury of 28 judges who also cited him for his technical perfection. Upon his return to New York the following week for the American Ballet's summer season, he was promoted to principal dancer.

Unfortunately for Bujones, his rise to eminence in ballet was overshadowed in the United States by the extensive publicity given by the press to another outstanding dancer, the Russian defector Mikhail Baryshnikov of the Kirov Ballet. However, in the early fall of 1974 Bujones made a tour of Central and South America with the Ballet Spectacular. Returning to the United States in October, he took part in the American Ballet Theatre's opening performance at the John F. Kennedy Center and then danced in its regular winter season at the City Center in New York. His arduous schedule of performances and rehearsals left him little time for other activities, but he squeezed in lead performances with a number of regional ballet companies as well.

Fernando Bujones remained with the American Ballet Theatre as a principal dancer until 1985, when a much-publicized quarrel with Baryshnikov, who was then the artistic director, led to his dismissal. Without an artistic home and without a regular appointment, he began a somewhat roving existence that took him to stages in 30 countries where he was sought after and welcomed as a great classical dancer. For six years, from 1987 to 1993, he danced with the Boston Ballet, leaving that position to take the position of artistic director of the Ballet Mississippi in Jackson. Due to lack of finances the job vanished after just one year when the company suspended operations, and he accepted appointment as artistic director of the Bay Ballet Company in Tampa, Florida. This time the troupe collapsed before he even arrived to take charge.

Meanwhile Bujones took the inevitable step, at his age, from dancing to choreographing and teaching. He has said that he looks forward to passing on his knowledge to the next generation of dancers. With this transition from dancing to choreography and instructing well under way, early in 1995 he scheduled a "farewell" ABT performance in New York on 2 June. His performance in *Giselle* was greeted by the audience with unusual fervor, and he even received a congratulatory letter from President Bill Clinton. He still has some earlier scheduled commitments to fulfill. Understandably enough, as he moves into his forties his days as an exciting principal dancer noted for his technical mastery are winding down.

Among notable achievements Bujones can count his appearances as guest artist with the Joffrey Ballet, Rome Opera Ballet, Stuttgart Ballet, Deutsche Oper Ballet, the National Ballet of Canada, and the Royal Swedish Ballet, among more than 55 companies worldwide. In addition to winning the Varna International Ballet Competition gold medal, in 1980 he was selected for the Outstanding Young Man of America award. In 1982 he received an award from *Dance* magazine and four years later was given the *New York Times* Award for Outstanding Artistic Talent of

Florida. In 1989 he was honored with the Hispanic Heritage Award and in 1991 was singled out on Library of Congress Honor Day.

Further Reading

Current Biography, 1976. New York: H. W. Wilson Co., 1976.

Dance 49 (January 1975): 56.

Harris, William. "Poised at 40 to Take the Leap and Turn to Guiding Others." *New York Times* 144 (9 April 1995): S2 H29(N), H29(L).

International Dictionary of Ballet, vol. A–K. Detroit: St. James Press, 1993.

Kisselgoff, Anna. "Celebration of 50 Years of Artistry." *New York Times* 144 (5 June 1995): C14(L).

New York Times 141 (28 May 1992): C18(L).

Variety 283 (12 May 1976): 466.

Who's Who among Hispanic Americans, 1991–1992. Detroit: Gale Research, 1991.

JULIA DE BURGOS

(1914–1953)

Puerto Rican Poet, Nationalist

Julia de Burgos is remembered by many, Puero Ricans and others, for her physical beauty, powerful intellect, and commanding presence as well as for the enigmatic melancholy that consumed her. Despite sad and unfortunate personal problems that plagued much of her adult life, she was recognized by everyone as a remarkable and exceptional woman. A precursor of feminism and an advocate of Puerto Rican independence, she was also unquestionably one of the greatest Puerto Rican poets of all time.

Julia Constanza Burgos García was born on 17 February 1914 in the Santa Cruz barrio of Carolina, a small area in metropolitan San Juan, Puerto Rico. She was the eldest of 13 children, 7 of whom survived into adulthood. Her parents were schoolteachers. From her father, Francisco Burgos Hans, she learned to develop her adventurous spirit and love of freedom. From her mother, who took her on long walks along the Río Grande de Loíza, she acquired a love for nature. This river became a constant symbolic presence in the poetry she wrote later in her life.

At age 3 Julia began grammar school in Carolina and later attended Muñoz Rivera School. She stayed with a family that cared for her during school days, returning to her family home only on weekends. She loved school and was an excellent student. After her graduation from grade school with honors in 1928, her family moved to nearby Río Piedras, a university town. This move worsened her family's financial situation. Among other problems, her family was unable to pay on time the admission fee required by the exclusive University of Puerto Rico high school. She was barred from attending classes, but her desire to learn was so great that she used to climb into the classroom through a window.

Julia completed her high school education in 1931 and two years later graduated from the University of Puerto Rico with a teaching degree. Influenced by the strong sense of nationalism among university students, she began to develop a deep awareness of Puerto Rico's struggle for independence, which would later motivate her to leave the island in an act of self-exile.

After her graduation in 1933 she worked in the town of Comerío at the Puerto Rico Economic Rehabilitation Agency (PRERA), which provided milk and other basic food to children. She also worked in the Cedro Arriba barrio in Naranjito as a teacher. In 1935 she married Rubén Rodríguez Beauchamp, a journalist. To complete her bachelor's degree in education, during the summer she continued her studies at the university, where she joined the Partido Nacionalista, a leftist group advocating independence. In 1936 and 1937 she worked for the Escuela del Aire, a radio program sponsored by the Department of Education. During 1937 she was divorced and also wrote a book of poems, *Poemas exactos a mí misma* ("Exact Poems to Myself"). As a result of the book she became well known among the San Juan literary elite.

In 1938 Burgos published *Poemas en 20 surcos* ("Poems in 20 Furrows"). During this period she met Juan Isidro Jiménez-Grullón, a Dominican intellectual who became the great love of her life. Under the influence of their relationship she wrote *Canción a la verdad sencilla* ("Song to Simple Truth"); published in 1939, it reflects an almost mystical affirmation of love. These poems won her the annual award given by the Institute of Puerto Rican Culture that year. Her joy at the award was lessened by her mother's death in 1939 after four years of illness.

In January 1940 Burgos departed for New York City, where she was feted, and then in June left for Cuba to join her lover. There she wrote *El mar y tu* ("The Sea and You"), which was published in 1954. It contains her most famous poem, entitled "Río Grande de Loíza." This poem is both a love song and an affirmation of the fellowship of mankind; in it she portrays herself as a free spirit yet the product of society. She so loved this river that she requested that the first five copies of her book *El mar y tu* be cast into the river as a symbolic act of union.

In Cuba she attended the University of Havana and the Havana Free

School, studying philosophy and enjoying the company of leading literary figures. She felt at home with Havana's Paris-like life-style of gaiety and frivolity. However, her relationship with Jiménez-Grullón began to deteriorate. He was unable to commit himself to marrying her but was domineering and possessive, discouraging her literary activity. Despite his opposition and their stormy relationship, she continued to write poetry. In 1941 she entered a pro-democracy literary competition for which she wrote three war-related poems; "Las voces de los muertos" received a prize in March 1942.

Because of the stifling emotional relationship, in 1942 she decided to leave Jiménez-Grullón and go to New York City. As a feminist she could not reconcile her feelings of self-worth with his view of her as a woman. Her feminism, however, was tempered by a profound humanism. Her poetry promoted fraternization between the sexes to attain full humanity. Her feminism made Burgos a rebel against the role of women in society, yet she did not hold men responsible for the historical oppression of women. She did not allocate blame; rather, she wished to liberate men from societal notions that victimized both men and women. She implicitly claimed an autonomous ethic for women, a liberation from customs and mores that represented obstacles to attaining self-actualization as human beings.

Although Burgos was not angry at her lover, she was devastated by his demands and his rejection of her. The affair took a permanent toll on her young life. In New York City she became destitute. She worked as a seamstress, sold lamps, and wrote for *Pueblos Hispanos*. She also experienced hunger and loneliness. In her despair she began to consume alcohol. The following year she married Armando Marín and moved to Washington, D.C., but returned to New York City soon thereafter. Between 1943 and 1945 she worked as a journalist for *Pueblos Hispanos*. By this time she was well on her way to becoming a hopeless alcoholic, spending hours in bars where she would write poems on napkins.

In 1946 the Institute of Puerto Rican Literature awarded her a journalism prize for the essay "Ser o no ser es la divisa," which reflected her sociopolitical ideas. During this year her severe alcoholism led to a diagnosis of cirrhosis of the liver. The illness marked the beginning of many periodic hospital confinements. She wrote the poem "Farewell in Welfare Island" while she was thus hospitalized; in it she bid good-bye to the world. Her poem tells of the solitude, the despair, and the emptiness that she felt. She was only 39 years old when she died of pneumonia in a Harlem hospital on 16 July 1953, just hours after collapsing into unconsciousness. At the hospital she identified herself as a teacher and a poet, but in the admissions forms she appeared as amnesiac. After her death her body lay unclaimed for three days before she was buried without being identified by family or friends, as she had carried no credentials. Publication of her picture later made positive identification possible. Friends collected money to send her body to Puerto Rico, where she had wished to be buried: "I hunger for freedom. If I die, I do not want this tragic country to swallow my bones. They need the warmth of Borinquén. At least let them strengthen the worms there and not here." Her remains were buried near the river that was her inspiration, El Río Grande de Loíza.

Julia de Burgos's poetry shows clearly that she lived before her time, a forerunner of Puerto Rican feminists. Yet although her feminism was militant and active, she held men in high esteem. She hoped that she could liberate them as well as women from society's mores that seemed to her to victimize both sexes. She believed that neither sex could attain full humanity or liberation without the other. An icon for Puerto Rican writers, Julia de Burgos was clearly a woman ahead of her time.

Further Reading

Flores, Angel. *Spanish American Authors: The Twentieth Century*. New York: H. W. Wilson Co., 1992.

González, José Emilio. *Julia de Burgos: La mujer y la poesía*. San Juan, Puerto Rico: Sin Nombre, vol. 7, no. 3.

Kanellos, Nicolás. *Biographical Dictionary of Hispanic Literature in the United States*. New York: Greenwood Press, 1989.

Lockert, Lucia Fox. "Vida, pasión y muerte de Julia de Burgos." *Letras Femeninas* 16:½ (Spring 1990): 121.

"Love and Death: The Thematic Journey of Julia de Burgos." In *Latin American Women Writers: Yesterday and Today*. Pittsburgh: LALR, 1977.

McLaughlin, A. T. "The Theme of the Self-Paralleled in the Poetry of Julia de Burgos." *Ceiba* 5 (1976–1977).

Vicioso, Sherezada. "Julia de Burgos: Our Julia." *Callaloo* 17:3 (Summer 1994): 674.

LYDIA CABRERA

(1900–1991)

Cuban American Short Story Writer, Folklorist, Ethnologist

Lydia Cabrera was a remarkable woman. Author of 23 books (including several short story collections) relating to Afro-Cuban culture, folklore, and religion, she was universally considered both the number one expert on Afro-Cuban life and the foremost woman practitioner of a favorite Cuban literary genre, the short story. Almost single-handedly she brought about the retrieval and appreciation of African contributions to Cuban culture. Her three decades of research among Cuban blacks resulted in a monumental collection of source material that today remains fundamental to any study of Afro-Caribbean folklore, history, linguistics, and ethnology. The writings of the last 20 years of her life in Miami completed the trajectory of her earlier works while often showing evidence of American influences as well as nostalgia for her "lost" homeland.

Lydia Cabrera was born on 20 May 1900 in Havana, Cuba, during the unsettled times just after the Spanish American War. On her second birthday Cuba became an independent country; she thought the celebration was for her. Her father, Raimundo Cabrera Bosch, was a writer and a highly respected and well-to-do jurist who had taken an active role in the struggle for Cuban independence ever since the Ten Years War of 1868–1878. Her mother, Elisa Bilbao Marcaida y Casanova, was a graceful and elegant beauty of Basque descent. Lydia was baptized several months after her birth in New York's St. Patrick's Cathedral on one of the family's many visits to the United States. As the youngest child in a very large family, she was her father's favorite and he indulged her every fancy and whim.

Lydia grew up in a household that frequently played host to the many distinguished intellectual and political friends of her father. In the drawingroom she was exposed to a world of patriotic enthusiasms and intellectual ideas; in the kitchen she listened, all agog, to the magical folk tales of talking animals, trees, and stones related by the black servants, particularly her nanny. She quickly developed an insatiable appetite for the marvelous legends of African gods partly Christianized by Catholicism in *santería*, the syncretic religion of many Cuban blacks.

Lydia first attended a private elementary school, which she detested so heartily that her father soon sent her to a semi-public school operated by the Sociedad Económica de Amigos del País in which he was an officer. After elementary school she was educated by tutors and an older sister, since in that era Cuban girls did not go to high school (*colegio*) or the university. She also educated herself by reading and studying a wide variety of works in her father's extensive library. She became deeply interested in art, especially Oriental painting, and, without her father's knowledge and without asking his permission, took classes at the San Alejandro Academy of Painting in Havana. As a youth she also wrote extensively and had published more than two dozen articles by the time she was 14 years old. Later she also had articles on Oriental art published.

While still in her late teens Lydia became interested in colonial architecture, historic buildings, and artifacts of bygone times. After her father died in 1923 she began collecting antiques and later opened the first antique shop in Cuba. In 1927 Lydia Cabrera decide to fulfill a longtime dream and go to Paris, which the family had often visited and which she loved, to study painting. She sold out her business interests in Havana, went to Paris, and enrolled in the École du Louvre. Although her studies were far from systematic, she graduated three years later. Except for brief visits to Cuba she remained in Paris (principally) for 17 years with her close friend, the Venezuelan poet Teresa de la Parra. During this time she studied a great deal about Eastern cultures and religions and became increasingly impressed with the parallels between Oriental religious folk stories and the tales she had heard as a child from black servants in Cuba.

Her years in Paris provided a time of gestation for her later intellectual endeavors. It was a time when an intense interest in African art and cultures was felt all over France and *negritude* became the buzzword of the day. On brief visits to Cuba at the end of the 1920s Cabrera began to develop contacts with the black Cuban community. In 1932 her mother died and de la Parra entered a Swiss sanatorium because of tuberculosis. To entertain her friend, Lydia began recomposing the Afro-Cuban folk stories she recalled from her childhood. In 1936 these stories were published in translation as *Contes nègres de Cuba*, Cabrera's first book. They met with a very positive reception.

Because of the Spanish Civil War and the coming of World War II, in 1938 Lydia Cabrera returned to Cuba, her friend Teresa having died two years earlier. In Cuba she buried herself in in-depth research among Afro-Cubans, interviewing thousands of blacks and collecting mountains of material. Two years after her return she published *Cuentos negros de Cuba* and in 1948 came out with *¿Por qué? . . . : Cuentos negros de Cuba*, another magisterial collection of 28 folk tales written in her poetic, almost lyrical language. Although they are simple fictional narratives presented in an oral style, her short stories are solidly based on folk tales. As a colleague said of her, she was a scholar with the magic of a poet.

After further intensive research all over the island, in 1954 Cabrera published what many consider her most important ethnographic work, *El monte: Notas sobre las religiones, la magia, las supersticiones y folklore de los negros criollos y del pueblo de Cuba*. A seminal work on *santería*, it became the bible for Afro-Cuban studies. During the 1950s she published three additional scholarly studies, primarily of Afro-Cuban folklore, religion, and linguistics.

After the triumphs of the Cuban revolution in 1959 and the coming to power of Fidel Castro, Cabrera left for the United States and took all her research materials with her. Having a deep love for her island, she found the break difficult, despite her strong anti-communist convictions. Except for a short stay in Spain she spent the remaining 31 years of her life in Miami, somewhat apart from the Cuban exile community. During this period of her life she raced against time, organizing the results of her vast research on Afro-Cuban life. While in her Miami exile she published the bulk of her research, 15 outstanding works that made her name synonymous with Afro-Cuban folklore and most of which still remains of utmost importance to the study of the Afro-Cuban—and by extension the Afro-Caribbean—experience.

Even in self-exile Cabrera remained a preeminent figure in Cuban literature, and her short stories were frequently reprinted in anthologies of Latin American literature. In 1991, against her expressed wishes, even the Castro government published a pirated edition of her major work, *El monte*.

In Miami Cabrera's home was a mecca and haven for young Cuban intellectuals and artists, for whom she was a guiding light and mentor. Rejecting a third world stance and surrounded by mementos of her beloved Cuba and by a select group of admirers, she was always ready to welcome the tired exile and the budding young writer. As her obituary pointed out, her death marked the end of an era; she was the last link to a fondly recalled time of Cuban gentility and grace.

Lydia Cabrera died on 19 September 1991 at 92 years of age. Among accolades for her literary and ethnographic work, she was given honorary doctorates in her adopted country by Denison University in Ohio, Redlands University in California, Manhattan College in New York, and Florida International University in Miami.

Further Reading

Alvarez, Lizette. "Afro-Cuban Scholar Lydia Cabrera Dies." *Miami Herald* (21 September 1991): 1A, 22A.

Castellanos, Isabel, and Josefina Inclán, eds. *En torno a Lydia Cabrera*. Miami: Universal, 1987.

Kanellos, Nicolás, ed. *Biographical Dictionary of Hispanic Literature in the United States*. Westport, Conn.: Greenwood Press, 1989.

Kanellos, Nicolás, et al., eds. *Handbook of Hispanic Cultures in the United States*, vol. 1. Houston, Tex.: Arte Público Press, 1993.

Lomelí, Francisco A., and Carl R. Shirley, eds. *Dictionary of Literary Biography*. Detroit: Gale Research, 1992.

Madrigal, José Antonio, and Reynaldo Sánchez, eds. *Homenaje a Lydia Cabrera*. Miami: Ediciones Universal, 1978.

Marting, D. E. *Spanish American Women Writers*. Westport, Conn.: Greenwood Press, 1990.

Morgado, Marcia. "Void Never to Be Filled." *Miami Herald* (5 October 1991): 23A.

Simó, Ana María. *Lydia Cabrera: An Intimate Portrait*. New York: Inter Latin American Gallery, 1984.

ARTHUR LEÓN CAMPA

(1905–1978)

Mexican American Folklorist, Teacher

For a quarter of a century before the 1960s Chicano renaissance, Arthur León Campa, along with *nuevomexicano* educator **George I. Sánchez** and *tejano* historian **Carlos E. Castañeda**, was one of a tiny group of leading Mexican American intellectuals. He was one of the first to discard the melting pot analogy for immigrants, replacing it with a fruit salad analogy that described a pluralistic society in which there was diversity within unity. At the same time, as a semi-immigrant himself, he was able to see the essential unity of Mexican Americans whether *nuevomexicanos*, *californios*, or *tejanos*. He saw folk culture as the heart and soul of a people and was one of the first to make a relevant connection between scholarship and the daily reality of Mexican American life.

Arthur León Campa was born on 20 February 1905 in Guaymas, Sonora, an important port on the northwestern coast of Mexico. He was the son of Mexican American Methodist missionary parents, Daniel Campa and Delfina López. He spent the first decade of his life in Guaymas in a middle-class Mexican environment. When the 1910 Mexican revolution broke out his father served as an officer in the forces of the old dictator, Porfirio Díaz. His father was killed in 1914 in an encounter with Francisco (Pancho) Villa's revolutionary troops, and the Campa family, headed by his mother, soon crossed over into the United States for safety. The Campas first settled in El Paso, where Arthur began his American education and also worked as a delivery boy to help support the family.

Later the Campa family moved to Albuquerque, New Mexico, where Arthur continued his education first in the local Methodist school and then in Albuquerque High School. After high school he entered the University of New Mexico (at Albuquerque), majored in modern languages with Spanish as his specialty, and in 1928 received his A.B. degree. Upon graduation he taught for a year at Albuquerque High and then with help of a [Bronson] Cutting Research Fellowship completed his master's degree in 1930. With his advanced degree he was able to obtain a position at the university teaching Spanish and French, but he realized that he needed to get a Ph.D. in order to succeed in higher education. Accepted in the doctoral program at Columbia University in New York, he completed the requirements for a doctorate in modern languages in 1940.

Campa continued to teach at the University of New Mexico, being promoted from instructor to assistant professor in 1932, to associate professor in 1937, and to full professor in 1942. In the mid-1930s he briefly participated in the Works Progress Administration (WPA) folk art program in New Mexico. In 1943 he enlisted in the armed services at age 38. During the last two years of World War II he served in the European and North African theaters as an Army Air Corps combat intelligence officer with the rank of captain. Upon his return to civilian life he accepted a position as chair of the division of languages and literature at the Methodist-related University of Denver in Colorado. He also was director of its center for Latin American studies. Except for leaves of absence, he remained there until his retirement in 1972.

As a result of his wartime experience Campa was employed in various capacities by the U.S. Department of State. In the mid-1950s he was appointed cultural attaché for the U.S. embassy in Lima, Peru. Because of his expertise in the folklore of the Hispanic people of the American Southwest, he was sponsored by the State Department to give a series of lectures in Spain; as a result he was honored with an appointment as corresponding member of the Real Academia Hispano-Americana. He took an extremely active part in western hemisphere language and folklore organizations and was a frequent speaker at their conferences.

Although he was trained primarily as a linguist, Campa's area of interest and research was folklore, particularly that of the Hispanic Southwest. He recognized that *nuevomexicanos* differed from *californios* and *tejanos* in their life experiences, socioeconomic status, cultural development, and degree of assimilation, but stressed similarities in their cultures rather than the differences. He rejected most *nuevomexicano* claims to aristocratic origins and their assertions of Spanish rather than Mexican origins.

Campa pointed out that it was the continuing frontier isolation of the New Mexican area that resulted in the retention of archaic language and other cultural elements from Spain, not any ethnic considerations. He used the term "Mexican" in a cultural rather than national or ethnic sense. Arguing that *tejanos* and *californios* were increasingly affected by the propinquity of Mexico and heavy immigration, he noted that *nuevomexicanos*, especially in the northern part of the state, continued to be withdrawn and isolated.

With a populist attitude toward scholarly activity, Campa saw his task as the combining of folklore and history in order to describe and explain New Mexico's popular culture. History, he said, provided the facts, whereas folklore made possible a more complete understanding of those facts. Making use of New Mexico's extensive oral traditions, he wrote voluminously on southwestern folklore. In addition to several Spanish-language textbooks and numerous articles, he published half a dozen books on popular lore in music, theater, poetry, religion, and language. His most important works were *A Bibliography of Spanish Folklore in New Mexico* (1930); *Spanish Religious Folktheatre in the Southwest* (1934); *Treasures of the Sangre de Cristos: Tales and Traditions of the Spanish Southwest* (1963); and *Hispanic Culture in the Southwest* (1979). The last was published posthumously.

Although moderate in his political views, in 1939 Campa was briefly the temporary national president of the fledgling, somewhat leftist Congreso del Pueblo de Habla Española. He stepped down when pressure was put on the University of New Mexico by conservatives. He was less active politically than some of his academic peers, but he supported efforts of the League of United Latin American Citizens (LULAC), the American G.I. Forum, and other moderate organizations to improve the social and economic position of Mexican Americans in U.S. society.

Further Reading

Campa, Arthur L. *Hispanic Culture in the Southwest*. Norman: University of Oklahoma Press, 1979.

Contemporary Authors: A Bio-Bibliographical Guide, vols. 17–18. Detroit: Gale Research, 1967.

García, Mario T. *Mexican Americans: Leadership, Ideology, & Identity, 1930–1960*. New Haven, Conn.: Yale University Press, 1989.

Sonnichsen, Philip. "Arthur León Campa." *La Luz* 7:12 (December 1978).

Who's Who in the West, 1972–1973, 13th ed. Chicago: Marquis Who's Who, 1972.

JOSÉ CANSECO

(1964–   )

Cuban American Professional Baseball Player

José Canseco unquestionably ranks among the all-time greatest power hitters in baseball. From early in his professional career, fans responded to his prowess by showing up in large numbers whenever he appeared. On the other hand, he also became widely known for his sizable ego, considerable arrogance, and abiding concern for the financial bottom line. He claims that this negative reputation is the result of ethnic prejudice—especially on the part of newsmen, with whom he has generally had a poor relationship since the beginning of his baseball career. Certainly some of the sports writers give indications of a less-than-impartial, evenhanded attitude toward Canseco, however valid their reasons may seem to them.

José Canseco was born on 2 July 1964 in a suburb of Havana, Cuba, just a few minutes after his twin brother Osvaldo (also a professional baseball player). He was the second son and third child of Barbara Capas and José Canseco Sr., members of one of Havana's prominent families. After the success of the Castro revolution in 1959, his father, who had been an important executive in an American petroleum company, lost his job and their home as a result of his staunch anti-communist stand. The Canseco family was finally permitted to leave Cuba in December 1965. Arriving in the United States, the Cansecos first settled with relatives in the town of Opa-Locka, just north of Miami. A decade later they moved into Miami proper.

José grew up in Opa-Locka and Miami, beginning his education in the former and completing grade and high school in the latter. His hard-working upper-middle-class parents encouraged him to do his best in school, and he claims he was an excellent student until he got his driver's license. Although he was active in basketball and soccer as a youngster, he did not play baseball until he entered high school. He tried out for the Coral Park High School baseball team all four years but made the varsity team only in his senior year. He failed to make the Florida high school all-stars that year, even though he had a high batting average that led to several college sport scholarship offers. He showed considerable promise as a hitter, but his physical build worked against him in the view of most pro scouts; he was 5 feet 11 inches tall and weighed 160 pounds. In the 1982 draft Canseco was selected only in the fifteenth round, by the Oakland A's whose scout in Miami had argued for his potential. He signed up.

Canseco spent the next four years playing in various minor league Oakland teams. In 1982 and 1983 he progressed at an average pace through the Miami and Idaho Falls rookie teams and the Madison, Wisconsin, and Medford, Oregon, minor league teams. Nothing spectacular. At the end of the 1983 season he played on the A's Arizona Instructional League team; his four home runs there tied him for first place on the team and his 26 runs batted in (RBIs) put him in the lead in that category. About this time he began a rigorous weight-training program that ultimately added inches to his height and increased his weight to over 230 pounds, making him one of the strongest athletes in baseball. Later it also led to unsupported rumors of steroid use.

In 1984 Canseco led the A's Modesto, California, team in home runs (15) and in RBIs (73); unfortunately, his strike-out record was equally impressive, 127 out of 410 times at bat. The following year his stepped-up weight-gain regime began to really pay off. His half-season hitting record with the A's farm team in Huntsville, Alabama, led to his being named most valuable player in the Southern Association. Promoted at mid-season to Oakland's Class-AAA team in Tacoma, Washington, he continued to give evidence of his batting skills, becoming the first batter in 26 years to hit a ball out of Tacoma's Cheney Stadium. Fans began coming to games early to watch him at batting practice, and *Sporting News* gave him its minor league player of the year award.

Called up to the Oakland A's at the beginning of September 1985, Canseco made a very unimpressive debut in the majors by striking out as a pinch hitter. However, he soon redeemed himself by hitting a ball up on the roof of Comiskey Park in Chicago and by ending his first major league year with a .302 batting average. In his first full season with the majors he attracted great attention by his power hitting. At mid-season he was number one in the American League in RBIs and home runs— which got him selected for the 1986 All-Star team. He finished the season in the number four position for home runs with 33, and second in RBIs with 117. *Sporting News* and the Baseball Writers Association both named him American League Rookie of the Year. Unfortunately, his strike-out and outfield error records were equally striking.

Despite a slow start in 1987 Canseco improved his earlier performance; his fielding was noticeably better and he raised his batting average from .240 to .257 while decreasing the number of his strike-outs. However, 1988 was Canseco's year. It began with his confident prediction that he would hit 40 home runs and steal 40 bases, a feat no one had ever achieved but a boast he fulfilled by the end of September. His 120 runs, 42 home runs, 124 RBIs, .307 batting average, and 40 stolen bases won him unanimous selection as Player of the Year by both the Associated Press and *Sporting News*.

In the following season Canseco's personality began to seriously hurt his image. Before the season even started he was severely criticized in the press for not fulfilling various commitments connected with his star status and for his strong emphasis on the monetary bottom line. Then in February he was arrested in Miami for racing his red Jaguar at 120 miles per hour and having a handgun in the car. Soon after again reporting late for spring practice in Phoenix, Arizona, he was arrested for running a red light. Many of his critics saw these occurrences as evidence of an arrogant and capricious attitude, but Canseco claimed his troubles arose from bigotry and bias, especially on the part of the news media. Although he made no apologies for his behavior, he began trying to improve his image by being more civil with reporters and by settling down a bit in his off-diamond activities.

On top of these problems, early in the 1989 season Canseco suffered a serious wrist injury. This accident led to surgery that necessitated a long rest. During his recuperation he was arrested in the northern California Bay Area for having a semi-automatic pistol in his car on a college campus. In July he returned to the A's with a bang. In 65 games he hit 17 home runs and was credited with 57 RBIs. His performance was an important factor in the A's winning the World Series that season. In the following year he signed a five-year, $23.5 million contract with the comment that he was worth more than that because of both his hitting skill and his popularity with the fans. A back problem and other injuries plagued him throughout the 1990 season, causing him to miss a third of the games. In 1991 Canseco had an excellent year, finishing up with 44 home runs and 115 runs scored. Unfortunately, he also ranked second in strike-outs with 152.

Meanwhile, his personal problems had not diminished. The deterioration of his marriage to the former Miss Miami, Esther Haddad, led to the announcement of divorce proceedings followed by a reconciliation early in 1991. In February 1992 after quarreling with his wife he expressed his feelings and made the front page by ramming her BMW with his Porsche and was arrested. Their subsequent divorce did not end his bickering with her.

Managerial unhappiness with what newspaper headlines characterized as "big bat, big ego, big pain" and his on-field performance, plus other considerations, led to Canseco's being traded by the Oakland team to the Texas Rangers later that year. "Three men for a baby" read a *New York Times* headline on 6 October 1992 as stories of the lack of popularity with his former teammates also began to appear. Clearly he had fallen into disfavor in Oakland. Canseco told reporters that he was happy with the Texas Rangers, and his record in 1994 seemed to confirm that statement; but in December he went to the Boston Red Sox. Happy in Boston, in 1995 he re-signed for two years at $9 million despite reported offers from Tony La Russa to join the St. Louis Cardinals. At Boston he has continued his impressive, albeit somewhat less spectacular baseball career despite injuries. In a March 1996 interview the much-subdued first baseman with exactly 300 home runs to his credit said he hoped to play until he had hit 500—which he figured would take him seven, "maybe eight," more seasons.

At Boston throughout the year 1995 Canseco seemed to be less the volatile, temperamental star of years gone by and more the team player. The newly modest, more reticent star has shed his youthful flamboyance and arrogance and is a cooperative player, aware that he has eight teammates. No longer does he blame all his troubles on racism and bias; nor does he drive fast cars anymore. He has even sold his two speedboats and now stresses his volunteer work with youth groups. At the end of Janurary 1997, Canseco was traded back to the Oakland A's.

Further Reading

"The Battle Is with Himself." *GQ* 59 (May 1989): 224–228.

Bloom, Barry. "Monster Basher." *Sport* 86:6 (January 1995): 87–91.

"Canseco Traded for Otis Nixon." *New York Times* 144 (10 December 1994): Sports 31, 36.

Chass, Murray. "Boston Hopes It Has a Straw for Its Drink." *New York Times* 144 (2 May 1995): B13.

Current Biography Yearbook, 1991. New York: H. W. Wilson Co., 1991.

Frey, Jennifer. "The Questions Are Lingering for Canseco." *New York Times* 141 (5 September 1992): 28(L).

Geracie, Bud. "An Older, Wiser Canseco." *San Jose Mercury News* (6 March 1996): 1D.

Montville, Leigh. "Texas-Sized Trade." *Sports Illustrated* 77:11 (14 September 1992): 36–39.

Mooney, Louise, ed. *Newsmakers, 1990: Cumulation.* Detroit: Gale Research, 1990.

Who's Who in America, 1990–1991. Chicago: Marquis Who's Who, 1990.

MARIAH CAREY

(1970–   )

Venezuelan American Singer, Lyricist

With the release in June 1990 of her debut album "Mariah Carey," the 20-year-old singer burst upon the popular music world like a Fourth of July rocket a bit ahead of its time. Carey impressed both critics and music lovers with the amazing range of her five-octave voice, leading to comparisons with the noted Peruvian singer Ima Sumac. Moreover, the soulful passion in her singing voice created deep emotional feeling, especially among young people, who rushed in record numbers to stores to buy the album. Her co-authorship of the lyrics of the 11 songs on the album met with less flattering comments from critics, some of whom characterized their sentimentality of personal crises and bankrupt relationships as trite, maudlin, and sophomoric. The lyrics may have been commonplace, but the voice was not. Mariah was clearly the outstanding new artist on the music scene and as a result received an extremely rare triple Grammy nomination: best female pop vocalist, best album, and best new artist. She won Grammies as Best New Artist and Best Female Pop Vocalist. In 1992 she received the American Music Award for favorite soul/

R&B artist, and in December 1995 *Billboard* named her the number one Top Billboard 200 Album Artist—Female.

Mariah Carey was born in 1970 in New York City, the youngest of three children of an interracial marriage. Her father, Alfred Carey, was a black Venezuelan aeronautical engineer; her mother, Patricia, was an Irish American singer and voice coach. Because Mariah was nearly a decade younger than her two siblings, both of whom left home at relatively early ages, she spent some of her most formative years virtually as an only child. Her parents experienced considerable marital stress, arising in part from terroristic acts by racist neighbors and frequent movings partly as a result. They separated and divorced when Mariah was 3 years old. She grew up living with her mother in limited economic circumstances, seeing her father infrequently.

When her mother, a former soprano with the New York City Opera, realized that Mariah was gifted with a remarkable singing range, she began giving her toddler voice lessons on a regular basis. Before Mariah turned 5 she knew that she wanted to become a professional singer and began directing her energies toward that goal. Her mother nourished her budding talent, provided support, instilled in her a strong belief in herself, and supplied a successful role model as a singer. She often took Mariah with her on gigs and encouraged her to participate in the impromptu jam sessions of musician colleagues. As a result, by the time Mariah entered first grade she felt quite grown-up and was, in fact, far more self-confident and sophisticated than fellow students of her age.

Often left alone at home as a child (her mother sometimes held as many as three jobs), Mariah spent hours listening to music on the radio and playing her older siblings' records. As a result, she says, her musical taste was influenced by gospel and soul as well as by Motown rock music. At this time her favorite singers were Stevie Wonder, Gladys Knight, Aretha Franklin, Al Green, Edwin Hawkins, and the Clark sisters—whose records formed the heart of her brother's and sister's collections. From her mother and her mother's musician friends she learned also to love the jazz patterns of Sarah Vaughn and Billie Holiday.

After various changes of residence, in the mid-1980s her mother settled in Huntington, a small town on the northern coast of Long Island. Because of the family's repeated moves and Mariah's absolute conviction that she would one day become a successful professional singer, she was an indifferent student, and her high school teachers had to struggle to keep her from dropping out. The frequent residential moves also resulted in few close friendships and a self-directive attitude. In addition, they reduced Mariah's involvement in music programs at school. However, at age 13, while still in junior high, she began writing songs in her spare time. Through her brother she later met the young composer Ben Margulies, with whom she began a successful song-writing collaboration that lasted nearly half a decade.

In 1987 when Mariah graduated from Harborfield High School at age 17 she left Huntington for New York City to begin her assault on the music world. She shared a one-bedroom apartment in Manhattan with two other young aspiring and struggling artists, sleeping on a mattress on the floor. The talented singer worked as a waitress, hat check girl, and restaurant hostess and spent all her free time making the rounds of record company offices with her demonstration tapes. Her persistence— or "abundance of attitude," as one critic was later to characterize it— paid off. Soon she was regularly being offered studio session work and ultimately became backup for the singer Brenda Starr, who recorded with Columbia Records. The two became good friends, and Starr helped Mariah get her tapes into the right hands.

At a Columbia Broadcasting Company party in late 1988 Mariah was introduced by Starr to Thomas D. (Tommy) Mottola of CBS Records, and she gave him one of her demo tapes. Mariah's voice greatly impressed Mottola, who shared the tape with other CBS executives. It happened that just then Columbia lacked a major female pop singer and was on the lookout for candidates to fill that void. Mariah was seen as ideal to meet the CBS need, and she was signed up in December.

Before her debut album, "Mariah Carey," was released, Mottola of Columbia Records mounted a carefully orchestrated publicity blitz that included a promotional tour, an appearance at a record industry convention, and the singing of "America the Beautiful" at the opening game of the National Basketball Association finals in Michigan. This last performance brought her intense voice to the attention of an estimated 16 million television viewers. "Mariah Carey" quickly reached number one in *Billboard* ratings, remained there for over five months, and eventually sold over seven million copies. Four singles from the album also reached number one position on the pop charts.

"Mariah Carey" was followed in September 1991 by Carey's second album, "Emotions," which met with mixed reviews from the critics. However, it sold over three million copies by the end of 1993, demonstrating that she was no flash in the pan as far as the public was concerned. Its title song became a number one single. Meanwhile, her third effort, "Mariah Carey MTV Unplugged," released in 1992, reached sales of two million in its first year and showed that Carey's ability was not limited to music studio performances. In 1993 she released her fourth album, "Music Box." The following year saw the issuance of "Merry Christmas" in time for the holiday season, and in October 1995 "Daydreams" came out with the usual saturation publicity. The "Daydreams" single, "Fantasy," led to Carey's debut in October as director of a video with the same title and to preliminary discussions with Sony about future releases under her own custom label. Her albums together have sold over 60 million copies worldwide, making her one of the world's top-selling artists.

On 3 November 1993 Carey began her first tour with the initial performance in Miami, Florida. The critics, underwhelmed by her performance, panned it. Recognizing that their criticism was valid and that her performance was impaired by the fact that as a studio performer she was unused to the dissimilar atmosphere of the concert stage, Mariah made the needed corrections. Her next concert appearance on the tour received rave reviews. In the early spring of 1996 Carey began a world tour with her first concert in the Tokyo Dome because of her great popularity in Japan. Although she was the top-selling foreign artist there in 1994 and 1995, nevertheless her performance was preceded by Columbia Records' usual all-encompassing publicity barrage.

In June 1993 Mariah Carey, the multi-talented multi-millionaire, wed Tommy Mottola, now president of the worldwide music division of Sony, which had acquired Columbia Records. To get away from the pressure of the music business and to savor the fruits of their accomplishments, the couple retreats as often as they can to their large wooded estate in rural upstate New York. In addition to enjoying her success, Mariah participates in charitable events and is concerned with the problems of inner-city youths, recurrently working with the Police Athletic League in Manhattan.

Further Reading

Current Biography Yearbook, 1992. New York: H. W. Wilson Co., 1992.

Dougherty, Steve. *People Weekly* 40:21 (22 November 1993): 82–88.

Dunn, Jancee. "Clown 'N' Dirty." *Rolling Stone* 721 (16 November 1995): 33.

Flick, Larry. "Columbia Blitz for Carey's 'Daydream' a Global Reality." *Billboard* 107 (9 September 1995): 1, 20.

Gates, David. "Starting Out at No. 1." *Newsweek* 116 (6 May 1992): 63.

Goodman, Fred. "The Marketing Muscle behind Mariah Carey." *New York Times* 140 (14 April 1991): 28, 30.

Holden, Stephen. "The Pop-Gospel According to Mariah Carey." *New York Times* (15 September 1991): 28, 30.

Johnson, Robert F. "Mariah Carey Says: My Mom Taught Me to Believe in Myself." *Jet* 85:12 (24 January 1994): 52–57.

"Mariah Carey: 'Not Another White Girl Trying to Sing Black.'" *Ebony* 46:5 (March 1991): 54–58.

McClure, Steve. "Japan Is Crazy for Carey." *Billboard* 108 (23 March 1996): 9, 18.

Norment, Lynn. "Mariah Carey." *Ebony* 49:6 (April 1994): 54–60.

Tannenbaum, Rob. "Building the Perfect Diva." *Rolling Stone* (23 August 1990): 33.

VIKKI CARR
(FLORENCIA BISENTA DE CASILLAS MARTÍNEZ CARDONA)
(1940–)

Mexican American Singer, Entertainer, Philanthropist

Vikki Carr, who was unable to go to college because of family poverty, has an overriding concern about education, especially for her fellow Mexican Americans. She has been quoted as asserting her belief that education is the real answer to three-fourths of the problems faced by Chicanos. Not only does she say this, but she also places her considerable talents and her purse in support of that belief. She is perhaps best known in philanthropic circles for the Vikki Carr Scholarship Foundation, which for the past three decades has provided scholarships to help young Mexican Americans reach their goals. However, she has other philanthropic irons in the fire as well.

Florencia Bisenta Cardona was born in San Juan, a suburb of El Paso, Texas, on 19 July 1940, the first of seven children of Florence and Carlos Cardona. While she was still a toddler the family moved to Rosemead, California, a small town on the eastern edge of Los Angeles. She grew up there in a family atmosphere in which music played a daily part. She sang while her father, a construction worker, played the guitar and inculcated in his children an awareness of and a pride in their Mexican culture, particularly its music. Her first occasion to sing in public took place at age 4 when she sang "Adeste Fideles" in a local Christmas program.

Still speaking only Spanish, Florencia entered the local Catholic grammar school and then attended Rosemead High School, where she joined the a capella choir, took all the music courses offered, and took part in all the plays. To improve her stage presence she also took drama classes. A bit of a tomboy, she was good at sports but preferred to spend most of her time with her music. As she grew older she began singing with small local bands on weekends while still in high school. Upon graduation she was offered a job by Pepe Callahan as vocalist with his Mexican-Irish band. Calling herself Carlita, the 18-year-old singer made her debut with the band at the Chi-Chi Club in Palm Springs, California. Because the name Carlita limited her repertoire largely to Spanish-language songs, she later changed her professional name to Vikki Carr, an abbreviation and adaptation she made from Bisenta (also spelled Vicenta) Cardona. As Vikki Carr she could sing songs in any language. She has always made a point of proudly announcing her Mexican heritage to her audiences.

While touring with the band, Vikki Carr made a sample recording of her singing and sent the record to agents and record companies. Finally her singing ability was recognized; in 1961 she signed a long-term contract with Liberty Records and made her first commercial recordings. Although not a smashing success in the United States, her records became very popular in England and Australia. In between moderately successful concert tours she continued to work in a local bank for several years. Then she toured Australia and on her return was hired as the vocalist with Ray Anthony's big band on television. This exposure led to engagements on the night club circuit: Las Vegas, Reno, Lake Tahoe. By the second half of the 1960s Vikki Carr had become one of the top female vocalists in the United States and was the featured guest on major television variety shows. She even filled in for Johnny Carson several times. She also did six English television specials in London.

In 1966 Vikki Carr recorded the song "It Must Be Him," which was immediately a huge success in England and a year later became equally popular in the United States. Her position as an international singing star was firmly established in 1967 when she was invited by Queen Elizabeth II of England to give a Royal Command Performance. There followed a wildly successful Vikki Carr Show at the London Palladium and then equally triumphant sold-out concert tours of the principal European countries, Japan, and Australia. Later she also toured Mexico and a number of South American countries. At the same time she expanded her musical horizons, making her musical comedy debut in Kansas City as the lead in *South Pacific* and in 1969 starring in *The Unsinkable Molly Brown*. Since then she has performed in numerous musicals.

After nine years with Liberty Records, in 1970 Vikki Carr switched to Columbia Records and two years later did her first album completely in Spanish, "Vikki Carr en Español." She soon became one of the leading voices in Latino music and has done television specials on the Mexican networks. A number of her Spanish-language recordings have reached gold and platinum status. In 1980 she signed with CBS/Sony Records. Her 1985 album for Sony, "Cosas de Mujer," won her a Grammy, as did "Cosas de Amor," cited as the Best Latin Pop Album of 1992. The title song was also named Single of the Year. In all, Vikki Carr has had 17 gold albums and over 50 best-selling records.

In 1968, while fulfilling a two-month engagement at San Antonio's

HemisFair, Vikki Carr was told of the financial difficulties of Holy Cross High School in the *mexicano* barrio. This opened up a whole new field of interest for her. She began a series of annual benefit performances that have since raised over a quarter of a million dollars for the school. In addition to her fund-raising for Holy Cross High and her scholarship foundation, she has raised money for scholarships at Southern Methodist University (Dallas), for the popular Cursillo movement (a Hispanic religious movement), and for the Denver chapters of the American G.I. Forum. She has also participated in benefit performances for organizations such as the March of Dimes, the American Cancer Society, the American Lung Association, the Tuberculosis Association, and St. Jude Children's Research Hospital. She averages more than one benefit per month.

In 1970 Vikki Carr was invited by President Richard M. Nixon to give a concert on June 2 at a dinner honoring Venezuelan president Rafael Caldera, who was visiting Washington. Subsequently she became the favorite of the Republican White House, singing at President Nixon's second inauguration in 1973 and at state dinners by invitation of presidents Gerald R. Ford, Ronald Reagan, and George Bush. In July 1990 she sang at the dedication of the Nixon Library in Yorba Linda. Among her albums in recent years are "Brinda a la Vida, al Bolero, a Ti," for Sony in 1992 and "Recuerdo a Javier Solís," in 1994, also for Sony. In 1996, although in the second half of her fifties, she continues her busy schedule of night club, concert, and theater appearances and has occasionally appeared in Latino television specials.

In addition to the laurels implicit in the command performances for presidents and royalty, Vikki Carr has been the recipient of numerous specific honors. In 1970 she was named Woman of the Year by the *Los Angeles Times* and Visiting Entertainer of the Year by Mexican authorities. In 1974 St. Edward's University in Austin awarded her an honorary doctorate in fine arts, and in the following year she received an honorary Doctor of Laws degree from the University of San Diego. In 1984 she was named Hispanic Woman of the Year by the Hispanic Women's Council. Four years later Nosotros, the association of Latino actors, selected her for its Golden Eagle award as Outstanding Performer, and in 1991 she was given the Girl Scouts of America Award. Among her many other accolades, unquestionably the most all-embracing is Woman of the World, given her by the International Orphans Fund.

Further Reading

Carr, Vikki. "Building Higher Horizons." *News–San Antonio* (14 September 1981).
Chacón, José. *Hispanic Notables in the United States of North America*. Albuquerque: Saguaro Publications, 1978.

Doviak, Joan, and Arturo Palacios. *Catorce personas lindas*. Washington, D.C.: Educational Systems Corp., 1970.

García, David, Jr. "Florencia Bicenta de Casillas Martínez Cardona: It Must Be Her." *Nuestro* 3:7 (Fall Special 1979).

Martínez, Al. *Rising Voices: Profiles of Hispano-American Lives*. New York: New American Library, 1974.

Telgen, Diane, and Jim Kamp, eds. *Notable Hispanic American Women*. Detroit: Gale Research, 1993.

LOURDES CASAL

(1938–1981)

Cuban American Writer, Poet, Political Activist, Intellectual

Like virtually all Cuban American writers who came to the United States as adults, Lourdes Casal's life was driven by her concern for the island of her birth and by her relationship to it and its government. This exile, rather than immigrant, consciousness sharply illustrates her refugee perspective and her hope of some day returning. Unlike most of her cohorts she did return at the end of her life, even though she recognized that living in America had changed her. She is representative of a small group of exiled Cuban writers who came to modify their views of Castro's government over the years and have described the process in their writings.

Lourdes Emilia Irene de la Caridad Casal y Valdés was born in 1938 in Havana, Cuba, into a family of middle-class professionals of combined European, African, and Asian ancestry. Her mother, Emilia Valdés, was a primary school teacher; her father, Dr. Pedro Casal, was a dentist and doctor of medicine. Lourdes grew up in Havana, first attending private primary and secondary schools. However, in her junior year in 1951 she moved to a public school, Instituto Número 2 in the Vedado district, from which she received her *bachillerato* in science and letters at age 16. Shy and introverted, she was also a very serious and highly intelligent student, as her parents recognized; to provide her with the best educational opportunity, after her graduation from the institute they enrolled her in the private Catholic University of Santo Tomás de Villanueva in the Marianao district of Havana.

At the university Lourdes began as a student of chemical engineering but decided that the discipline was too dry and limiting and in 1957 switched to psychology, which she had found much more interesting and exciting. During her seven years, 1954 to 1960, at Santo Tomás she became much less self-conscious and shy, and she soon stood out in student affairs, writing for several student publications. She was a regular contributor to the newspaper *El Quibú*, subdirector of the *Revista Insula*, secretary general of the Asociación Cultural, and president of the women's group of the Juventud Universitaria Católica. She also underwent an extensive period of religious crises at this time.

Because this was a time of widespread Cuban opposition to the dictator Fulgencio Batista, especially at the universities, Lourdes inevitably became involved in the anti-Batista plotting. By the late 1950s she also joined her fellow students in revolutionary activities in support of Fidel Castro's 26th of July movement. When Castro and his followers came to power in 1959, she became a member of the Revolutionary Student Directorate. The subsequent leftward tilt of the Castro government led her to become critical of its ideology and methods, but not its objectives. After working in the anti-Castro underground for a while, in 1961 she was forced to flee Cuba.

As a director in the Consejo Revolucionario Cubano (CRC) in exile, Casal made a trip to Africa underwritten by the CIA. After the disbanding of the CRC as a result of the missile crisis of late 1962, Casal settled in New York where she resumed her graduate studies in psychology at the New School for Social Research. In 1962 she received her master's degree in psychology and 13 years later completed the work for her doctorate. Deeply concerned with the widening gulf between Cuban intellectuals and the revolutionary government, during this time she put together a collection of documents that were published in 1971 under the title *El caso Padilla: Literatura y revolución en Cuba*. Her book outlined the increasingly difficult and tense relationship between the revolution and Cuban writers as exemplified in the case of the poet Heberto Padilla, who was harassed for his views by officials of Castro's government and finally forced into exile. In the late 1960s and early 1970s Casal was writing poetry and short stories as well as publishing the results of her psychological studies. In 1973 she published a collection of her short stories titled *Los fundadores: Alfonso y otros cuentos* with Ediciones Universal in Miami.

During the 1960s Casal became an American citizen and also became deeply involved in the civil rights movement, a participation that eventually helped lead her to completely rethink her position toward the Castro revolution and the radical government that had evolved from it. Her new attitude was that of a friendly critic. Like most other Cuban American writers who had reached adulthood before leaving the island, she was also deeply concerned about the potential loss of Cuban culture by the Cuban American generation. She was a leader in helping found the literary magazine *Areito*, which she hoped would become the focal point for Cuban culture in the United States by taking a less partisan view of Castro's attempt at social reformation.

In the 1970s Casal was also active in academia, teaching social psychology at several universities in the United States. Among them were Rutgers University in Newark, New Jersey; Brooklyn College of the City University of New York; and Dominican College of Blaufeld, in Blaufeld, upper New York state. As part of her academic persona she wrote and edited numerous articles and monographs on psychology as well as on societal and political topics. In 1974 she was awarded a Cintas fellowship by the Institute for International Education, and three years later she won a Ford Foundation competition on the Movement of Caribbean Peoples. In 1978 she obtained a Social Science Research Council summer grant to do further research in Cuba; in 1978 and 1979 she was a Woodrow Wilson Fellow at the Wilson International Center for Scholars at the Smithsonian Institution in Washington, D.C.

Meanwhile, at the invitation of the Cuban government Casal made an exploratory research trip to Cuba in September 1973, a logical accompaniment to her reevaluation of Castro's revolution and her interest as a social psychologist in its efforts to change Cuban society. A short time later on her second visit she participated in a conference of Cuban intellectuals at the University of Havana, an experience that changed—or at least considerably modified—the views expressed in her *Padilla* book and also her attitude toward the Castro government. When pressed for her reasons for the change, she replied that she was convinced that on balance the revolutionary government was a positive force for Cuba. The journal *Areito* now became a vehicle for the expression of more favorable views toward the Cuban government as Casal pursued a course of fostering better relations between the refugees and Cuba. This bridge-building now became the heart of her interests. As a result she became intensely involved in the Círculo de Cultura Cubana, the Institute for Cuban Studies, and Cuban Studies/Estudios Cubanos, among others. In 1978 she played a major role in the discussions between exiled Cuban intellectuals and the Cuban government; this dialogue resulted in a Cuban agreement to permit exiles to visit their families on the island.

Although many of her fellow Cuban refugees, despite their strong emotional attachment to Cuba, had reconciled themselves to spending the rest of their lives in the United States, Casal had not. Aware that she was suffering from a terminal kidney ailment (she went on dialysis in 1977), she returned to Cuba in December 1979 in order to die and be buried in her beloved homeland. After a lengthy and excruciating illness she expired there on 1 February 1981, too soon to see publication of a volume of her Casa de las Américas Prize–winning political poetry, *Palabras juntan revolución*, issued by the Casa in Havana later that same year.

Further Reading

Burunat, Silvia. "Lourdes Casal." In *Biographical Dictionary of Hispanic Literature in the United States*, Nicolás Kanellos, ed. Westport, Conn.: Greenwood, 1989.

Casal, Lourdes. "Cubans in the United States: Their Impact on U.S.–Cuban Relations." In *Revolutionary Cuba in the World Arena*, Martin Weinstein, ed. Philadelphia: Institute for the Study of Human Issues (ISHI), 1979.

de la Cuesta, Leonel, and María Cristina Herrera, eds. *Itinerario ideológico: Antología de Lourdes Casal*. Miami: Ediciones Diáspora, 1982.

Fradd, Susan. "Cubans to Cuban Americans: Assimilation in the United States." *Migration Today* 11:4/5 (1983): 34–42.

Rivero, Eliana. "From Immigrants to Ethnics: Cuban Women Writers in the U.S." In *Breaking Boundaries: Latina Writing and Critical Readings*, Eliana Ortega et al., eds. Amherst: University of Massachusetts Press, 1989.

Telgen, Diane, and Jim Kamp, eds. *Notable Hispanic American Women*. Detroit: Gale Research, 1993.

PABLO CASALS

(1876–1973)

Spanish American Musician, Cellist, Conductor, Composer, Teacher

Pablo Casals is the only man in history to give two recitals at the White House—with nearly 60 years in between! The first was for President Theodore Roosevelt in 1904 and the second for President John F. Kennedy in 1961. Beyond cavil the greatest cellist of the 20th century, his fame as a cellist, conductor, and composer began in the 19th century and spanned most of the 20th. When Casals moved to Puerto Rico in 1957, Governor **Luis Muñoz Marín** welcomed him to the island with a one-hour panegyric that not only extolled his numerous artistic and personal virtues but included him with Albert Einstein and Albert Schweitzer as one of the three most important figures of contemporary history.

Pablo Casals was born in the province of Catalonia on 29 December 1876 in the small town of Vendrell, about 44 miles south of Barcelona.

He was born into an undistinguished middle-class family. His father, Carlos Casals, belonged to a family that had been paper manufacturers for years. When his father's older brother took over the paper business, Carlos chose to become a church organist and teacher of piano because he had shown a natural talent for music. Pablo's mother, Pilar Ursula Defilló y Amiguet, had been born on the then Spanish island of Puerto Rico, where she had received an above-average general education. Although shy and retiring, Pilar was also firm in her views and resolve. She instilled this sense of personal strength in young Pablo.

The second of 11 children, Pablo grew up in a musical milieu. For Casals the everyday household noises were juxtaposed to and blended with the sound of music, particularly the piano. "I remember when I was 2 or 3," Pablo said, "sitting on the floor and resting my head against the piano to hear better what my father was playing." Musical rhythms and discipline were central to his intellectual and musical development. Young Pablo learned to read musical scores with the same ease that he later learned to read Spanish. His father guided him musically, teaching him to play the piano, violin, and organ before he was able to read and write. By the time he was 8 years old he was skilled enough to substitute for his father at the church organ.

Pablo's childhood was essentially happy and carefree; generally his parents enveloped him in security and their love. However, as he grew up he was often disturbed by the fact that they quarreled over his future. His father, a humble man, believed that a life in music would be financially hazardous and that his son should apprentice to a carpenter. His mother, on the other hand, recognizing his musical genius early on, always supported and nurtured his musical career; she even took him to Barcelona, where he studied for two years at the Municipial School of Music. While studying in Barcelona he helped support himself by playing for dances in a local café.

At the same time Pablo did not neglect the enjoyment of life. As a young man he made friends easily as he explored the culture of Barcelona's streets and barrios and entered the world of endless discussions on music, politics, and society. Casals matured as a high-spirited young man, yet he never strayed from his parents' code of right and wrong. From his father and his early music teacher he learned concentration and the discipline of study. Throughout his life he adhered to a lengthy daily routine in which his music was always the first consideration. On the other hand, he also developed a feeling for adaptability and flexibility. This youthful view of flexibility remained with him throughout his life.

Pablo Casals began his concert career while still in his mid-teens. Accompanied by his mother and two brothers, he studied in Madrid from 1894 to 1897. Then after an extremely brief period of study in Paris he returned to Barcelona, where he taught at the municipial music school.

As a young musician he revolutionized the way the cello was played by developing a new, relaxed technique of freedom and naturalness in the finger and elbow movements to make cello playing easier, more fluid. While teaching in Barcelona he also seized every opportunity to play in the opera, on the concert stage, and at fashionable resorts. With his savings from this playing he then returned to Paris to study and in November 1899 made his official concert debut there. It was an immense success.

For the next two decades Casals constantly toured Europe and the Americas from his base in Paris, making more than a dozen trips to the United States. Returning to his native Catalonia after World War I, in Barcelona he founded and underwrote a symphony orchestra that he conducted. He also continued his world tours, appearing as a guest conductor with such orchestras as the New York Symphony and the London Symphony. Guided by his strong sense of integrity, he refused to perform in Russia as a protest against the brutality of the communist regime. When General Francisco Franco led the revolt in 1936 against a duly elected Spanish government, Casals declared himself in opposition, refused to play in Spain, and went into voluntary exile in southern France. Despite numerous offers to play in the United States, he remained with his fellow exiles in southern France throughout World War II.

After the end of the war Casals resumed his concert touring for a while and then decided to accept no more foreign engagements in protest against the democracies' acquiescence to Franco. After nearly nine years of quasi-retirement, in 1956 he returned to the concert stage in Mexico and then spent three months visiting his mother's birthplace in Puerto Rico. In the following year Pablo Casals married Marta Montañez, a native of Puerto Rico and one of his most brilliant students. He was only a few months shy of his 81st birthday and she was just 21. She brought spirit, humor, gaiety, and companionship into his life and kept it organized as well. Marta, a gifted musician, often joined him in musical performances as he continued to tour the world.

Pablo and Marta moved from Paris to Puerto Rico and built a home there. Casals founded the Casals Festival in 1957 and conducted its annual concerts. After the festival each year he would conduct in Carnegie Hall and then teach and conduct in the summer program at the Marlboro School in Vermont. Casals found the key to his "fountain of youth" in continued teaching and constant learning and in playing the cello. He firmly believed that every time he played a piece of music he could find something new in it, no matter how many times he had performed the music before. In short, he established flexibility and adaptability within routine.

Casals received the U.S. Presidential Medal of Freedom in 1963 and eight years later was awarded the United Nations Peace Medal. No matter the international acclaim, the tributes, all the decorations that came his way from 1900 onward; Casals considered that he was, as he said: "a man first, and an artist second. As a man, my first obligation is to the welfare of my fellowman. I will endeavor to meet this obligation through music—the means which God has given me—since it transcends language, politics, and national boundaries. My contribution to world peace may be small. But at least I will have given all I can to an ideal [peace, fraternity, fellowship] I hold sacred."

During the latter years of his life until his death in 1973, Casals never slowed down his pace of work. By the time of his last concerts in the late 1960s and very early 1970s, Pablo Casals had completely fused his music and his personal philosophy. In classical music he found not only the common soul of humanity but love for life. He knew who he was—a man who loved peace and freedom, and a citizen of the world through his music. "Humanity," he said, "is far more important than music. You can do much for humanity with music, with anything noble. But greater than all is love, love for all the living."

Further Reading

Blum, David. *Casals and the Art of Interpretation*. New York: Holmes & Meier, 1977.

Corredor, José María. *Conversations with Casals*, trans. André Mangeot. New York: E. P. Dutton, 1958.

Hargrove, Jim. *Pablo Casals: Cellist of Conscience*. Chicago: Children's Press, 1991.

Kahn, Albert E. *Joys and Sorrows: Reflections of Pablo Casals*. New York: Simon and Schuster, 1970.

Katchen, Julius. "The Miracle of Pablo Casals." *Music and Musicians* (January 1961): 14.

Kirk, H. L. *Pablo Casals: A Biography*. New York: Holt, Rinehart and Winston, 1974.

CARLOS CASTAÑEDA

(1896–1958)

Mexican American Historian, Teacher, Author

Only a handful of American historians have achieved the academic stature attained by Dr. Carlos Castañeda. In a lifetime devoted to the study of history he wrote a dozen outstanding books and over six dozen jour-

Carlos Castañeda. Photo courtesy of the
University of Texas at Austin.

nal articles on the history and culture of the U.S. Southwest and Mexico.
Central to his scholarship was his seven-volume *Our Catholic Heritage in
Texas, 1519–1936*, published between 1936 and 1950. In addition to his
publications he was important for the many enthusiastic graduate students he trained to share his dedication to southwestern history.

Few American historians have received more honors than Carlos Castañeda. In recognition of his great historical contributions he was made
a knight commander in the Order of Isabel La Católica by the government of Spain and a knight of the Equestrian Order of the Holy Sepul-
chre of Jerusalem by Pope Pius XII. The Academy of American
Franciscan History gave him the Serra Award of the Americas for 1951.
Among the many other tokens of the high regard in which he was held
were honorary memberships in various historical societies of Central and
South America as well as in the Texas Philosophical Society.

Carlos Eduardo Castañeda was born on 11 November 1896 in the small
town of Ciudad Camargo on the Rio Grande in the Mexican border state
of Tamaulipas. He was the seventh of eight children born to Elisa and
Timoteo Castañeda, a Mexican civic leader and schoolteacher of Yuca-

tecan birth and Texas education. To escape the impending Great Revolution of 1910 the family moved first to Matamoros and then, when Carlos was 12 years old, across the river to Brownsville, Texas. He entered the local school and also enrolled in summer school in order to perfect his mastery of English. His parents died two years later within months of each other. Despite this trauma Carlos was able to go on to Brownsville High School; after school hours he worked as a clerk in a general store. In addition to his work and school he found time for sports. He graduated from high school in 1916, valedictorian and the only Mexican American in his senior class.

During his high school years Carlos Castañeda showed the passion for learning instilled in him by his parents; his conscientious work and outstanding grades won him a scholarship to the University of Texas at Austin, where he enrolled as an engineering student. A year after the United States entered World War I in 1917 he enlisted in the army, where he served as a machine gun instructor. Upon mustering out of the service he returned to the university, only to be forced to drop out again for financial reasons. For a year he worked in the Tampico (Mexico) oilfields as an engineer for Mexican Gulf Oil Company and then returned to Austin.

When he entered the university Castañeda had obtained a student job working for the preeminent Texas historian Eugene C. Barker, who became both his mentor and friend. From Tampico he wrote to Barker about his intention to become a historian. Excited and fascinated by history, especially that of Mexico and Texas, he switched from engineering to history after his junior year. With funds from the George Tarleton scholarship and an anonymous donor, he was able to complete his historical studies in record time. In 1921 he graduated from the University of Texas, Phi Beta Kappa, with a B.A. in history.

Unable to find a college position as he had hoped, Castañeda began his teaching career in the public high schools of Texas, first at the Beaumont high school and then at Brackenridge High School in San Antonio. With the counsel and support of Professor Barker and by dint of working 16 hours a day, he also completed his studies and thesis for an M.A. in history, which he received in 1923. He then took a job as an associate professor in modern languages, teaching Spanish for four years at the College of William and Mary southeast of Richmond, Virginia. Although he enjoyed teaching there, financial difficulties and his wife's serious illness plagued his spirit. Besides, his heart was still in Texas and he continued to importune Barker about job possibilities there. When he was offered a position in the University of Texas library in 1927 as head of its new Latin American Collection, he quickly accepted.

Back again in Austin, Castañeda also enrolled in the university's doctoral program in history, working under Barker. In 1928 he published

The Mexican Side of the Texas Revolution, based on his translations of eye-witness Mexican documentation of the 1836 event. Four years later, having completed the requirements, he received his doctorate in history. His "thesis" was an annotated translation of Fray Juan Agustín Morfi's "lost" *History of Texas*, which was published three years later. His work on Morfi's *History* brought him considerable publicity and an appointment from the Texas Historical Commission of the Knights of Columbus to write a history of the Catholic Church in Texas for the upcoming Texas centennial in 1936. This project expanded to eventually become the heart of his research and publishing; between 1936 and 1950 he published the seven volumes of his monumental narrative history, *Our Catholic Heritage in Texas, 1519–1936*, a far broader work than its title indicates.

In 1939 Carlos Castañeda accepted an invitation to join the history department of the University of Texas, part-time. With his typical tremendous energy he retained his library position half-time and was working on *Our Catholic Heritage*. In that same year he was elected president of the American Catholic Historical Association. And, of course, he was teaching classes. Over the years he served as editor for the *Hispanic American Historical Review*, *The Handbook of Latin American Studies*, and *The Americas*. He also participated actively in local, regional, state, national, and international historical meetings and worked to develop better relations between scholars and universities on both sides of the Rio Grande.

Because of his detailed knowledge of borderland history and his excellent reputation, Castañeda was recruited during World War II by the chairman of the Fair Employment Practices Committee (FEPC). The FEPC had been created by an executive order of President Franklin D. Roosevelt to enforce his prohibition of discrimination in defense industries and government employment. Castañeda took a leave of absence from the university and was appointed special fact-finding assistant to the chairman and director of Region 10 in Texas. At the end of the war he returned to his jobs at Austin.

Although immersed in Texas history, Castañeda was not isolated from contemporary issues and was fully aware of racial discrimination. A member of the middle class, he participated in moderate Mexican American organizations such as the League of United Latin American Citizens, which were concerned with ethnic prejudice. He believed the American system was basically sound and advocated a pluralistic society with deeper understanding between Anglo and Mexican Americans. His contribution was the rewriting of Texas history to stress what the two groups held in common rather than what divided them.

In 1946 Castañeda was promoted from associate to full professor in the history department, where he remained for the rest of his life, researching and chronicling the history of his beloved Texas. After a very productive lifetime devoted to historical studies he died on 4 April 1958.

Further Reading

Almaraz, Félix D., Jr. "Carlos Eduardo Castañeda, Mexican-American Historian: The Formative Years, 1896–1927." In *The Chicano*, Norris Hundley Jr., ed. Santa Barbara, Calif.: Clio Press, 1975.
"Carlos Castañeda." *La Luz* 3:10–11 (January–February 1975).
Cattell, Jacques, ed. *Directory of American Scholars*, 3rd ed. New York: R. R. Bowker Co., 1957.
García, Mario T. *Mexican Americans: Leadership, Ideology, and Identity, 1930–1960.* New Haven, Conn.: Yale University Press, 1989.
Mecham, J. Lloyd. "Carlos Castañeda, 1896–1958." *Hispanic American Historical Review* 38:3 (August 1958): 383–388.

LAURO CAVAZOS JR.

(1927–   )

Mexican American Presidential Cabinet Member, University President, Educator

Lauro Cavazos was the first U.S. Latino to be appointed a cabinet officer, secretary of education for President Ronald Reagan. His qualifications as an educator were of the highest and his goals as secretary the noblest. He wanted every child in America to be educated to his or her fullest potential. He favored bilingual education with the clear goal of English proficiency and supported affirmative action despite a White House lack of enthusiasm for, and sometimes outright opposition to, such programs.

Lauro Fred Cavazos Jr. was born on 4 January 1927 on the famous King Ranch in southern Texas, the eldest son of one of the foremen who was a descendant of an 18th-century Mexican land grantee. His father, Lauro Fred Cavazos, and his mother, Tomasa Quintanilla Cavazos, had limited formal schooling but a great appreciation of the importance and value of education. Cavazos received his first two years of schooling in the small one-room school for *mexicanos* on the King Ranch. Then his father bought a house in the nearby town of Kingsville so that his children could have better educational opportunities. Lauro (or Larry, as he was known to most Anglos) and his siblings became the first Mexican American students in the Kingsville elementary school. Despite some prejudice and hostility, the Cavazos children did well in school, encouraged and urged on by their father's insistence on the paramount importance of education.

Upon his graduation from high school in 1945 young Lauro enlisted, at age 18, in the U.S. army and served in the infantry during the last months of World War II. When he was mustered out a little over a year later, he enrolled (at his father's insistence and over his youthful objections) in the Texas Arts and Industries College (now University) in Kingsville. Later, taking the advice of one of his teachers, he transferred to Texas Technological University at Lubbock. There he completed his undergraduate work in three years, graduating in 1949 with a B.A. in zoology. Securing an appointment as a teaching assistant, he then began working on a master's degree, specializing in cytology, the study of cell formation, structure, and function. In 1952 he was awarded his master's degree and also obtained a fellowship to Iowa State University of Science and Technology at Ames to study for his doctorate.

In 1954 with his Ph.D. in physiology in hand, Cavazos accepted an offer to teach anatomy at the Medical College of Virginia in Charlottesville. In the ensuing decade between 1954 and 1964 he was promoted from instructor to assistant professor and then to associate professor. With a basic interest in cell replication he authored numerous articles on the topic, some of which were reprinted in textbooks. He also published two guides on dissection in human anatomy. In 1964 he was offered the chairmanship of the Department of Anatomy at Tufts University School of Medicine at Medford, Massachusetts, with the rank of full professor. He accepted. In the early 1970s he was advanced from departmental chairman to associate dean of the medical school and then soon to acting dean and in 1975 to dean.

In his 16 years at Tufts, Lauro Cavazos also served on the faculty of the New England Medical Center Hospital, on a National Board of Medical Examiners advisory committee, and on several editorial boards. While at Tufts he achieved his long-term professional ambition to have an impact on medical policy. And then he received an offer he could not turn down. In 1980, while being considered by President-Elect Ronald Reagan for the post of secretary of education, he was offered the presidency of his alma mater, Texas Tech. He accepted.

As president of Texas Technological University from 1980 to 1988 Cavazos provided efficient and financially cautious leadership, cutting the administrative costs per student to a little more than one-half of the state average. He also traveled tirelessly over the entire state, giving talks in high schools to encourage more students to go to college. He especially pushed for greater Mexican American and black enrollment in the University and also worked energetically to reduce the dropout rate of minority students. He was more successful at the former than the latter.

In 1983 the Texas LULAC (League of United Latin American Citizens) named Lauro Cavazos the Hispanic Educator of the Year, and in the following year President Reagan bestowed on him the Outstanding Leadership Award in education. In addition to these tributes, 11 honorary degrees from various universities and colleges, and other honors, he was named to the Hispanic Hall of Fame by the national LULAC in 1987. Later he was awarded the Medal of Honor by the University of California, Los Angeles. However, not everything he did was well received. His tendency as president of Texas Tech to establish policy unilaterally without consulting the faculty offended its sense of collegiality. With morale at a low ebb, in the fall of 1984 the faculty formally declared its lack of confidence in President Cavazos. However, he managed to weather the academic turbulence for the time.

In 1988, a few months after announcing that he was stepping down as president and would return to teaching after a sabbatical, Cavazos was tapped by President Reagan for the post of secretary of education. His selection was almost certainly a political move. Cavazos was a Texas Democrat, and the presidential campaign of Reagan's heir, George Bush, was faltering in Texas. Cavazos believed his national leadership might help prevent further erosion of the federal education budget, which was under bitter attack within the Reagan administration. With his eminent qualifications for the post, Cavazos's appointment was unanimously confirmed by the Senate, making him the country's first Hispanic cabinet member. Two months later, in November, President-elect Bush named him to his cabinet.

As secretary of education, Cavazos continued his efforts to encourage minority enrollment in college and to reduce the dropout rate. Less than two years later he resigned as the result of tremendous pressure from the arrogant White House chief of staff, John Sununu. Cavazos's goals for the Department of Education were certainly at variance with those of the president, and he was criticized as being ineffectual as secretary of education. Since his resignation he has been active as a teacher as well as a business and education consultant. In April 1993 he was named to the board of directors of Luby's Cafeterias, Inc., a Texas chain, and he remains an adjunct professor at Tufts School of Medicine in Medford, Massachusetts.

Further Reading

"The Amazing Cavazos Family." *Texas* [*Houston Chronicle* Magazine] (5 February 1989): 5–7.
Current Biography Yearbook, 1989. New York: H. W. Wilson Co., 1989.

Hernández, Antonia. "La Educación: El Secretario Cavazos está equivocado."
    Réplica 21 (July 1990): 14–15.
Kanellos, Nicolás, ed. *The Hispanic Almanac.* Detroit: Visible Ink Press, 1994.
"Luby's Cafeterias, Inc." *Wall Street Journal* (15 April 1993): B12(E).
Mooney, Louise, ed. *Newsmakers: The People behind Today's Headlines.* Detroit: Gale
    Research, 1989.
Who's Who in American Politics, 1993–1994, 14th ed., vol. 2. New Providence, N.J.:
    R. R. Bowker, 1993.

CÉSAR CHÁVEZ

(1927–1993)

Mexican American Social Activist, Union Organizer

César Chávez's struggle for the human dignity of workers in harvest agriculture made him a world-recognized Mexican American leader and a national metaphor for equality, humanity, and social justice. Both as a symbol and as an individual he was an energizing force bringing to the attention of all Americans the many injustices suffered by farm workers. Because of his leadership and dedication, powerful agribusiness interests were forced to face issues of social responsibility, decent wages, humane work and housing conditions, and pesticide abuse. He touched millions of lives; his life made a difference.

A quiet unpretentious man, Chávez was not charismatic in the generally accepted use of that word. His charisma derived from his personal moral goodness and his deep concern for the suffering of individuals. An intense, ascetic person, a man of contrasts, he had a gentle sense of humor combined with a will of steel. He was a great admirer of Mohandas Gandhi and Martin Luther King Jr. and their commitment to nonviolence. His simplicity of manner belied the ego that any great leader must have to be successful.

César Estrada Chávez was born on 31 March 1927 on a small farm homesteaded in 1909 by his Mexican grandfather Cesario near Yuma, Arizona. He was the second child of Juana Estrada and Librado Chávez, who eked out a precarious living on the farm. When the Great Depression of the 1930s occurred, the Chávezes like thousands of other Americans lost their land because they could not pay their taxes. Piling their meager possessions in and on their old Studebaker, they joined the long procession heading for California.

César grew up following the harvests in California and Arizona. At best his home was a tarpaper-covered shack in a farm labor camp, and at worst a tent, the Studebaker, or shelter under some overpass. César and his brothers endured, learning independence from their father and compassion from their mother. But they learned little in school. By his own count César attended at least 30 schools before he dropped out in the seventh grade. He could scarcely read and write.

At the end of the 1930s the Chávez family was living in the Sal Si Puedes ("Get Out If You Can") barrio of San Jose, California, and César worked alongside his parents and siblings in the harvest fields. Here he first became acquainted with labor unions when his father became active in one. Although these early unions were unsuccessful, the lessons of unionism were impressed upon young César.

In 1944 17-year-old César enlisted in the U.S. navy and spent two years of World War II on a destroyer escort in the Pacific. Returning to San Jose after his discharge, the young veteran courted Helen Fabela from Delano, and in 1948 they were married. They worked in harvest agriculture with the Chávez clan.

In the summer of 1952 there occurred an event that changed César Chávez's life. Through a local priest, Rev. Donald McDonnell, he became acquainted with Fred Ross Sr., an organizer for the Community Service Organization (CSO). The CSO taught people how to solve their own problems. Although skeptical at first, Chávez quickly became a "convert" and joined the CSO as an unpaid volunteer, working in voter registration. By observing Ross carefully he learned techniques of recruiting and organizing, of holding meetings, of creating power among the powerless. At the same time, with help from his wife he began to read and study in order to improve his poor education and thereby become a more effective organizer.

By 1958 Chávez was a director in the CSO. During the next few years he became increasingly convinced that the organization had strayed from its earlier goal of mobilizing the very poor. Because workers in agriculture were among the poorest, he believed that the CSO should concentrate its efforts among them. The CSO board of directors disagreed. When his proposal to organize a farm workers' union was again voted down in 1962, Chávez resigned from the organization and moved to Delano in California's central valley. Here he began to build his National Farm Workers Association (NFWA). Helped by Fred Ross, **Dolores Huerta**, and others, Chávez spent 16 to 18 hours a day, 7 days a week, talking to workers about the need for organization. In three years he enrolled some 1,700 families in the union and had achieved some minor successes.

On 16 September 1965 the NFWA voted to join some 800 Filipino grape workers in their strike for higher wages and better working and living conditions. Realizing that his fledgling union with its $100 treasury was far from ready and would need all the help it could get, César sought and obtained support from the student movement, from civil rights and church groups, as well as from established unions and national leaders. He also converted La Huelga ("The Strike") from a mere labor dispute to a civil rights crusade—La Causa ("The Cause"). He strongly stressed its moral basis and dramatized it by making the Virgin of Guadalupe its unofficial symbol along with the black eagle; by organizing a long march from Delano to the state capital, Sacramento; by undertaking a 25-day fast to reaffirm his commitment to nonviolence; and by declaring a nationwide grape boycott that soon spread overseas.

At the end of the march to Sacramento in April 1966 Chávez's United Farm Workers Organizing Committee, as the union was now known, won contracts from 11 major wine grape companies, but growers of table grapes held out. Even with a conscience-stirring national and international boycott of California table grapes, it took Chávez until 1970 to bring them to the bargaining table. In July, with the help of the Catholic Bishops Committee on Farm Labor, three-year contracts were drawn up with 26 growers; the five-year strike had ended in success. Unfortunately, the United Farm Workers (UFW) sorely lacked a professional staff needed to successfully implement the contracts.

When the three-year UFW contracts expired, 59 California grape growers signed with the Teamsters Union. Meanwhile Chávez attempted to organize workers in the Salinas Valley lettuce fields but encountered the Teamsters union there and failed after eight years of boycott. In announcing the boycott's end, Chávez declared it had served its purpose of calling attention to the workers' plight.

In spite of Chávez's continued vigorous leadership and the union's wide range of services to its members, UFW membership began to decline in the second half of the 1970s. By the end of the decade Chávez's union had shrunk to about 20 percent of the 90,000–100,000 California farm workers earlier enrolled. The promise of the 1975 state Agricultural Labor Relations Act, which provided statutory support for secret ballot union elections, was quickly sabotaged by the legislature's control of its funding. Two years later Chávez's leadership suffered another blow when a serious internal UFW split resulted in the loss of some of the union's most experienced organizers and staff. On top of this, by the 1980s unionism generally was running into hard times all over the country.

To counter rising anti-union sentiment and to recapture the dream of the 1960s, in the early 1980s Chávez turned to expanded objectives and new tactics such as mass mailings with computerized lists. Among his goals was the reduction of excessive use of pesticides; in 1984 he initiated a new grape boycott because of pesticide abuse. In July 1988 Chávez went on his third fast—his "act of penance," as he referred to it—to publicize the boycott and to bring the pesticide issue dramatically to the attention of the American people. His 36-day fast left him greatly weakened physically.

The grip that Chávez, the tireless fighter, held over the imagination of so many idealists of the 1960s and 1970s had also weakened. The Delano grape strike was a remarkable personal victory, but by the 1990s it seemed to many to be largely symbolic in its benefits. There was some criticism, even by friends and family, of his absolute and personal domination of the UFW. By the beginning of the 1990s the union had perhaps 20,000 members and about 100 contracts; statewide its influence appeared marginal. The grape boycott was still in place, but few consumers seemed aware of it. However, César Chávez still had a devoted following.

In 1976 there was some talk of Chávez being a possible candidate for a Nobel Prize. In November 1990 Mexican president Carlos Salinas Gotari conferred on him the highest award Mexico can give to a foreigner, the Aguila Azteca. César Chávez died unexpectedly in his sleep on 23 April 1993 while in Arizona testifying in a UFW court case. In August the San Jose (California) City Council by a unanimous vote declared the Chávez home at 53 Scharff Avenue a historical landmark. One year later U.S. president Bill Clinton honored Chávez with the nation's highest civilian award, the Presidential Medal of Freedom. At the end of March 1995, after a two-decade campaign by Mexican Americans and others, New Haven Middle School in Union City, California, was formally renamed the César Chávez Middle School. A well-attended commemorative march at San Jose, California, in late March 1996 seemed to some observers to be another sign of the recent resurgence of Chávez's union, the UFW.

Further Reading

García, Richard A. "César Chávez: A Personal and Historical Testimony." *Pacific Historical Review* 63:2 (May 1994): 225–233.

Goodwin, David. *César Chávez: Hope for the People*. New York: Fawcett Columbine, 1991.

Griswold del Castillo, Richard and Richard Garcia. *César Chávez: A Triumph of Spirit*. Norman: University of Oklahoma Press, 1995.

Hammerback, John C., et al. *A War of Words: Chicano Protest in the 1960s and 1970s*. Westport, Conn.: Greenwood Press, 1985.

Levy, Jacques E. *César Chávez: Autobiography of La Causa*. New York: W. W. Norton, 1974.

London, Joan, and Henry Anderson. *So Shall Ye Reap: The Story of César Chávez and the Farmworkers Movement*. New York: Thomas Y. Crowell Co., 1971.

Pitrone, Jean M. *Chávez: Man of the Migrants*. New York: Pyramid Communications, 1972.

DENNIS CHÁVEZ

(1888–1962)

Latino Leader, U.S. Senator from New Mexico, 1935–1962

From the 1930s until his death in 1962, Dennis Chávez was the only Mexican American of note on the national political scene. He was, in other ways as well, a unique political figure in Washington, D.C. A New Deal liberal by conviction, he supported President Franklin D. Roosevelt's 1937 plan to liberalize the U.S. Supreme Court by enlarging its membership from 9 to a maximum of 15 justices. He voted for U.S. ratification of the United Nations charter, but against American participation in a proposed post–World War II peace-keeping force. He was sponsor of, and strongly supported, an Equal Rights Amendment; yet he endorsed a bill outlawing strikes in plants operated by the government during the war. In all he was a paradoxical, and sometimes seemingly illogical, political leader.

Dennis Chávez came from an extensive clan with old New Mexican roots; one of his ancestors came to this northernmost province of New Spain (Mexico) in 1691, and later ones played important roles in *nuevomexicano* government and economy. Dennis was born on 8 April 1888 in a dirt-floor adobe home in Los Chávez, a small settlement east of Albuquerque in Valencia County, the eldest son of eight children born to David Chávez and his wife Paz Sánchez Chávez. Baptized Dionisio, he found his name was changed to Dennis when he entered the local school; he used that Anglo name for the rest of his life and named his only son Dennis Jr.

When Dennis was 7 years old the Chávezes moved to Albuquerque. Because they were very poor he worked as a newsboy and dropped out of school in the eighth grade to drive a grocery delivery wagon. Working from 6 o'clock in the morning until sundown, the 13-year-old earned $2.75 a week. Four years later, in 1905, having studied surveying at night, he got a job in the engineering department of the city of Albuquerque at five times that salary.

Dennis Chávez. Photo courtesy of the Center
for Southwest Research, General Library, University of New Mexico.

Although Dennis had left school, he had by no means ended his education. Nearly every evening after work he went to the Albuquerque
library, where he read voraciously. For the rest of his life he remained
an avid reader of history and biography. He was particularly attracted
to Thomas Jefferson and devoured every word he could find on his hero.
Through reading about Jefferson he developed an early interest in politics.

The year before New Mexico became a state in 1912, Dennis married
Imelda Espinosa. He took great interest in the statehood process and four
years later ran for county clerk but lost. He also acted as Spanish interpreter for Andreius A. Jones, a successful Democratic candidate for the
U.S. Senate. Senator Jones rewarded him with a job as a Senate clerk in
1918 and 1919. While clerking, Dennis was accepted in Georgetown University law studies by special examination in lieu of a high school diploma. Constantly encouraged by Imelda, after three years of night law
classes he earned his Bachelor of Laws (LL.B.) degree in 1920 at age 32.

Chávez returned to Albuquerque and established a law practice as a
base for his political career. The ambitious young lawyer soon ran, suc-

cessfully, for the state House of Representatives. He also campaigned regularly for Democratic candidates, and in 1930 he was elected as New Mexico's single voice in the U.S. House of Representatives. Two years later he was re-elected as part of the Democratic New Deal landslide. In a bitter, hard-fought campaign in 1934 he tried to unseat New Mexico's popular senator, the liberal Republican Bronson F. Cutting. Narrowly losing the election, he filed charges of voting fraud against Cutting. While his lawsuit was still pending, Cutting was killed in an airplane crash in May 1935 and Chávez was appointed to replace him until elections in the following year. Chávez easily won the election. In 1940 he was re-elected and thereafter was regularly returned to the Senate, election after election.

Originally Dennis Chávez was elected as a Hispanic candidate by *nuevomexicanos* who were beginning a massive switch in the early 1930s from the Republican to the Democratic Party. However, by the end of World War II in 1945 less than 40 percent of New Mexicans were Hispanos, and he needed the votes of the Anglo newcomers as well. From the 1940s until his death he achieved a remarkable balancing of these two often antagonistic conservative political blocs.

As a freshman senator in the 1930s Chávez was quickly plunged into the mounting tensions created by the rise of Adolf Hitler in Germany. A Western isolationist, he disagreed with many of President Franklin D. Roosevelt's more internationalist positions. In 1939 he urged recognition of General Francisco Franco's fascist government in Spain. Yet he favored creation of a government radio station to offset Nazi propaganda in Latin America and argued for trade expansion to counter German economic influence there. In March 1941 he voted against the first Lend-Lease bill to aid the allies fighting Hitler, but reversed his stand on the second bill in October. A month later he opposed the arming of merchant ships although he supported their right to sail in combat zones and to enter belligerent ports. These seeming inconsistencies resulted in part from rapidly changing events in Europe between the outbreak of World War II in September 1939 and U.S. entrance after Pearl Harbor in December 1941.

Chávez saw his role in the Senate as advancing New Mexican interests. A reserved and quiet man, he infrequently spoke on the floor and tried to avoid public debate. His political interests were reflected in his committee memberships. He was a member of the committees on Indian Affairs, Irrigation and Reclamation, Education and Labor, and Territories and Insular Affairs. (He had a special interest in Puerto Rico.) Through committee memberships, especially on the Appropriations Committee and Post Office and Post Roads, he developed considerable power. As one of the last great individualist politicians, he often took independent stands and sometimes irked many of his loyal conservative supporters with his advocacy of liberal social legislation.

During the post–World War II years Senator Chávez did some of his most statesmanlike work. He worked quietly to improve the lot of Native Americans. He exerted forceful leadership in writing a bill and spearheading a fight to establish a permanent federal Fair Employment Practices Commission (FEPC). Although he was frustrated in this effort by southern Democratic filibustering, he continued the struggle through his influential position on Senate committees. Only after his death was a permanent federal FEPC established in the 1960s. His most important contribution, especially to his Hispanic American constituency, was his advocacy and support of education and civil rights. Yet in 1960 he voted to send a civil rights bill back to committee, thereby effectively killing it.

Senator Chávez was a key figure in national defense, strongly supporting U.S. preparedness. Asserting "There can be no price tag on freedom," he opposed efforts to reduce the size of the army and air force after World War II and vigorously advocated increased defense appropriations. He laid the groundwork for establishing U.S. military bases in Spain, and he proposed consideration of sending U.S. troops into Cuba at the time of the Bay of Pigs fiasco in 1961.

In the early 1960s Chávez continued his busy schedule, even participating in the 1962 political campaign in New Mexico although he was not up for re-election and was ill with cancer. (The senator was a very heavy smoker—as many as 12 cigars a day.) On 18 November 1962 he died in Georgetown University Hospital at age 74 of complications arising from cancer of the throat. His body was returned to Santa Fe for an official lying-in-state, and he was buried in Albuquerque. When New Mexico was invited to select its most distinguished son for a statue in the Statuary Hall of the Capitol, the New Mexico Historical Society chose Dennis Chávez.

Further Reading

Current Biography, 1946. New York: H. W. Wilson Co., 1947.

Keleher, William A. *Memoirs: 1892–1969, A New Mexico Item.* Santa Fe: Rydal Press, 1969.

Perrigo, Lynn I. *Hispanos: Historic Leaders in New Mexico.* Santa Fe: Sunstone Press, 1985.

Popejoy, Tom. "Dennis Chávez." In *Hall of Fame Essays.* Albuquerque: Historical Society of New Mexico, 1963.

Vigil, Maurilio E. *Los Patrones: Profiles of Hispanic Political Leaders in New Mexico History.* Washington, D.C.: University Press of America, 1980.

Linda Chávez

(1947–)

Mexican American Political Commentator, Educator, Author

Long active in politics, Linda Chávez has been a participant in the Successor Generation Conference in France, 1981; Young Leaders Conference in Germany, 1984; Monitoring Panel on UNESCO, 1984; United Nations Conference on Women in Nairobi, 1985; American Young Leaders Alumni in Sicily, 1989. She is a complex individual who marches to an interesting sociopolitical drummer. An outspoken opponent of affirmative action for minorities, she has been accused of favoring the denial to others of what she herself has benefited from. Although she makes pronouncements as a Latina, she rejects being identified with the Latino community. In the long run her forthrightness and strongly conservative views have probably hurt her career.

Linda Chávez was born on 17 June 1947 in Albuquerque, New Mexico, the daughter of Velma McKenna and Rodolfo Chávez, whose family had come to the northern Mexican frontier in the 1600s. After spending her early years in Albuquerque, at 10 years of age Linda moved with her family to Denver, Colorado, where she attended parochial schools. In both cities she grew up in working-class Mexican American barrios; at home her father stressed the family's colonial Spanish background.

In high school Linda first became acutely aware of racism and discrimination and joined both the Congress of Racial Equality (CORE) and the National Association for the Advancement of Colored People (NAACP). She even walked the picket line at a segregated Woolworth's lunch counter in Denver. After high school she entered the University of Colorado at Boulder just as the Chicano *movimiento* was getting under way. However, she was never attracted to its rhetorical radicalism and confrontational tactics. Instead she concentrated on studying hard and getting good grades; as an English major and an honor student she also volunteered to tutor Mexican American students who had difficulties with English.

After graduating with a B.A. in English in 1970, Linda Chávez entered a doctoral program in English and Irish literature at the University of California, Los Angeles. She was also persuaded by the administration to teach a class in Chicano literature despite her lack of enthusiasm for the course. Unwilling to accept the validity of Chicano literature as a college subject, she found herself pressured and harassed by campus militants. Faced with this situation, in 1972 she gave up academia and joined her husband, Christopher Gersten, in Washington, D.C.

In Washington Linda worked for the Democratic National Committee to offset Richard Nixon's wooing of the Latino vote and soon became a professional staffer for liberal Republican congressman Don Edwards of California on the subcommittee on civil and constitutional rights, House of Representatives Judiciary Committee. After a year and a half in that position she moved to the liberal National Education Association (NEA) as a lobbyist. In 1975 she undertook the job of assistant director of legislation for the more conservative American Federation of Teachers union (AFT). Two years later, in February, she accepted an appointment from the new president, Jimmy Carter, to the Department of Health, Education, and Welfare as special assistant to the deputy assistant secretary for legislation. A few months later she was briefly a consultant to the president's Office of Management and Budget reorganization project.

In 1977 Linda Chávez was offered the dual position of director of research for AFT and editor of its influential quarterly publication, *American Educator*. As editor of the *American Educator* from 1977 to 1983 she authored and published a series of articles on the need to teach traditional values in the public schools. Her conservative views attracted favorable attention in the Reagan administration, and in August 1983 she received appointment as staff director of the U.S. Commission on Civil Rights, the first woman to hold that position.

As director for the next two years Linda did her best to assist Ronald Reagan in his attempts to raze the commission. She made a drastic shift in the agency's research goals, seeking to discredit affirmative action and opposing quotas as a remedy for racial and sex discrimination, although she herself had benefited from both goals. In less than two years she converted the commission from a reasonably bipartisan agency into a propaganda arm of the administration.

Linda Chávez's leadership role in the commission was not unnoticed in the White House, and in 1985 she was appointed to the powerful position of director of the White House Office of Public Liaison, becoming thereby the highest-ranking woman in the Reagan administration. After less than a year in her new prestigious job she resigned because, she said, the position offered her little policy-making opportunity.

Instead, having switched from the Democratic Party to the Republican, Chávez decided to run for the U.S. Senate from Maryland. With the help of her former boss, President Reagan, she obtained the Republican nomination in September 1986. However, in November, despite Reagan's assertion that failure to elect Linda Chávez might mean the end of the

United States as we know it, she lost by more than 20 percent of the votes cast. An intense campaigner, she earned the label of dirtiest politician of the year from the Coalition of Labor Union Women for her innuendo and mud-slinging against her female Democratic opponent.

In 1987, with her failed bid for the U.S. Senate behind her, Linda Chávez accepted the presidency of U.S. English, a well-financed right-wing organization with headquarters in Washington, D.C., that has as one of its objectives the legislating of English as the official language of the United States. It also opposes bilingual and bicultural education programs and ethnic quotas. Despite her general agreement with U.S. English goals, Linda resigned her presidency in October 1988 as the result of public anti-Latino and anti-Catholic remarks by co-founder John Tanton.

After U.S. English, Linda Chávez's next step was to become a senior fellow at the Manhattan Institute for Policy Research, a conservative Washington-based think tank. She is director of the Center for the New American Community, which seeks to counter the alleged threat of multiculturalism. As a result of her work at the Institute, in 1991 she published *Out of the Barrio: Toward a New Politics of Hispanic Assimilation*, which presents her views on affirmative action, ethnic political involvement, and multiculturalism. She has also acquired status as a political guru, writing articles for the *Wall Street Journal, Fortune*, and the *Los Angeles Times* and appearing on the *MacNeil-Lehrer Newshour, CBS Morning News, Good Morning America*, and other television shows. She is also a frequent guest on National Public Radio and Cable News Network (CNN). Currently she is working on a new book on multiculturalism. She believes immigrants can succeed only when they are able to function fully in American society; for her, that means learning to speak English.

Further Reading

Aitken, Lee. "Barbara Mikulski and Linda Chávez Stage a Gloves-Off Battle . . ." *People* (3 November 1986): 115–116.

Barrett, Paul M. "Linda Chávez and the Exploitation of Ethnic Identity." *Washington Monthly* 17 (June 1985): 25–29.

Chávez, Linda. "Hispanics: Just Another Immigrant Story?" *Fortune* 118 (21 November 1988): 188.

Saavedra-Vela, Pilar. "Linda Chávez: Commentary by a Political Professional." *Agenda* 7:5 (September/October 1977).

Telgen, Diane, and Jim Kamp, eds. *Notable Hispanic American Women*. Detroit: Gale Research, 1993.

HENRY CISNEROS

(1947–   )

Mexican American Political Leader, Businessman

Henry Cisneros made his political reputation as the high-energy mayor of San Antonio from 1981 to 1988. Then, after months of mounting rumors, newspaper headlines blared "Cisneros Stuns City, Nation with Admission of Affair." The mayor publicly admitted his indiscretion with a former fund-raiser. Despite his fall from grace, Henry Cisneros remains one of the most prominent Mexican American political leaders today. His success in politics is a story of discipline and education.

Born into a middle-class Mexican American family, Cisneros made the best possible use of resources available to him. He was strongly influenced by both his upwardly mobile father, a migrant farm worker from Colorado who had risen through the ranks to become a colonel in the U.S. army, and his maternal grandfather, Rómulo Munguía, a Mexican newspaper owner-editor who left Mexico in 1926 after the great revolution. Charismatic, eloquent, and urbane, Henry Cisneros tends to be moderate to conservative in his positions, but with liberal concerns about most social issues. He retains a common touch that offers an example for middle-class Mexican Americans and hope for the poor.

Henry Gabriel Cisneros was born on 11 June 1947, a year after the end of World War II, in San Antonio, Texas. He was the eldest of five children born to Elvira Munguía and J. George Cisneros; his father, a youthful migrant worker and orphaned son of a sharecropper, through education and perseverance had broken the cycle of poverty in the Cisneros family. Both parents held strong convictions about education and instilled in Henry and their other children a belief in self-improvement, industry, and their special potential. Growing up in an extremely supportive nuclear family in Prospect Hill, a middle-class Mexican American barrio, Henry attended Little Flower parochial school and later graduated from Catholic Central High School while still only 16 years old.

In the fall of 1964 Henry Cisneros enrolled in Texas A&M (Agricultural and Mechanical) University at College Station. Despite his youth and a heavy involvement in extracurricular activities including Reserve Officers Training Corps, he graduated four years later with an A.B. degree in city planning and an award as Distinguished Military Graduate. Returning to San Antonio, he went to work in the Model Cities program and in January 1969 was promoted to assistant director. A year and a half later, having completed graduate program requirements, he received his master's degree in urban and regional planning at Texas A&M. He then began to work on a doctorate at George Washington University.

In Washington, D.C., Cisneros expanded his horizons by taking a job with the National League of Cities; and in 1971 he was named a White House Fellow, working for Elliot Richardson, secretary of health, education, and welfare. A Ford Foundation grant took him to Harvard University in Boston, where he earned an M.A. in public administration at the John F. Kennedy School of Government in 1973. Turning down a teaching position at the Massachusetts Institute of Technology where he was doing doctoral research and was also a teaching assistant, he returned to San Antonio in the following year and began lecturing at the University of Texas. Later he also joined the faculty at Trinity University as a visiting professor. In 1974 he received his doctorate in public administration.

Only months after his return from Washington, Cisneros was elected to the San Antonio city council at a time of great political turbulence in the city. At age 27 he became the youngest councilman in the city's history. Six years later he was chosen mayor over his Anglo opponent by a solid majority, the first Mexican American mayor of San Antonio since Juan Seguín over a century and a quarter earlier. He was re-elected mayor for three more terms, with 94, 73, and 67 percent of the votes cast.

Cisneros's principal goal as mayor was to bring jobs and economic opportunity to San Antonio. He energetically pursued the agenda of economic development he had outlined in his campaign. For San Antonio he sought tourism, high-technology businesses, light manufacturing, and other job-creating industries. At the same time he worked with an aggressive local advocacy group, Communities Organized for Public Service (COPS), to increase the political potential of Mexican Americans, who constituted over 50 percent of the city's population. His success at balancing the various constituencies that supported him was best illustrated by his Target '90 plan, a comprehensive program of goals for the various issues confronting San Antonio in the 1990s. His 10- to 12-hour days in a part-time job that paid barely $4,000 a year explain his success as much as does his well-publicized charisma. As mayor he gave the city direction with impressive leadership and brought its Anglo and Mexican American communities closer together.

From the mid-1970s onward Cisneros was the recipient of numerous "outstanding" awards, citations, medals of merit, and honorary memberships. During the 1980s he received honorary degrees from universities and colleges too numerous to list here. Ideologically very much middle of the road, in 1983 he was appointed by Republican president Ronald Reagan to the National Bipartisan Commission on Central America headed by Henry Kissinger. Cisneros issued a strongly dissenting minority opinion that condemned U.S. policy and involvement in Nicaragua and El Salvador. This public exposure and his outstanding reputation as mayor made him one of the top contenders for the Democratic vice-presidential nomination in 1984. Although he lost out to Geraldine Ferraro, his national recognition was further enhanced and expanded.

In 1987 the Cisneros's third child, a son, was born with a heart defect. As a result of the financial demands created by their son's illness, Cisneros announced that he would not be a candidate for re-election to a fifth term as mayor. In this context in 1989 he formed Cisneros Assets Management Company, of which he is chairman of the board. In 1993 Henry Cisneros accepted appointment to President Bill Clinton's cabinet as secretary of housing and urban development. In that position he ordered a reversal of federal policies that he argued not only tolerated but even encouraged racial segregation in housing. Calling racism a malignancy at the heart of big-city problems, he advocates suburban public housing projects to reduce the concentration of minorities in inner-city ghettos.

In November 1991 Cisneros's wife, Mary Alice, filed for divorce; later a reconciliation was effected. Neither his extramarital affair nor foundering marriage appear to have done much damage, short or long term, to his political career. He remains a leading young Mexican American in public life. In August 1995 he announced that because of the high price of political life he was leaving politics at the end of 1996. Cisneros had a burning desire to make the Department of Housing and Urban Development better serve the people, and most observers think that he did just that. In January 1997 he became the president and chief executive officer of Univision Communications, Inc., the largest Spanish language television broadcaster in the United States.

Further Reading

Burka, Paul. "Henry B. and Henry C." *Texas Monthly* 14:1 (January 1986): 182, 218–230.

Chavira, Richard, and Charlie Ericksen. "An American Political Phenomenon Called Cisneros." *La Luz* 19:6 (August–September 1981).

Current Biography Yearbook, 1987. New York: H. W. Wilson Co., 1987.

Díaz, Katherine. "Henry Cisneros: Our Hope for Today and Tomorrow." *Caminos* 4:3 (March 1983).

Diehl, Kemper, and Jan Jarboe. *Cisneros: Portrait of a New American.* San Antonio: Corona Publishing, 1985.

Gillies, John. *Señor Alcalde: A Biography of Henry Cisneros.* Minneapolis: Dillon Press, 1988.

Lehman, Nicholas. "First Hispanic." *Esquire* 102:6 (December 1984): 480–486.

SANDRA CISNEROS

(1954–   )

Mexican American Short Story Writer, Poet

Sandra Cisneros first came to the attention of the American reading public with the publication, in 1984, of *The House on Mango Street*, a collection of interrelated portrayals of barrio life and personalities, of growing up and coming of age, all told from a sensitive feminine viewpoint as seen through the eyes of 11-year-old Esperanza. *House* won the Before Columbus Foundation American Book Award for 1985 and, having caught the attention of Random House, was reissued in a Vintage edition six years later. In that same year Cisneros's *Woman Hollering Creek and Other Stories* brought her further mainstream recognition and was selected by *Library Journal* as one of the "Best Books of 1991."

Sandra Cisneros was born in a Chicago, Illinois, barrio on 20 December 1954, the only daughter (with six brothers) of Elvira Cordero and Alfredo Cisneros. Her mother's family came from the central Mexican state of Guanajuato, driven northward by the forces of the 1910 revolution to Chicago, where her maternal grandfather found railroad employment and to which he later brought his family. Her father, from a middle-class Mexico City family, ran off to the United States rather than face his military father's anger when he failed his first year at the university. With his brother, her father rambled around the eastern United States, planning on going to California but stopping to take a look at Chicago. There he met Elvira and they later married.

Although Sandra's father never returned to the university and worked the rest of his life as an upholsterer, he stressed the value and importance of education to Sandra and her six brothers. From her mother, who had not completed high school but who read voraciously, Sandra acquired the habit and love of reading. Even before she could read, her mother took her to the local library to get a library card, and she quickly became a habitual patron, taking out as many as eight books a week. Her library reading helped her create a fantasy world quite different from barrio reality. Today she regularly schedules talks at libraries because she feels she owes them a debt of gratitude.

Sandra remembers her early years growing up in a working-class family as being dominated by moving from house to house. Partly because her father was her grandmother's favorite child, the family visited Mex-

Sandra Cisneros. Photo copyright Rubén Guzmán.

ico City every few years and on return to Chicago always rented a different apartment—which often meant a new school as well. She started out in a public school but later transferred to a Catholic parochial school. She has negative memories of the nuns who taught her in grade and high school; she feels they had a tunnel vision that stressed conformity and dismissed her as a minority person lacking in worth.

The family's moving so much was upsetting to Sandra, and she developed a certain shyness and retreated within a fantasy world of her own creation. When she was 11 years old her parents' purchase of a small two-story bungalow on the north side of Chicago in a Puerto Rican neighborhood at last brought her some sense of security and a feeling of pride in their home. Later the neighborhood and its spectrum of Latino residents were to provide a basis for her stories.

When she was 10 years old Sandra Cisneros began creating poetry. After doing a bit of writing in the seventh and eighth grades, she wrote for an audience for the first time in high school. She joined the staff of the school literary magazine and ultimately became its editor. During her high school years she read a great deal of poetry outside of class and became acquainted with the works of English and American poets through an inexpensive book club. From her sophomore Spanish class she also became aware of leading Latin American writers.

After high school, despite her father's lack of enthusiasm for her decision, Sandra entered Loyola University in Chicago, where as an English major she deepened and widened her literary horizons, especially in poetry. In her junior year she enrolled in a writing workshop. After receiving her A.B. in English, she went from Loyola to the well-known University of Iowa Writers' Workshop at the recommendation of one of her professors. She spent two years in Iowa City, earning her Master in Fine Arts (M.F.A.) degree in 1978. While there, she published some of her poetry in *Nuestro* and *Revista Chicano-Riqueña*. Her Iowa master's thesis, revised, was published nine years later under the title *My Wicked, Wicked Ways* by a small publisher, Third Woman Press.

Upon graduation Sandra returned to Chicago, where she became involved in the Movimiento Artístico Chicano (MARCH). Through MARCH she got a job teaching for the Illinois Arts Council; she also taught a variety of subjects at an alternative Latino high school for dropouts in Pilsen, one of Chicago's many ethnic neighborhoods. During the three years she taught there, 1979–1982, she was also reading her poetry in libraries, schools, and coffeehouses.

In 1982 Cisneros was awarded a National Endowment for the Arts (NEA) fellowship, which she used to travel in Europe, and in the following spring was artist-in-residence at the Foundation Michael Karolyi in Vence, France. A job in San Antonio as an arts administrator took her to Texas and helped persuade her later to make her permanent home there. After quitting her San Antonio job she spent a summer in Mexico through an Illinois Arts Council grant; however, she returned to Texas to accept a Texas Institute of Letters Dobie Paisano fellowship at Austin.

Scrambling for a job after her Dobie Paisano residency, Cisneros went from Texas to Chico State University in northern California as a visiting lecturer. At this low point both professionally and emotionally, her confidence was revived by an NEA fellowship in fiction writing that led to publication of *Woman Hollering Creek* in 1991. As a leading American writer she has since taught her specialty as a visiting professor at several major universities. She also visits local schools and libraries, where she inspires young writers to persevere by showing them her fifth-grade report card with its Cs and Ds and assuring them that they too can succeed as writers.

Although more widely known for her prose, Sandra Cisneros began her literary career as a poet. Her first publication was a book of poems titled *Bad Boys*, printed in 1980 by Mango Publications in San Jose, California, through the good offices of Chicano poets Gary Soto and Lorna Dee Cervantes. Four years later *The House on Mango Street*, a novel about a teenage girl's neighborhood, was published by Arte Público Press in

Houston. It was followed in 1987 by *My Wicked, Wicked Ways*, printed by Third Woman Press in Bloomington, Indiana, and reprinted by Random House in 1992.

Meanwhile, Random House's 1991 reprinting of *The House on Mango Street* had made Cisneros the first Chicana published by a mainstream press. *House* was immediately followed by *Woman Hollering Creek and Other Stories*. Her perceptive and often lyrical vignettes of courageous, strong-willed Latinas caused her to be hailed as the new star on the literary horizon. *Woman Hollering Creek* was given the PEN Center West Award Best Fiction of 1991 as well as several other prestigious awards. The *New York Times*, the *Los Angeles Times*, and the *American Library Journal* singled it out as outstanding fiction writing, and reviewers vied with each other to find words of sufficiently high praise—"unforgettable", "stunning", "compelling", "poignant", "matchless"—for her work. Some have applauded her for breaking the stereotypical portrayal of passive, fatalistic Latinas; others have criticized her for perpetuating stereotypes of the Latino male.

Sandra Cisneros's works have been translated into ten languages and published abroad as well as in the United States. Her poems and short stories have been included in numerous anthologies and textbooks. *Mango Street*, a text in many college literature and ethnic studies classes, has sold over a quarter of a million copies. Her most recent work, *Loose Woman*, a collection of her poems about assertive Latinas, was published by Alfred A. Knopf in 1995. Knopf is also publishing her first children's book, *Hairs/Pelitos*, and a tenth anniversary hardback edition of *Mango Street*. Cisneros is presently working on a novel tentatively titled *Caramelo* and on a book of poetry.

In June 1995 Sandra Cisneros was one of 24 people in the United States awarded "Genius Grants" by the MacArthur Foundation.

Further Reading

Binder, Wolfgang, ed. *Partial Autobiographies: Interviews with Twenty Chicano Poets*. Erlangen, West Germany: Verlag Palm & Enke, 1985.

Cisneros, Sandra. "Do You Know Me? I Wrote *The House on Mango Street*." *Americas Review* 15:1 (Spring 1987): 77–79.

Los Angeles Times Book Review (28 April 1991): 3.

Magill, Frank N. *Masterpieces of Latino Literature*. New York: HarperCollins, 1994.

Medina, David. "The Softly Insistent Voice of a Poet." *Onward* (11 March 1986).

New York Times Book Review (26 May 1991): 6.

"Only Daughter." *Glamour* (November 1990): 256–257.

Sagel, Jim. "*P W* Interviews: Sandra Cisneros." *Publishers Weekly* 238:15 (29 March 1991): 74–75.

"Sandra Cisneros." *Authors & Artists for Young Adults*, vol. 9. Detroit: Gale Research, 1992.

"Sandra Cisneros: Giving Back to Libraries." *Library Journal* (January 1992).
Walters, Laurel Shaper. "One Writer's Bicultural Blend." *Christian Science Monitor*
    85 (12 March 1993): 12.

ROBERTO CLEMENTE WALKER

(1934–1972)

Puerto Rican Baseball Great, Humanitarian

To many baseball fans, Roberto Clemente Walker was at times something of an enigma. He suffered from numerous injuries and illnesses, including a curved spine, bone chips in his elbow, loose spinal discs, pulled muscles and a strained tendon, hematoma on his thigh, malaria, insomnia, headaches, and nervous stomach. But his athletic ability, his dedication to the game of baseball, and his unfailing good humor helped him overcome these ailments. Although he often moaned as he trotted out at the start of a game, he would then amaze fans with his towering athletic achievements. Once he explained that he had scored all the way from first on a single base hit because "I had a sore foot and wanted to rest it."

Roberto Clemente Walker was born on 18 August 1934 in Barrio San Antón in the small Puerto Rican town of Carolina, a suburb of the capital, San Juan. He was the youngest of five children born to Luisa Walker and Melchor Clemente, who was a foreman on a sugar cane plantation. A thin, dark-skinned boy, Roberto Clemente became enamored of baseball early in life even though his athletic skills were not exceptional. During the Great Depression of the 1930s he made his own baseballs, using as a core an old golfball that he then wound with string and covered with tape. He played in his first organized game of softball at age 8. After grade school he entered Julio Vizcarrado High School in 1949, but baseball remained his passion and as a teenager he played with various amateur softball teams on the island. When he was 17 years old the owner of the Santurce Cangrejeros, a professional hardball team in Puerto Rico, signed him for three years.

While playing left field with the Cangrejeros, Roberto became acquainted with Willie Mays, who was the center fielder. Mays coached him in some finer points of baseball, and Clemente paid close attention to and followed his advice. Soon his high batting average caught the attention of Brooklyn Dodger scouts, and he was signed up with a $10,000 bonus. This was more money than the Dodgers had ever paid a Latin American player.

Roberto was assigned to the Dodgers' International League farm team. The manager was instructed to use him sparingly for fear his outstanding batting abilities would be recognized by scouts from other teams. This tactic confused Roberto, making him angry as well as frustrated. He used to complain that if he struck out the manager kept him in the lineup, but if he played well he got benched. Ultimately the management strategy failed. Clemente was noticed by a scout for the Pittsburgh Pirates. The Pirates, with first choice in the round-robin draft because they had finished last in the National League in 1954, chose Roberto.

Clemente's first five seasons in the National League were solid but not outstanding. His yearly batting averages were .255, .311, .253, .289, and .296. During these early years with the Pirates he had many barriers to overcome. He was a black Puerto Rican on a team that had only just begun to integrate. Because of his skin color he often could not stay in the same hotels as his teammates, nor eat in the same restaurants. He was also held back by his limited command of English. A direct and outspoken person, he was frequently frustrated because he was not able to express to reporters what he felt and often did not relate well to the press as a result. Among his peeves was that often he was referred to as Roberto Walker instead of Roberto Clemente (Walker) by reporters.

In 1960 Clemente was important in the Pirates' winning the National League pennant; this became a turning point for him. During the season he batted .314, hitting 16 home runs and bringing in 94 runs. In the World Series against the Yankees he had 9 hits in 29 times at bat, for a .310 average. Yet he felt restless and dissatisfied. He made the hits, the runs, and the outstanding plays, but other players seemed to get the rewards. He was greatly disappointed and unhappy when he was voted only eighth in the Most Valuable Players balloting that year. But he believed he just had to play harder and better. The result: in 1961, 1964, 1965, and 1967 he led the National League in batting.

In 1965 Roberto Clemente and Vera Zobala were married and built a home in Rio Piedras, Puerto Rico. Married life agreed with Roberto, and each spring he returned to Pittsburgh refreshed. In 1966 he was voted the League's Most Valuable Player.

In the following year *Sports Illustrated* magazine polled the general managers of major league teams on the question: Who is the best player in baseball today? Of 18 managers, 8 chose Roberto Clemente Walker; the runner-up got only 5 votes. In 1968 one general manager called Clemente "a one man team . . . one of the most amazing athletes of all time." Sandy Koufax, the great Dodger pitcher, paid highest praise to Clemente's batting skills by saying, "Roberto can hit any pitch, anywhere, at any time . . . with both feet off the ground!"

During 1970 Clemente hit a resounding .352, and in the next year he became a national as well as Puerto Rican hero because of his performance throughout the season and in the World Series. He had clearly become a giant in the world of baseball. Clemente was hopeful that during 1972 he would become the 11th player in baseball history to achieve 3,000 hits. His historic 3,000th hit came on 30 September 1972 in a late season game against the New York Mets.

At the end of the 1972 baseball season Clemente returned to Puerto Rico to spend the winter and to consider whether or not to retire from baseball and actively pursue his humanitarian dream of constructing a huge sports complex for young Puerto Ricans. On New Year's Eve, 1972, he set out for Nicaragua to help provide relief aid for those made homeless by a devastating 6.2 earthquake that had killed more than 6,000 Nicaraguans. The plane was filled with medical and food supplies that Clemente had helped collect. Soon after take-off the aircraft plunged into the sea off northern Puerto Rico, apparently because the improperly loaded cargo had shifted. Clemente's body was never found.

Within three months of his death, Roberto Clemente Walker was inducted into baseball's Hall of Fame. The rule that a player had to have been out of the game for at least five years before becoming eligible was waived. His longtime dreams of assisting poor Puerto Rican youths came true when the long-planned 600-acre Roberto Clemente Sports City Complex in San Juan was completed at a cost of more than $13 million. This memorial to Clemente was designed to give underprivileged children the chance to learn baseball and other sports. In Nicaragua, Clemente's memory was honored by naming two hospitals after him. In Pittsburgh, the home of the Pirates, on 18 August 1994 a statue of Clemente was dedicated on what would have been his 60th birthday.

It is a measure of Clemente's character that he once said in an interview that he kept himself in the best physical condition possible because if he had a bad season he would be stealing people's money, and his conscience would not let him do that.

Further Reading

Christie, Bill. "Remembering Roberto." *Los Angeles Times* (25 December 1992): Section C.

Feldman, Jay. "The Legend and Legacy of Roberto Clemente." *Smithsonian* 24:6 (1 September 1993): 128.

Gerber, Irving. *Roberto Clemente: The Pride of Puerto Rico*, American Destiny Series: Puerto Rico. Oceanside, N.Y.: Irving Berger, 1978.

Moritz, Charles, ed. *Current Biography Yearbook, 1972*. New York: H. W. Wilson Co., 1972.

Newlon, Clarke. *Famous Puerto Ricans*. New York: Dodd, Mead and Co., 1975.
Wulf, Steve. "Arriba Roberto." *Sports Illustrated* 77:27 (28 December 1992): 114.

IMOGENE COCA

(1908–   )

Spanish American Comedian

Noted for her outstanding talent and many skills as a performer, her subtle and almost imperceptible shadings, the arched eyebrow, a movement of the nose, a scowl, a glint in the eye, and her mischievous, almost lunatic touch, Imogene Coca was a shy, gentle, petite actress. Characterized by a silly grin and somewhat prominent eyes, the elfin entertainer let little escape her sharp wit. She was a keen satirist and mistress of pantomime and whimsy, poking fun at everything from Hollywood's *femmes fatales* to New York's ballet, to fashion shows and all-girl orchestras. In a career that spanned nearly 70 years and was firmly based on early experience in vaudeville and nightclub circuits, Imogene Coca is best remembered for her starring role in the 90-minute weekly television program *Your Show of Shows*, which kept America laughing from 1950 to 1954.

Imogene Coca was born in Philadelphia, Pennsylvania, on 18 November 1908. She was the only child of dancer and vaudeville entertainer Sadie Brady and Joseph [Fernández y] Coca, an orchestra conductor of Spanish descent at the local opera house. Growing up in an entertainment-oriented atmosphere, Imogene started her training for the stage early. As early as age 5 she began to take instruction on the piano, a year later started voice lessons, and at age 7 was studying dance. With this grooming, the encouragement of both parents, and her father's theatrical connections, at age 9 she got her first stage job as a tap-dancing juvenile in vaudeville, followed two years later by an engagement as a singer in a local theater.

When Imogene completed grammar school in 1922, two avenues were suggested to her by her parents: to begin to work in earnest on a career in the theater, or to go on to high school. Her choice was for the former, and the 14-year-old began intense training in tap, acrobatic, and ballet dancing. At the end of the following year she left Philadelphia for New York City with her parents' blessing and encouragement and with a sense of confidence about her future in show business. Her first job was as a chorus girl in the short-lived *When You Smile*, a Broadway musical of the 1925–1926 season. There followed a series of nightclub engagements in New York and Philadelphia as a dancer and then brief employment again as a chorus girl on Broadway and as a dancer in vaudeville. She then joined dancer Leonard Sillman as his partner in a vaudeville act at the Palace theater in New York.

The advent of talking pictures and the Great Depression of the 1930s combined to cause the decline and eventually the demise of vaudeville, and Coca returned to the New York stage in secondary roles in musicals and revues. Coca's rise to stardom as a comedian began in 1934 when Sillman, now turned producer, hired her for his revue, *New Faces*. In the course of rehearsals she ad-libbed a delightfully ludicrous spoof of a striptease using a large-sized man's polo coat, which swamped her 5-foot, 3-inch frame. Sillman added it to the program and also included several of her other pantomime bits. The audiences and the critics loved her performances. As a result, between 1935 and 1940 Coca worked for Sillman, with featured spots in seven of his productions. Now in great demand, she also played the Rainbow Room in New York in 1937 and toured with George Olson's orchestra in the following year.

In 1939 Coca got a leading part in *Straw Hat Revue* directed by Max Liebman in the Taminment Summer Playhouse at Bushkill, Pennsylvania. When Liebman brought an expanded version of the revue to Broadway that fall, Coca starred in one-third of the 25 sketches and met with an enthusiastic reception. In the following year she appeared in the musical *A Night at the Folies Bergère*, followed by a stint at the New York nightclub La Martinique. Then World War II interrupted both her career and her personal life.

When Coca's husband of six years, Robert Burton, who was also her music arranger and advisor, joined the armed forces after the Pearl Harbor attack, she returned to Philadelphia to live with her mother. Somewhat discouraged with her career at this point, she withdrew from entertainment activity and considered abandoning the musical theater altogether. In 1943 she was asked to audition for a role in the Broadway musical *Oklahoma* but was turned down for the part. However, the renewed contact with the theater aroused her desire to return to performing, and she began a series of nightclub engagements that lasted for five years and brought renewed plaudits for her artistry. Performed in top clubs, two of her acts—a satire on 20 years of Hollywood vamps titled "Cavalcade of Oldtime Movie Stars," and a spoof of the well-known Phil Spitalny All Girl Orchestra—were particularly big hits with her audiences.

Coca's next stroke of good fortune came in 1948 when she was selected by Max Liebman for a feature part in the *Admiral Broadway Revue*, a television show he was writing and producing for the National Broadcasting Company (NBC). The show teamed her with comedian Sid Caesar, and the two quickly developed a rare comedic chemistry. Her portrayal of a zany, impish innocent beautifully complemented Caesar's serious, harassed everyman. Two years later the comic duo starred in Liebman's weekly 90-minute television program *Your Show of Shows*, in which Coca did pantomimes, monologues, and dances by herself and also shared hilarious skits with Caesar. Together the duo poignantly portrayed the sometimes hapless humor of the human condition as illustrated in ordinary, everyday events. The program was and still is considered one of the best shows in television's "Golden Age." Coca was named "Tops in TV" in a 1951 poll by the *Saturday Review of Literature* and was nominated for an Emmy as "Best Television Actress" by the Academy of Television Arts and Sciences. She also received an Award of Merit from the Federation of Jewish Philanthropists.

Coca's run of good luck ended in 1954 when NBC canceled the *Show of Shows*. *The Imogene Coca Show*, which followed, survived only one year and then she suffered the further blow of her husband's death. Nevertheless, she continued her career in entertainment. Returning to Broadway, in the ensuing 30 years Coca appeared in nearly 40 stage presentations, most of them revues or variety shows. In the 1960s and 1970s she took part in a number of television series, including *The Brady Bunch*, and also appeared in various made-for-television movies including *Nothing Lasts Forever* in 1985. Two years later, at age 79, she did a five-month tour of the United States in *On the Twentieth Century*, and in 1990 she celebrated the 40th anniversary of *Your Show of Shows* by re-teaming with Sid Caesar in a television revue entitled *Together Again*. As a result of its warm reception, Music Television (MTV) obtained rights to *Your Show of Shows* and organized the programs into half-hour segments for a generation of adult viewers who had been too young for the original.

Further Reading

Conniff, Richard. "In Iowa: Rolling toward Peoria." *Time* 129:16 (20 April 1987): 11–13.

Current Biography, 1951. New York: H. W. Wilson Co., 1952.

"Girl with a Rubber Face." *Life* (2 February 1951): 53–63.

Klein, Robert. "Humorous Sages of the Human Condition." *New York Times* (15 April 1990): Sec. 2, pp. 7, 14.

Telgen, Diane, and Jim Kamp, eds. *Notable Hispanic American Women*. Detroit: Gale Research, 1993.

MARGARITA COLMENARES

(1957–)

Mexican American Engineer

Margarita Colmenares is a dynamic young woman of firsts. In most of
the positions she has held as an engineer, she has been the first woman
in that job. In addition, in 1989 she became the first female national
president of the Society of Hispanic Professional Engineers (SHPE), an
overwhelmingly male organization. Two years later she was the first
Latina engineer and the first Chevron employee to be named a White
House fellow in the entire quarter-century of the highly respected and
successful fellowship program. At her request she served in the Department of Education.

Margarita Hortensia Colmenares was born in Sacramento, California,
on 20 July 1957. She is the eldest of five children of Hortensia and Luis
S. Colmenares, who immigrated to the United States from the moun-
tainous southern Mexican state of Oaxaca. She grew up in a multicultural
middle-class neighborhood not far from the California capitol building.
Her playmates and schoolfellows spoke both English and Spanish, so
she grew up feeling comfortable in both languages. Her parents believed
very strongly in the value of education, and although the family was
poor she was sent to Catholic parochial schools to get a better education.
When she reached high school age she got a part-time job in the evening
to help with the family finances.

By the time Margarita entered Sacramento's Bishop Manogue High
School in 1971, the Chicano *movimiento* was well under way and she had
her first experience in leadership by founding the Asociación Juvenil
Mexicano Americana at school. Despite increasing awareness by school
administrators of Chicano educational needs and demands, she found
herself being counseled away from college preparatory courses into typing, shorthand, and other office skills classes—apparently because she
was Mexican American. Upon graduation from the all-girl high school
in 1975, she decided to enter California State University at Sacramento.
In this decision she received strong parental support.

Although she enrolled as a business major, in her first year at the
university Margarita discovered engineering and decided it was meant
to be her life's work. However, she also discovered that she lacked the
solid background courses needed for acceptance as an engineering major.

So she turned to junior college, taking courses in calculus, physics, and chemistry at Sacramento City College to prepare herself. At the same time she began to look for a part-time job in engineering and was successful in finding one with the California Department of Water Resources. She also secured a number of scholarships and subsequently entered the school of engineering at Stanford University.

At Stanford Margarita developed a fairly balanced life, dividing her time between her studies, work, and recreational interests. She found her classmates highly competitive, her research assistantship and tutoring helpful in gaining a deeper understanding of engineering, and her dancing and teaching of dance a welcome change of pace from engineering studies. For one year she was co-director of the Ballet Folklórico de Stanford University.

After her junior year at Stanford Margarita opted to enter Chevron Corporation's co-op education program and spent nine months working for the company in California and Texas. In 1981 she graduated from Stanford University with a B.S. in civil engineering and took a job with Chevron. In the ensuing dozen years she worked for the company in an amazing variety of capacities. She began by working as a field construction engineer in northern California's Bay Area for Chevron USA, Marketing Operations division. Later she was named recruiting coordinator. After a tour out of the Denver, Colorado, regional office as a field construction engineer in four western states, she returned to the San Francisco headquarters where she was selected by the Management, Planning, and Development division as foreign training representative. While working in the Bay Area, Colmenares founded the San Francisco chapter of the Society of Hispanic Professional Engineers and was chapter president for two years. She also found time to dance with Los Lupeños, a folkloric group in nearby San Jose, about 50 miles south of San Francisco.

Colmenares's next move was to Houston, Texas, where she accepted a position in Marketing Operations as a compliance specialist because of her longtime interest in and concern for protection of the environment. Her experience there stood her in good stead for her next job, which was heading a multimillion-dollar environmental cleanup at the Chevron USA, Manufacturing division plant at El Segundo in southern California. In 1989 she was promoted to air quality specialist at the El Segundo refinery. During her stint as a compliance specialist in Houston she was active in the Hispanic Women's Network of Texas and from 1987 to 1988 served on its board of directors.

As Colmenares gained in engineering experience, she also participated actively in professional organizations. While in Texas she was elected regional vice-president of the Society of Hispanic Professional Engineers and two years later served a term (1988–1989) as national chairwoman of SHPE's leadership development and civic affairs programs. In 1989 she became the first woman elected SHPE national president, a position she took very seriously. To provide sufficient time to achieve the goals she set for herself she obtained a year's leave of absence from Chevron. She then set about her program; she visited nearly all of SHPE's 130 chapters, urging members to become active leaders in their communities, especially in environmental issues. While traveling about the country she also visited high schools, colleges, and universities stressing her strongly held belief that education is the foundation of technological leadership and urging Latino students to consider careers in engineering and the sciences.

A staunch believer in the vital importance of leadership, she was a participant in the National Hispana Leadership Initiative program in 1989, attending special conferences at the Center for Creative Leadership and the Kennedy School of Government at Harvard University. In the following year she took part in the Leadership America training project and also participated in several national and international conferences.

After her SHPE presidency, at the suggestion of friends Colmenares made an application to the White House fellowship program. She was selected, becoming one of 16 fellows for 1991–1992. At her request she was assigned to the Department of Education, where she became special assistant to Deputy Secretary David Kearns. In the department she worked on federal government plans to develop long-term programs in mathematics and science education. After her year as a White House fellow she returned to work for Chevron.

Margarita Colmenares was selected for three important awards in 1989: the Community Service Award, from the journal *Hispanic Engineer;* Hispanic Role Model of the Year, from SHPE; and Outstanding Hispanic Woman of the Year, from *Hispanic* magazine. She was also the keynote speaker at the University of Southern California's Engineering and Science Day, 1989.

Further Reading

Hispanic Business (October 1992): 78.

"Hispanic Women in Technology." *Hispanic Engineer* (Fall 1985).

"Margarita H. Colmenares." *Réplica* 21 (July 1990): 23.

"Profiles in Leadership." *Hispanic Engineer* (Fall 1989): 22–25.

Telgen, Diane, and Jim Kamp, eds. *Notable Hispanic American Women.* Detroit: Gale Research, 1993.

Unterburger, Amy, ed. *Who's Who among Hispanic Americans.* Detroit: Gale Research, 1992.

Gregorio Cortez

(1875–1916)

Mexican American Folk Hero

A single but complex event that occurred in midsummer 1901 in southeastern Texas made Gregorio Cortez famous. At the beginning of this century the Texas Rangers with their maxim "Shoot first and ask questions later," their practice of shooting *mexicanos* who had nothing to do with the criminals the rangers were pursuing, and their penchant for wholesale annihilation of alleged accomplices of miscreants created a certain attitude among some less submissive border *mexicanos*. The latter's mental stance of "What do we have to lose?" and its combative reaction lay at the heart of Gregorio Cortez's astounding feat and made his achievement the stuff of border ballad and legend. His deed became a symbol of the oppressed *mexicano*'s resistance to his Anglo oppressor.

Gregorio Lira Cortez was born in 1875 not far from Matamoros in the northeastern Mexico border state of Tamaulipas, the seventh child in a family of eight. His parents, Rosalía Lira Cortinas and Román Cortez Garza, belonged to that special breed of border dwellers who had never fully accepted control by the government in Mexico City. In 1887, when Gregorio was 12 years old, the family crossed over the Rio Grande River and settled a few miles northeast of Austin in Manor, Texas. As a young unmarried male with little formal education, for more than a decade Gregorio followed the migrant life of an itinerant cowboy, ranch hand, and farm worker with his inseparable older brother Romaldo. But marriage and the responsibility of children caused Gregorio to seek greater security. As a result, at the end of the 19th century he and his brother, with their families, settled down in Karnes County about 70 miles southeast of San Antonio on adjoining farms rented from a W. A. Thulemeyer.

Here the legend began. On 12 June 1901 Karnes County's experienced sheriff, W. T. Morris, attempted to arrest Gregorio and Romaldo (neither of whom had any previous encounter with the law) in connection with a horse-stealing, which according to Anglos was a favorite Mexican proclivity. Gregorio spoke little English, the sheriff knew only a few words of Spanish, and his "interpreter" was at best inadequate. When Gregorio protested their innocence to the sheriff, a fracas ensued; Morris shot at and wounded Romaldo and fired at and missed Gregorio. Gregorio in return fired at the sheriff, wounding him. There was a further exchange

Gregorio Cortez. Photo courtesy of the University of Texas at Austin.

of shots that left the sheriff with a mortal wound. Gregorio then sent his family to the home of friends to protect them from vigilante "justice" and later that night took Romaldo in for medical care.

Aware of the summary treatment he might expect from the large posse now searching for an imagined "Cortez gang," Gregorio fled northward on foot, hoping to lose himself in northern Texas. After walking nearly 100 miles he had an encounter with a large posse at Belmont during which he shot and killed Robert Glover, the Gonzales County sheriff. He decided to head for the Rio Grande border. Pursued by various Anglo posses, some of them numbering as many as 300 men, he rode southward by circuitous routes.

Until 22 June he managed to outwit and elude his pursuers through his knowledge of the terrain and clever evasive tactics. In this frantic second half of his efforts to avoid capture he traveled over 400 miles on two stouthearted mares. His remarkable resistance and refusal to submit to Anglo injustice caused him to be seen as a symbol in the Mexican American struggle for equality before the law. In his flight he was often helped by *mexicanos*. However, almost within sight of the Rio Grande he was betrayed by an acquaintance and taken prisoner by Captain J. H. Rogers of the Texas Rangers. He was taken back to join his family, including his four young children, in jail. Because nearly everyone thought he would surely be hanged after a trial, there was little interest in lynching him, although the effort was made.

Gregorio Cortez endured a series of trials that lasted nearly four years and took him to 11 Texas counties. His defense was financed by donations from *mexicanos* on both sides of the Rio Grande, from all levels of society, and from rich and poor alike. Undoubtedly many Mexican Americans in Texas saw him as their proxy in the fight for social justice. Many Anglo Americans who came to admire his engaging personality and charm, as well as his courage and endurance, came to his aid. Gregorio was tried on three murder charges, ultimately found not guilty in the killing of Sheriff Morris and a member of the posse at Belmont, but was convicted of murder in the death of Sheriff Glover. During the trials his wife, Leonor, who was early a chief witness, divorced him, apparently when several of his "sweethearts" came to his support.

On 2 January 1905 Gregorio Cortez began serving a life sentence in Huntsville Penitentiary, eight days after marrying, in the jail, one of his "sweethearts," Estéfana Garza of Manor, Texas. At Huntsville he adapted himself and continued to make friends, impressing nearly all who came into extended contact with him and winning them over by his cheerful, straightforward attitude. Most came to be convinced that he did not belong in jail. Repeated appeals for his release were made over the years by his many ardent well-wishers and supporters—including Esther Martínez, whom he spoke of as a girlfriend he planned to marry upon his release. After serving eight years of his life sentence he was finally given a conditional pardon by Texas governor Oscar B. Colquitt on 8 July 1913—although the pardons board had recommended a full pardon with restoration of citizenship. In Texas the popular reaction to his release was quite mixed.

After convalescing and traveling around Texas to thank the many people responsible for his release, including the governor, he headed for the border. Within three months of his discharge from prison Gregorio Cortez had crossed the Rio Grande and joined the federal army of the Mexican dictator-president Victoriano Huerta, apparently as a gesture of gratitude to some of his supporters. In subsequent fighting against the 1910 Mexican revolutionaries he was wounded and then crossed over into Texas to recuperate. Three years later while celebrating his latest wedding at Anson, near Abilene in northern Texas, he died quite suddenly at age 41, apparently of either a heart attack or a stroke.

Gregorio Cortez, by his fantastic flight and his various trials, became enshrined as a border folk hero in southern Texas, fixed indelibly in the minds of *mexicanos*. The memory of his exploits and his challenge to Texas racism is kept forever verdant in the border ballad "El Corrido de Gregorio Cortez."

Further Reading

Castillo, Pedro, and Albert Camarillo, eds. *Furia y muerte: Los bandidos chicanos*. Los Angeles: University of California, Chicano Studies Center, 1973.

Limón, José E. "Healing the Wounds: Folk Symbols and Historical Crisis." *Texas Humanist* (March–April 1984).

Paredes, Américo. *With His Pistol in His Hand; A Border Ballad and Its Hero*. Austin: University of Texas Press, 1958.

———. "With His Pistol in His Hand." In *Chicano: Evolution of a People*, Renato Rosaldo et al., eds. Minneapolis: Winston Press, 1973.

Webb, Walter P. *The Texas Rangers*. Austin: University of Texas Press, 1965.

JUAN CORTINA

(1824–1892)

Mexican American Bandit-Revolutionary,
Rancher, Politician

Juan Cortina was born into a prominent *mexicano* border family at the beginning of Mexico's independence from Spain, grew up in the turbulent decades of the separation of Texas from Mexico and the war between the United States and Mexico, and spent the rest of his adult life amid the chaotic border conditions of the late 1800s. He has been seen as a kind of Robin Hood or social bandit by many, certainly by nearly all *mexicanos* of his time and later. Neither fully a saint nor a complete rogue, he seems to have been largely a product of the border conditions of his day. During his lifetime he was a very controversial figure; even today his motives, objectives, and loyalties remain a matter of debate.

Juan Nepomuceno Cortina was born on 16 May 1824 at Camargo on the southern side of the Rio Grande (Rio Bravo del Norte) midway between Nuevo Laredo and Matamoros. His parents, Estefanía Cavazos and Trinidad Cortina, owned ranches on both sides of the river. Upon his father's death his widowed mother moved the family to a small ranch she owned on the northern (later U.S.) side of the river near Brownsville. Juan grew up here, preferring to spend most of his time with the vaqueros and learning their cowboy skills. Although he had little formal schooling, from his mother he learned the basics of reading, writing, and arithmetic as well as the fundamentals of ranch management. From her he also imbibed a sense of duty toward his fellow *mexicanos*, the humble ones as well as the rancheros.

When the war between the United States and Mexico broke out in 1846, young Cortina joined with other local *mexicanos* to oppose the invading American forces under General Zachary Taylor. Throughout the war "Cheno," as he was called, filled the role of a Mexican officer and often acted as a courier or spy. He was witness to much robbery, torture, rape, murder, and other atrocities by undisciplined soldiers on both sides. After the war he became part of an ill-defined, easy-going ranch society on the border.

Having become an American national under the Treaty of Guadalupe Hidalgo in 1848, Cortina turned to political organization to secure protection for *mexicanos*, many of whom were being despoiled of their property by force and dubiously legal means. As they lost their lands, he saw his fellows reduced to an inferior economic and social role. One of his ideas and objectives was the creation of a separate territory or independent buffer republic between Mexico and the United States that would be controlled principally by border *mexicanos*. During the 1850s Cortina's political goals often became embroiled in the sometimes violent struggles among Anglo groups to control southern Texas.

In midsummer 1859 there occurred an incident that was to affect the course of the rest of Cortina's life. According to the generally accepted version of the story, in Brownsville he wounded a Texas marshal who was abusing a drunken employee from one of his mother's ranches. As a result, Cheno became the center of a growing *mexicano* (*tejano*) movement to resist by force the efforts of Anglos to dominate the heavily

Spanish-speaking border region. To avoid capture and almost certain lynching, he fled southward across the border into the Mexican state of Tamaulipas.

In September Cortina and 50 or so followers made a raid on Brownsville in which a number of *mexicanos* were released from jail and several people were killed. Having proclaimed a buffer Republic of the Rio Grande, Cortina fled to his family's Rancho del Carmen in Cameron County, from which, in the following month, he issued a statement about the raid and his determination as a *tejano* to defend the rights of his fellows. This episode marked the beginning of Cortina's career as a border fighter.

Cheno Cortina established his headquarters at Matamoros just across the Rio Grande from Brownsville. As a vocal leader of a *mexicano* rights movement, he attracted increasingly large numbers of followers and was successful in fighting off early attempts to defeat his forces. Early in 1860, however, he was overcome by a large force made up of Texas Rangers and the U.S. army under Colonel Robert E. Lee. During the American Civil War his sympathies lay primarily with the North, but he refused to fully commit himself and his men. At times he actively supported the Union against the Confederacy, probably as much because Texans supported the South as for other, political reasons. At the end of the Civil War in 1865 he served as a general and as military governor of Tamaulipas, actively helping President Benito Juárez expel the French invaders from Mexico.

At the beginning of the 1870s just before President Juárez's death, Cortina returned to Matamoros. From there he and some of his friends, citing his anti-Confederate stance during the Civil War, petitioned the Reconstruction governor of Texas to allow Cheno to return to his Texas land holdings. His request was denied, largely because of opposition from the cattle barons who circulated stories that he was a cattle thief. Ultimately in 1875 he was arrested by Mexican authorities who were pressing to control the unruly border region and feared a separatist movement. He was imprisoned, first under President Sebastián Lerdo de Tejada and later under President Porfirio Díaz as well. His friends interceded for him with Díaz; as a result he was able to avoid the firing squad and was allowed out of prison on parole, which required him to remain in the federal district around Mexico City.

In 1890 Cortina was allowed by Díaz to visit relatives and friends in the border region; at Matamoros he was feted with a banquet and was greeted by many of his old comrades. He then left the border for the last time, returning to Mexico City. In 1892 the old warrior contracted pneumonia and died. He was buried in the capital with full military honors from the Díaz administration. His last wish, to be buried in Texas, was never carried out despite several efforts to obtain permission to do so.

Further Reading

Canales, José T., ed. *Juan N. Cortina Presents His Motion for a New Trial*. San
    Antonio: Artes Gráficas, 1951.
Castillo, Pedro, and Albert Camarillo, eds. *Furia y muerte: Los bandidos chicanos*.
    Los Angeles: Chicano Studies Center, University of California, 1973.
Cortina, Juan N. "The Death of Martyrs." In *Aztlán*, Luis Valdez and Stan Steiner,
    eds. New York: Alfred A. Knopf, 1972.
Goldfinch, Charles W. *Juan Cortina, 1824–1892: A Reappraisal*. Brownsville, Tex.:
    Bishop's Print Shop, 1950.
Larralde, Carlos. *Mexican American Movements and Leaders*. Los Alamitos, Calif.:
    Hwong Publishing, 1976.
Webb, Walter Prescott. *The Texas Rangers*. Boston: Houghton Mifflin, 1935.
Webster, Mike. "Juan N. Cortina, defensor de la raza." In *Aztlán: historia del
    pueblo chicano (1846–1910)*, David Maciel and Patricia Bueno, eds. Mexico:
    SepSetentas, 1975.
Woodman, Lyman L. *Cortina, Rogue of the Rio Grande*. San Antonio: Naylor Co.,
    1950.

CELIA CRUZ

(1920s?–   )

Cuban American Singer, Entertainer

Celia Cruz refuses to tell the year of her birth, and efforts by a number
of writers to discover it have proved fruitless. But we do know that she
was born in Havana, Cuba, on 21 October, probably in the late 1920s.
She was the second-oldest of four children born to Catalina Alfonso and
Simón Cruz; she and her three siblings shared their humble home in the
Santa Suárez barrio with ten cousins, nieces, and nephews whom her
parents took in. Because she loved music even as a small child, she was
given the chore of singing to lull the children to sleep. However, the
songs she sang to them, many learned from the chants of street peddlers,
tended instead to keep them awake and brought the neighbors over to
listen at the door. She was an avid listener to music on the radio and as
a young girl accompanied one of her aunts to dances at ballrooms, where
she became acquainted with the musicians.

Although it was very clear early on that Celia had a talent for singing,
she was encouraged by her father to study for a "respectable" career, so

she planned to become a teacher. After completing her studies in the República de México public school in Havana, she enrolled in the Escuela Normal para Maestros to study for a teaching credential. While she was a student there in the early 1940s she was entered in a local radio talent show by an older cousin. She won first prize, a cake, and the die was cast. There followed an intoxicating round of amateur show appearances, and her success in them led to offers of singing jobs.

Her father objected to the music business as somewhat disreputable. However, he was overruled by his wife, and Celia accepted the offers and sang professionally on Radio Progreso Cubano and Radio Unión, always accompanied by a female relative as chaperone. According to Celia, when one of her teachers at the Escuela Normal pointed out that as a singer she might expect to earn far more than she could as a teacher, she began to become serious about music.

Her father having been persuaded by Celia and her mother that her career in music would not disgrace the family, she matriculated at the Havana Conservatory of Music, where she had studied music theory and voice for three years. An enthusiastic and hard-working student, she continued to accept singing engagements while attending school. After her music studies her first long-term singing job was with a dance group called Las Mulatas de Fuego; her role was to keep the audience entertained during the troupe's costume changes. She also began singing with a group calling itself La Gloria Matancera ("The Glory of Matanzas"— a Cuban province close to Havana) and on Cuban radio. Her big opportunity came in the late summer of 1950 when she was chosen to replace an extremely popular radio singer who left Cuba's number one orchestra, La Sonora Matancera, to return to her native Puerto Rico. By 1951 Celia was the top female singer in Cuba, on radio and in record sales.

Celia Cruz sang with La Sonora Matancera for 15 years, her first stretch of long, exhilarating popularity. With the band she sang on radio, at Havana's premier nightclub, La Tropicana, and in the new medium of television. She also performed extensively in Latin America and the United States. The group also appeared in five movies made in Mexico. In 1960, after the Castro revolution, they quietly left Cuba, acting as if they were going on a Latin American tour. After a year and a half in Mexico, Celia and the band moved to a permanent base in the United States to entertain U.S. Latino audiences. Unfortunately for Celia, in the 1960s the Latino youth of the United States were obsessed with rock and roll and had no interest in Latin music, particularly the Matancera sound. As a result her outstanding position as a singer gradually eroded.

In mid-1962 Celia married one of the Sonora Matancera orchestra members, Pedro Knight. They had known each other for 14 years and had been courting for two. From then on Knight became her personal manager and musical director. With his counsel, in the early 1960s Celia signed with Seeco Records, cutting 20 albums of the Matancera sound. Sales were less than sensational. In 1966 she switched to Tico Records, with whom she made 13 more albums. The band having split up, she also toured the United States and Latin America and, most important, began to sing with the upcoming king of salsa, **Tito Puente**, with whom she recorded 8 of her 13 Tico albums. They have since performed together over one thousand times.

In the 1970s the popularity of salsa, to which Celia was an outstanding contributor, among Latino American youths and their reminiscing old-country parents put her star on the rise again. In 1973 she had the lead role in a pop opera at Carnegie Hall. Her powerful voice, outrageously incandescent costumes, and boundless energy thrilled young and old alike. When Cruz's contract with Tico Records expired she joined with the well-known rumba band leader Johnny Pacheco on the Vaya label to make what was to be her first gold record, "Celia and Johnny." She followed this heartwarming success with several more highly successful albums for Vaya Records, in collaboration with various musicians. One that she cut in 1974 with conga player Ray Barretto won her a Grammy award. In addition to her recording activity, she sang in concert all over the world with Pacheco, Barretto, Puente, and others. From 1975 to 1982 she was named every year as best female vocalist by the magazine *Latin N.Y.*; she was similarly cited in 1977 and 1979 by the *New York Daily News* and in 1978 by *Billboard* magazine.

During the 1980s Celia Cruz remained a dynamic salsa singer, constantly on the move. To meet the demands of her devoted fans she continued to give concerts, cut record albums, and appear on television. In 1982 she was reunited with La Sonora Matancera in an updated album. Later that year with the group and many other old friends, such as Pacheco and Puente, she did a retrospective concert in Madison Square Garden that was televised worldwide via satellite. In 1986 she was awarded the Ellis Island Medal of Honor and in the following year won another Obie, an award for Best Latin Artist, and received her fourth nomination for a Grammy award. In 1988 she did a concert for her old friend and fellow musician Frank Grillo, "Machito," and a year later starred in a triumphant birthday (her own) concert in Harlem accompanied by many old musician friends. She concluded the decade of the 1980s by winning yet another Grammy. During half a century as a singer she has recorded more than 70 albums, which continue to delight her devotees and most Latinos, young and old.

In 1991 Celia had her first English-speaking role in a film, *The Mambo Kings Play Songs of Love*. During the 1990s, despite her nearly 70 years, she continues to perform as vigorously as ever. In October 1994 she participated in a four-hour salsa show in Madison Square Garden, titled La

Combinación Perfecta, singing with her usual verve and vitality and making "much of what had gone on before seem superficial," in the words of one critic. That same year she was one of 12 artists—including Julia Harris, Pete Seeger, and Gene Kelly—who were awarded the National Medal of Arts by the National Endowment for the Arts and President Bill Clinton.

Further Reading

"Celia Cruz y su estrella." *Más* 3:6 (November–December 1991): 77.
Current Biography, 1983. New York: H. W. Wilson Co., 1983.
"In Performance." *New York Times* 144 (25 October 1994): C16(L).
Kanellos, Nicolás, ed. *Handbook of Hispanic Culture in the United States*, vol. 1. Houston: Arte Público Press, 1993.
Telgen, Diane, and Jim Kamp, eds. *Notable Hispanic American Women*. Detroit: Gale Research, 1993.
Variety (5 November 1990): 90.
Watrous, Peter. "La combinación perfecta." *New York Times* 144 (25 October 1994): C16(L).

XAVIER CUGAT
(1900–1990)

Spanish American Violinist, Dance Band Leader, Composer

Although Xavier Cugat was born near Barcelona, Spain, and died in Barcelona, he was a U.S. citizen for 75 years and spent 66 of those years in the United States. Known almost as much for his many marital problems as for his musicianship and showmanship, he married five women in his lifetime and had a reputation of being something of a womanizer. Because of his music and early life he was thought of by many as a Cuban American. He was not; but for his activities in behalf of Cuban music and musicians, in October 1941 the Cuban government awarded Xavier Cugat the Orden de Honor y Mérito de la Cruz Roja Cubana with the rank of commander.

Francisco de Asís Xavier Cugat was born on 1 January 1900 in the small town of Tirona in northeastern Spain not far from the leading

Catalan city of Barcelona. His parents, Mingall de Bru and Juan Cugat, left Spain two years later and settled in Havana, Cuba. From a very early age Francisco de Asís Xavier seemed destined for a career in music like his contemporary fellow Spaniard, **José Iturbi**. At about age 5 he began to play the violin and to study classical music, and before he was 7 he appeared with the Cuban Symphony. He continued his instruction in classical music in Berlin, Paris, and New York, studying in the last city with Walter Damrosch. He then returned to Cuba, where he played in the Havana Symphony at age 12. In that same year, 1912, he and the family moved from Havana to New York City. Three years later he was sworn in as an American citizen.

During the second half of his teen years, the talented young concert violinist got his first long-term job; for five and one-half years he toured with the world-famous Italian tenor Enrico Caruso as supporting artist. After Caruso's death in 1921 he played violin with the Vincent López dance band in New York for a year. Determined to try his luck once again in classical music, he obtained a position with the Los Angeles Philharmonic, but his violin solos met with lackluster reception from the critics. The scarcity of employment for classical violinists, combined with Cugat's satiric sense of humor, art training, and considerable talent as a caricaturist, led him to accept a post as staff cartoonist on the *Los Angeles Times*. He specialized in caricature, a skill he allegedly learned from his time with Caruso. He became well known for his often barbed characterizations, which he achieved economically with a minimum number of lines.

After a year or so of meeting deadlines, Cugat found being amusing on demand too taxing and in 1928 quit the newspaper business and started a small six-man band called the Gigolos. Later that year the group opened at the Coconut Grove nightclub in Hollywood as the relief band for the main orchestra. In 1933 Cugat was invited to bring his band to New York City as the relief band at the opening of the Hotel Waldorf Astoria's new Starlight Roof. From this modest start he and the band continued there as the main orchestra for 16 years, becoming the Waldorf's highest-paid attraction. During these years they spent about six months of the summer and early fall at the Starlight Roof, sometimes referred to as the Cugat Room. The rest of the year they scheduled tours of colleges, hotels, and theaters, played radio engagements, and did work in Hollywood films. Among the band's vocalists who later became well known in their own right were **Desi Arnaz** and Miguelito Valdez.

One of the pioneers in introducing Latin American music in the United States, Cugat had the facility to simplify the complex, intricate rhythms of the rumba, tango, conga, samba, bolero, and the like for American audiences. He quickly became known as the "Rumba King," and his name became closely identified with all Latin American music. For example, when the American composer Cole Porter wrote "Begin the Beguine," he first gave it to Cugat to play. Cugat and his orchestra helped make the song famous along with "Perfidia," "Frenesí," the folk tune "El Manisero" ("The Peanut Vendor"), and other Latin American songs. Cugat also wrote a number of the songs that the band played. He once said that giving people joy through his dance band music was just as satisfying as playing classical violin in concert.

Xavier Cugat made his debut on the airwaves in 1921 in the very early days of radio, but not until he and the band went to the Waldorf Astoria in 1933 did radio appearances become an important part of his career. Riding on a tide of American interest in Latino music, in the next year Cugat and his band began performing on a weekly network radio program. By the beginning of the 1940s he and his band had achieved a national reputation because of their radio appearances; for some years they were the heart of a program called "The Camel Caravan."

In addition to his radio work and making a great number of recordings Cugat appeared with his orchestra in various films between 1936 and 1949, after which time the appeal of Latin American music went into a decline for several decades. He added spice to *Go West, Young Man* (1936) and *The Heat's On* (1943), both with Mae West. Then he signed up with Metro-Goldwyn-Mayer, where he played his music in several films starring the famous swimmer Esther Williams. Two of her films especially, *Bathing Beauty* and *Neptune's Daughter*, helped make his name a household word.

In 1958 Cugat opened his own nightclub, Casa Cugat. During the 1960s and 1970s he continued a heavy schedule of musical activity that included tours, recordings, and appearances on radio and the new medium of television. He often appeared on television talk shows with the last of his five wives, the singer, dancer, and guitarist Charo Baeza. Because of heart problems he began to slow down and in 1978 left the United States for retirement in Barcelona, Spain. However, a decade later, at age 88, he organized another band with which he began touring Spain.

On 27 October 1990 Xavier Cugat died of arteriosclerosis at the Quirón Clinic in Barcelona.

Further Reading

Alford, Harold. *The Proud People.* New York: David McKay Co., 1972.

Current Biography, 1942. New York: H. W. Wilson Co., 1942.

Current Biography Yearbook, 1991 [obit.]. New York: H. W. Wilson Co., 1991.

Mooney, Louise, ed., *Newsmakers: The People behind Today's Headlines,* 1991 Cumulation. Detroit: Gale Research, 1991.

Reyes, Luis, and Peter Rubie. *Hispanics in Hollywood.* New York: Garland Publishing, 1994.

The World of Music, vol. 1. New York: Abradale Press, 1963.

"Xavier Cugat, 90, the Bandleader Who Rose on the Rumba's Tide." *New York Times* [obit.] (28 October 1990): I28.

OSCAR DE LA RENTA

(1932–)

Dominican American Fashion Designer, Entrepreneur

Internationally renowned for his dress designs, Oscar de la Renta is especially acclaimed for his dramatic, elegant, and not infrequently elaborate creations for high society patrons, among whom he counted Jacqueline Kennedy Onassis and most other women of the Kennedy family. His designs are generally noted for their graceful and sophisticated, yet conservative, lines suitable for women from their teen years to old age. However, his typical aristocratic styling has not noticeably hindered him from presenting daring designs to the fashion world at times, particularly in his ready-to-wear dresses. He has become particularly known for his romantic and delicately jewel-trimmed ballroom gowns.

Oscar de la Renta was born on 22 July 1932 in Santo Domingo, the capital of the Dominican Republic, the eastern half of the Caribbean island of Hispaniola. He was the only son (with six sisters) of María Antonia Fiallo and Oscar de la Renta, an insurance agent on the island. Oscar's early life was unexceptional for the son of a family belonging to the small Dominican middle class. After his lower school education he enrolled in the Escuela Normal at the national university, a teacher-training institution in Santo Domingo from which he graduated in 1950. While at the university he had developed an interest in painting, and after graduation he entered the Academia de San Fernando, the national art school in the capital. Having completed his classes at San Fernando he went to Madrid, the capital of Spain, to further his training in painting. After finishing his formal studies there he remained in Madrid, becoming a struggling young painter of abstract canvases, a career choice that, after a while, seemed to hold no great promise for the future.

As one facet of his art studies, de la Renta had become increasingly interested in women's fashion design, sketching various ideas when he became bored with painting. Some of his sketches for evening gowns came to the attention of the wife of John Lodge, the American ambassador to Spain in the 1950s, and she asked him to design a gown for her daughter's society debut. When a photograph of the debutante, dressed in her de la Renta creation, appeared on the cover of *Life* magazine, Oscar's future was determined. Abandoning his painting career, the young artist obtained a position on the staff of the well-known Madrid custom couture house of Balenciaga. After training for several years as an apprentice designer with Balenciaga, he "graduated" to a position as assistant to world-famous clothing designer Antonio Castillo of Lanvin-Castillo in Paris, working there from 1961 to 1963. Having completed his "postgraduate courses" in women's fashion, he left Paris for the United States.

De la Renta found his first American job in New York City as a designer for the Elizabeth Arden cosmetics and women's clothing firm. There he designed chic romantic, yet sophisticated, clothing for young women of the jet set as well as for elegant, sophisticated women of all ages. Two years later, early in 1965, he left Elizabeth Arden and bought into the wholesale clothing firm of Jane Derby, Inc., as a partner. With Derby he began to design simple, conservative, ready-to-wear clothing with a custom look and also with a clear de la Renta flair. In 1966 he opened up a new and much larger market area by creating a boutique line of daytime and evening dresses for the woman of taste with about $100 to spend. This new line also allowed him the keen pleasure of experimenting with more venturesome and audacious stylistic ideas, which he had earlier not dared to incorporate into his high fashion creations.

When Jane Derby retired, the company became his, but de la Renta retained the Derby label for several more years. Meanwhile he began to make changes in the boutique line, until at the beginning of the 1970s the dresses had become moderately priced versions of the high fashion designs that he continued to turn out. In addition to the boutique clothing line he expanded his offerings by introducing his own designs in costume jewelry and furs, as well as collections of attractive handbags, belts, and other leather accessories carrying his label. He had clearly become one of the most influential couture designers and a pacesetter in both American and world fashions.

In 1969 de la Renta's firm was acquired by the large conglomerate Richton International as part of its holdings in fashion, jewelry, and other accessories. De la Renta remained chief executive of Richton's Oscar de la Renta Couture. In 1991 de la Renta surprised the world of fashion by moving to the prestigious couture house of Balmain. In January 1993 he became the first American since Mainbocher to show his collection of gowns in Paris, at L'École Nationale Supérieure. The couture collection showed that de la Renta still had the touch. In August 1996 his "Oscar Fall '96 Collection," a new "bridge" collection of affordable simplified designs for the professional woman, received high praise from fashion critics. In January 1997 First Lady Hillary Rodham Clinton chose Oscar de la Renta to outfit her for her husband's second presidential inaugural.

De la Renta has been the recipient of a number of prizes and awards for his designs featuring both stylish, sophisticated opulence and daring, often provocative extravagance. One fashion critic, recalling J. Pierpont Morgan's famous statement about yacht ownership, said that anyone concerned about price or serviceability should probably forget de la Renta. However, for two years straight—in 1967 and 1968—he received the Coty American Fashion Critics Award, the Winnie, and five years later was inducted into the Coty Hall of Fame for his influence on the world of fashion over the years. From Joaquín Balaguer, president of the Dominican Republic, he received El Orden de Juan Pablo Duarte (the hero of the Dominican independence movement) *grado Caballero*; he also was awarded the Tiberio de Oro by the Italian government in 1968. In that same year he received the Nieman Marcus Award, and ten years later the Fragrance Foundation Award. For his support of the Dominican Childhood Center in Santo Domingo he was awarded the Order of Cristóbal Colón, and in 1988 he was presented with the Jack Dempsey Award for Humanitarianism. He is also the proud recipient of a Lifetime Achievement Award from the Council of Fashion Designers of America.

Further Reading

Christian Science Monitor (18 November 1963): 10.

Cue 35:10 (12 March 1966).

Current Biography, 1970. New York: H. W. Wilson Co., 1970.

Moukheiber, Zina. "The Face behind the Perfume." *Forbes* 152:7 (27 September 1993): 68.

"Stocking Stuff." *New York* 28:48 (4 December 1995): 60.

Unterburger, Amy, ed. *Who's Who among Hispanic Americans, 1994–1995*. Detroit: Gale Research, 1994.

Van Zuylen, Vanessa. "Fashion . . . and the Oscar Goes to . . . Balmain." *Town & Country* 147:5156 (May 1993): 112.

Who's Who in the East, 1989–1990, 2nd ed. Chicago, Ill.: Marquis Who's Who, 1990.

JUSTINO DÍAZ

(1940–   )

Puerto Rican Opera Singer

To young bass-baritone Justino Díaz, premiere performances that opened the "new" Metropolitan Opera House at the Lincoln Center and Kennedy Center were "a piece of cake." Díaz was only 26 years old when he starred in Samuel Barber's *Antony and Cleopatra* in 1966, sharing the stage with Leontyne Price. Reminiscing later about this act of bravura, he marveled at his own youthful chutzpah. As a young singer Díaz did not envision becoming an opera great; even today, after three decades of success, he has the air of someone who does not quite believe what has happened to him.

Justino Díaz was born of privilege in the elegant Condado district of San Juan, the capital of Puerto Rico. He was the only child of Gladys Villarini and Justino Díaz Morales, who taught economics at the University of Puerto Rico. At age 5 Justino traveled with his parents to Philadelphia, Pennsylvania, where he resided for one year while his father obtained his master's degree. The family returned to Puerto Rico soon thereafter.

Díaz made his first public appearance at Robinson grammar school in San Juan at age 6, singing a solo in a school music presentation. He sang "Old Black Joe"—in English! Throughout his childhood Díaz embraced every available opportunity to sing, joining school choruses and the church choir. At the urging of the Robinson school music teacher, who recognized the quality of his voice early on, he practiced and began voice training.

In 1954 Justino's family moved to Cambridge, Massachusetts, for a year and a half while his father worked on his doctoral dissertation at Harvard University. This move served young Justino well. In the States he sang in his high school glee club and also perfected his English.

When the Díaz family again returned to Puerto Rico, Justino attended San Ignacio de Loyola Jesuit High School in San Juan. Here, during the local opera company's annual season he made his first operatic appearance as a member of the chorus in *La Forza del Destino*. This experience prompted the 17-year-old high school student to consider an operatic career seriously for the first time. With the help of his father's persuasive efforts to influence the opera company's managers, Díaz was tentatively admitted to the chorus and later became a permanent member. He performed his first solo at age 18 in *La Traviata*, singing just one line to announce that dinner was being served.

After high school Díaz attended the University of Puerto Rico, where he majored in psychology and continued voice training under soprano María Esther Robles and Augusto Rodríguez, who directed the University chorus. At age 19 he sang his first leading role in a Puerto Rican company's production of Gian Carlo Menotti's *The Telephone*. In 1959 he transferred to the New England Conservatory of Music, where he continued his studies in voice and languages, music theory, counterpoint, and piano. He fondly recalls his days in Boston, where he was an indifferent student of the piano who also felt no need to slave over theoretical subjects because he knew he had a "hell of a voice." He took voice lessons from Frederick Jagel, who was connected with the Metropolitan Opera in New York. While at the Conservatory he sang at churches and in festivals, and joined the New England Opera directed by Boris Goldovsky. He recalls performing in Rossini's *The Barber of Seville*, playing three different roles.

During the period Díaz worked with Goldovsky he was on tour three or four times a week, traveling as much as 100 miles each day. In 1962 Díaz dropped out of the New England Conservatory and left for the Met studios in New York City. With him he carried a letter from Goldovsky that earned him an audition and admission to further training. Díaz soon became a member of the Met Studio, a company of young professionals who took one-hour versions of such operas as *The Barber of Seville* and *Cosi Fan Tutte* to schools in greater New York City. Having noticed Díaz's talent, the Met's musical director and assistant manager persuaded him to try out in the Metropolitan Opera auditions.

In 1963, at age 23, Díaz entered two singing contests and won first prize in both, one of which offered a cash prize of $2,000 and the opportunity to sing with the Met. He was unaware that he exactly fitted the Met's need at that moment for someone young, talented, and inexpensive. Díaz came to international attention that year when he made his debut at Carnegie Hall opposite Joan Sutherland and Nicolai Gedda in a concert version of *I Puritani*.

In October of that year Díaz appeared for the first time with the Metropolitan Opera as Monterone in *Rigoletto*. The handsome bass-baritone made an impressive debut; *Opera News* noted: "Everything about him suggests a basso profundo: his hair, eyes and generous eyebrows are almost black, his voice dark and velvety, his speech earnest." He became responsible for 29 roles at the Met, including the King in *Aïda* and Prince Gremin in *Eugene Onegin*.

Díaz's first Metropolitan appearance was followed by events that became highlights of his career: appearances in the Casals Festival in

Puerto Rico and debuts in Salzburg, Austria, and Tanglewood, Massachusetts. Then, in 1965 he made his debut at the famous La Scala Opera House in Milan, where he had the honor of singing the title role in the premiere Italian performance of Menotti's *Death of the Bishop of Brindisi*. His greatest operatic honors took place in 1966 and 1971 when he was chosen to sing opening night at the Metropolitan Opera House in New York City and for the opening week of the Kennedy Center in Washington, D.C. In the latter debut he performed the role of Count Cenci in *Beatrix Cenci* by the Argentine composer Alberto Ginastera, who so admired Díaz's voice that he wrote this opera and the part of the Count specifically for Díaz.

Among the roles that have served Díaz well is the lead character in *Don Giovanni*, which he has performed over 150 times in the past three decades. Díaz sees the opera *Don Giovanni* as a morality play about a man who reflects on how life has caught up with him, rather than as the story of a seducer of women.

Díaz appeared as Iago in Franco Zeffirelli's film of Giuseppe Verdi's opera *Otello*. The movie was considered a financial flop. However, it proved a windfall for Díaz since the film did more to bring his voice and name to wider public attention than had 20 years of singing in opera houses all over the world. Iago became Díaz's signature role. He sang this part in all the Met's performances of *Otello* following the film's release. Díaz's recollection of the film is lighthearted and breezy.

In 1993 Díaz was honored with the Award for Excellence in Singing from the New York Singing Teacher's Association. A few years earlier the New England Conservatory of Music had awarded him an honorary degree. Díaz is now engaged in a new career as a baritone and looks forward to exploring new roles in opera.

Further Reading

Abdul, Raoul. "Award for Excellence Given to Bass-Baritone Justino Díaz." *New York Amsterdam News* (27 March 1993): 6H.

Graeme, R. "Justino Díaz Mozart Arias." *Opera Quarterly* 7:3 (1990): 204–208.

Newlon, Clarke. *Famous Puerto Ricans*. New York: Dodd, Mead and Co., 1975.

Opera News, Winners Two (11 January 1964): 29.

Press Kit for Justino Díaz. New York: Robert Lombardo Associates, 1994.

LINCOLN DÍAZ-BALART

(1954–   )

Cuban American Politician, Lawyer

Most Cuban Americans who were born in Cuba have a great love for the island as they remember it. Many still hope, after nearly four decades of Castroism, to return with the help of the United States. So it is not surprising that Lincoln Díaz-Balart, Cuban American representative of the 21st District in Florida, has as his principal (if not sole) political objective as a member of the U.S. House of Representatives to bring about the downfall of Fidel Castro's dictatorship. Like many of the voters he represents, Díaz-Balart's life and daily actions continue to center on his and their Cubanness, an essential element in the surrogate homeland they have created in Greater Miami, Dade County, Florida.

Lincoln Díaz-Balart was born in Havana, Cuba, on 13 August 1954 into a well-to-do and politically active middle-class family. Both his father and grandfather had served in the Cuban House of Representatives, and his father was president of the Senate under the dictator Fulgencio Batista. When the Fidel Castro–led revolution overthrew Batista in 1959 and took over the government, the Díaz-Balart family, including 5-year-old Lincoln, left for the United States. Lincoln received his primary education in Miami public schools and attended high school in the American School in Madrid, the capital of Spain. During his high school years he was elected president of the student government. After high school he enrolled in the New College of the University of South Florida in Sarasota, where he received his bachelor of arts in international relations in 1976. Subsequently he studied British politics in Cambridge, England, and in 1979 obtained his doctorate in jurisprudence (J.D.) from Case Western Reserve University in Cleveland, Ohio.

Upon graduating from law school Díaz-Balart began to practice law in Miami and later served as an assistant state attorney in the office of the Florida state attorney, at that time Janet Reno. Almost inevitably he became active in Florida politics. In the early 1980s he was head of the Florida Young Democrats and in 1982 ran unsuccessfully for the state House as a Democrat. Although he remained in the Democratic Party after the failure of the Bay of Pigs invasion, he later became disenchanted by what he considered its "soft policy on communism" in Nicaragua and El Salvador and left the party to become a Republican. He also recognized that he could never be elected from District 34 as a Democrat.

Lincoln Díaz-Balart.

With the help of the solid ethnic vote of the Cuban American community, Díaz-Balart won election to the Florida House of Representatives in 1986 with the largest margin of votes ever cast for any candidate for state representative. He was the first Latino to be elected chairman of the Dade County delegation to the Florida legislature. During his freshman term at the state House he was noted by his colleagues for his persuasiveness in debate. Two years later he was re-elected. Except for fiscal policy, in the House he sometimes deviated from the Republican Party position and voted with the Democrats, especially on social issues such as accessibility of health care. He also became known as an advocate for farmworkers, many of whom were Latinos. In 1989 he ran in a special election for an open seat in the state senate, taking a strong stand on taxes and other budgetary issues that he felt were of prime importance to his Cuban American constituents. He won and in the following year was re-elected. In the Florida senate he worked unceasingly to make sure that Miami would get a second district with a Latino majority when the area was to be redistricted as a result of the 1990 census.

Ultimately the courts drew the new 21st District boundaries much as Senator Díaz-Balart had argued, creating a district in western Dade

County that was nearly 70 percent Latino; he ran for the newly created position in the U.S. House of Representatives. The primary elections saw a bitter campaign in which he ran against Javier Souto, a fellow Cuban American state senator, who questioned his anti-Castro credentials and accused him of being a tool of wealthy Cuban Americans. Díaz-Balart nevertheless won in the primaries with 69 percent of the votes cast; in the general election he ran unopposed.

During his first term in Washington, D.C., Díaz-Balart served on the House Foreign Affairs Committee, where he worked strenuously to protect national security. He also used his position there to lead the fight to strengthen the 30-year-old embargo of Cuba and to prevent any relaxation of sanctions against the Castro dictatorship. He helped bring about the closure of a loophole by which foreign-located subsidiaries of American companies avoided the embargo, and he called for an international embargo sanctioned by the United Nations. Consistent with his pro–Cuban American views he was opposed to the Latin American Free Trade Association (LAFTA), principally because of the political and economic ties that both Canada and Mexico maintain with Cuba. He also secured all the federal aid he could get for Miami to offset the ravages of Hurricane Andrew.

In 1994 Díaz-Balart was re-elected to the House without opposition. In his second term he was named to the very powerful 13-member House Rules Committee by Speaker Newt Gingrich, who echoed Lincoln's freshmen Florida colleagues in praise of his eloquence on the floor of the House. He became vice-chairman of the subcommittee on rules of the House and was selected as a member of the House Oversight Committee. He is also chairman of the Congressional Hispanic Task Force on Housing and Development. In the House he continues to be in the mainstream of Republican thought, strongly concerned about taxes, spending cuts, jobs, and federal help for employers and incentives for investors.

Díaz-Balart has found useful the highly politicized Cuban *municipios* organized in Dade County, which help to account for the higher-than-average political activism of Cuban Americans. Their principal objective (as it is of a large majority of the more than one million Cuban Americans) is the overthrow of Fidel Castro. The remarkable demographic concentration of Cuban Americans in Dade County and their focus on a single issue has undoubtedly helped Díaz-Balart in his political career, as it has helped other Republican Latinos in the greater Miami area. Also helping him are the ten local Spanish-language radio stations, headed by Station WQBA, which calls itself La Cubanísima. But his success is also the result of his playing the political game very astutely.

Díaz-Balart has been honored with awards by the Florida Epilepsy Foundation, the Dade County Fair Campaign Practices Committee, and the Dade County Public Schools.

Further Reading

Azicri, Max. "The Politics of Exile." *Cuban Studies/Estudios Cubanos* 11:12 (July 1981–January 1982).

Boswell, Thomas D. "The Cuban-American Homeland in Miami." *Journal of Cultural Geography* 13:2 (Spring 1993):133–147.

Bragdon, Peter. "Cuban-Americans Poised to Succeed Pepper." *Congressional Quarterly Weekly Report* 47:25 (24 June 1989):1571–1572.

Clymer, Adam. "Minority Candidates See Congress as a Useful Tool." *New York Times* 142 (20 September 1992):15N, 26L.

Congress, A to Z, 2nd ed. Washington, D.C.: Congressional Quarterly, 1993.

Kanellos, Nicolás, ed. *The Hispanic Almanac*. Detroit: Visible Ink Press, 1994.

"Lincoln Díaz–Balart, Republican, Florida 21st District." *Congressional Quarterly* 51 (15 January 1993):72.

Olson, James S., and Judith E. Olson. *Cuban Americans: From Trauma to Triumph*. New York: Twayne Publishers, 1995.

Unterburger, Amy, ed. *Who's Who among Hispanic Americans, 1994–95*. Detroit: Gale Research, 1994.

PLÁCIDO DOMINGO

(1941–   )

Spanish American Opera Star, Singer, Conductor, Administrator

Plácido Domingo is one of the world's great opera singers, comparable to such immortals of the past as Enrico Caruso and currently rivaled as a lyric-dramatic tenor only by Luciano Pavarotti and José Carreras. His voice is a voice for all seasons, all peoples, and all music. The center of his world is opera. He wants everyone to become acquainted with opera, to get to know him, and above all to appreciate the world of aesthetics. He is a workaholic, an overachiever, a man of great ambition and boundless energy. He loves to sing. "The more I sing the better I sing," he says. Since he sang his first operatic role at age 19, he has sung more than 70 roles in 55 operas as well as solo parts in 8 choral-orchestral works. He has recorded over 60 operas, and by his 43rd birthday he had to his credit more than 1,700 performances in major operas: *Aïda, La Bohème, Madame Butterfly, La Traviata, Tosca, Faust, Carmen, Rigoletto*, and many others. In all these major performances he was triumphant.

Plácido Domingo was born on 21 January 1941 in Madrid, Spain. His father, also Plácido, was of Catalan and Aragonese descent; his mother, Josefa Embil, was Basque. Both parents were devoted to the theater, taking active roles in it first in Spain and then in Mexico. Plácido's father studied the violin and played in opera and zarzuela orchestras in his home town of Zaragoza in northeastern Spain. The zarzuela, sometimes described as a popular form of opera, is a theatrical form that combines music with dialogue, not unlike operetta. Plácido's father and mother sang in a zarzuela company that traveled throughout the various Spanish regions and then in Mexico after they moved there. Plácido was reared in this aesthetic milieu of popular culture and learned to love music and singing and to appreciate their appeal to the general public. "I owe my love of music," he once said, "to the zarzuelas I so often heard from the time I was a small boy." However, as he grew up he was disturbed by the sometimes low quality of the singing. He longed for perfection in the music, the story, and the singers. As a result, he has constantly been driven to seek flawlessness in his performances. He believes that he owes the audience his best.

When Plácido was about 8 years old the family moved to Mexico, where his parents eventually organized an operatic company in the capital. Plácido grew up in Mexico City, going from primary school to the Instituto México, where he learned to love soccer. Since his parents traveled a great deal Plácido lived with his aunt Augustina, who emphasized punctuality, proper behavior, and keeping faithfully at lessons from his piano teacher, Manuel Barajas, as more important than playing soccer. Plácido has always remembered his aunt as his "second mother" and gradually internalized her emphasis on disciplined behavior and punctuality. Upon Barajas's untimely death, the 14-year-old Plácido was enrolled in the National Conservatory of Music in Mexico City. He believes that this was a crucial turning point in his life. If Barajas had not died, he probably would have become a concert pianist because of his facility at the keyboard and his ability to "sight-read" music. He remains convinced that his career path as well as his love of opera was determined by this *forza del destino*, or force of fate. Plácido has always held a strong belief in the Hispanic concept of fate as an underlying force in the lives of individuals.

While retaining his love of soccer, at the world-famous National Conservatory Plácido studied both musical and academic subjects, pursuing courses in literature and mathematics as well as musical composition, harmony, and singing. Although Plácido studied with various well-known faculty members, none of them ever filled the role of mentor. Believing that he would find his own path, he gravitated toward classes, lessons, and coaching sessions offered by the National Opera. However, he did not appear to be interested in "learning" and "studying" the world of music and opera in an academic fashion. No pedantic high-brow, Plácido Domingo wanted to learn by "doing." He was pragmatic, almost in the American sense. From the time he watched his first opera, *Rigoletto*, he knew what he wanted to do with his life.

Plácido believed that opera was the art form that provided a point at which childhood emotions, the element of play, fantasy, imagination, and the desire to be at the center stage of life intersected. He has pointed out that "the artist is likely to have maintained into adulthood something valuable from childhood that many people lose as they mature, something of the freshness of response of the child, the inclination to use 'play' as a means of trying to impose order upon a stubbornly inchoate world, and the capacity to create imaginative fantasy out of reality." For Domingo opera merges aesthetics, cultural representations of life and passions, and the private with the public self.

In 1961 Plácido Domingo made his first appearance on the opera stage in the northern Mexican industrial city of Monterrey in Nuevo León and later that same year made his U.S. debut with the Dallas Civic Opera. After appearing the following year with the Fort Worth Opera, he decided to accept employment with the Israel National Opera but returned to the United States in 1965. From 1965 onward his operatic career has been based in the United States. After a successful audition he joined the New York City Opera and early in the next year was "discovered" by the critics in a stunning opening of the 1966 season at Lincoln Center. From the New York City Opera it was only a short step for Domingo to the Metropolitan Opera's summer productions at Lewisohn Stadium in Manhattan. In 1968 he officially debuted at the Metropolitan, continuing his triumphant operatic career. In the 1996 season he sang his 400th performance at the Metropolitan.

In addition to his singing, Domingo has moved into other musical areas. In the mid-1980s he took a position as artistic consultant to the Los Angeles Music Center Opera and at about the same time began an additional career as a conductor. Most of his conducting has been with the L.A. Music Center Opera and the Metropolitan Opera. He has said that he finds conducting both difficult and immensely rewarding. Most recently, in the mid-1990s he accepted the post of artistic director designate (beginning in July 1996) of the Washington Opera at Kennedy Center. He also plans to embark in June 1996 on a four-continent tour of some of the world's largest outdoor arenas with fellow tenors Pavarotti and Carreras.

From 1961 through 1995 the United States, Europe, and Latin America have embraced the "Age of Domingo." This success occurred not only because he is a leading operatic tenor but also because he has reached out to all social classes, all age groups, and all geographical areas through his operas, recordings, operatic films, popular songs, television appearances, and radio interviews. Domingo once told a reporter, "I love to sing anything that is good music. The best zarzuela songs, or those of Lennon and McCartney or Sammy Cahn or John Denver . . . and I want to sing these just as much as the greatest operas." He sees his ventures into popular music as creating a cultural bridge.

Domingo has extended the world of aesthetics to all Americans, to everyone in the world. He believes that through his reaching out to different audiences he can ultimately win larger audiences for his special love, opera. One musical audience that especially concerns him is the Latino community of the United States. For the Hispanic communities he would like to sing the music of the zarzuela and the Mexican music of Jorge Negrete and Pedro Infante, as well as the music of the rest of Latin America. Domingo ultimately wants everyone to share his love of singing, which, for him, is a metaphor for living. He believes that music links everyone within a single aesthetic human chain that still allows all members to follow their own paths in life. Plácido Domingo wants all persons to discover their humanity through music and, of course, especially through opera.

Further Reading

"Arias, Songs and Tangos." *Time* 139:17 (27 April 1992): 71.

Current Biography, 1972. New York: H. W. Wilson Co., 1972.

Domingo, Plácido. *My First Forty Years.* New York: Alfred A. Knopf, 1983.

Gunther, Louise T. "Conquistador." *Opera News* 60:13 (16 March 1996): 8–11, 47.

Jellinek, George. "Plácido Domingo: Mozart, Arias, Duets." *Opera News* 57:3 (September 1991): 51.

Livingstone, William. "From the Official Olympic Games Ceremony: Domingo, Carreras, Caballé." *Stereo Review* 57:9 (September 1992): 98.

Mark, Michael. "Plácido Domingo." *American Record Guide* 57:1 (January–February 1994): 193.

Snowman, Daniel. *The World of Plácido Domingo.* New York: McGraw-Hill, 1985.

Sunier, John. "Plácido Domingo, Grandissimo." *American Record Guide* 56:2 (March–April 1993): 204.

de Toledano, Ralph. "Carreras, Domingo, Pavarotti." *National Review* 3:2 (11 February 1991): 57.

JAIME ESCALANTE

(1930–)

Bolivian American Teacher

Growing up is never easy, but growing up amid poverty and political chaos is especially difficult. Jaime Escalante grew up in Bolivia in the 1930s in a world of political uncertainty, economic chaos, and social impoverishment. As a result of chaotic conditions during his youth, Escalante learned to hate disorder and sought to create for himself a world that was ordered and controllable. He quickly learned to turn to what he has called his four natural "talents for survival": a love of mathematics, a sense of showmanship, an impatience with rules, and an athletic competitiveness and urge to win. Because he nurtured these qualities he gained confidence and ultimately a feeling of power and control, so much so that he once exclaimed he could "teach rope-climbing to sea lions."

Jaime Alfonso Escalante was born in 1930 in La Paz, Bolivia's capital city, but his family soon moved to a small village in the Bolivian highlands. Jaime's parents, Sara Gutiérrez and Zenobio Escalante, were teachers in the Bolivian educational system. It was a rudimentary system in which the poorly paid teachers were made to move wherever the government felt they were needed. The Escalante family was ordered from one poor village to another until at last they were permanently assigned to an impoverished but pleasant Andean town with the typical small plaza, a few shops, a church, and the school. It was a simple village populated by Quechua and Aymara Indians who traced their ancestry back to the Inca "empire." Consequently Jaime grew up in a place that was a quiet backwater in the turbulence of toppling Bolivian juntas, a declining economy, and social disaster in the worldwide depression of the 1930s.

Young Jaime spent most of his first nine years learning word games and creating games of imaginary numbers and distances with his maternal grandfather, José Gutiérrez, a retired teacher and self-proclaimed philosopher. A man of exuberant personality and all-embracing inquisitiveness, his grandfather introduced Jaime to a world of imagination, curiosity, and discovery that contrasted sharply with the drudgery and oppression of the 1930s Bolivia. However, if his grandfather served as the liberator of his mind, Jaime's father served as a damper. Zenobio

Escalante was a man of tremendous energy who succumbed to suppressed anger and depressive moods and often resorted to alcohol as a refuge. Zenobio ruled his family with patriarchal violence, frequently striking his wife and children, especially Jaime because his young son's brightness and optimism irritated him. In his attempt to control the world outside himself Zenobio made use of anger and violence, whereas the defenseless Jaime sought self-control and order.

To give order to his world, Jaime used his imagination and his skill at arithmetic as well as at soccer, handball, and basketball. The neighborhood handball court, the *frontón*, became—as it would remain in adulthood—the special arena where he would work out his frustrations, his problems, and his anxieties, and most of all, would exercise his high level of energy and competitiveness. At the *frontón* he learned that victory ultimately came to the player who had more *ganas*, loosely translated as an intense urge, a deep desire to win. This spirit of *ganas*, so central to athletic competition, served as his central philosophical axiom in dealing with life. When he was unable to attend engineering school for financial reasons, he studied to become a teacher.

By 1961, at age 31, Escalante had become a Bolivian success: he was a school mathematics teacher, he owned a house and a blue DeSoto sedan, and he was earning a salary that placed him above the average rural and small-town Bolivian. He had, it seemed, control over his world, his life, and his classroom—especially his classroom, where he had "routinized" his world. His students studied long hours, underwent quizzes and tests, and worked on projects. They especially relished his additional personal "motivating lessons" on the handball court and his sincere interest in them as individuals. In his classes Escalante not only energized them and cajoled them through problems, methods, and concepts but used "fear"—the fear of being mediocre—as a motivating tool. He frequently told them, *"Lo mediocre no sirve"* ("Mediocrity is worthless").

Escalante emphasized not only the subject matter but also the process—the transmission of knowledge. He believed that his class was to be used for motivating and guiding the students toward a faith in themselves and a belief in mathematics and science as a key to the world. Above all, he created a unifying spirit built on class teams that worked and studied together to win the ultimate prize: the annual national San Andreas science and mathematics contest. The teams practiced daily on countless mathematics problems because of Escalante's belief that students learn by doing. Above all, he taught his students to be focused, disciplined, and dedicated. This pedagogy and philosophy he later brought with him to the United States.

As he reached his early thirties Escalante began to feel that there might be more to life than the San Andreas contest, more than Bolivia. In 1963 Escalante told his wife, Fabiola, and his brothers Fêlix and Raúl, "I cannot progress here. Fabiola is right. My friends always call me up, have me out for a drink. I'm drinking too much. I am going to succeed. I am going down there to America and I'm going to start from zero."

Selling everything and leaving his wife and son with relatives, he left Bolivia to make a new life in the United States. In May 1964 he was able to send for his wife and son. For years he worked as a cook at Van de Kamp's in Los Angeles, California, and attended evening classes at Pasadena Community College. In 1967 Fabiola suggested that he apply for a job in electronics at the Burroughs plant where she worked on the assembly line. He did and was immediately hired when he scored 100 percent on the application test. He spent a decade working as a cook and electronics technician, at the same time taking night classes in order to obtain a college degree and a U.S. teaching credential. Having transferred to the California State University system, in 1973 Escalante applied for and received a National Science Foundation scholarship that enabled him to complete the degree requirements and obtain his teaching credential in one year.

Escalante stated his goal simply: "I am going to teach. That is the only thing I can do." In 1974 he began teaching mathematics at Garfield High School in the Mexican American community of East Los Angeles. During the next two decades Escalante gained national acclaim for Garfield High School and its Latino students. Through his teaching methods, his work habits, and his need for an ordered but intellectually exciting world, he became a brilliant teacher in the United States. Between 1979 and 1992 fully 711 of his students passed the rigorous and prestigious Advanced Placement Calculus examination for college. Behind his success was his underlying drive—the *ganas*—to teach and to continue to challenge life.

In 1991 Escalante left Garfield High to take a position at Hiram Johnson High School in Sacramento, California. He cited faculty politics and petty jealousy in the mathematics department at Garfield as the reasons for his departure. At Johnson he played a subdued role, teaching only introductory math courses for his first two years. Then he taught beginning calculus for two years. Only in 1995 did he begin to teach advanced calculus. Meanwhile he introduced all the techniques and strategies that had gained him fame at Garfield as well as Saturday review sessions and a summer program financed by one of the foundations he works with.

Escalante's strength, according to his colleagues, is first his mastery of mathematics and then his ability to teach his students complex concepts while still keeping them relaxed and beguiled. By 1994 Escalante had won the Presidential Medal for Excellence in Education, a Special Recognition Award for Teaching Excellence from the American Association of Community and Junior Colleges, and the Andrés Bello Prize from the Organization of American States. Escalante's work was portrayed in the 1988 **Edward James Olmos** film *Stand and Deliver*.

Escalante has summarized his teaching success by saying that he teaches his students not only mathematics but also responsibility, self-respect, and the need to have *ganas*. He also presents an image of success. Ultimately Escalante, the "Bolivian Showman," wants his students to make maximum use, as he did, of their own natural talents channeled by an intense desire to succeed.

Further Reading

Di Rado, Alicia. "Math, Minus Escalante, Suffers." *Los Angeles Times* (23 October 1992): BI.

Hopkins, Kevin R. "The Escalante Math Program." *Business Week* 3241 (25 November 1991): ED67.

Hubbard, Kim. "Beating Long Odds, Jaime Escalante Stands and Delivers." *Peoples Weekly* 29:14 (11 April 1988): 57.

Libman, Gary. "Success Keeps Multiplying for Jaime Escalante." *Los Angeles Times* 114 (23 May 1995): E1, E6.

Mathews, Jay. *Escalante: The Best Teacher in America*. New York: Henry Holt, 1988.

———. "Escalante Still Stands and Delivers." *Newsweek* 190:3 (20 July 1992): 58.

Meek, Anne. "On Creating GANAS: A Conversation with Jaime Escalante." *Educational Leadership* 46:5 (February 1989): 46.

Monroe, Sylvester. "Escalante: The Best Teacher in America" [book review]. *Washington Monthly* (May 1989): 59.

Woo, Elaine, "Math Teacher Escalante Quitting Garfield High." *Los Angeles Times* (14 June 1991): BI.

GLORIA ESTEFAN

(1958–)

Cuban American Singer, Composer, Entrepreneur

Through her vocal recordings with the Miami Sound Machine band, Gloria Estefan first became a well-known singer of popular songs in Latin America and Europe. When the band added English-language songs to its early Latino orientation, she quickly became a leading figure in top ten lists in the United States as well. Her tragic automobile accident injury in 1990 created widespread sympathy for her, as did her long, valiant, and ultimately successful recovery efforts and musical comeback struggle.

Gloria María Fajardo was born in Havana, Cuba, on 1 September 1958. She was the daughter of Gloria García, a schoolteacher, and José Manuel Fajardo, a soldier who served in the security guard for the family of the widely detested Cuban dictator, Fulgencio Batista Zaldívar. When the revolution headed by Fidel Castro overthrew Batista's regime at the end of 1958, the Fajardos found it expedient to leave the island. In the United States Gloria's father supported the family for a time by continuing his military career, first as a recruit in the ill-fated attempt to overthrow Castro in the 1961 Bay of Pigs (Playa Girón) invasion by a CIA-financed Cuban refugee force, the 2506 Brigade. He was among those captured and was imprisoned for 18 months in a Cuban jail. After his release by Cuban authorities he joined the U.S. army, where he ultimately reached the rank of captain. As a result of his army service in Vietnam between 1966 and 1968 her father became a complete invalid, compelling her mother to seek work outside the family. Gloria, still a child, found herself caring for her seriously ill father and a younger sister. Completely tied down by her family responsibilities, she grew up in Miami, Florida, with a limited social life until her father later was admitted to a VA hospital.

After grade school Gloria attended all-girls Lourdes Academy, a parochial high school. In addition to the regular classes she took music lessons, although at the time she seemed to have no more than the normal teenager's interest in music. She sometimes sang in school assemblies but was also interested in poetry and composed poems. And to pass the time at home when caring for her father, to overcome the tedium and her recurring depression, she sang to herself for hours at a time as an emotional release. After graduating from Lourdes in 1975 she entered the University of Miami on a partial scholarship.

When she was 17 years old Gloria met young Emilio Estefan, a fellow Cuban refugee, a salesman for Bacardi Imports, and on the side the leader of a four-piece band, the Miami Latin Boys. After several chance encounters between the two young people at events where the Latin Boys furnished the music and she was asked to sing, he asked her to join the band as its singer. Although deeply concerned about her education and very timid and self-conscious, Gloria finally accepted the offer. On weekends she sang with the quartet and during the week attended university classes and studied. In 1978 she graduated from Miami with a bachelor of arts degree in psychology, and in that same year she and Emilio were married. Meanwhile the band changed its name to the Miami Sound Machine and also recorded its first album, "Renacer," a collection of Spanish-language ballads and disco tunes sung by Gloria. As she gained self-confidence she developed into a polished, spirited performer and began assuming an increasingly important role with the band.

By 1980 the Cuban American quartet plus Gloria were doing so well that Emilio quit his marketing job with Bacardi to devote full time to the band. That same year the Miami Sound Machine signed a recording contract with Discos CBS International, the Spanish-language branch of CBS Records. During the next three years the band cut four albums, playing a variety of Spanish-language and popular American music with Gloria doing the Spanish and English vocals. The combination of American pop rock and Spanish was unusual at the time. By the mid-1980s Gloria Estefan and the Miami Sound Machine had become well known in Spanish-speaking countries around the world, especially in South and Central America, but remained little known in the United States. By this time Emilio had taken on the job of managing and promoting Gloria and the band.

With several dozen hit songs abroad, in 1985 Gloria and the band cut "Age of Innocence." The switch to an all-English album resulted in popularity that gave the band a new impetus and modified its direction; also it caused CBS Records to move the group to its top label, Epic. There followed a number of highly successful albums, heavily credited to Gloria's singing: "Primitive Love," 1986, which had phenomenal acceptance; "Let It Loose," 1987; "Cuts Both Ways," 1989; and "Into the Light," 1991. Many of the songs Gloria sang on these albums made *Billboard* magazine's top ten list.

Managed and promoted by Emilio, Gloria and the band made music videos and went on extensive tours, giving concerts in huge stadiums as well as in more modest music halls. Gloria began to be more than just the lead singer; she became increasingly the principal attraction, developing a wide following. If Emilio was the band's head, she was its heart. She composed the music to some of the songs in the albums and the lyrics to more. She also became closely involved in planning and producing the recordings. Soon the Estefans branched into production and recording with the creation of Estefan Enterprises, Inc., in Miami.

While on tour late in the winter of 1989–1990, accompanied by Emilio and their young son Nayib, Gloria suffered a severe back injury when the band's bus was involved in an accident with a large tractor trailer on a snow-covered Pennsylvania freeway. The crash left her with a broken vertebra that required a lengthy operation and the insertion of two 8-inch steel rods in her back. Although the probability of complete recovery was doubtful, Gloria immediately began an intensive program of physical therapy. After a long and sometimes faltering period of mending, Gloria's firm determination, the strong support of her husband and family, and encouragement from her many caring fans enabled her to achieve nearly complete recovery. In January 1991 she returned to her career, appearing on TV's American Music Awards program.

Two months later, in March 1991, Estefan began a major concert trek to promote her comeback album, "Into the Light." The nearly year-long tour was hard on her physically, but her determination and Emilio's strong support and understanding enabled her to complete it. The album was received with moderate enthusiasm. In 1993 she turned out two albums, "Mi Tierra," a tribute to her Cuban heritage, which won her a Grammy, and "Christmas through Your Eyes," both of which went platinum. In the following year she issued "Hold Me, Thrill Me, Kiss Me," also platinum, and took time out from her career to give birth to a second child, daughter Emily. Her album "Abriendo Puertas," a collection of salsas, merengues, sones, and other Latin American musical forms, came out in late 1995 to wide popular and critical acclaim.

On 1 September 1995, her birthday, Gloria gave a concert at the U.S. naval base at Guantanamo, Cuba, for about 14,000 Cuban refugees. Supported by actor Andy García on bongos and bassist Israel "Cachao" López, she celebrated her "journey of the soul," her return to the spiritual home, Cuba. In 1996 she continued her heavy schedule. In addition to her albums and videos, in July 1996 she kicked off an extensive concert tour of the United States, Europe, and Central and South America titled "Evolution." A month later at the closing of the Olympic games in Atlanta, Georgia she sang "Reach," a single from her latest album, "Destiny," before a television audience estimated at three billion people.

Among the things that Gloria Estefan is proud of, in addition to her family and her songs, are the numerous honors and awards given her. In 1986 she was named Top Pop Singles Artist and *Billboard* magazine rated her the best new pop singer. Two years later she represented the United States at the Tokyo Music Festival and also headlined the 1988 Olympic games at Seoul, South Korea. In 1989 she was named songwriter of the year by Broadcast Music, Inc., and at the beginning of the 1990s she was named Crossover Artist of the Year by Lo Nuestro Latin Music Awards. In 1992 she was named Humanitarian of the Year by the B'nai B'rith, in the next year she was cited by the Alexis de Tocqueville Society for her outstanding philanthropy, and in 1994 she was titled Musicares Person of the Year. In May 1996 Estefan won top honors in Univision's Premio Lo Nuestro with four awards. She has been cited as the most positive role model in the music business.

Further Reading

"Amazing Gloria!: A Portrait of Success." *GTVE* [San Juan, P.R.] (December 1995): 18–20.

Brady, James. "Gloria Estefan." *Parade* [*San Jose Mercury News*] (28 April 1996): 18.

Current Biography Yearbook, 1995. New York: H. W. Wilson Co., 1995.

McLane, Daisann. "The Power & the Gloria." *Rolling Stone* (14 June 1990): 73–74, 79–80.

Mooney, Louise, ed. *Newsmakers: 1991 Cumulation.* Detroit: Gale Research, 1991.

Niurka, Norma. " 'Abriendo Puertas', un canto a Latinoamérica." *El Nuevo Herald* [Miami] (26 September 1995).
People 35:6 (18 February 1991): 21.
Telgen, Diane, and Jim Kamp, eds. *Notable Hispanic American Women.* Detroit: Gale Research, 1993.
Unterburger, Amy, ed. *Who's Who among Hispanic Americans.* Detroit: Gale Research, 1992.
Wall Street Journal (20 May 1992): B12(W), B5(E).

DAVID GLASGOW FARRAGUT

(1801–1870)

Spanish American Naval Officer, First Admiral in the U.S. Navy

David Glasgow Farragut was the first naval officer in U.S. history to hold the ranks of vice-admiral and admiral, the latter rank established especially for him. His naval career began when he was only 10 years old and, despite recurrent serious health problems resulting from his service in tropical waters, lasted until his death at age 69. Among the highlights of his early years in the navy was an occurrence off the Pacific coast of South America. There during the War of 1812 at age 12, he was briefly placed in charge of a captured whaler as prizemaster.

David Farragut's father, George Anthony Magín Farragut, was born on the Spanish island of Minorca and later emigrated. In 1775 as the 19-year-old master of a small ship trading between Cuba and Mexico he sailed into the then Spanish port of New Orleans, where he offered his services in the struggle for American independence. (Spain was helping the American revolutionaries.) He later fought in the Carolinas alongside various officers of the American Revolution. In 1795 he married Elizabeth Shine and subsequently they produced five children; the second oldest was named by them James Glasgow, but he later changed his first name to David.

James Glasgow Farragut was born on 5 July 1801 in a large log cabin on the family's 640-acre tract near Knoxville, Mississippi. In addition to doing some frontier farming, James's father operated a ferry on the adjacent Holston River. James spent his early years here on the riverbank, subject to the various hazards of frontier life including occasional incidents with Indians. When he was 6 years old his somewhat peripatetic father was appointed a sailing master in the U.S. navy and left for his post in New Orleans. James and the rest of the family followed by rafting down the Tennessee, Ohio, and Mississippi rivers, a two-month voyage of almost 1,700 miles. The trip greatly impressed the young lad, who still remembered it vividly late in life.

In 1808 James's mother died of yellow fever. As a result, all except the oldest son were parceled out temporarily to different families to be cared for. Early in the following year young David Porter Jr., commander of the New Orleans Naval Station, offered to care for one of the children as a gesture of thanks for the Farraguts' nursing his father during the latter's fatal illness. James, age 8, quickly volunteered. He was taken into the Porter home in New Orleans where he was treated as a son, although he was never legally adopted by the Porters. While the Porters remained in New Orleans, James often visited his father and frequently sailed with him on Lake Pontchartrain. He also accompanied David Porter on sea trips and other naval excursions, developing a love for boats and the sea.

In 1810 the Porters were transferred to Washington, D.C., and young Glasgow, as he was usually referred to, went with them—by sea, of course. He was never to see his father again but did keep in touch with his siblings. In Washington he was put into school. On 10 December 1810, at age 10, he was appointed a midshipman (the lowest rank for anyone aspiring to become an officer) in the U.S. navy, apparently through the good offices of his guardian. Shortly afterwards, the 11-year-old lad changed his name from James to David out of gratitude toward his foster father.

David Farragut was to spend the rest of his life in the U.S. navy. After serving under Porter on the frigate/man-of-war *Essex* in a training cruise toward the end of 1811, the young midshipman participated in the War of 1812 against Great Britain and suffered the indignity of being taken prisoner as the result of a battle off the coast of Chile. Back in the United States on parole, Farragut continued his education under a tutor. After the war he served in the Mediterranean Sea during the war declared on the Dey of Algiers, who was demanding tribute and was seizing American ships. Then in 1823 he again served under Porter in an action against pirates in the Caribbean. While on this duty he contracted yellow fever and became seriously ill, spending weeks recovering in a naval hospital as a result.

After 14 long years as a midshipman, in January 1825 Farragut was commissioned a lieutenant and later that year was assigned to the frigate *Brandywine*, which took the Marquis de Lafayette back to France after his 50th anniversary visit to the United States. Subsequently Farragut served in the South Atlantic and the Gulf of Mexico. In time of peace there was a scarcity of sea duty, but in 1838 he was able to get service with the West India Squadron and soon was given command of the sloop *Erie*, his third command up to that time. He then spent some months along the Mexican gulf coast protecting American citizens and interests during Mexico's "Pastry War" with France.

During 1841 Farragut again returned to sea duty, this time as executive officer of a ship of the line, the *Delaware*, and was promoted to commander after 16 years as a lieutenant. During the cruise along the coast of South America he was ordered to take command of the sloop *Decatur* in the harbor of Rio de Janeiro. From then on he was always to be in command of the ships on which he served. Returning to the United States early the next year, Farragut found active ship commands even more scarce than earlier because of the peacetime decline of the navy. He also found shore duty boring.

As the difficulties between the United States and Mexico began to heat up in the mid-1840s, Farragut again asked for sea duty, pointing out his earlier service along the Mexican coast and his acquaintance with Mexican coastal defenses as a good reason to be returned to active sea duty. It was not until March 1847 that his request was granted. He was given command of the sloop *Saratoga* and was assigned to blockade duty and other noncombatant activity, possibly because of an earlier feud with his superior, Captain Matthew Perry. Unhappy and disappointed that his knowledge was not being put to use, he felt that his participation in the war with Mexico was, in his words, "most mortifying."

Upon his return to the United States, Farragut was appointed second in command of the Norfolk Navy Yard in April 1848. Shortly thereafter he fell ill of Asiatic cholera and nearly died. Following his recovery he returned to the monotonous daily routine of the Navy Yard and continued to request sea duty. As a result of his abiding interest in gunnery, in 1850 he was sent to Washington, D.C., to create a book of ordnance regulations for the navy. While in Washington he regularly attended evening lectures at the Smithsonian Institution, which he found very educational. After a year in the capital he returned to Norfolk as ordnance officer; among his duties was superintending experiments in gun design and construction. During the Crimean War (1853–1856) his request to be sent as an observer of new naval developments was ignored by the Navy Department in spite of the need for modernizing and the fact that he spoke Spanish, Italian, and French.

In 1854 Farragut was selected to go to California to establish a naval station at Mare Island in the bay north of San Francisco; four years later, having completed construction of the yard, he again asked for sea service. Before his request reached Washington he was ordered back to Norfolk, now as a captain, the highest rank in the navy. At the end of 1858 he was given command of the *Brooklyn*, the first of five new steam sloops-of-war, a vessel that was to become the backbone of the navy during the impending Civil War. Farragut gave the ship a rundown cruise and wrote a report critical of its complete unlivability. Two years later, after several cruises in the Gulf of Mexico, he requested to be relieved of command. He returned to shoreside duty.

Meanwhile the Civil War was brewing. Following the lead of South Carolina, by early 1861 the southern states one by one seceded from the Union. Although Farragut was a native of Tennessee, lived in Virginia, and had close relatives in the deep South, he opposed secession. Because of his Union sympathies he soon found his situation in Norfolk untenable and moved with his family to the North. Here he quickly found his patriotism was held suspect. However, finally in December 1861 he was placed in command of the West Gulf Blockading Squadron and ordered to capture New Orleans. After two months of meticulous preparation, Farragut with 43 ships succeeded in obtaining the city's surrender in April 1862. His impressive performance won him promotion to rear admiral in July, as well as a commendation from the U.S. Congress.

For the rest of the year Farragut was active on the Mississippi, where his efforts in conjunction with ground forces were unable to bring about the capture of the Confederate stronghold at Vicksburg, Mississippi. In the Gulf, although he tightened the blockade and captured Galveston and Corpus Christi on the Texas coast, the naval base at Mobile, Alabama, still held out. In 1864 he was directed to make the capture of Mobile his main objective, and after his usual careful preparation he achieved its surrender in August. It was Farragut's grandest hour and the battle in which he allegedly issued his famous order, usually cited as: "Damn the torpedoes. Full speed ahead." Upon his return to the East Coast he was given a hero's welcome and a $50,000 purse by the city of New York to buy a home there. In December he was promoted to vice-admiral and two years later became the navy's first admiral.

After the Civil War Farragut commanded the European Squadron in 1867 and 1868. While on a tour of inspection at the naval base in Portsmouth, New Hampshire, he died of a heart attack on 14 August 1870.

Further Reading

Adams, William H. Davenport. *Farragut and Other Great Commanders*. London: Rutledge, 1880.

Farragut, Loyall. *The Life of David Glasgow Farragut: First Admiral of the United States Navy*. New York: D. Appleton and Co.: 1879.

Frothingham, Jessie Peabody. *Sea Fighters from Drake to Farragut*. New York: C. Scribner's Sons, 1902.

Lewis, Charles Lee. *David Glasgow Farragut*, 2 vols. Annapolis, Md.: U.S. Naval Institute, 1941–1943.

Mahan, Alfred Thayer. *Admiral Farragut*. New York: D. Appleton and Co., 1892.

JOSÉ FELICIANO

(1945–)

Puerto Rican Singer, Musician, Composer

For his performance in the 1968 World Series at Detroit's Tiger Stadium, José Feliciano was both booed and applauded. The next day the *New York Times* received letters from enraged readers protesting the singer's rendition of the "Star-Spangled Banner." Some of the protesters considered his performance insulting and unpatriotic. Yet all José had done was to tailor the U.S. national anthem to his singing style, an emotional Latin-jazz-soul mix. His interpretation was admittedly unconventional. Many young people liked it. The *Detroit Free Press* called it "tear-wrenching, soul-stirring and controversial." José Feliciano became briefly a national whipping boy, but he held his course.

Frustration and endurance have characterized much of José Feliciano's life. He was born with congenital glaucoma on 10 September 1945 in the small agricultural town of Lares in the western foothills of Puerto Rico. José Moserrate Feliciano was the second child born in a family of 12 children. In 1950 his parents, José Feliciano and Hortensia García, abandoned farming in Puerto Rico and moved to New York City.

José's memories feature a blind child who lived crammed into a tiny apartment with his large family and who spent a great deal of time listening to music on the radio. The Hit Parade became his early music teacher, providing him an opportunity to develop his talent. As a toddler he liked to beat a soda cracker tin to the rhythms on the radio.

From early on a love of music became the guiding force in Feliciano's life. At age 6 José learned to play a second-hand accordion, following the tunes of a few scratchy records his mother had bought him. Because of his blindness he did not play outside with other boys, so radio music became his constant companion. At age 9 he began playing an old guitar and shortly thereafter, in 1954, made his first public appearance as a guitarist at El Teatro Puerto Rico in the Bronx. The delighted audience gave a standing ovation to him and his unique musical style, an eclectic mix of flamenco, folk, pop, and rock.

As a young student in the public schools of New York City, Feliciano learned Braille. His early realization that he might face discrimination as a blind Puerto Rican aroused in him a persistent determination to overcome his physical limitations. As an adolescent he seized every opportunity to use his music to entertain his peers in school.

By the time he entered high school Feliciano had hit upon the acoustic guitar as his instrument and decided he also wanted to sing. He began to develop his own signature style, combining the sounds of Latin American musicians and American pop singers. Vocally, he was greatly influenced by Sam Cooke and Ray Charles. He identified with their pain and instinctively knew that singing was their way of coping with life. At Charles Evans Hughes High School he often performed at school assemblies and talent shows. By age 16 Feliciano was able to assist his family financially by performing in Greenwich Village coffeehouses.

His early exposure to appreciative audiences and his desire to help his unemployed father prompted Feliciano to quit school at age 17 in order to perform full-time at places like Cafe Id. His first professional job was in a Detroit nightclub, the Retort Coffee House. Upon his return to New York City late in the summer of 1963 he was "discovered" by Robert Shelton of the *New York Times* in an article that described him as a "ten-fingered wizard." Because of Shelton's prestige, the RCA Victor recording company offered Feliciano an exclusive contract and in 1964 released his first single, "Everybody Do the Click." It was a success.

Feliciano was invited to perform at the 1964 Newport Jazz Festival, where he was recorded by Vanguard Records. Many critics believed that among all the artists at Newport, his performance stood out. In mid-1965 Feliciano made his first national television appearance on the Al Hirt show. That same year his performance at the Marifex Hotel in Washington, D.C., received a rave review in the *Washington Post*.

The accomplished musician recorded his first solo album, "The Voice and Guitar of José Feliciano," in both English and Spanish. The album was greeted enthusiastically by disc jockeys and some important critics, as well as by Latino Americans generally. International stardom quickly followed. In 1966 Feliciano played to an Argentine audience of 100,000 people at the Mar del Plata Festival.

In that same year RCA Victor released Feliciano's second album, "A Bag Full of Soul," mostly blues numbers. Music critics now began to recognize his talents as a self-taught youthful artist. In June 1966 he made his New York concert debut at Town Hall. Meanwhile he continued gaining fame among Spanish-speaking audiences both in the United States and abroad. RCA International released three Spanish-language albums.

The year 1968 saw several major events in Feliciano's career. RCA released the album "Feliciano!" which included his soul version of "Light My Fire," notable for its sensuous Latin influences. The song immediately became a favorite on jukeboxes from coast to coast. Now a classic, "Light My Fire" sold over one million as a single, peaked at number three on pop music charts, and made Feliciano a mainland household celebrity overnight. The album reached number two and gave Feliciano his first gold album. In August he made a Las Vegas nightclub debut, and in October before television cameras he sang his controversial rendition of the national anthem for 53,000 baseball fans at Tiger Stadium.

Following his quick climb to stardom Feliciano in 1969 appeared in his first television special, "Feliciano—Very Special." In April of that year "Light My Fire" earned him two Grammy awards, one for best new artist and one for best male pop vocal performer. He had been nominated in four different categories. After this wide recognition Feliciano appeared in numerous television shows and specials with big-name singers and performed in sold-out concerts, including appearances as featured soloist with the Cleveland and Pittsburgh symphony orchestras.

On the concert circuit Feliciano's soul-inflected tenor, his Latin-jazz-rock-pop Spanish and classical blends, and his trademark appearances with his dark glasses and guide dog captured the popular imagination and soon made him an icon. At the beginning of each concert the dog led Feliciano to his stool in center stage and returned with him to take a bow at the end.

Soon after becoming recognized as a musical artist of high caliber Feliciano took to song writing. He defined his songs as lyrics with a message, rather than songs of "protest," which were much in vogue at the time. He has always considered himself to be a musician who can work at all levels of music; he credits his training in classical music for his successful innovative musical blends. Besides the guitar, Feliciano plays the mandolin, bass violin, banjo, and keyboard instruments. He regards his voice also as an instrument contributing a passionate, high, quavery tenor. He has recorded songs in Spanish, English, Italian, and Portuguese.

In looking back at his youth, Feliciano remembers dropping out of high school because he saw the family's financial need and felt at the time that school would not bring him musical success. Yet he stresses his wish to have completed his high school degree. He has since seriously studied many subjects because he feels that learning is an important component in both personal and artistic success. To Feliciano, talent has limited value unless the mind is developed along with it.

Although Feliciano is better known internationally than in the United States, in 1974 he recorded the theme for the television show *Chico and the Man* and the bilingual Christmas staple "Féliz Navidad." He has had 40 gold or platinum albums and won Grammy awards for best Latin pop performance in 1983, 1986, 1989, and 1990. In 1990 Harlem High School was renamed José Feliciano Performing Arts School, and in the next year he received from the First Annual Latin Music Expo its Lifetime Achievement Award, the first it has given out.

José Feliciano continues to perform in Greenwich Village and travels on the nightclub circuit. He recently recorded "Latin Street '92," which received a nomination for best Latin pop album. To mark his 30 years of success in music he plans to record a live concert album and a double-album set of new music and old favorites. Tenacity and determination have enabled him to overcome almost impossible odds and to become a world-famous guitarist.

Further Reading

Moritz, Charles, ed. *Current Biography Yearbook*. New York: H. W. Wilson Co., 1969.

Oeste, Marcia. "El hombre–el artista: José Feliciano." *La Luz* 3:2 (May 1974): 18–21.

Rubiner, Julie M., ed. *Contemporary Musicians*, vol. 10. Detroit: Gale Research, 1994.

Rule, Sheila. "The Pop Life." *New York Times* (26 January 1994): C13.

Stambler, Irving, and Grelun Landon, eds. *Encyclopedia of Rock, Country and Western Music*, 2nd ed. New York: St. Martin's Press, 1983.

GIGI (BEATRIZ) FERNÁNDEZ
(1964–   )
Puerto Rican Tennis Star

Since 1991, doubles tennis champion Gigi Fernández has been considered the number one women's doubles tennis player worldwide. With Dominican American **Mary Joe Fernández** as her partner she has won two Olympic gold medals, in 1992 and 1996. The first Puerto Rican woman athlete to turn professional in the international arena, Gigi has been noted for her strong serve and vigorous volley game, for power as well as finesse. She is arguably the most entertaining woman tennis player today. A trailblazer of the world's outstanding women's doubles team, she has also enlivened the courts with her sometimes audacious and brazen actions. She and her partner, Natasha Zvereva, have won 9 out of 12 recent Grand Slam doubles titles. Their match score for the 1994 season was 60–4.

Beatriz (Gigi) Fernández was born in San Juan, the capital of Puerto Rico, in 1964. She was the eldest daughter of four children born to Beatriz and Tuto Fernández, the latter a well-to-do medical doctor, a gynecologist. The self-styled spoiled rich girl grew up in a pampered, permissive atmosphere in which she seldom heard the word no. On her eighth birthday she received from her parents, who played recreational tennis, the gift of tennis lessons. Before she turned 10 her tennis feats were covered by newspapers all over the island. Two years later as a junior player she was ranked number one in Puerto Rico after winning the doubles of the Puerto Rico Open. As a teenager she was equally well known for her tennis ability, her black Camaro sports car, and the chic clothes she bought on various tournament and shopping trips to the mainland. When she graduated from high school her tennis skills made several college scholarships available to her, although at the time she was not focusing wholly on tennis.

Of the athletic scholarships she was offered, Gigi picked the one from Clemson University in South Carolina. While attending Clemson on her tennis fellowship she quickly developed into a seriously competitive and outstanding player. Before the end of her freshman year she reached the National Collegiate Athletic Association (NCAA) singles championship finals. In 1983 she turned professional at the age of 19. One year later she represented Puerto Rico at the 1984 Olympics.

But things did not always go smoothly for Gigi. Although an excellent technical player, her bravura performances seemed to come in spurts. She soon became known as an undisciplined player whose outbursts of temper at times seriously stood in the way of her singles game. (She has been known to make a deposit in advance on anticipated fines.) Her peers have tended to look on her as either a moody, blunt fire-eater or a breath of fresh air. She recalls that Martina Navratilova once praised her performance and encouraged her at a time when she desperately needed a boost. She had lost 14 matches in a row, was ranked 150th in the world, and was out of shape because in her despondency she was going on eating binges. Besides praising her, Navratilova advised her to discipline herself and to work hard at her game; this counsel prompted Gigi Fernández to change her habits when she became frustrated. She switched from her eating sprees to shopping sprees. Today she continues to be famous on the courts for her expensive outfits, Armani and others.

Her lucky break took place in 1988. In that year she teamed with fellow tennis professional Robin White to win the U.S. doubles Open. Two years later she repeated her victory, this time with Martina Navratilova as her partner. The following year she won her third Grand Slam title in the French Open, paired with Jana Novotna.

Gigi Fernández's best year was 1992. Paired with **Mary Joe Fernández** (not related) in the 1992 Olympic Games at Barcelona, Gigi won a gold medal, becoming the first Puerto Rican ever to win an Olympic gold. That year she also won three Grand Slam doubles crowns; with partner Natalia Zvereva she won at Wimbledon, and in the French and U.S. Opens. In 1993 the team of Fernández and Zvereva captured the Australian Open doubles, the French Open doubles, and the Wimbledon doubles. They also won the Virginia Slims doubles championship that year. Fernández and Zvereva are opposites in both temperment and behavior, and they complement each other on court. The one is volatile and tends to be explosive; the other is stolid, determined, and dependable. Since 1992 the team of Fernández and Zvereva has dominated women's doubles. In 1994 Fernández and Zvereva won the Australian and French Opens and the Wimbledon crown as well, just as they had the year before. However, just as happened the year before, they failed to win the U.S. Open and thereby make the Grand Slam doubles. In 1995 the defending doubles team came in second best in the Australian Open, thus ending their possible third bid for the Grand Slam. Later that year they came back to win their fifth consecutive French Open doubles title.

Fernández has been criticized in the press, especially on the island, for her decision to compete for the United States rather than Puerto Rico in the Federation Cup and Olympic tournaments. She agonized over this decision yet felt she had little choice because her game is doubles and there was no Puerto Rican partner available. If she had represented Puerto Rico in the singles she would have lost in the first round, according to Fernández.

Gigi Fernández is an enthusiastic fund-raiser for various charitable causes. In December 1993 she both organized and competed in the Gigi Fernández International Cup, a tennis exhibition that featured Gigi Fernández versus Martina Navratilova. This event benefited three benevolent groups: the National Hispanic Scholarship Fund, Yo si Puedo ("Say No to Drugs"), and the Puerto Rico Tennis Association. During 1983 Gigi was cited in the *Congressional Record* by a member of the House of Representatives as a Puerto Rican woman who exemplified an American "Model of Excellence."

As the undisputed queen of Puerto Rican tennis courts, she is a very popular figure on both the island and the mainland. Since very early in her career she has endorsed products and been a spokesperson for various commercial companies, from Hawaiian Punch and Honda to Rolex and Yonex Racquets. She has also posed for magazines like *Vogue, Glamour, People,* and *Sports Illustrated*. Perhaps because of these photographs people sometimes confuse her with Princess Caroline of Monaco, owing to their considerable physical resemblance. In 1989 she settled down in Aspen, Colorado, where her face is less well known, affording her a degree of anonymity. She expects to retire there in the not too distant future.

To this date Gigi Fernández has accomplished her two goals: to retain her number one world ranking in tennis doubles and to rank among the first 20 women in the world in tennis singles. In 1994 at Wimbledon she reached the semifinals in singles and was ranked 17th, the highest she has yet reached. Of course, she hopes to better that standing. Partnered again with **Mary Joe Fernández**, in August 1996 at Atlanta, Georgia, she won her second Olympic gold medal, repeating the Barcelona performance of four years earlier. Meanwhile, tennis has been very kind to her financially; she has earned more than $2.5 million in prize money.

Gigi encourages all Puerto Rican girls and young women to emulate her enthusiasm for sports. Although she is currently deeply committed to professional tennis, she also shares dreams held in common with other young women. She feels that someday she would like to get married and have children, but that's sometime in the future, along with retirement.

Further Reading

Finn, Robin. "Notebook." *New York Times* 143 (10 September 1994): 30(L).

Hahn, Cindy. "Talking About: Gigi Fernández and Natalia Zvereva." *Tennis* 29:5 (1 September 1993): 58.

Higdon, David. "Glamour." *Tennis* 31:6 (October 1995): 48, 50, 52, 54.

Jenkins, Sally. "Terrible Two." *Sports Illustrated* 82:7 (20 February 1995): 156–163.

"Score an Upset in Doubles." *New York Times* 144 (27 January 1995): B11(L).

Thomas, Irene M. "Olympic Dreams." *Hispanic* (1 August 1994): 14.

MARY JOE FERNÁNDEZ

(1971–   )

Dominican American Professional Tennis Player

At the 1992 Olympics in Barcelona, Spain, Mary Joe Fernández and her partner, Puerto Rican tennis star **Gigi Fernández** (not related) won the Gold Medal in women's doubles tennis for the United States. At Atlanta in 1996, they repeated that performance. Mary Joe has a habit of winning tennis matches. She won her her first tournament in 1981, walking away with the winning score at the U.S. Tennis Association Nationals for players age 12 and under. She was 10 years old. In 1984 she won both the U.S. Tennis Association championship and the U.S. Clay Court championship for players age 16 and under. That same year at age 13 she became the youngest player ever to participate in a professional tournament. This child tennis prodigy won the National Girl's Tennis Title and Orange Bowl titles in the categories of 12, 14, 16, and 18 years old and under. In 1990, her first full year on the professional tour, she won two tournaments and 80 percent of her 50 singles matches.

María José Fernández was born in the Dominican Republic on the island of Hispaniola in 1971. Her parents were Sylvia and José Fernández. Her mother had emigrated from Cuba, and her father was a Spanish-born employee of an American investment company. She was less than a year old when the family left the Dominican Republic for the United States, settling in Miami, Florida. When her father, who played tennis regularly, took her older sister Sylvia to the tennis courts, 3-year-old María José tagged along. While her father and sister played sets, she kept herself out of mischief and amused by hitting tennis balls against a wall with a racquet her father had bought her. She showed good physical coordination and at age 5 began taking tennis lessons.

While still in grade school Mary Joe won the U.S. Clay Court championship and the U.S. Tennis Association championship, both for age 16 and under. While in the eighth grade she was invited to play in a field of professionals competing at the Lynda Carter-Maybelline Tennis Classic at Fort Lauderdale, Florida. After grade school she went on to the Carrolton School of the Sacred Heart in Coconut Grove, Florida, virtually a suburb of Miami. In high school the level-headed 14-year-old was determined to be a good student, despite advice at times from agents, coaches, and some other tennis professionals to join the professional tour full-time. At one point even her parents, who suffered a severe financial crisis in the mid-1980s, apparently favored the idea.

Mary Joe did turn pro—part-time. With some help from school authorities and her classmates, who provided her with class notes, she got her education and also got in some tournament tennis during her high school years. In a much scaled down tournament schedule she participated in four Grand Slam tourneys and even took time out at the end of her sophomore year to play at Wimbledon. Between matches she studied her lessons in her hotel room and faxed her homework to her teachers. At Sacred Heart she was a straight-A student and in 1989 graduated with honors after four years—even though she missed her graduation ceremony because she was playing in the French Open in Paris. She reached the semi-finals there.

After high school Mary Joe joined the professional tour full-time. She soon found that her failure to undertake a regular conditioning program caused her to be physically out of shape for a full tournament schedule. She lacked the necessary stamina to play well in matches on several consecutive days. Also over the months she developed various injuries, including tendonitis, damage to knee cartilage, and a wrenched back; as a result she was forced to begin to do more exercising and muscle conditioning, at least on a minimum scale. Her coach had her do moderate weightlifting exercises as she began to work out to improve her physical endurance.

Ranked twelfth among women tennis players at the beginning of 1990, in February Mary Joe made the Top Ten although she still had not won a professional title. In that year she also changed her tennis style, a baseline game of attrition rather than power, based on the approach of her idol, Chris Evert. In addition, she began trying to change her basic attitude toward the game, which her coach described as hoping to win, happy to win, but not determined and expecting to win. In January 1990 she had been a finalist (for the first time ever in a Grand Slam) in the Australian Open and was a semi-finalist later that year in both the U.S. Open and the Virginia Slims tournament.

By late summer, still not having won a Grand Slam, Mary Joe moved up to number 8 position, and then in September at the Tokyo Indoor Tournament, despite severe cramps alleviated by acupressure, she won her first singles professional tournament title. Three weeks later she won her second pro title, in the Porsche Tennis Grand Prix at Filderstadt, Germany. She finished the year 1990 having won the two tournaments and 40 of her 50 singles games. She also finished the year a 19-year-old millionaire from her tournament earnings and her endorsement of various products. All this in spite of four serious injuries during the year—one of them severe enough to keep her off the courts for a month.

In 1991, encouraged by her coach to be more aggressive, Mary Joe reached the semi-finals at Wimbledon and again made it to the Australian Open finals. Her earnings for the year were again more than $1 million. At the 1992 Barcelona Olympics she won a bronze medal in the singles and, teamed with **Gigi Fernández**, won the gold in women's doubles. After reaching the finals at the French Open in 1993 she developed endometriosis, a painful inflammation of the uterus that left her weakened in health and susceptible to other illnesses. As a result she missed the U.S. Open altogether and made a poor showing in the next six Grand Slam events she played in. At the French Open in 1995 she failed in straight sets during the first round. However, with her health problems overcome, she then came back to reach the quarter-finals at Wimbledon. At the U.S. Open in September 1995 she upset the prognosticators by defeating the defending champion, Arantxa Sánchez Vicario, in the fourth round with three straight sets, but she failed to make it to the finals. At the French Open in 1996 she fell in the fourth round to number one–ranked Steffi Graf.

Further Reading

Clarey, Christopher. "Fernández Ends Sanchez's Bid to Repeat." *New York Times* 144 (4 September 1995): 27(L).

Goldaper, Sam. "13-Year-Old Plays Tennis Like a Pro." *New York Times* (21 September 1984): A21, A24.

"Mary Joe Fernandez." *New York Times* 143 (14 March 1994): C7(N), D8(L).

Murphy, Austin. "The Graduate." *Sports Illustrated* (11 February 1991): 76–79.

Telgen, Diane, and Jim Kamp, eds. *Notable Hispanic American Women*. Detroit: Gale Research, 1993.

"Women of '91: Healthy, Wealthy, and Wiser." *World Tennis* (February 1991): 24–26.

LUIS FERRÉ

(1904–)

Puerto Rican Industrialist, Politician, Philanthropist, Humanist

Don Luis, as he is affectionately referred to by many Puerto Ricans, is a person of numerous talents, activities, and avocations. He is a highly successful businessman; an outstanding political leader; an accomplished pianist, art connoisseur, and sponsor of culture; and a widely recognized humanist. He strongly believes that business success implies social and civic obligation.

On 17 February 1904 Luis Alberto Ferré became the second of five children born to Antonio Ferré and Mary Aguayo Casals Ferré in the Puerto Rican city of Ponce, the second largest and most prosperous city on the island. When Ferré was a teenager his father, an engineer of French ancestry, began developing Industrias Ferré. His iron foundry was a family business in which young Luis and his brothers José, Herman, and Carlos actively participated.

From very early in life Luis Ferré was an outstanding student. He attended public elementary and middle schools in Ponce. His high school years were spent at the prestigious Morristown School in Morristown, New Jersey, where his parents had sent him to further his education. At graduation he earned the highest honors in mathematics, physics, history, and English. Since his father's aspiration was for all his sons to become educated in various business areas, Luis followed his oldest brother José's footsteps to the Massachusetts Institute of Technology (MIT), where he pursued an undergraduate degree in science. He graduated in 1924, and in the following year he completed a master's degree in electromechanical engineering at MIT. While living in the Boston metropolitan area he also attended the New England Conservatory of Music, where he developed his talents as a classical pianist.

After college Ferré returned to Puerto Rico to work as a junior engineer in his father's business in Ponce. His brother Herman was a civil engineer and later became production chief; his youngest brother, Carlos, became a chemical engineer and also joined his brothers in the family business.

In 1931 Ferré married Lorencita Ramírez de Arrellano, who bore him two children. Ferré's family life was stressful at times because of his wife's frequent illnesses. Ferré loved her deeply and was intensely concerned for her comfort when she was sick. He once referred to her as his "inspired light and spiritual strength."

Demonstrating an early interest in public service, Ferré ran for mayor of Ponce in 1940 but was defeated. By the early 1940s he became the chief engineer of the newly founded Puerto Rican Cement Company. The family industrial conglomerate received a boost during the 1940s as a result of World War II. When the U.S. government began the construction of Roosevelt Roads, a Puerto Rican naval base, the Ferré family asked the U.S. government for capital to establish the Ponce Cement Corporation. This company became the supplier of cement for the project, providing the government with much-needed raw materials for its construction. At the end of the decade Ferré acquired several unprofitable local government companies in paper, clay, and glass, all of which soon became profitable under his direction.

In line with his ethical beliefs, in 1954 Ferré founded the Luis A. Ferré Foundation, incorporated two years later as a nonprofit corporation dedicated to charitable, scientific, literary, and educational purposes. The Museo de Arte de Ponce, which opened in 1959 and became the leading museum in Puerto Rico, was a product of this foundation. Ferré proudly announced that the museum's role—in addition to acquiring, exhibiting, and interpreting artworks—was "to inspire creativity and artistic sensibility and to broaden knowledge and understanding of our culture."

In the political arena during the 1940s and 1950s Ferré consistently provided support for Puerto Rico's Republican Party by actively participating in rallies and supporting its candidates. The party was pro-statehood and opposed **Luis Muñoz Marín's** commonwealth program, which in 1952 gave Puerto Rico local autonomy with U.S. protection, imposed no federal taxation, but excluded Puerto Ricans from voting in U.S. presidential elections. Ferré viewed commonwealth status as transitional to eventual statehood.

Ferré's first political victory came in 1952 when he was elected to the insular House of Representatives as a representative-at-large. He served until 1956, in which year he ran unsuccessfully for governor against **Muñoz Marín**. After his defeat he continued to actively promote his candidacy for the next election while continuing to serve as vice-chairman of the Puerto Rican Cement Company.

Luis Ferré's political efforts paid off a decade later. In 1964, after 14 continuous years of service, **Luis Muñoz Marín** stepped down from the governorship and backed the candidacy of maverick politician Roberto Sánchez Vilella. With **Muñoz Marín**'s help Sánchez Vilella won, but he also gave Ferré an opportunity. Sánchez Vilella was not universally liked and became the object of numerous attacks, even by members of his own party.

Meanwhile Ferré continued his political involvement as a member of the U.S. Republican National Committee in Puerto Rico, which sent delegates to the National Republican Convention on the mainland. This position gave him great visibility to voters. In 1965 the political status of Puerto Rico came under review, leading to the appointment of a joint commission composed of Puerto Rican and U.S. congressional appointees. The commission concluded that Puerto Ricans should have a plebiscite to choose among the three possible alternatives: independence, statehood, or commonwealth status. The commission scheduled the referendum for July 1967.

This major political event created divisions in the island's Republican Party. When party leaders recommended that voters boycott the referendum, Ferré boldly disagreed. He left the party, organized El Partido Nuevo Progresista, and urged voters to participate in the referendum. Although the statehood option that he supported lost, his bold and decisive leadership inspired his followers with a renewed spirit of hope.

With the slogan *La Nueva Vida* ("The New Life"), Ferré advocated fresh solutions to social and economic problems. His party's catchy jingle, *Esto tiene que cambiar* ("This must change"), and the baby blue palm tree party symbol captivated many voters. Ferré also toned down his statehood rhetoric and concentrated on local economic issues. His political momentum coincided with a demoralizing period for the Partido Popular Democrático and Governor Sánchez Vilella, who succumbed to political betrayals and marital scandals.

At the time of the 1968 elections, Ferré took advantage of the charged political climate and his recent political momentum to capture the governorship. He served only one four-year term during which his wife died, causing him great distress. His administration faced serious economic problems and some damaging scandals. Among his notable deeds as governor was the appointment of the first woman in Puerto Rico's history as secretary of the governor's cabinet; he also appointed other women to prominent positions.

In 1976 Ferré was elected to the island Senate. After 1980 he participated moderately in local politics and was appointed a member of the Presidential Task Force on Private Sector Initiatives in 1981. He has since continued active in his party but has not run for office. Despite his great successes, Don Luis remains an unpretentious man who still loves to play the piano. He has described himself as "revolutionary in my ideas, liberal in my objectives, and conservative in my methods."

Among the honorary degrees he has received are: Doctor of Laws from Harvard University in 1970; Doctor of Laws from Amherst College, also in 1970; Doctor of Music from the New England Conservatory of Music in May 1975; and a Ph.D., *Honoris Causa*, from the University of Puerto Rico in 1984. He has been given the following additional marks of recognition: Knight of the Holy Sepulcher from Pope John XXIII, 1959; the 1965 Antilles Personnel Administration Award; the Eugenio María de Hostos Award, 1962; the Hoover Medal, 1971; the Eugene McDermott Award of the Council for the Arts at Massachusetts Institute of Technology, 1980; plaque at the Julius Adams Stratton Student Center, Massachusetts Institute of Technology, 1984; the Americas Foundation Award, 1991; and the Presidential Medal of Freedom, 1991.

Further Reading

Current Biography Yearbook, 1970. New York: H. W. Wilson Co., 1970.
"Ferré Honored at Concert." *Nuestro* 6:4 (May 1982): 12–13.
Mejías-Rentas, Antonio. "Reflections on Fathers: My Three Fathers." *Nuestro* 7:5 (June/July 1983): 61–62.
"Partisan Politics in Puerto Rico" [Letters to the Editor]. *Washington Post* (16 April 1991).
Personalities Caribbean, 7th ed. Kingston, Jamaica: Personalities Ltd., 1983.
Press Kit. *Luis A. Ferré*. August 1994.
Who's Who in America, 1970–1971. Chicago: Marquis Who's Who, 1970.

JOSÉ FERRER

(1912–1992)

Puerto Rican Actor, Director, Producer

"At one point or another I think I killed every single person that I loved, and I saw them lying there bleeding before me." After contemplating his relatives, friends, and pets mournfully he added, "I even ran over strangers." The actor once told the *Washington Post* this was his way of arousing his emotions each night to act dramatically after playing the same kind of roles year after year. His technique paid off. José Ferrer was considered a major stage actor who attained fame primarily for his roles portraying sensitive persons, often with physical deformities. He was especially attracted to plays with a social message.

José Vicente Ferrer de Otero y Cintrón was born on 8 January 1912 in Santurce, Puerto Rico. His father was a successful and well-to-do lawyer. His parents were Spaniards who became naturalized U.S. citizens. Ferrer visited the U.S. mainland at an early age for an operation on his palate, and his family left Puerto Rico permanently for New York City when he was 6 years old. As a youngster he attended public and private schools in Manhattan. Always a good student, Ferrer passed Princeton's entrance exam at the age of 14 but was advised to attend a prep school in Switzerland for a year first. There he distinguished himself as a promising young pianist and seemed destined to become a concert performer.

Soon after his arrival at Princeton University Ferrer discovered he liked architecture. He also played piano in a school jazz band that he founded, calling it "José Ferrer and His Pied Pipers." The 14-member band, which included actor Jimmy Stewart, played locally and also toured Italy, France, and Switzerland during the summer.

In addition to his musical interests, Ferrer started acting in Princeton's Triangle Club. Seduced by the magic of the limelight, he soon abandoned his avocation of music for drama. His first assignment was as director of *Fol-de-Rol*, the Triangle Club's annual musical. The production was so successful that he took it on tour. Ferrer's many extracurricular activities forced him to spend an extra year at Princeton to earn his architecture degree. He graduated in 1933 and did some postgraduate language studies at Columbia University.

The next year José Ferrer made his first professional appearance in a showboat on Long Island, where he debuted in a melodrama, *The Periwinkle*. In 1935 he began working as an assistant stage manager for Joshua Logan, a member of his former jazz band. That same year he appeared on Broadway in the modest role of second policeman in *A Slight Case of Murder*, and in the following year he got a more important part as one of a trio of Virginia Military Institute cadets in the Broadway comedy *Brother Rat*. As he established a reputation for versatility, he slowly progressed to more prominent roles.

Four years later, in 1940, Ferrer starred in *Charley's Aunt*, garnering favorable reviews. He also began to direct summer shows at the Westchester Playhouse. His first golden opportunity came when he took over comedian Danny Kaye's part in Cole Porter's musical *Let's Face It*. Performing with established stage celebrities gave him greater self-confidence and helped him gain wider recognition in the theater as well.

Ferrer's next big chance came in 1943. He played Iago to Paul Robeson's Othello in one of the longest-playing runs ever of William Shakespeare's drama *Othello*. Critics hailed his performance, and soon he began to expand his repertory of plays. In 1946 he played in *Cyrano de Bergerac* on Broadway, portraying the gallant 17th-century French swordsman famed for his eloquence and large nose. Ferrer won a Tony award for this role in the following year.

His film debut in *Joan of Arc* with Ingrid Bergman proved dissatisfying for Ferrer. He later said that it was "one of the most boring films ever made." Yet he received the first of three Oscar nominations for his performance. After this Hollywood experience he returned to New York and the stage, taking over as director of the New York City Theater Company. As general director he acted in and directed Shakespeare's *Richard III* and a Eugene O'Neill play and also had roles in a program consisting of four one-act plays by Anton Chekhov.

Hollywood again called to Ferrer. Among other films, he starred in a version of *Cyrano*, which in 1950 won him an Oscar for best male performance, the first for a Latino actor. The demand for his acting skills soared. On stage he played opposite Gloria Swanson in *Twentieth Century*, as she stipulated in her contract. The year 1952 marked the peak of Ferrer's career; his name appeared on three Broadway marquees. He produced and directed *Stalag 17*, *The Fourposter*, and *The Shrike*, in which he also played the lead. He won his second Tony Award for direction, and also a third Tony Award for his lead role. The three plays ran for a total of 1,265 performances!

Praised for his versatility, commanding presence, energy, and bravura style, Ferrer had become known as an outstanding stage actor. He ended 1952 by starring in the film *Moulin Rouge*, in which he walked on his knees with his legs strapped up to portray the famous stunted French painter Henri Toulouse-Lautrec. He was nominated as best actor for this film but lost the Oscar to Gary Cooper. During that year he also received the Donaldson Award for acting and directing. In the following year he further expanded his talents by becoming film composer for *Love Is a Beautiful Stranger*.

Despite these successes, Ferrer was never comfortable with film acting. To him, acting had to be done before a live audience. In spite of his intellectual and theatrical skills he did not project much warmth in films; on screen he was interesting rather than exciting. Yet he made over 40 feature films and several television movies. Much of his appeal on film was his rich, husky voice, which tended to get him typecast in serious or dour roles.

Ferrer always accepted challenges. In 1960 he did not hesitate to try opera; he sang the title role in Puccini's *Gianni Schicchi* at Santa Fe, New Mexico. In 1965 at Palm Beach he played the mime role of Dr. Coppelius in the ballet *Coppelia*. He also sang opera with the Brooklyn Academy of Music and the Beverly Hills Opera. Ferrer was nominated for television's Emmy awards three times and once for a Grammy for the 1958 children's recording of "Tubby the Tuba." Ferrer the director never proved as successful as Ferrer the actor, and in 1960 he gave up directing. In his later years he played memorable and diverse film characters in *The Caine Mutiny, Lawrence of Arabia, Ship of Fools*, and Woody Allen's *Midsummer Night's Sex Comedy*.

After *Lawrence of Arabia* in 1962 he continued to appear regularly on screen, yet his roles were relatively small ones, sometimes mere cameo appearances. He felt disdain for his cameos and his supporting roles, which he referred to as "bit parts to earn a fast buck." He once commented he regretted his decision not to work in Europe, where older actors are held in higher regard than in the United States. He also deplored the fact that he had been reduced to doing television voice-overs. What he failed to realize was that his voice was so distinctive and well known that his voice-overs were readily identified.

In 1985 President Ronald Reagan awarded the National Medal of Arts to Ferrer, one of 12 winners and the first actor to receive that honor. He was also honored by Princeton University with an honorary M.F.A. degree, as well as with honorary doctorates from the University of Puerto Rico and Bradley University in Illinois.

Toward the end of his life one critic summed up his career, saying José Ferrer was a jack of all trades and master of most of them. After a brief illness José Ferrer died in Coral Gables, Florida, just after his 80th birthday, on 26 January 1992.

Further Reading

Folkart, Burt A. "Stage, Film Actor José Ferrer Dies." *Los Angeles Times* (27 January 1992): B7(L).

International Directory of Films and Filmakers, 2nd ed., vol. 3, Actors and Actresses. Detroit: St. James Press, 1992.

"José Ferrer." *People Weekly* 37:5 (10 February 1992): 61.

Moomey, Louise, ed. *Newsmakers: The People behind Today's Headlines*, 1992 Cumulation. Detroit: Gale Research, 1992.

Reyes, Luis, and Peter Rubie. *Hispanics in Hollywood*. New York: Garland Publishing, 1994.

Variety Obituaries. New York: Garland, 1993 [3 February 1992].

Weil, Martin. "Oscar Winner José Ferrer Dies." *Washington Post* (27 January 1992).

PATRICK FLORES

(1929–)

Mexican American Archbishop, Religious and Ethnic Leader

On Cinco de Mayo, 5 May 1970, amid mariachi music, the plaintive sounds of folk hymns, and fervent shouts of *Viva la raza*, the Reverend Patrick Fernández Flores was consecrated auxiliary bishop of the San Antonio archdiocese. Behind the altar a huge banner proclaimed the maxim that the new bishop had selected for himself: *Trabajaré no por mí mismo, pero para otros* ("I shall work not for myself, but for others"). The bilingual event took place in the San Antonio convention center in the presence of a standing-room-only crowd of over 7,000, mostly Mexican Americans and including **César Chávez** and **José Angel Gutiérrez**, who read the two epistles of the mass. Flores was the first Mexican American and the second U.S. Latino priest to be appointed a bishop in the Roman Catholic Church.

Patrick Flores was born in the tiny town of Ganado, just north of Lavaca Bay in southeastern Texas, on 26 July 1929. His parents, Trinidad Fernández and Patricio Flores, were sharecroppers who lived in a small house without plumbing or electricity and worked a small farm that provided a subsistence living for the parents and nine children of the Flores family. As a result, to earn extra income the family annually followed the vegetable and cotton harvests from southern Texas all the way to the panhandle of the state, 700 miles to the north. As soon as he was old enough, young Patrick joined his older siblings and parents in this family undertaking each year. Along with their mother's washing machine and small stove, the children packed into a small house trailer that Patrick's father hitched to the ancient family pickup truck. They slept in the trailer or in barns or sheds provided by the farmers whose crops they picked.

Although Patrick's parents were illiterate and the migrant life-style made getting an education extremely difficult, his parents believed in the importance of education and urged their children to attend school and get as much education as they could. Patrick's schooling was understandably sporadic; although he took assignments with him on the migrant circuit, it was difficult to study after a 12-hour day in the fields and without electric lights in their sleeping quarters. A very bright stu-

Patrick Flores. Photo courtesy of Reverend Patrick Flores.

dent, Patrick managed to complete grade school, usually passed "conditionally," and attended high school in Houston and Galveston.

During World War II Patrick's father used the family's lifetime savings and a small bank loan to buy a house and 80-acre farm outside of the tiny rural town of Pearland, just south of Houston. With his siblings Patrick walked more than 2 miles every day to a substandard school for Mexican Americans. Since his older brothers had left home for the armed services, Patrick dropped out of high school in his sophomore year to help his ailing father. Determined to get an education, he returned to high school after a couple of years of helping his father develop the farm.

During these late teen years Patrick came to the decision that he had a vocation to become a priest. Now he had to consider how he might be able to achieve that goal. Fortunately he had come to the attention of a traveling nun who taught catechism classes in Pearland, Sister Mary Benitia. She arranged a meeting between Patrick and Christopher Byrne, bishop of Galveston, whom the young man impressed with his sincerity. Bishop Byrne agreed to finance his high school education provided he maintained a high grade point average. Patrick graduated from the

Christian Brothers Kirwin High School at age 20, the oldest student and top scholar in his class.

From Kirwin High Patrick Flores entered the diocesan seminary, Saint Mary's, at La Porte. Later he attended St. Mary's Seminary in Houston. During the summers he worked at a wide variety of jobs, from picking cotton to singing in local cantinas. After seven years of rigorous study, in 1956 at age 27 he was ordained to the priesthood and immediately assigned as an assistant pastor at Holy Name Church in Houston. Here he became deeply involved with the Cursillo movement, a charismatic religious movement that started in Spain and came to the U.S. Southwest via Mexico. He was profoundly influenced by the *cursillistas*, who stressed communal prayer and singing, participation as a family, and simplicity and personal style in their religious observation. And the language of the Cursillo movement was Spanish, which he thought should be used in church. When he became pastor of his own church with many Mexican American parishioners, first Guardian Angel in 1963 and then St. Joseph and St. Stephen in 1967, he introduced Spanish and Cursillo attitudes into church services and became widely known for mariachi masses.

During his 14 years as a parish priest, Patrick Flores worked largely with poor Mexican American parishioners in the barrios. Among his secular concerns for them were jobs, housing, and educational opportunities. He strongly supported the *movimiento* in the areas of education and civil rights, where, he declared, change was long overdue. He saw the movement as an effort on the part of Chicanos to achieve self-identification and to define their goals. He also lent his support to **César Chávez** and the Delano grape strike, urging Texas *mexicanos* not to go to California as strikebreakers. Later, as bishop, he visited Chávez in his cell when César was jailed for rejecting a court order. In 1968 he was one of the founders of the Mexican American priests' organization PADRES—Padres Asociados Para Derechos Religiosos, Educativos, y Sociales ("Priests Associated for Religious, Educational, and Social Rights")—and at the beginning of the 1970s was elected its national chairman.

Fortunately Flores's views on social justice were supported by his new archbishop, Francis Furey, who soon strongly urged Rome that he be appointed auxiliary bishop. The result was the joyous outpouring in 1970 at the convention center, attended by many Catholics and non-Catholics alike. Almost exactly eight years later Patrick Flores was installed as bishop of the El Paso diocese, and in October 1979 he became the fourth archbishop of San Antonio. In 1990 he celebrated his 20th anniversary as the first Mexican American bishop. As bishop and archbishop he has proved to be an effective and innovative administrator as well as a religious leader.

While at heart a moderate who believed in working within the system, Bishop Flores continued to actively pursue the goal of greater civil rights, especially for Mexican Americans. He was chairman of the Texas Advisory Committee to the U.S. Civil Rights Commission and personally involved himself in the legal defense of Chicanos accused of crime. A staunch believer in the organizing ideas of Saul Alinsky's Industrial Areas Foundation, on whose board he served, he was instrumental in establishing the Mexican American Cultural Center (MACC) in San Antonio to train barrio people to help themselves and find their own solutions to problems. To raise money for MACC in 1974 he recorded an album of songs titled "The Singing Bishop," and in that same year he helped bring about the founding of Communities Organized for Public Service (COPS), a neighborhood organization to achieve greater civil rights and to improve the quality of life for people in the barrios. Always one to stand up for what he believed right, in 1972 he became involved in the Farah Company strike, which eventually he and four other bishops endorsed. He also established an Office of Catholic Services for Immigrants and the National Hispanic Scholarship Fund to encourage and assist young Chicanos to study for the professions and the priesthood. Education is his obsession.

In addition to local involvement, Archbishop Flores has shown his concerns for the larger Latino church in his chairmanship of the U.S. Bishops Committee on the Church in Latin America. In 1985 he was one of three American prelates invited to visit Cuba to observe relations between Fidel Castro and the church. In the following year he was the only U.S. bishop invited to a week-long conference. He came away with positive impressions and hope for the future of Catholicism in Cuba.

Archbishop Flores has been the recipient of numerous awards and honors, including three honorary doctorates and the Medal of Freedom.

Further Reading

American Catholic Who's Who, 1980–1981, vol. 23. Washington, D.C.: N.C. News Service, 1980.

Casey, Rick. "Patricio Flores." *S.A., The Magazine of San Antonio* (December 1979).

Doviak, Joan, and Arturo Palacios. *Catorce personas lindas*. Washington, D.C.: Educational Systems Corp., 1970.

Martínez, Al. *Rising Voices: Profiles of Hispano-American Lives*. New York: New American Library, 1974.

McMurtrey, Martin. *Mariachi Bishop: The Life Story of Patrick Flores*. San Antonio, Tex.: Corona Publishing, 1985.

Morey, Janet, and Wendy Dunn. *Famous Mexican Americans*. New York: E. P. Dutton, 1989.

"Patrick Flores: The Barrio Bishop." *La Luz* 1:4 (August 1972).

María Fornés

(1930–)

Cuban American Playwright, Producer, Director, Teacher

Winner of six Obies (Off-Broadway theater awards), María Fornés is widely considered one of the leading contemporary American playwrights and play producers. She has been called one of the top five playwrights in the United States today. Her plays, her own outstanding direction of her plays, and her "sustained achievement" account for her Obies. In the past 34 years she has written over three dozen plays, including several musicals, making her one of the most prolific of modern playwrights. Better known to people within the theater than to theatergoers, she is noted for introducing into her plays new theatrical techniques, many borrowed from the film medium. Both the striking forms used in her plays and their significant content have contributed to her stature as a champion of Latinos and especially of women. Her plays aim at supporting and inspiring both groups, and by her own life she has provided them with an inspiring and impressive role model.

María Irene Fornés was born in Havana, Cuba, on 14 May 1930, the daughter of Carmen Hismenia Collado and Carlos Fornés. Her father, a Cuban government employee and somewhat of a maverick for his day, believed in educating his six daughters, teaching them at home. However, María did attend number 12 Escuela Pública in Havana for four years; the rest of her education came largely from her father's tutoring and her extensive reading. While she was still in her early teens her father died.

When María was 15 years old her widowed mother left Cuba, taking the family to New York. The young girl, who spoke no English, took a factory job to help support the fatherless family. When she had learned sufficient English she was able to get work as a translator and later also worked as a doll maker. In 1951 she became a citizen of the United States at age 21 and about this time became seriously interested in painting and began her studies and training. Four years later she went to Europe to pursue a career as a painter. After three years of studying and painting there she returned to the United States, where she obtained a position in New York as a fabric designer. She continued to paint but increasingly felt her interest lagging and found it necessary to establish a disciplined, regular schedule for her painting efforts.

Somewhere around 1960 María Fornés had an epiphany. She discovered that she enjoyed writing so intensely that she soon had to discipline herself to eat and sleep while in the grip of literary creation. In 1961 her first play, *La viuda*, was published in a collection of works by four Cuban writers, and later that year she was awarded a John Hay Whitney Foundation fellowship. For the following year she received a Centro Mexicano de Escritores fellowship as well. In 1963 her play *There! You Died* (later also titled *Tango Palace*), with its debut in San Francisco, became her first work produced on stage. Its considerable success set in motion her career as a serious playwright.

In 1965 Fornés saw three more of her plays produced and won her first Obie for distinguished play writing. Her "protest" musical, *Promenade* (a humorous social satire about two prisoners, their journey out into the world, and their return to jail), had its premiere production in April that same year. The critics found this virtually plotless musical attractive and illustrative of Fornés's wit and compassion. During the years between 1966 and 1970 she was extremely busy as a dramaturgist. To give voice to her protest against U.S. involvement in Vietnam she wrote *A Vietnamese Wedding*, which she produced in 1967 and again in 1969. In 1968 her second play protesting the U.S. role in Vietnam, *The Red Burning Light or Mission XQ*, was first produced in Switzerland and then in early spring 1969 saw production off Broadway.

Supported by fellowships from various institutions (Cintas Foundation in 1967; Yale University, 1967–1968; and Boston University in 1968), Fornés was able to write a half dozen new plays by the end of the 1960s, most of them produced off Broadway. In 1971 these plays plus *Promenade* and *Tango Palace* were published by Winter House in New York under the title *Promenade and Other Plays*.

During the 1970s Fornés wrote 8 more plays and in the decade of the 1980s followed this record production with 14 more. In this impressive creativity she was given a tremendous helping hand by two Rockefeller Foundation grants, 1971 and 1984; a Creative Arts Public Service grant as well as a Guggenheim fellowship, 1972; another Creative Arts Public Service grant, 1975; a New York State Council on the Arts award 1976; two National Endowment for the Arts grants, 1974 and 1984; and the highly prized American Academy and Institute of Arts and Letters award in literature, 1985.

Although nearly all her plays from this period met with highly positive critical acclaim, the feminist play *Fefu and Her Friends*, 1977, was by far the most outstanding and won her two of her six Obies. It is the virtually plotless story of eight women who have come together to make plans for a fund-raising and who tell of their regrets for the past and hopes and yearning for the future. Its vignettes have been described as the dramatic equivalent of a collection of poems, and Fornés has been called America's truest poet of the theater. Her 1979 play, *Eyes on the Harem*, a collection of feminist tales based on ancient Turkish legends, won her another Obie.

In addition to her roles as playwright and director, María Fornés has taken pride in her long career as a teacher. She has been especially interested in teaching young Latino writers and in helping them get a foothold in the theater. She taught with Theatre for the New City in New York from 1972 to 1973 and for INTAR (International Arts Relations, a New York Latino American theater group) after that. At INTAR she has been of utmost importance in teaching and mentoring a whole generation of Latina playwrights. She has also given workshops at many universities. Perhaps her most important teaching has been at the Padua Hills Festival in Claremont, California. In addition, beginning in 1978 she wrote a number of her plays specifically for the festival and produced most of them as well.

Although most of Fornés's plays have been produced off-off-Broadway, in regional theaters, and at INTAR, in the mid-1980s her works began to find a revived interest among regional theater directors. From the beginning they have always found a warm welcome in university theaters.

Fornés has donated a collection of her papers to the Lincoln Center Library of the Performing Arts in New York City.

Further Reading

Betsko, Kathleen, and Rachel Koenig. *Interviews with Contemporary Women Playwrights*. New York: William Morrow, 1987.

Contemporary Authors, New Revision Series, vol. 28. Detroit: Gale Research, 1990.

Cortina, Rodolfo. *Cuban American Theater*. Houston, Tex.: Arte Público Press, 1991.

Fornés, María Irene. *María Irene Fornés: Plays*. New York: PAJ Publications, 1986.

The Oxford Companion to Women's Writing in the United States. New York: Oxford University Press, 1995.

Telgen, Diane, and Jim Kamp, eds. *Notable Hispanic American Women*. Detroit: Gale Research, 1993.

ERNESTO GALARZA

(1905–1984)

Mexican American Autobiographical Historian, Farm Labor Organizer, Economist, Educator, Poet

Ernesto Galarza was a man of both staunch beliefs and decisive action. He was the first Mexican American to be accepted for graduate studies at Stanford University, one of the first to achieve a doctorate, and the first to be suggested for a Nobel Prize. His life history is the story of a Mexican immigrant who was determined to succeed in the Anglo world and who struggled with high principles toward that goal. In some ways it is a typical story of the immigrant from Mexico; in some ways it is unique. It is also the insightful story of post–World War II agricultural unionism as Galarza, the first important Chicano farmworker union leader, experienced it—especially in California from 1947 to the end of the bracero program in 1964.

Ernesto Galarza was born on 15 August 1905 in Jalcocotán in the west-coast Mexican state of Nayarit, the only child of Henriqueta Galarza. His autobiographical *Barrio Boy* recalls what it was like as a small boy grow-ing up in the friendly atmosphere of a tiny Mexican mountain village. When the Great Revolution of 1910 swept over Mexico his mother, two uncles, and he were forced by the lawlessness to begin a three-year flight, first to nearby Tepic, then to Mazatlán where Ernesto began his school-ing, across the northern border to Tucson, Arizona, and from there fi-nally to Sacramento, California.

In the Sacramento barrio he continued his education and began his adaptation to American society. Although his mother and one uncle died in the great influenza epidemic of 1917 when he was 12 years old, Er-nesto was able, by dint of hard work at a wide variety of odd jobs, to continue in Lincoln Elementary School. Six years later he graduated from Sacramento High with a scholarship to Occidental College in southern California.

Active in debate and on the college paper, in 1927 Galarza graduated from Occidental with a degree in history, specializing in Latin America, and qualified for Phi Beta Kappa. Through a fellowship from Stanford University in northern California he was able to continue his graduate education at that institution. During summers he continued to work in harvest agriculture. In 1929 Stanford awarded him an M.A. in political

Ernesto Galarza. Photo courtesy of Mae Galarza.

science and history. With his new wife, Mae Taylor Galarza, he went to New York where he had been accepted in Columbia University's doctoral program. After publication of his dissertation on the Mexican electric industry by Fondo de Cultura Económica in Mexico, he was awarded the Ph.D. with Honors in 1944.

Meanwhile, with the family enlarged by two young daughters, Ernesto also had to earn a living. Between 1932 and 1936 he and Mae taught and were co-directors of Gardner Year-Long School, a private progressive institution on Long Island. At the same time Ernesto did research for the Foreign Policy Association in New York. During the following four years he held a research position at the Pan American Union (PAU) in Washington, D.C., because of his interest in labor and expertise in Latin American affairs. Then he was promoted to director of the PAU's newly formed Division of Labor and Social Information, an appointment that involved extensive travel in Latin America. The result was a lifelong focus on Latino workers, especially in agriculture. He became intimately acquainted with the World War II bracero (Mexican farm worker) program in the United States and wrote a scathing report on its exploitative aspects.

In 1947 Galarza resigned from the PAU and took a job as research director and Spanish-speaking field organizer for the Southern Tenant Farmers Union (later the National Farm Labor Union, or AFL), which was planning to organize agricultural workers in California. The family moved back to California, to San Jose. Galarza spent the next dozen years trying to unionize farm workers, most of them *mexicanos*, in the face of two serious obstacles: "right to work" legislation, and a large agricultural labor surplus created by braceros and undocumented workers. The 20-some strikes he led during these years were uniformly unsuccessful in achieving immediate major objectives. However, his involvement led to two books on abuses of the bracero program: *Strangers in Our Fields*, 1956, and *Merchants of Labor*, the latter published by Galarza himself with borrowed funds in 1964, the year the bracero program ended. Of passing interest, although he and **César Chávez** pursued the same objectives with equal fervor, they were never close to each other. Galarza was basically a labor leader; Chávez was more a civil rights organizer.

Having left the AFL in 1959, Galarza worked at a variety of jobs related to urban workers during the 1960s. He acted as consultant to a number of important federal agencies, the government of Bolivia, and the Ford Foundation. He also became involved in the growing Chicano movement, serving as a member of the Mexican American Legal Defense and Education Fund's board of directors. Increasingly recognized as a Mexican American intellectual, he became an active educator-scholar, accepting appointments to teach about labor and labor migration at Harvard University, Notre Dame, and several California state universities.

Harking back to his own early experience and impelled by a lifelong concern for education, by the early 1970s Galarza was also becoming involved in bilingual and bicultural education as an author and administrator. He founded a bicultural resource center for the San Jose (California) school district and also began writing a series of bilingual books in poetry and prose for children. In all, Galarza wrote and published 12 of these mini-*libros*, half prose and half poetry, and sometimes was humorously referred to as Father Goose. In 1979 these mini-books led to his being suggested as a nominee for the Nobel Prize in literature. During the last decade of his life he was a frequent and active participant in conferences and workshops, in spite of poor health. He died on 22 June 1984 in San Jose.

Out of his involvement with labor came a large number of important publications. He wrote over a dozen books and numerous reports and articles. In addition to those already mentioned, his best-known books include *Spiders in the House and Workers in the Field*, 1970; *Tragedy at Chualar*, 1977; and *Farm Workers and Agri-Business in California, 1947–1960*, 1977. His last work, published just two years before his death, was *Kodachromes in Rhyme*, a lyric outpouring of his poetic soul. Galarza will probably be remembered longest for *Barrio Boy*, the poignant story of his family's uprooting by the Mexican revolution and its adaptation to American society, the saga of thousands of other Mexican families.

Further Reading

Chabrán, Richard. "Activism and Intellectual Struggle in the Life of Ernesto Galarza (1905–1984) . . ." *Hispanic Journal of Behavioral Sciences* 7:2 (June 1985): 135–152.

Galarza, Ernesto. *Barrio Boy*. Notre Dame, Ind.: University of Notre Dame Press, 1971.

———. *Farm Workers and Agri-Business in California, 1947–1960*. Notre Dame, Ind.: University of Notre Dame Press, 1977.

Guilbault, Rose del Castillo. "Scholar, Labor Leader, Poet, Hero." *San Francisco Chronicle This World* (23 September 1990): 3–4.

London, Joan, and Henry Anderson. "Man of Fire: Ernesto Galarza." In *Chicano: The Evolution of a People*, Renato Rosaldo et al., eds. Minneapolis: Winston Press, 1973.

Martínez, Julio A., and Francisco A. Lomelí. *Chicano Literature: A Reference Guide*. Westport, Conn.: Greenwood Press, 1985.

RUDY (VALENTIN JOSEPH) GALINDO

(1970–   )

Mexican American Ice-Skating Champion

In four and a half minutes Rudy Galindo passed from a penniless, virtually ignored figure skater to the soon-to-be well-off U.S. national Figure Skating champion. Americans have always had a soft spot for the underdog, the Horatio Alger figure, any heart-warming story of rags to riches. So it is no surprise that they loved the triumph of Rudy Galindo over the various adversities that beset him and that they took him to their hearts. At the ripe old age (for a figure skater) of 26 he overcame lassitude, depression, and a degree of despair and went on to win the national championship and to become a Mexican American role model, a hero nationwide, and the U.S. hope in the following World championship trials. A modest hero, he has been quoted as saying, "If you have a dream—if you want something badly enough—and you work hard, it will come true. Look at me; I'm proof."

Rudy Galindo was born in East San Jose, California, in 1970. His mother, Margaret Galindo, and his father, Jess Galindo, a truck driver, named him Valentin Joseph after two uncles in a close-knit nuclear family. However, his father preferred to call him Rudy and the name stuck. He grew up in the lower middle-class environment of a trailer park in East San Jose, where uncles and aunts were frequent visitors and where his widowed mother still lives. Wanting his children to be accepted, his father insisted that English be spoken at home as well as in school, with the unfortunate result that today Rudy speaks almost no Spanish. After grade school he attended J. W. Fair Middle School in San Jose.

The youngest of three children, baby brother Rudy tagged along after his older sister Laura, who often had the task of keeping an eye on him. He went along everywhere she went, even when she began taking ice-skating classes. He listened in on her lessons and did his best to follow her teacher's instructions. It was soon evident that he felt at home on the ice, and he quickly developed into an adept skater. When his aptitude became clearly evident he began to take lessons and Laura stepped aside, since the family could afford lessons for only one of their children. She became his first fan. His first competition was in the beginners "Papoose Boys" category at Squaw Valley; he won first place. By age 13 through hard work and constant practice Rudy had become the reigning national junior solo champion. He soon decided that he wanted to skate with a partner rather than solo; he selected shy, promising 11-year-old Kristi Yamaguchi for his partner.

From 1986 to 1991 Galindo partnered with Kristi Yamaguchi. In 1988, in Australia, the pair became the first American duo to win the World Gold Medal in the junior category. Their success pushed them into senior level competition, where for the next two years they won the national championships. As they were about to begin training for the Olympic tryouts in 1991, Kristi decided she wanted to pursue a solo career. Her decision devastated Rudy, who had his heart set on the Olympics, and gave him feelings of crushing defeat and abject failure. His spirit was broken and his confidence in himself completely destroyed. His dream for the Olympics went out the door with Yamaguchi.

As a result of his emotional feelings, Rudy did poorly on the ice during the next years. Plunged into the depths of self-pity, he blamed everybody but himself for his inability to rise quickly to the top again as a solo performer. It seemed to him that the system and everybody in it were against him. His frustration was sometimes apparent in his off-ice statements to reporters. He was quoted in the press as saying that he felt he was discriminated against in skating competitions because he was Mexican American and also openly gay.

Until January 1996, the 1990s did not seem to be Rudy Galindo's decade. In 1993, with his father's death from a heart attack weighing heavily upon him, he placed fifth in national competition. In the following year he was cruelly distressed by the fact that his brother George and his coach were both dying of AIDS. Rudy finished seventh at the finals in Detroit and made an even poorer showing the next year after his brother's death. His eighth place in the 1995 national competition brought on a long bout of depression. Discouraged and apparently giving up any hopes to become champion again, he stopped figure skating for over seven months in 1995. He holed up in his mother's home watching soap operas all afternoon, day after day. Although he was not skating, he went to the gym every morning to work out. Without any income, in order to make ends meet he joined his sister Laura in teaching ice-skating to youngsters.

During this self-imposed "sabbatical" Galindo had time to give serious thought to himself and his future. He concluded that for him, skating was more than physical exercise, a source of income, or a way to glory and fame; it was, he decided, his way of expressing himself artistically; it was simply soul-satisfying. Then with his sister Laura acting as his coach and encouraging him, he buckled down to serious daily practice, the results of which soon became evident in his performance. In the 1996 preliminaries for the U.S. men's title in January, Rudy won third place. Then came the finals.

In the national finals Galindo drew the 17th, the last, position. Despite the tension of waiting, of skating last, he skated superbly. After eight triples—Axels, Salchows, Lutzes, flips, and loops—he finished his four and a half minutes of figure skating to the music of Swan Lake and to the thunderous applause of 11,000 spectators. He received the first-place votes of seven of the nine judges, with the first perfect 6.0s awarded by judges since 1988 (two of them). It was the greatest upset ever in U.S. figure skating. Rudy had become the first Latino American national men's figure skating champion and the second-oldest ever national men's champion.

Rudy's hometown was as ecstatic as he about his success. In his honor January 23 was declared Rudy Galindo Day by the mayor of San Jose, and he was feted with an elegant reception by the Saint Moritz Ice Skating Club, of which he was a member. He was inundated with various offers—a book contract, a starring role in a television sitcom, endorsements. His win also brought numerous other financial proposals, including a five-figure fee for an appearance in Moscow. Five days after his win he received a contract to skate with the Campbell's Soup Tour of World and Olympic Figure Skating Champions. He accepted, with the idea of getting away from all the distractions that San Jose insisted on heaping upon its hometown hero. He skated eight performances with the tour and then returned to San Jose to prepare for the World competition in Edmonton, Canada, in March.

On 20 March 1996 at the World Figure Skating Championships in Edmonton, Rudy Galindo finished fourth in the men's short program, thereby putting himself in a position to compete and possibly win a medal in the long program. The next day in the finals he drew first position, his favorite position in contests. He skated flawlessly, did six triples, and took third place. After being presented with the bronze medal he took it off and placed it around his sister Laura's neck. Third place, but after all, third best in the world!

In September 1996 Rudy Galindo turned professional.

Further Reading

Cone, Tracie. "Axels to Grind." *West, San Jose Mercury News* (3 March 1996): 13–19.

Killion, Ann. "Rudy Bags a Bronze." *San Jose Mercury News* (22 March 1996): 1A, 24A.

Galindo, Rudy, with Eric Marcus. *Icebreaker: The Autobiography of Rudy Galindo.* New York, NY: Pocket Books, 1997.

———. "Still in the Hunt." *San Jose Mercury News* (21 March 1996): 1A, 18A.

Longman, Jere. "After Years of Struggle, the Veteran Galindo Lands an Upset for the Ages." *New York Times* 145 (21 January 1996): S2(L).

Martínez, Katynka Zazueta. "A Natural Talent." *El Andar* 6:9 (March 1996): 22–25.

Meacham, Jody. "Rudy's Ride." *San Jose Mercury News* (31 March 1996): 1H.

CRISTINA GARCÍA

(1958–   )

Cuban American Novelist, Journalist, Teacher

Seldom has an author's first novel so impressed and moved literary critics as has *Dreaming in Cuban* by Cristina García. She has written a novel that has been compared to the work of such towering literary figures as Gabriel García Márquez and Anton Chekhov. It clearly places her in the generation of young Cuban Americans whose cultural consciousness, as indicated in their writing, reflects both their growing up in the United States and a recollection of their parents' overwhelming nostalgia for the lost island home. She also clearly belongs to that group of Cuban-origin writers who have come of age intellectually in the United States. Having grown up in New York where she was immersed in the melting pot, García has written convincingly about the ethnic realities of urban America.

Cristina García was born on 4 July 1958 in Havana, Cuba, the daughter of Esperanza Lois and Francisco M. García, a cattle rancher. For political reasons her parents emigrated to the United States two years later when the leftward turn in Fidel Castro's government became apparent, particularly in its confiscation of private property. Because they had family in New York they settled there, going into the restaurant business.

Cristina grew up in Brooklyn Heights in New York City. After grade school she attended and graduated from Dominican Academy in Manhattan. From there she entered Barnard College at Columbia University, from which she graduated in 1979 with a B.A. degree in political science. With the goal of entering the foreign service she continued her education in the School of Advanced International Studies at Johns Hopkins University in Washington, D.C., where she earned a master of arts in European and Latin American studies two years later. While at Barnard she tutored and also worked in her parents' restaurant; at Johns Hopkins she enjoyed a partial scholarship, which she supplemented by working.

In the four years from 1980 to 1983 Cristina served her apprenticeship as a reporter intern on the *Boston Globe*, as a reporter for United Press International, and as reporter–arts critic for the *Knoxville Journal* as well as a news assistant for the *New York Times* in Washington, D.C. Between 1983 and 1990 she worked on various assignments for *Time* magazine. Reporting and writing articles on medicine, the environment, business, law, and technology, she was a national correspondent in New York, San Francisco, and Los Angeles. From 1987 to 1988 she was Miami, Florida, bureau chief with responsibility for news and feature coverage of Florida and the Caribbean. Early in 1989 she began writing her first novel, a goal she had nurtured since high school days.

In 1992 Alfred A. Knopf published *Dreaming in Cuban*. This chronicle of an extended Cuban family on the island and in the United States has been characterized as a jewel of a first novel. Although García does not consider herself a feminist writer, it focuses on three generations of formidable female members of the Del Pino family. Against a background of Cuban politics that constantly lurk barely beneath the surface, it details the melodrama of the family members in their own words and thoughts. This technique enables García to present a variety of political and social views. She relates the thinking and postures of all the family members, as well as their religious convictions or lack thereof. In the novel *santería*—the mixture of Catholicism and African tribal religion, with its secret rituals and animal sacrifices—appears almost as pervasive an element in Cuban life, whether on the island or in New York, as Castro's revolution.

Beyond the human interest, García's novel is about ethnic identity and belonging. The longed-for Cuba of traditional grace and gentility that the emigrés dream about no longer exists at the end of the twentieth century. While the exile generation tries to hold on to the old island ways, its members find it increasingly difficult to communicate with or understand their children who are conversant with Spanish but speak English. García sees language as playing an important part in the Cuban American experience.

To some degree *Dreaming in Cuban* is emotionally autobiographical. Pilar, like Cristina García, was born in Cuba and came to New York City as a child. Here she grows up, not sure of her identity. Lamenting her lost Cuban heritage and identity, she rejects her mother's blind faith in the capitalist American dream. She tries to achieve an equilibrium between her dreamed-of Cubanness and her actual Americanness, a balance between the two cultures that struggle in a tug of war within her. Even though Brooklyn does not quite feel like home, she is not at all sure that Cuba will. Eventually she comes to the conclusion that she is definitely neither Cuban nor completely American, but an amalgam, the Cuban American. In Havana, Pilar says of New York, "I know now it's where I belong—not instead of here but *more* than here."

Dreaming in Cuban seems to place Cristina García among those Cuban American writers whose work is marked by an ethnic memory that orients them toward the past, largely as a result of a continuing political and historical commitment to the island. However, she is completely aware of her bipolarity, of belonging to an ethnic minority as well as to the dominant society. Her writing in English, rather than Spanish, clearly sets her apart from most other emigré Cuban writers.

For Cristina García, *Dreaming in Cuban* is a first giant step in the process of establishing herself on the multicultural American literary scene. It was a finalist for the National Book Award of the National Book Foundation in 1992 and was anthologized in *Iguana Dreams* published by HarperCollins in that same year. It brought García a Hodder fellowship at Princeton University in 1992–1993 as well as a Cintas fellowship from the Institute of International Education in the same period. In 1994–1995 she was awarded a prestigious Guggenheim Foundation fellowship.

In 1992 Cristina García began teaching creative writing for University of California, Los Angeles Extension, and two years later taught a similar course in the College of Creative Studies, University of California, Santa Barbara. In the fall of 1995 she began teaching in the English department of the University of Southern California—all these positions largely the result of *Dreaming in Cuban*. Currently she is working on her second novel, tentatively titled *The Agüero Sisters*.

Further Reading

Agosin, Marjorie. "Dreaming in Cuban" [book review]. *Christian Science Monitor* 84:82 (24 March 1992): 13.

Alvarez-Borland, Isabel. "Displacements and Autobiography in Cuban American Fiction." *World Literature Today* 68:1 (Winter 1994): 43–49.

Contemporary Authors, vol. 141. Detroit: Gale Research, 1994.

Contemporary Literary Criticism, Yearbook 1992, vol. 76. Detroit: Gale Research, 1993.

García, Cristina. *Dreaming in Cuban*. New York: Random House, 1992.

Hospital, Carolina. "Los atrevidos: The Cuban American Writers." *Linden Lane Magazine* 6 (1987): 22–23.

Magill, Frank N., ed. *Masterpieces of Latino Literature*. New York: HarperCollins, 1994.

The Oxford Companion to Women's Writing in the United States. New York: Oxford University Press, 1995.

Taboada, Antonio. "That's Who We Are: Cuban American Literature . . ." *Dispositio* 17 (January 1991).

Weiss, Amelia. "Fantasy Island." *Time* 139:12 (23 March 1992): 67.

HÉCTOR PÉREZ GARCÍA

(1914–1996)

Mexican American Physician, Political Activist, Community Leader, Ambassador

Héctor Pérez García is one of the few U.S. Latinos to be awarded the Presidential Medal of Freedom, given to him by President Ronald Reagan in 1984. Two decades earlier President John F. Kennedy had named him a member of the U.S. delegation to sign the 1961 Mutual Defense Agreement with the newly established Federation of the West Indies. Three years later President Lyndon B. Johnson appointed Dr. García as special ambassador to represent the United States at the inauguration of Dr. Raúl Leoni as president of Venezuela and in 1967 named him an alternate delegate to the United Nations with the rank of ambassador. Meanwhile García was awarded the Vasco Núñez de Balboa medal by President Marco Robles of Panama in 1965 in recognition of his services to humanity. He also was honored with appointments to a number of important government commissions on which he served with distinction. Clearly Dr. García is a national Latino leader.

Héctor García was born on 17 January 1914, just months before the outbreak of World War I, in Llera, a small village in the Mexican border state of Tamaulipas. His parents, Faustina Pérez and José García, took the family across the Rio Grande into Texas in 1918 in order to get away from the disorder and violence of the Mexican revolution of 1910, but more important, in order that their children might have access to a better education. The Garcías settled in Mercedes, Hidalgo County, almost on the Rio Grande in the extreme southern corner of Texas not far from Brownsville. Here Héctor grew up in a close-knit family in which the importance of education was constantly stressed.

Héctor García attended the Mercedes public schools. After graduating from Mercedes High School he enrolled in the University of Texas at Austin and obtained his A.B. there in 1936. Influenced by his parents' emphasis on the importance and value of education and by the example of an elder brother (there are five physicians in the García family), he entered the University of Texas School of Medicine. Four years later he completed his M.D. degree and then found it difficult for a Mexican American to get an internship in Texas. He did his two years of general and surgical internship at Creighton University's St. Joseph Hospital in Omaha, Nebraska.

When the United States entered World War II after Pearl Harbor in December 1941, Héctor García volunteered for service in the army, serving first in the infantry, then in the Corps of Engineers, and last in the Medical Corps as a combat surgeon. His service earned him the Bronze Star with six battle stars. After the war and his release from the army, he returned to Texas and set up a family practice in Corpus Christi with his office near the Veterans Administration (VA) building. He quickly established himself as a physician and contracted with the VA to provide medical care to former servicemen. He soon became sharply conscious of the fact that Mexican American veterans were often subjected to discrimination in the VA and received poor service from it.

When the mortuary at Three Rivers, Texas, refused to handle the reburial of the body of veteran Félix Longoria, who had been killed in the Philippine Islands, Dr. García took a prominent role in the protest by Mexican American veterans that followed. In order to do something about the treatment of members of *la raza* as second-class citizens, he called for a meeting of Mexican American veterans. As a result, in March 1948 the American G.I. Forum (AGIF) was organized. He was elected its first president.

During the 1950s Dr. Héctor García continued his activities, positioning the G.I. Forum in the forefront of the civil rights movement. He played a major role in other civil rights cases involving Mexican Americans as well as in the Longoria affair. He traveled all over Texas helping to organize voter registration drives among adults and urging their children to complete their high school educations. At the same time he founded new chapters of the AGIF, soon making it one of the largest

Mexican American organizations in the United States. Despite threatening telephone calls and some physical harassment, Dr. García continued his activism and expanded his interests by becoming a spirited participant in an older civil rights organization, the League of United Latin American Citizens (LULAC). Inevitably he became involved politically.

During the 1960 presidential campaign Dr. García was named national coordinator of the Viva Kennedy clubs and served on the Democratic National Committee. In the aftermath of the election he was one of the leaders in the movement to create a nationwide Hispanic organization and as a result helped to organize the Political Association of Spanish Speaking Organizations (PASSO). He was elected its first president.

With a reputation as a moderate reformer, Héctor García acted as consultant and advisor to presidents Kennedy, Johnson, and Carter. Presidents Kennedy and Johnson appointed him to various commissions including the National Advisory Council on Economic Opportunity, the National Commission on UNESCO, and the U.S. Civil Rights Commission (from which Republican president Richard M. Nixon later removed him). He also served on the Advisory Council to the Veterans Administration and was vice-president of the Catholic Council for Spanish Speaking People in the Southwest. Along with his intense involvement in numerous civil rights and political activities, Dr. García continued his practice of medicine into his sixties. After suffering with cancer for more than a decade, on 26 July 1996 Dr. García died at age 82 in Corpus Christi, Texas, from congestive heart failure and pneumonia.

Because of his long and intimate involvement with civil rights, during this period Dr. García was honored by such disparate groups as the Alba Club, 1949; the Texas Council of Negro Organizations, 1955; the American Cancer Society, 1962; the Veterans of Foreign Wars, 1964; the National Council of La Raza, 1990; the 8th Marine Corps District, 1967; and the National Association for the Advancement of Colored People, 1969. Twenty years later, in 1989 the Texas Senate formally recognized him for a lifetime of work on behalf of civil and human rights for all Americans and especially for Mexican Americans.

Further Reading

Chacón, José. *Hispanic Notables in the United States of North America*. Albuquerque: Saguaro Publications, 1978.

Palacios, Arturo. *Mexican-American Directory*. Washington, D.C.: Executive Systems Corp., 1969.

"President Honors G.I. Forum Founder." *Nuestro* 8:4 (May 1984): 27–31.

Sinott, Susan. *Extraordinary Hispanic Americans*. Chicago: Children's Press, 1991.

Fabiola Cabeza de Baca Gilbert
(1898–1993)
Mexican American Teacher, Home Economist, Author, Folklorist

Fabiola Cabeza de Baca Gilbert became virtually a legend in her own lifetime. Her outstanding achievements in nutrition and home economics garnered her numerous awards at home and abroad. She was extremely active in a wide variety of community organizations. Her fame was such that in 1951 the United Nations Educational, Scientific, and Cultural Organization (UNESCO) chose her to develop a home economics program among the Tarascan Indians in the state of Michoacán, Mexico, and to teach her techniques to other Latin Americans. She set up shop on the edge of Lake Pátzcuaro and established training centers in some 18 villages around the shores of the beautiful lake.

Fabiola Cabeza de Baca was born on 16 May 1898, just a month after the beginning of the Spanish American War, at La Liendre, the family ranch in northeastern New Mexico near the college town of Las Vegas. She was the daughter of Indalecia Delgado and Graciano Cabeza de Baca. Both her parents came from distinguished *nuevomexicano* ranching families that had come to Mexico's northern frontier in the 1600s and had received extensive land grants from the Spanish and Mexican governments. Her mother died when she was 4 years old, and she was brought up by her paternal grandparents on their large ranch.

Fabiola's early formal education was under the Sisters of Loretto in their school at Las Vegas, to which town the family moved when she and her three siblings reached school age. Upon completing high school she began teaching and also entered New Mexico Normal School (today Highlands University) at Las Vegas. In 1921 she graduated with a degree in general education. She then devoted a year to enriching not only her academic training but also her life by immersing herself in the study of art, history, and the elegance of the Spanish language at the Centro de Estudios Históricos in Madrid, Spain.

Fabiola spent the next few years teaching in the public schools of New Mexico, mostly in rural schools of the northern part of the state. Among the subjects she was assigned to teach was domestic science; she became so impressed with its importance for poor rural *nuevomexicanos* that she returned to the university classroom to study it in depth. In 1929 she

received her second degree, a B.S. in home economics, from the College
of Agriculture and Home Economics of the New Mexico State University
at Las Cruces. Upon graduation she went to work for the New Mexico
State Extension Service. Her next 30 years were to be spent as a home
demonstration agent among the poverty-stricken Hispanos and Indians
of northern New Mexico's ranches and villages. She developed a deep
respect for their traditional ways of preparing foods. In the early 1930s
she was the first extension service agent to be assigned to the Pueblo
Indians.

The emphasis of Fabiola Cabeza de Baca (Gilbert after she married)
was on teaching her students the Anglos' way of preserving food—can-
ning, rather than the drying that was widely practiced in southwestern
culture. She even taught the use of the pressure cooker, which spread
like wildfire despite limited family budgets in the Depression years. In
the severe drought of 1933–1934 and 1934–1935, the worst in New Mexican history, her promotion of family gardens and her food preservation
program were credited with mitigating desperate food shortages and
even avoiding outright starvation.

Cabeza de Baca also took upon herself the role of community organizer; she sought out leaders, set up youth clubs and associations for
women and children, and taught new cottage industries—all desperately
needed in the Depression years of the 1930s. In her reports she indicated
that although at times these activities might be limited in immediately
visible material results, their psychological and social value was great.
Even after her right leg was amputated as the result of an automobile
accident, she continued the sometimes strenuous trips to her beloved
mountain villages. Her deep involvement was a two-way street and in
the process she learned much: to appreciate the positive aspects of rural
Hispano and Indian cultures, to speak the Tewa and Tiwa languages.
She also collected recipes, herbal remedies, and folklore as she became
ever more deeply steeped in the culture and culinary traditions and practices of the Southwest.

The education that Fabiola Cabeza de Baca acquired through her work
led to another important aspect of her life—her literary career. Her new
knowledge enabled her to become the author of articles for popular journals as well as of numerous informative bulletins and pamphlets for the
extension service. Her first book-length publication was *Los alimentos y
su preparación*, published by the New Mexico State University Extension
Service in 1934 and thereafter revised and expanded several times. A
year later her *Boletín de conservar* came out; it also was revised in 1937
and 1941. In 1939 she published her *Historic Cookery*, which (like its pred-
ecessors) became a best seller, resulting in several printings and going
through a number of editions. It won her renown as the number one
expert on New Mexican food preparation.

As a result of her long acquaintance with rural *nuevomexicanos*, Cabeza de Baca developed a deep interest in their traditions and folklore. In 1949 she authored *The Good Life*, a folkloric story describing the yearly cycle of work and fiesta in a New Mexican village and including much material on food, herbs, and folk medicine. It stressed the stamina and resourcefulness of Hispanic women and included many recipes. In it she tended to romanticize southwestern life and, as a result, has been accused of perpetuating the so-called "fantasy heritage" of heroic Spanish dons, beautiful señoritas, and noble Indians. Five years later her book that became best known outside the Southwest, *We Fed Them Cactus*, was published. The title refers to the strategy employed to keep cattle alive during severe drought; the work is a mixture of history, memoir, and folklore.

In 1959 Fabiola Cabeza de Baca retired from the extension service after 30 years. However, she continued to be active, lecturing widely and writing articles for newspapers and magazines on southwestern food, culture, and folklore. She wrote a weekly column in Spanish on nutrition and regional recipes for the newspaper *El Nuevo Mexicano* of Santa Fe and had a weekly bilingual radio program. In the 1960s she acted as consultant for the Peace Corps and helped train its volunteers. Her later years were spent in a convalescent home in Albuquerque, New Mexico. She died in 1993. In the following year the University of New Mexico Press brought out a second edition of her book *We Fed Them Cactus*.

Further Reading

Alford, Harold J. *The Proud People: The Heritage and Culture of Spanish-Speaking Peoples in the United States*. New York: David McKay Co., 1972.

Jensen, Joan M., and Darlis Miller. *New Mexico Women: Intercultural Perspectives*. Albuquerque: University of New Mexico Press, 1985.

Lomelí, Francisco A., and Carl R. Shirley, eds. *Dictionary of Literary Biography*, vol. 122, Chicano Writers, Second Series. Detroit: Gale Research, 1992.

Perrigo, Lynn I. *Hispanos: Historic Leaders in New Mexico*. Santa Fe: Sunstone Press, 1985.

Walsh, Marie T. "New Mexico's Famous Home Economist." *California Farmer* 201 (16 October 1954): 371.

ROBERTO GOIZUETA

(1931–)

Cuban American Businessman

Roberto Goizueta has been quoted as saying, "the things you carry in your head, no one can take away from you. . . . Don't attach too much importance to material things, because, as I know so well from my own experience in Cuba, one individual can take all those material things away from you." Nevertheless, as chief executive officer and chairman of the board of the Coca-Cola Company he strongly defended his 1991 compensation package of more than $86 million in pay and stock bonus when it was criticized in the press. At the annual stockholders' meeting in April 1992 he pointed out that during the decade of his presidency Coca-Cola's worth had increased fourteenfold and that according to company guidelines he might have been awarded nearly twice the amount he received. Not one of the 4,000 shareowners attending the meeting in Atlanta's Georgia World Congress Center was critical of his stewardship or his pay package. In fact, he was publicly praised by a couple of the attendees.

During the early stages of the Great Depression, Roberto Goizueta was born in Havana, Cuba, on 18 November 1931. His parents, Aida de Cantera and Críspulo Goizueta, belonged to the Cuban urban upper middle class, so he grew up in comfortable circumstances. He attended primary and secondary schools in Havana and was chosen valedictorian of his high school graduating class. At the end of the 1940s he was admitted to Yale University in New Haven, Connecticut, where he majored in chemical engineering. Upon receipt of his B.S. in 1953 he returned to Cuba and in the following year obtained a position as a quality control chemist in the technical department of Compañia Embotelladora Coca-Cola, S.A., in Havana, a wholly owned subsidiary of the Coca-Cola Company.

In October 1960 the Cuban government took over the Havana Coca-Cola plant and thereby drove the young chemical engineer into exile. Leaving behind his diploma from Yale, the family photographs on the wall, and wedding gifts on the shelves, Goizueta fled Cuba with his wife and children and with little more than the clothes on his back. In 1961 Goizueta was transferred to Nassau in the Bahamas by the Coca-Cola Company as a chemist in the Caribbean Area Office of the Coca-Cola Export Corporation. Two years later his hard work and dedication paid

Roberto Goizueta.

off, and he was named staff assistant to the senior vice-president for Latin America.

In 1964 Roberto Goizueta continued his rapid rise through the ranks in Coca-Cola's U.S. headquarters. He was transferred to the Coca-Cola Company offices in Atlanta on special assignment with the Technical Research and Development Department and in the next year was named assistant to the vice-president of that department. In 1966 his abilities were recognized anew by election to the vice-presidency of Technical Research and Development. Three years later in the federal building in Atlanta he was sworn in as an American citizen on what he recalls as a hot, muggy Georgia afternoon. In 1974 he made another large step up the corporate ladder by his election as senior vice-president of the Technical Division; just one year later he was elected executive vice-president. In his new position Goizueta had expanded responsibilities in management, with supervision of three of the company's divisions: Administration, External Affairs, and Legal and Technical departments.

His outstanding qualities of enterprise, industry, and intellect having long been recognized by his associates and superiors, Goizueta was elected vice-chairman of the Coca-Cola Company late in November 1979 and six months later was elected president, chief operating officer (CEO), and a director of the company, thereby ending a six-way race in which he was the darkest horse. Despite the fact that he had had no direct operational experience, less than a year later, on March 1, he became chairman of the board and CEO. He continues to carry out the duties of the two positions 15 years later. As chief executive during this period he transformed the Coca-Cola Company, chiefly by selling off most of its enterprises not connected to soft drinks. His business expertise and acumen have been recognized by membership on the board of directors of Ford Motor Company; Eastman Kodak Company; SONAT, Inc.; the Trust Company of Georgia; and SunTrust Banks, Inc.

At the beginning of 1994, as Goizueta moved toward the normal retirement age for Coca-Cola employees, succession fever began to appear in the company's offices. In April speculation as to who might be the next president was ended by the announcement that Goizueta had agreed to remain at the helm for an indefinite period past his 65th birthday. Coke's directors saw no reason to dispense with his experience and expertise simply because he was to turn 65. Goizueta himself has humorously suggested that he would remain at least until the end of the century.

Roberto Goizueta believes strongly that opportunity is always accompanied by obligations. He is firmly convinced that immigrants coming to the United States have the chance to work hard and apply their skills, thereby earning or creating opportunity. Having benefited by America's open society and its economic opportunity, he has tried to repay his debt by being active in civic organizations. He is a member of the board of the Atlanta Symphony Orchestra and serves as a trustee of the Robert W. Woodruff Arts Center, Emory University, and the American Assembly. He is also a board member of the Boys & Girls Clubs of America. He belongs to the Business Roundtable Policy Committee and the Business Council and is a founding director of the Points of Light Initiative Foundation.

Goizueta has been the recipient of honors and awards far too numerous to be listed in their entirety. In 1984 he was presented with the Herbert Hoover Humanitarian Award by the Boys & Girls Clubs of America and was elected a Gordon Grand Fellow by Yale University. In the following year the American Academy of Achievement awarded him "The Golden Plate," and in 1986, along with 82 other recipients, he was invested with the Ellis Island Medal of Honor. In 1990 Emory University gave him an honorary Doctor of Laws degree and four years later renamed its business school the Goizueta Business School in recognition of his deep interest in and many contributions to the university. Meanwhile he had also received the Equal Justice Award from the NAACP

Legal Defense Fund in 1991, and a year later was honored with an honorary Doctor of Business Administration degree from Boston College.

Much in demand as a speaker, in 1995 Roberto Goizueta received an honor he deeply appreciated. He was selected to deliver the keynote address at the swearing in of 67 new American citizens on 4 July at Monticello, Thomas Jefferson's home in Virginia. Three months later he was the principal speaker at the Global Quality Leadership Forum in Palm Beach, Florida.

Further Reading

"The Boss Stays." *Wall Street Journal* (3 May 1994): A1(W), A1(E).
"Coke Chief's Pay Rises 19%." *New York Times* 144 (6 March 1995): C2(N).
Gilder, George. "Miami's Cuban Miracle." *Reason* (November 1984): 21–28.
Kanellos, Nicolás, ed. *The Hispanic Almanac*. Detroit: Visible Ink Press, 1994.
Llanes, José. *Cuban Americans: Masters of Survival*. Cambridge, Mass.: ABT, 1982.
Unterburger, Amy, ed. *Who's Who among Hispanic Americans, 1992–93*, 2nd ed.
    Detroit: Gale Research, 1992.

CORKY (RODOLFO) GONZALES

(1928–   )

Mexican American Community Organizer, Chicano Activist, Prizefighter, Politician

For Mexican Americans, and especially for the 90 percent who live in large cities, Corky Gonzales was arguably the most important leader who arose in the 1960s. An extremely complex person, he is a romantic, a poet, an activist, and the very embodiment of the frustrated and sometimes bewildered Chicano youth from the urban barrio. In addition to his accomplishments as a civic leader and reformer, he is widely known as the author of the 1967 epic poem, *I Am Joaquín*, which inspired thousands of young Mexican Americans during the years of the Chicano movement as nothing else did. In the end, it may be his most enduring legacy to *la raza*.

Rodolfo Gonzales was born on 18 June 1928 in the Denver, Colorado, barrio, the son of a Mexican immigrant father who worked in the southern Colorado coal mines and in agriculture, primarily in the Colorado sugar beet fields northeast of Denver. His mother died before his third birthday; from age 10 he grew up working in the sugar beet fields along-side his father and siblings during the late spring and summer and spent the rest of the year amid the poverty and prejudice of Denver's barrio environment. He attended nearly a dozen schools before graduating from high school at age 16, by which time he was also working part-time in a Denver slaughterhouse. As a possible way out of the slaugh-terhouse, the barrio, and poverty he began to develop an interest in boxing even before he left school.

Young Corky became a very successful boxer. While still in his teens he won both the national and international Golden Gloves amateur championships. In 1947 at age 19 he turned professional. Of his 75 pro-fessional fights he won all but 10, and one of those was a draw. Toward the end of his boxing career he was being spoken of as a likely contender for the world featherweight championship. Partly because of his wife's opposition to the sport, after eight years in the ring he left boxing—still a hero, an idol—to go into business.

The young businessman opened a neighborhood tavern called Corky's Corner and soon was also operating a bailbond business and an auto-mobile insurance agency. Later he became general agent for the Summit Fidelity and Surety Company of Colorado. With his large following of sports fans and his developing rhetorical skills, Gonzales was a natural for politics. He became active in the Democratic Party and before his 30th birthday had been elected captain of the Third District in Denver, the first Mexican American to be a district captain. During the 1960 pres-idential electioneering he was the state coordinator for the successful Viva Kennedy campaign.

After the election of John F. Kennedy to the presidency, Gonzales be-came deeply involved in various federal and local poverty and social services agencies. By 1965 he was being mentioned as a possible candi-date for state or federal office. Disillusioned by the hurly-burly of politics and lacking the necessary thick skin, he resigned from all political in-volvement when a Denver newspaper accused him in 1966 of practicing discrimination in administering Denver's War on Poverty program.

Now he turned his attention wholly to the problems of Colorado's Mexican Americans. He had already formed a Denver organization called Los Voluntarios, which he now used as the basis for La Cruzada Para la Justicia ("The Crusade for Justice") with the goal of securing civil rights and economic and political equality for Chicanos. He established the Crusade's headquarters in an old red brick church and school com-plex, which he converted into a cultural center, classrooms, library, din-ing room, gymnasium, nursery, and theater.

In 1968 Gonzales and **Reies López Tijerina** led a group of several hundred Mexican Americans in the Poor Peoples March to Washington,

D.C., where he issued a series of Chicano demands under the title Plan del Barrio. In the following year he used the Crusade for Justice to convene a Chicano Youth Conference in Denver to discuss political, educational, and social issues affecting young Mexican Americans.

At the conference Corky and the 1,500 young Chicano delegates representing one hundred organizations drew up the Plan Espiritual de Aztlán, which stressed self-identification and self-determination with a "national" homeland in the Southwest to be called Aztlán. During this time Gonzales was deeply involved in the problems besetting many young Chicanos. He bitterly criticized the American educational system, organized and supported school walkouts, protested police brutality toward Chicano students, and defended those arrested. His ideas were especially appealing to Chicano youths, and he spread his views by giving talks around the country at colleges and universities.

In 1970 Corky formed the Colorado La Raza Unida Party (LRUP) to further his ideas of national self-determination and became its first state chairman. Two years later at the first national LRUP convention in El Paso he engaged in a power struggle for the national chairmanship with Texas LRUP leader **José Angel Gutiérrez**. Although a majority of the delegates seemed to favor much of Corky's ethnic nationalism at least in theory, he lost out to Gutiérrez's more pragmatic political ideas.

As the Chicano movement, in which he played such an important role, subsided in the second half of the 1970s, Gonzales's preeminent position weakened. His strong nationalism and confrontational activism found less support. He remained head of a flagging crusade, largely limited to Colorado and centered on the languishing Denver complex and its useful services. Meanwhile he returned to boxing as a trainer and promoter of Golden Glove amateurs; during the 1980s he began training young men for professional boxing careers. In October 1987 he was severely injured in an automobile accident that left him with a long-drawn-out and difficult recovery beset with numerous medical complications. Early in 1996 a subdued gray-haired Corky Gonzales appeared in PBS documentary about the Chicano movement and reminisced about his dream of an independent Raza Unida party, still speaking out for civil rights.

Further Reading

Castro, Tony. *Chicano Power: The Emergence of Mexican America*. New York: Saturday Review Press, 1974.

Doviak, Joan, and Arturo Palacios. *Catorce Personas Lindas*. Washington, D.C.: Educational Systems Corp., 1970.

Gonzales, Rodolfo. *I Am Joaquín: An Epic Poem*, [Denver, Colo.?]: R. Gonzales, 1967.

Hammerback, John C., et al. *A War of Words: Chicano Protest in the 1960s and 1970s*. Westport, Conn.: Greenwood Press, 1985.

Larralde, Carlos. *Mexican American: Movements and Leaders*. Los Alamitos, Calif.:
    Hwong Publishing, 1976.
Marín, Christine. *A Spokesman for the Mexican American Movement: Rodolfo "Corky"
    Gonzales*. San Francisco, Calif.: R&E Research Associates, 1977.
Steiner, Stan. "Epilogue: The Poet in the Boxing Ring." In *La Raza: The Mexican
    Americans*. New York: Harper and Row, 1969.

PANCHO (RICHARD ALONZO) GONZALES

(1928–1995)

Mexican American Tennis Great

"He was a guy who would never give up," a competitor once said of
Pancho Gonzales. The powerfully built, 6-foot, 3-inch athlete has been
called the best tennis player of all time by fellow players and sports
writers. Over his years on the tennis court his extensive repertoire of
strokes, plus his dazzling power and speed, slowly won him a faithful
following despite his ethnic isolation. He not only broke the color and
caste barrier in a sport then dominated by well-to-do Anglos but also
was important in making tennis a popular spectator sport. He showed
a deep enjoyment of tennis, often playing with amateurs purely for the
fun of it. On court he was sometimes moody, often contentious and
snarly; off the court he liked to tinker with cars and play cards; in retirement he liked to spend much of his time with his youngest son.

Richard Alonzo Gonzales was born in Los Angeles on 9 May 1928, the
first child of Carmen Alire and Manuel A. Gonzales, both immigrants
from Mexico. To support their seven children his father worked as a
movie set painter and furniture finisher, and his mother from time to
time worked as a seamstress. Large for his age, Gonzales was active in
sports as a youngster and in his freshman year at Edison Junior High
School in Los Angeles won certificates in basketball and football. To de-
flect him from the hazards of football his mother, despite family poverty,
gave him an inexpensive second-hand tennis racquet when he was 12
years old. The racquet opened up unimagined vistas for young Gonzales.

Richard Alonzo began practicing with his newly acquired racquet on
the cracked asphalt public courts in Los Angeles and made friends with
a high school tennis player named Charles Pate, who, in exchange for
help on his paper route, passed on to him a better racquet, some tennis

balls, and a few fundamentals of the game. This was the full extent of Pancho Gonzales's tennis training. Like **Lee Treviño** in golf, he was completely self-taught. Without taking a lesson he developed his game by observing other players and adopting those techniques that seemed to work best for him. Within three years his natural talent and intense self-training had made him the ranking teen-age tennis player in Southern California. However, in 1944 he was barred from tournament competition by the Southern California Tennis Association because of poor school grades—largely the result of a high absenteeism rate and a life-long difficulty in accepting any discipline that he himself had not imposed. He preferred to be on the public courts perfecting his tennis game.

Early in 1945 16-year-old Gonzales dropped out of school to devote his time to tennis; in the autumn, after his 17th birthday, he enlisted in the U.S. navy. He served 18 months in the Pacific; in the navy he again experienced difficulties with externally prescribed discipline. He was discharged in January 1947 and immediately returned to the tennis courts. In May he entered the Southern California championship tournament and reached the finals; he then joined an all-expenses-paid tour of eastern tournaments. Although he played well he won no major matches. However, in the fall he defeated three top players but was then suspended by the U.S. Lawn Tennis Association for violating the association rule (of which he was unaware) prohibiting acceptance of invitations to more than eight tournaments per year. During his suspension he was promised a college education and a lifetime job by the government of Mexico if he would become a Mexican citizen and represent Mexico in tennis tournaments. He rejected the offer.

In the 1948 U.S. tennis rankings Gonzales advanced from number 17 to number 8. His marriage in March of that year was seen as a steadying influence on Pancho, and six months later he won the tournament at Southampton, New York. In September the 20-year-old Gonzales became a national celebrity by winning the U.S. singles title at Forest Hills, making him the second-youngest champion in the history of the game. He went on early the next year to become concurrent national champion on clay, turf, and indoor courts. At midyear he was named to the Davis Cup team and won his two singles matches. He turned pro in September and joined a tour organized by famed tennis player–promoter Jack Kramer, who judged Gonzales to be the finest tennis player in the world.

Pancho Gonzales's record as a professional was never ordinary, but less than consistent; some years were better than others. From 1953 to 1962 his powerful serve, sure placement, and amazing control dominated professional tennis, winning him a spate of world championships and earning him a reputation as a fiercely aggressive, overpowering opponent and probably the best tennis player of the century.

At the end of the 1950s and in the early 1960s Gonzales twice retired from play and came back. In 1962 he stepped down to become the successful coach of the U.S. Davis Cup team and to work as a tennis pro for a luxurious resort in the Bahamas. In the mid-1960s he started his own 8-acre Pancho Gonzales Tennis Ranch at Malibu, California, and in the 1980s he was the tennis pro at Caesar's Palace in Las Vegas, Nevada.

Gonzales's various retirements did not last very long; the lure of competition and the joy of winning brought him back. In 1968 he reached the semi-finals in the French Open and in that same year was named to the International Tennis Hall of Fame. In the following year the 41-year-old grandfather, in the twilight of his career, played against Charles Pasarell in the longest match in Wimbledon history. It went 112 games, played over a span of two days. And Gonzales won! At the beginning of the 1970s he again left retirement and returned to the pro tour and to the cheers of the crowds who came to see him. The older he got, the harder and more craftily he played. His indomitable spirit and intuitive court sense enabled him to compete against much younger players. In 1971, having first won the Pacific Southwest Tournament at age 43, he also won the World Series of Tennis. A year later, a quarter of a century after first placing in the top ten of world tennis, he still ranked as number 9.

During the 1980s and early 1990s, in his late fifties and mid-sixties, the man described as the most natural tennis player who ever lived still occasionally sallied forth from his Las Vegas retirement to play exhibition tennis. It was perhaps a part of his persistent struggle for recognition and respect. It took the quiet, socially isolated Gonzales many years to be accepted by his peers, whom he consistently beat. On 3 July 1995 he died, defeated by stomach cancer.

Pancho Gonzales was the author of a number of books on tennis, including one entitled *Tennis Begins at Forty: A Guide for All Players Who Don't Have Wrists of Steel or a Cannonball Serve, Don't Always Rush the Net or Have a Devastating Overhead, But Want to Win* (New York: Dial Press, 1976).

Further Reading

Current Biography, 1949. New York: H. W. Wilson Co., 1949.

Doviak, Joan, and Arturo Palacios. *Catorce personas lindas.* Washington, D.C.: Educational Systems Corp., 1970.

Frayne, Trent. *Famous Tennis Players.* New York: Dodd, Mead, 1977.

Gonzales, Pancho. *Man with a Racket: The Autobiography of Pancho Gonzales.* New York: Barnes, 1959.

Inside Tennis (August 1993): 13.

Obituary. *New York Times* (5 July 1995): A15.

HENRY BARBOSA GONZÁLEZ

(1916–)

Mexican American Political and Governmental Leader, Lawyer

Although Henry González has made newspaper headlines often in his long political career, he probably came to the attention of more Americans because of his criticism of certain Chicano activists as "reverse racists" during the *movimiento* of the 1960s–1970s. He was particularly upset by the (Texas) Mexican American Youth Organization and La Raza Unida Party, and especially by the strident verbal anti-gringo rhetoric of their militant leader, **José Angel Gutiérrez**. González's views turned many Mexican Americans against him; but many others to some degree agreed with his criticism. He stood by his assessment and continued to be re-elected. Congressman González has always shown himself to be fiercely independent, supporting what is right as he sees it. His dedication to principle has sometimes reduced his effectiveness. Some critics have viewed his political style as not unlike that of his *jefe político* Mexican ancestors.

Henry González was born in San Antonio, Texas, on 3 May 1916, just a year before the United States entered World War I, to Genevieve Barbosa and Leonides González. Just five years earlier his upper middle-class parents had fled from the Mexican revolution in the state of Durango, where his father was the mayor of the small mining town of Mapimi. Although his father worked hard and became an editor of the newspaper *La Prensa* in San Antonio, life in the United States was difficult for the González family with their six children; while still in grade school Henry began working part-time to contribute to family support.

Henry's parents strongly stressed the value of education and the satisfactions of learning; after learning English in the first grade he became a frequent visitor to the public library in his studious pursuits. He always accepted his parents' view that education was the key to a better future. After graduating from San Antonio public schools and the local junior college, in 1936 he realized a long-cherished dream by entering the University of Texas at Austin to study engineering. However, because the world was still in the middle of the Great Depression, he was unable to find sufficient work to support himself while at the university and had to return to San Antonio. Henry did not give up his educational goals;

Henry González.

he soon enrolled at St. Mary's University in San Antonio, where he completed the requirements for a bachelor of laws degree. Over 20 years later, in 1965 St. Mary's added an honorary Doctor of Jurisprudence degree to his earned LL.B.

After his graduation from St. Mary's, Henry González worked at a variety of jobs: he taught English and government to immigrant workers in an ILGWU (International Ladies Garment Workers Union) education program, he developed a Spanish-English translation service with his father, he was a public relations officer for an insurance company. During World War II he served in army and navy intelligence as a civilian employee. From 1946 to 1950 he was a juvenile probation officer, rising to chief probation officer of Bexar County (in which San Antonio is located).

In 1950 González entered politics by running for the state House of Representatives virtually on pocket money. He lost by a small margin, but three years later he was elected to the San Antonio city council. As a council member he proposed and got passed an ordinance ending segregation practices in the city's recreation department. Firmly committed now to a political career, in 1956 he was elected to the state Senate by

300 votes, the first Mexican American to serve in that body in over 100 years. In the Senate he quickly developed a reputation as a champion of civil rights for minority citizens and as a vigorous foe of racist legislation. Although he lost some battles, he was admired for his ideals and his fighting spirit.

In the late 1950s González became the best-known political figure in Texas and attracted national press attention by leading the longest filibuster in Texas history in order to defeat racist bills being considered by the Senate. Only two of ten were ultimately passed, and one of those was shortly thereafter declared unconstitutional. During his five years in the Senate he aligned himself clearly with the poor, supporting slum clearance and opposing a state sales tax, extension downward of the state income tax, and a large increase in college tuition.

In 1961 Henry González won the special election held to fill an unexpired term in the U.S. House of Representatives for the San Antonio area, thereby becoming the first Mexican American from Texas ever to be elected to a national office. Since then, he has been regularly re-elected to the House every two years, on occasion receiving as much as 90 percent of the votes cast. In the House he continued his concern for the poor and the disadvantaged, his constituents in the 20th Congressional District. His interests were, therefore, both broad and varied: education, housing, equal economic opportunity, a higher minimum wage, protection and benefits for workers, and industry for San Antonio.

González pursued his objectives both by his action on the floor of Congress and through his work on a variety of committees. He combined an active, well-trained mind with tireless working habits. He sponsored and supported many bills, including Puerto Rican rights, basic adult education, educational benefits for Vietnam veterans, manpower training, and a conservation corps for youths. In 1964 he was one of the leaders in bringing about the end of the Mexican bracero program, because he believed it held down U.S. agricultural wages. He was a member, and after 1988 chairman, of the House Banking and Currency Committee; and a member of various subcommittees including Housing and Community Development, International Finance, Urban Growth, and Consumer Affairs. He has been a member of the U.S. delegation to the Mexico–United States Interparliamentary Conference held every year.

In 1965 González began writing a weekly column for the San Antonio *Express News* and has been both a popular and a prolific writer, publishing numerous articles on a wide variety of topics related to his legislative interests in the *Wall Street Journal, U.S. Banker, Business Week,* and other periodicals. A liberal Democrat, he is also a popular speaker—especially in election years—and was co-chairman of the Viva Kennedy clubs during the 1960 elections. Four years later he took an active role in the Viva Johnson movement. After the election of Democrat Jimmy Carter to the presidency in 1976 he was, along with Congressman **Edward Roybal** of California, one of the founders of the Congressional Hispanic Caucus.

Now nearing the end of a long career in government service, in 1993 González spearheaded a movement to reform the Federal Reserve banking system, which he believes is holding back economic growth. He introduced a bill that would have the president appoint and the Senate confirm the presidents of the 12 regional Federal Reserve banks, who currently are selected by private sector banking interests.

Further Reading

Burka, Paul. "Henry B and Henry C." *Texas Monthly* 14:1 (January 1986): 182, 218–230.

Castro, Tony. *Chicano Power: The Emergence of Mexican America*. New York: Saturday Review Press, 1974.

Chacón, José. *Hispanic Notables in the United States of North America*. Albuquerque: Saguaro Publications, 1978.

Conroy, Ed. "Give 'em Hell, Henry." *Mother Jones* 16:4 (July–August 1991): 12.

Ehrenhalt, Alan, ed. *Politics in America*. Washington, D.C.: Congressional Quarterly, 1983.

González, Henry. "Reverse Racism." In *Aztlán: An Anthology of Mexican American Literature*, Luis Valdez and Stan Steiner, eds. New York: Random House, 1972.

Palacios, Arturo, ed. *Mexican American Directory, 1969–70*. Washington, D.C.: Executive Systems Corp., 1969.

"Profile of a Public Man." *Nuestro* 2:13 (March 1983).

Rodríguez, Eugene. *Henry B. González: A Political Profile*. New York: Arno Press, 1976.

Chelo (Consuelo) González Amezcua
(1903–1975)
Mexican American Artist, Poet, Composer

Chelo González Amezcua remained an obscure, self-taught artist until relatively late in her life, being virtually unknown outside of her home town of Del Rio, Texas, until she was in her sixties. Only in the last decade of her life did her unusual visual art talents become widely recognized. Her pen and ink drawings, usually on cardboard or paper, interweave delicate serpentine swirls and intricate linear geometric patterns that are sometimes vaguely reminiscent of detail in the paintings of **Alfredo Arreguín** yet are functionally different from them. Some of them include architectural elements. In an apt phrase, Chelo often referred to her work as *filigranas*, or filigree art, a new Texas culture. Inspiration for her sometimes shamanistic drawings came from stories of Pre-Columbian American Indian leaders and imposing figures from the Bible and secular history.

Consuelo González Amezcua was born at the beginning of the 20th century on 13 June 1903 in the northern Mexican border town of Piedras Negras, Coahuila, directly across the Rio Grande from Eagle Pass, Texas. She was one of two daughters and four sons born to Julia Amezcua and Jesús González Galván, both of whom had been teachers in the town of Monclova farther south in Coahuila. When Chelo was 10 years old the family moved to *el norte*, crossing the Rio Grande to Del Rio, Texas, in large part because of the uncertainty and violence that accompanied the great Mexican revolution of 1910. Chelo was to remain in Del Rio for the rest of her life.

For six years Chelo attended Del Rio schools, showing considerable aptitude for artwork and freehand drawing. At a very early age she began sketching and coloring. As a child she enjoyed sitting on the banks of the San Felipe River watching the swirling waters and observing nature. She also loved to draw on cardboard, paper, and scraps—whatever came to hand. The family was poor, but her home life, she later said, was a happy one. Her parents enjoyed music, playing the guitar and singing folk songs. They also told the children stories from old Mexico, some of which much later formed the basis for Chelo's poems and drawings. Although her parents were not particularly supportive of her artwork and gave her little encouragement, she continued drawing and writing poetry that indicated a deep interest in things magical, mystical, and religious.

In the mid-1930s Chelo sent some examples of her drawings to President Lázaro Cárdenas of Mexico and asked for a scholarship to the Academia Nacional de Bellas Artes in Mexico City. At that time Diego Rivera was the director of the academia's Escuela Central de Artes Plásticas. Chelo received notification that she had been awarded the scholarship three days before the death of her father. As a result, she was, perhaps unfortunately, unable to accept it. She and her sister Zaré remained at home, taking care of their mother, and were forced to seek employment to support themselves. Over the years Chelo continued to spend countless hours making her pen and ink drawings, writing poems, and composing songs.

Using ballpoint pens, Chelo developed her unique art form without any formal training and continued to write poems to accompany her drawings despite the somewhat cynical criticism of her efforts by her sister. According to the Chicano art historian Jacinto Quirarte, Chelo was probably better off without outside influence or formal training in art, because such training might well have blighted or even destroyed her simplicity as well as her sensitivity and openness to nature and to the world around her. Zaré reinforced this judgment, describing her in somewhat different terms as unconventional, even a bit eccentric at times.

It has been said that Chelo González Amezcua viewed the universe with the heart and eyes of a child; her vision, as expressed in her drawings, has been described as both naive and baroque. The inspiration for her work came largely from the Bible, sermons, and the stories she remembered her parents telling their children. Her reading was limited; only occasionally did her inspiration come directly from literary sources.

Starting with a general idea of what she wanted to do, Chelo would then give long thought to how she might express it, working out the details thoroughly before beginning to put anything on paper. Without making any preliminary sketches she would outline the sharply defined major forms of her drawing and then meticulously fill in the tiny details. Sometimes while working on a drawing, which could take from two weeks to a month, she might be inspired to write a poem to be included in the work. In her earlier drawings she used black or blue ballpoint pens only; later she also used red and green, and less frequently other shades.

In addition to her art and caring for her mother, González Amezcua had one outside activity. She served as a sort of mascot for the Del Rio chapter of the Knights of Columbus and sometimes accompanied the knights on their trips to meetings with fellow knights in nearby towns. At these meetings she would often entertain the knights by singing songs of her own composition.

Early in 1968 the well-known Marion Koogler McNay Art Institute in San Antonio mounted an exhibition of Chelo's drawings, marking the first appreciation of her work outside of Del Rio. Subsequently she exhibited in Dallas, New York, and Springfield, Massachusetts, as well as in Monterrey, Mexico. Her poetry also won prizes and expanded her recognition. Unfortunately she did not have many years to enjoy her newly found renown. She died in June 1975.

Further Reading

Lee, Amy Freeman. "Filigree Drawings by Consuelo González Amezcua." Exhibition Catalogue, Marion Koogler McNay Art Institute, San Antonio, 1968.

Quirarte, Jacinto. "Chelo González Amezcua." *Quetzal* 1:2 (Winter 1970–1971).

———. *Mexican American Artists*. Austin: University of Texas Press, 1973.

Telgen, Diane, and Jim Kamp, eds. *Notable Hispanic American Women*. Detroit: Gale Research, 1993.

JOSÉ ANGEL GUTIÉRREZ

(1944–)

Mexican American Activist, Organizer, Politician, Educator

Of the four outstanding Mexican American leaders at the end of the 1960s—**César Chávez, Reies Tijerina, Corky Gonzales**, and José Angel Gutiérrez—the last named unquestionably showed the greatest promise. Of the four he was by far the best educated; he was bright and could be a pragmatic politician. Moreover, he provided a role model (and symbol) illustrating the importance to the Chicano movement of the intellectual and the student. A fiery and sometimes unrestrained speaker, he was the preeminent student leader in the late 1960s and early 1970s. Yet he was perhaps the least successful in achieving his goals. Ultimately he fell into relative obscurity as the Chicano *movimiento* declined. Possibly he set his goals too high. Or maybe he antagonized the establishment too much. Unfortunately for him, many persons, both Mexican American and Anglo, perceived him as an extremist rather than as a rhetorical radical and the political pragmatist that he was.

José Angel Gutiérrez was born on 25 October 1944 in the small (population about 10,000) southern Texas town of Crystal City, the "Spinach Capital of the World." He came from an upper middle-class family, the only child of Concepción Fuentes and Dr. Angel Gutiérrez, M.D. His physician father, who died while José was still in grade school, had participated in the Mexican revolution of 1910 and then emigrated. As a result of his father's death the family fell on difficult days and José Angel at times worked in the harvest fields around Crystal City. A studious and highly motivated youngster, he did well in both grade and high school. With the help of some of his teachers he distinguished himself in high school by leading the school debating team to victory. One of five Mexican Americans in a class of 30, he was elected student body president in his senior year.

From high school Gutiérrez entered Uvalde College and then Texas A & I (Texas Arts and Industries University) in Kingsville, about 30 miles southwest of Corpus Christi. After earning his undergraduate degree with a major in political science in 1966, he continued his studies and obtained a master's degree in the same field at St. Mary's University in San Antonio two years later. In 1976 he completed the requirements for a doctorate in political science at the University of Texas, Austin, and 12 years later earned a second doctorate at the University of Houston, this one in law. An impressive intellectual record.

While at St. Mary's University, Gutiérrez was one of the student leaders who worked for social and economic change by forming a local chapter of the Mexican American Youth Organization (MAYO) on campus. He was elected its first president. After receiving his master's degree he decided to return to Crystal City to put into practice his theories about organizing its 80 percent Mexican American population to use the political system in order to achieve social and economic objectives. In 1969 a high school walkout and boycott over the issue of Anglo control in the selection of cheerleaders and the homecoming queen provided the occasion for Gutiérrez to organize a new political force, La Raza Unida Party (LRUP).

With support and votes from LRUP, José Angel and two additional *raza* candidates were elected to the school board, and two other Mexican Americans were elected to the city council in 1970. Gutiérrez subsequently was named president of the school board. Despite great political and economic pressures by Anglos (many Mexican Americans found themselves without employment or without customers in their places of business), he and his supporters were able to bring about changes in the educational system, particularly by introducing bilingual and bicultural programs. In addition, they instituted improvements in public health and legal services, in hiring on public works and in the educational system, and in police-Chicano relations.

The success in Crystal City put pressure on Gutiérrez to take La Raza Unida national. Despite his strong belief that La Raza Unida Party had a glorious future of growth and success ahead, he felt that a move at that time to a national organization would be at least premature, if not counterproductive. In 1972 at the national LRUP convention in El Paso his supporters struggled against the followers of **Corky Gonzales** for control of the party and won a clear but divisive victory for his pragmatic approach to politics. LRUP candidates were successful only in limited areas in the ensuing 1972 elections. Gutiérrez himself was elected to a judgeship in Zavala County two years later. As a judge he soon found himself in a power struggle, trading charges and countercharges with Anglo members of the judiciary. His trip to Cuba at Fidel Castro's invitation not only further antagonized Anglos but also split his Mexican American followers in the rapidly shrinking and disintegrating Raza Unida Party. Finally in 1981, after a long feud with the judicial commission over his absences from commission meetings and other matters, Gutiérrez handed in his resignation.

Meanwhile José Angel Gutiérrez had taken a job teaching at Colegio César Chávez in Mt. Angel, Oregon, and then accepted an associate professorship in the social sciences at Western Oregon State College in Monmouth. From there he returned to Texas in 1986 to assume the directorship of the Greater Dallas Legal and Community Development Foundation. Having received his J.D. (Doctor of Law) degree in 1988, he became an administrative law judge for the city of Dallas two years later.

In 1993 Gutiérrez entered the race for the U.S. Senate seat given up by Lloyd Bentsen when he became Treasury secretary. Although Gutiérrez stormed the state in his van, taking his message in Spanish and English to Dairy Queens, courthouses, and smalltown weekly papers, he failed to convince the voters that he was the best of two dozen candidates. He continues to operate the José Angel Gutiérrez legal center. He has been the recipient of various awards and is the author of several books.

Further Reading

Castro, Tony. *Chicano Power: The Emergence of Mexican America.* New York: Saturday Review Press, 1974.

Dubose, Louis. "Senate Race, Texas Style." *Christian Science Monitor* 85L:103 (23 April 1993): 18.

García, Ignacio. *United We Win.* Washington, D.C.: University Press of America, 1989.

Hammerback, John, et al. *A War of Words: Chicano Protest in the 1960s and 1970s.* Westport, Conn.: Greenwood Press, 1985.

Martínez, Al. *Rising Voices: Profiles of Hispano-American Lives.* New York: New American Library, 1974.

Muñoz, Carlos, Jr. *Youth, Identity, Power: The Chicano Movement.* New York: Verso, 1990.

Shockley, John S. *Chicano Revolt in a Texas Town.* Notre Dame, Ind.: University of Notre Dame Press, 1974.

RITA HAYWORTH
(MARGARITA CARMEN CANSINO)
(1918–1987)

Spanish American Dancer, Actress

Rita Hayworth died in 1987 at age 69 lacking memory and having no perception of her daily life. She died of Alzheimer's disease, a malady that ultimately reduces its victims to an infantile state. Some psychoanalytic historians have seen her Alzheimer's as a kind of metaphor for her life, which left her severed from her Hispanic roots. She was born Margarita Carmen Cansino but was transformed into Rita Hayworth, the 1940s "sex goddess" whose photograph appeared in the barracks of every U.S. World War II camp. She lived a life of conflict between being Margarita Cansino and Rita Hayworth, and in her more introspective moments she suffered considerable inner torment.

Margarita Carmen Cansino was born of Spanish-Irish-English ethnic heritage on 17 October 1918 in New York City, the first child of the "Dancing Cansinos" team. Her mother, Volga Haworth, came from an English theatrical family; her father, Eduardo Cansino, who was born in Seville, Spain, came from a long line of Spanish dancers. When Margarita was 9 years old the family moved to Los Angeles, California, where her father found employment with the movie studios as a dance director and also gave private dancing lessons. Margarita attended Cathay School and then went to Hamilton High School. At her father's behest she took dancing and acting classes and at age 11 had a part in her first school play.

When Margarita was born, her father was extremely disappointed. He had hoped for a boy to carry on the Cansino family tradition of dancing. Later, when his two sons, Eduardo Jr. and Vernon, showed little talent for dancing, it became clear to him that Margarita, who did have talent, was the one who could be trained to continue the time-honored family practice. She became the focus of his attention. In his demanding and domineering fashion he taught her stage presence, dancing techniques, and a wide variety of dance steps from tap to tango.

Tired of being just a choreographer to stars like Betty Grable and James Cagney, in 1932 Eduardo decided to make the physically mature 12-year-old Margarita his dancing partner in a new "Dancing Cansinos" team. Because Margarita was too young to dance in U.S. clubs, he moved the family to San Diego and got a dancing contract across the border in the Foreign Club of Tijuana, a border town that attracted thousands of Americans with its horse racing, bullfights, nightclubs, gambling, and brothels.

For their Tijuana engagement Eduardo made up and costumed Margarita with a more Mexican appearance, giving her a swarthy, sensual look. He often presented her as his wife; in fact, she later told her second husband, Orson Welles, that her father sometimes beat her and abused her sexually. She learned to accept his demands and patiently followed his instructions, hanging on his every word. She sought his advice and approval on everything she did and became whatever he wanted her to be. She became her father's creation, sensual in public performance but otherwise shy in personal demeanor. In all her subsequent relations with men, particularly with her five husbands, she exhibited a basic passivity—a need to please.

While dancing in Mexico Margarita came to the attention of Winfield Sheehan of Fox Films, who hired her for a small role in a film starring Spencer Tracy and then signed her to a one-year contract. After a handful of dancing parts in various Fox films, her contract was not renewed at the end of the year. She spent the next year doing ethnic bit parts. Her life became dichotomized: practicing, training, acting, dancing, and being her father's pliant doll; or existing in a world of silence sitting on the porch, not talking, reading romance novels or just staring into space. Although she often seemed detached from the world around her, Margarita generally took life as it came without complaint. She once observed, "I think my father's strictness was well justified and certainly indicated his love and concern for my well-being."

But the worm turned. In 1937, at age 18, in a filial rebellion Margarita married her business manager, Edward C. Judson, a man 40 years her senior. Her father objected to the marriage, so she broke with her family. Judson decided she was lacking in personality and was too tied to her Catholic religious background and traditional upbringing. Above all, she was too "Mexican." A dominating man like her father, Judson stifled Margarita's personality and tried to physically alter her ethnicity by changing not only her name but her supposedly "Mexican" hairline and eyebrows with electrolysis. Using her mother's maiden name slightly modified, she became Rita Hayworth. Like her father, Judson assured her he would take care of everything and began to display her at Hollywood parties and in nightclubs, where her new persona could be photographed and made public. The result was a long-term contract with Columbia Pictures.

After numerous "B" movies, at the end of the 1930s Hayworth was given a leading part in a Cary Grant film, *Only Angels Have Wings*, released in 1939. *Strawberry Blonde* with James Cagney followed in 1941, and *Blood and Sand* with Tyrone Power came out in the same year. These films catapulted Hayworth into the elite ranks of Hollywood's glamour stars. Her picture as the "sex goddess" of the era appeared on the covers of *Time* and *Life* magazines in 1941 and later papered army barracks' walls and navy bulkheads. Men wanted her and women wanted to be like her.

Appearing as Fred Astaire's dance partner in *You'll Never Get Rich* in 1941 clinched Hayworth's position as a Hollywood celebrity. An immense success, she followed it with an equally successful series of films: *My Gal Sal, Tales of Manhattan*, and *You Were Never Lovelier*, all in 1942. In all three Hayworth received praise for the quality of her acting as well as her dancing. Finally getting credit for her acting ability, she learned self-discipline and developed a strong work ethic, a desire to succeed, and a competitive spirit. Paradoxically, because of this she often appeared aloof and distant, in a state of private shyness that sharply contrasted with her public image. At times she tried to find her real identity in the area between "Margarita" and "Rita."

Hayworth divorced Judson in 1942, but she still craved affection and felt a need for direction. She turned to Orson Welles, the brilliant young Renaissance man of American theater, who promised her the personal space to discover her authentic self. She married him in September 1943. She sought to build with Welles what she so earnestly desired: family, love, and loyalty—especially after she gave birth to her first child, Rebecca. In spite of her sincere wish to construct a family life, Rita returned to the sound stage soon after Rebecca's birth. In a series of movies— *Cover Girl*, 1944; *Tonight and Every Night*, 1945; and *Gilda*, 1946—she reasserted her position as America's glamour girl while still seeing herself as a dutiful wife and mother. Friends, and her five husbands, often encountered but did not understand this duality in her character.

After her divorce from Welles, in her search for a man to guide her Rita Hayworth met the playboy-millionaire Aly Khan in 1948 and soon became pregnant and married. However, Khan had married the image "Gilda," not "Margarita." In spite of the birth of their daughter Jasmin, she divorced Khan in 1953 primarily because he had continued his marital escapades and failed to give her the sense of home and family that she sought. Naively, perhaps, she had simply hoped for a home, love, and a sense of self. These seemed to exist only when she was with her daughters Rebecca and Jasmin.

However, Hayworth was unable to live without male guidance, without a man to dominate her life. At age 35 she married crooner Dick Haymes in 1953; their marriage quickly degenerated into a turbulent, abusive, alcohol-saturated relationship. Ironically, during these years she received accolades for her acting in several films, especially *Pal Joey* and *Fire Down Below*, both in 1957. Now older, she no longer felt herself under professional obligation to the "sex goddess" image. In 1958 at age 40, having divorced Haymes three years earlier, Rita married James Hill, a movie executive. This, her fifth and final marriage, was no more successful than the first four; in 1961 they were divorced. She remained, however, highly vulnerable and continued to be influenced by domineering men.

In the late 1950s and early 1960s Rita Hayworth made some outstanding films, such as *They Came to Cordura* with Gary Cooper in 1959 (considered by some critics her best film) and *The Money Trap* in 1966 with Glenn Ford. Altogether, she appeared in more than 40 films between the late 1930s and the mid-1960s. In her last few films, critics found her looking tired and sometimes drawn but also giving the best performances of her long career. However, her acting career was coming to an end as American culture changed, as she aged, and as she gradually lapsed into Alzheimer's. In her last years, unable to function on her own, she was cared for by her second daughter, the princess Jasmin Aga Kahn. She died in New York City on 14 May 1987.

Further Reading

Current Biography Yearbook, 1960. New York: H. W. Wilson Co., 1960.

Current Biography Yearbook, 1987 [obit.]. New York: H. W. Wilson Co., 1987.

Hill, James. *Rita Hayworth: A Memoir*. New York: Simon and Schuster, 1983.

Kobal, John. *Rita Hayworth: The Time, the Place, and the Women*. New York: Berkeley Books, 1982.

Leaming, Barbara. *If This Was Happiness: A Biography of Rita Hayworth*. New York: Viking Press, 1989.

McLean, Adrienne L. "I'm a Cansino: Transformation, Ethnicity, and Authenticity in the Construction of Rita Hayworth, American Love Goddess." *Journal of Film and Video* 44:3–4 (Fall–Winter 1992): 8.

Morella, Joe, and Edward Z. Epstein. *Rita: The Life of Rita Hayworth*. New York: Delacorte Press, 1983.

Ringgold, Geme. *The Films of Rita Hayworth: The Legend and Career of a Love Goddess*. Secaucus, N.J.: Citadel Press, 1974.

Steinem, Gloria. "Women in the Dark: Of Sex Goddesses, Abuse, and Dreams." *Ms* 1:4 (January–February 1991): 35.

OSCAR HIJUELOS

(1951–)

Cuban American Novelist, Short Story Writer

Although he had written only two novels up to 1989, the first published in 1983, Oscar Hijuelos was considered one of the top U.S. Latino writers by the beginning of the 1990s. Hijuelos is American-born, but his novels and short stories have been described as reflecting the perspective of one who shows affectionate but not uncritical feelings for Cuban culture. His four novels have been characterized by critics as sensitive and moving in their portrayal of misremembered recollections about a lost island-paradise and the wistful, unrealistic dreams of a new Eden in the United States. Writing only in English, he is one of a mere handful of Latino writers whose universal themes have successfully reached a broad American reading audience.

Oscar Hijuelos was born on 24 August 1951 in New York City, the son of working-class parents Magdalena Torrens and Pascual Hijuelos, who had emigrated from Cuba in the 1940s seeking greater economic opportunity than the island provided under the dictatorship of Fulgencio Batista. Oscar belongs therefore to the second generation of Cuban Americans. His early years were spent in the ethnically nurturing atmosphere of Spanish Harlem. He might have grown up speaking only Spanish, but fate intervened. When he was 4 years old he developed a serious illness (nephritis) that put him in the hospital, where he spent nearly two years. He entered the hospital a monolingual Spanish-speaker and was discharged speaking mostly English and communicating with his parents only imperfectly as a result. He emerged with an almost totally new identity.

Growing up in the urban environment of Spanish Harlem, he heard constant talk about the Pearl of the Antilles (Cuba) and innumerable refugee reminiscences as his self-exiled elders fondly recalled earlier times. Hijuelos particularly remembers the stories, accompanied by photographs, that his musician uncle Pedro told about playing in **Xavier Cugat's** orchestra during the 1930s. The picture young Oscar unconsciously formed was filled out by hearing the music of the Caribbean in the barrio and by the family's devotion to **Desi Arnaz** and the *I Love Lucy* television show, watched with religious dedication every week. Although his father was occasionally a heavy drinker and his parents quarreled with some regularity, he says there was a good deal of love in the family.

Oscar received his early education in the New York public schools. At this time he was interested in drawing and dreamed of becoming a cartoonist. On graduating from high school in 1969 he entered the work force, undertaking a variety of jobs running the gamut from Latino band musician to farmworker. At the beginning of the 1970s he returned to New York and entered City College, completed his undergraduate degree in English, and in 1976 earned his M.A. from City University of New York (CUNY), also in English with emphasis on creative writing. At CUNY he came under the influence of a successful and prominent short story writer-teacher who nurtured his literary talent. From 1977 to 1984 he worked as advertising media traffic manager for Transportation Display, Inc. Meanwhile he wrote short stories, which he had little trouble getting published, and began work on his first novel.

One of the few Latino American writers with formal creative writing training, Hijuelos was extremely successful and fortunate in obtaining writing fellowships and awards. In 1978 he received an outstanding writer accolade from the editors of Pushcart Press for a short story of his that they had published. That honor was followed by an Oscar Cintas fiction writing grant, 1978–1979; a scholarship at the prestigious Breadloaf Writers Conference workshop in 1980; and further fiction writing grants in 1982 and 1983.

Oscar Hijuelos completed his first novel, *Our House in the Last World*, in 1983. An ethnic story of Cuban alienation and assimilation, it was greeted enthusiastically by the critics as a sensitive human story of social and economic difficulties met and overcome. Although it is closely based on Hijuelos's youthful experiences in the family, the story stresses issues of identity and Cubanness and aspects of the community exile personalities that Hijuelos was exposed to daily. Many critics have found it to be harshly realistic. In 1985, mainly because of the critical success of *Our House*, Hijuelos won both the American Academy in Rome fellowship in literature and a National Endowment for the Arts fellowship for creative writers.

Four years later Hijuelos's second novel, *The Mambo Kings Play Songs of Love*, was brought out by a major publisher, Simon and Schuster, who gave it intensive promotion with a $50,000 marketing campaign. It is the story of two Cuban musician brothers and their immigrant experience told against the background of New York City life in the 1950s. It enjoyed great popularity and was an outstanding success both financially and critically. It was made into both English- and Spanish-language films.

In gathering background material for the book Hijuelos interviewed numerous people involved in the Latino music scene, including the widow of the famous Cuban musician "Machito" Frank Grillo. The use of historical figures and real events enabled Hijuelos to create an intense feeling for the New York City and the times he wrote about. Critics have credited his thorough research for a strong sense of realism in his work.

The Mambo Kings made Hijuelos a literary lion and was nominated for the National Book Critics Circle award and the National Book Award in 1989. In the following year it was awarded the Pulitzer Prize for fiction, the first novel by a Latino American to be so honored. Also in 1990 Hijuelos became the recipient of a highly valued Guggenheim fellowship in fiction.

The Fourteen Sisters of Emilio Montez O'Brien, Hijuelos's third novel, centers less on Cuban exile alienation and more on the roles of women in the Cuban American family. Hijuelos has said that he wanted to portray a society, a family, in which women were strong and powerful. Published in 1993 by another mainstream house, Farrar, Straus, & Giroux, it solidified his position as a leading Latino novelist. Hijuelos recently completed his fourth novel, *Mr. Ives' Christmas*, published in 1995 by HarperCollins. Based on the author's experiences during the 1950s and his Catholic beliefs, it is the story of a father in Spanish Harlem whose faith in America is destroyed by his son's murder.

Hijuelos continues pursuing his avocations, which include working out, listening to jazz, playing various musical instruments, and puttering around with graphics and pen and ink drawing.

Further Reading

Chávez, Lydia. "Cuban Riffs and Songs of Love." *New York Times Magazine* 112 (18 April 1993): 22.

Fein, Esther. "Oscar Hijuelos's Unease, Worldly and Other." *New York Times* (1 April 1993): B2.

Honnewell, Susannah. "A House Filled with Women." *New York Times Book Review* (7 March 1993): 6.

Kanellos, Nicolás, ed. *The Hispanic Almanac.* Detroit: Visible Ink Press, 1994.

Mosle, Sara. "Father and Son." *New Yorker* 71:25 (21 August 1995): 120.

Pérez Firmat, Gustavo. "Qué rico el mambo." *Más* (November–December 1991): 78–81.

Ryan, Bryan. *Hispanic Writers.* Detroit: Gale Research, 1991.

Stavans, Ilán. "Oscar Hijuelos, novelista." *Revista Iberoamericana* 57:155–156 (April–September 1991): 673–677.

Watrous, Peter. "Evoking When Mambo Was King." *New York Times* (11 September 1989): C17, C19.

ROLANDO HINOJOSA-SMITH

(1929–   )

Mexican American Writer, Educator, Poet

One of the most widely known Mexican American authors, Rolando Hinojosa enjoys an enviable international reputation. Although he began to write seriously only after his 40th birthday, his output since has been impressive. He is the author of numerous short stories, essays, and poems and has written a dozen books. His novels generally lack a strong plot or a dominant character, but rather are composed of a series of linked vignettes forming a vivid tapestry of the *mexicano* experience in the lower Rio Grande valley, based chiefly on his recollections of growing up there in the 1930s and 1940s. The vignettes are pervaded by a feeling of socioeconomic and political inequity between Anglo and *mexicano.*

Born on 21 January 1929 in the small town of Mercedes, Texas (population a few thousand), just off the Rio Grande River about 30 miles

Rolando Hinojosa-Smith. Photo courtesy of the University of Texas at Austin.

northwest of Brownsville, Rolando Hinojosa-Smith came from a middle-class bicultural border family. His ranch-hand father, Manuel Guzmán Hinojosa, descended from ancestors who had settled in the lower Rio Grande valley during the mid-1700s in what today are the states of Texas and Tamaulipas (Mexico); his Anglo mother, Carrie Effie Smith, who came to the area from the Mississippi valley as an infant, grew up on the border and was bilingual (Spanish and English), as was his father. Rolando's language at home was predominantly Spanish. His mother, a schoolteacher, kept the home while his father participated, at first indirectly and then actively, in the Mexican revolution of 1910.

Growing up in a *mexicano* barrio, the youngest of five children, Rolando first attended a barrio school taught by Mexican exiles who viewed themselves as sojourners rather than as immigrants and tended to be staunchly nationalistic. He later transferred to the public elementary school in which the teachers were Anglo but the student body was overwhelmingly *mexicano*. His classmates from both barrio and elementary school served to reinforce his bilingualism and biculturalism. Only in junior high school did he become more closely acquainted with Anglo youths.

Like other Mercedes high school students, Rolando played football; he also acted in several school plays and began writing. By this time he had developed the habit of reading voraciously whatever came to hand—from Spanish pulps to modern American and British novels. In 1946 at the end of World War II he graduated from high school and soon enlisted for a three-year hitch in the army. After his military service he entered the University of Texas but was called back to active duty at the outbreak of the Korean conflict in 1950. After serving in Korea he was returned stateside, where he began editing an army camp newspaper. His next assignment was in the Caribbean Defense Command; here he served as a radio announcer and newspaper editor. His army service gave him ample time and opportunity to continue reading extensively.

Out of the army, Hinojosa completed his undergraduate degree in Spanish, graduating in 1954 from the University of Texas where he had maximized his reading opportunities by working as a student employee in the reserve book section of the university library. Upon graduation he took a job teaching a variety of subjects, including typing, at Brownsville High School. He soon quit that for a better-paying job in an oil refinery and later worked for a local clothing manufacturer. Possibly influenced by his mother and siblings, who were all teachers, he taught high school for two more years, after which he decided to enter graduate school at Highlands University in northern New Mexico. He earned his M.A. in Spanish literature there and in 1963 entered the Ph.D. program in modern languages at the University of Illinois, Urbana. At the end of the 1960s he completed his doctorate, specializing in Spanish literature with history and Portuguese as minor fields. He then took a position teaching at Trinity University in San Antonio.

From Trinity Hinojosa went to Texas Arts and Industries University in Kingsville, where he became chairman of the modern languages department, then dean of the College of Arts and Sciences, and finally vice-president for academic affairs. In 1976 he moved from Kingsville to the University of Minnesota in Minneapolis as professor of English and chairman of the Department of American and Chicano Studies. After twice accepting a visiting professorship at his alma mater, the University of Texas at Austin, in 1981 he returned to his native Texas as the Ellen Clayton Garwood Centennial Professor in Creative Writing and English at the university.

While teaching at Trinity University, Hinojosa had begun seriously to write what later became *Estampas del valle y otras obras*, based on his early experiences and recollections in the lower Rio Grande valley. At this time he also began what subsequently developed into a close friendship with **Tomás Rivera**, who encouraged him to continue his literary pursuits. In 1973 *Estampas del valle* was selected for the third annual Quinto Sol award as an outstanding Chicano novel. His next book, *Klail City y sus alrede-*

dores, received even higher acclaim and in 1976 won Hinojosa a coveted international prize, the prestigious Premio Casa de las Américas.

Hinojosa-Smith has been the recipient of numerous other honors, among them a handful of prestigious scholarships in graduate studies; Premio Quinto Sol for best novel, 1972; Best Book in the Humanities award, 1981; appointment as Ellen Clayton Garwood Professor, 1986; and the Mari Sabusawa Michener Chair, 1992.

Since *Klail City*, Rolando Hinojosa has written and published a number of books: a volume of poetry titled *Korean Love Songs*, 1978; *Generaciones, notas y brechas*, 1980; *Mi querido Rafa*, 1981, which won the 1981 Best Book in the Humanities award given by the Southwest Conference on Latin American Studies; *Rites and Witnesses*, 1982; a revamped English version of *Estampas del valle* called simply *The Valley*, 1983; *Dear Rafe*, 1985, a revised English rendition of *Mi querido Rafa*; *Partners in Crime: A Rafe Buenrostro Mystery*, 1985, a detective story based on the protagonist of his earlier novels; and *Claros varones de Belken*, 1986. In the following year an English-language edition of *Klail City y sus alrededores* was issued by Arte Público Press under the title *Klail City: A Novel*; and in 1992 *Korean Love Songs* was published in a German translation.

In 1993 Hinojosa's latest work, *The Useless Servants*, was published by Arte Público Press. Written in the form of the Korean War diary of Rafe Buenrostro, it paints a grippingly realistic picture of a Chicano's reaction to the pain and horror of that conflict. Obviously it is based on Hinojosa's own experience and in some ways is the flip side of *Korean Love Songs*, 1978.

Like his friend **Tomás Rivera**, in his writings Hinojosa has set high literary standards. He is equally at home writing in English and in Spanish, but prefers to write in Spanish, partly because of his subject matter. Some literary critics have characterized his works as regional, but in fact they go far beyond any such limitations.

Although best known for his novels, Rolando Hinojosa exhibits his pungent wit in an ongoing satirical literary endeavor that seems based closely on the concept of Ambrose Bierce's 1906 *Cynic's Word Book*, better known as *The Devil's Dictionary*. Hinojosa calls it *El Grito*, or *Devil's Dictionary*. A few sample definitions:

BARBECUE: A religious gathering wherein Chicanos are invited to participate . . . [in election years]. The barbeque meat is cooked by hot air.

BRIBERY: Interchangeable with "apple pie" and "mother."

HONESTY: A nonmarketable item.

MINIMUM WAGE: A phrase noted for its exemplary candidness to those who are paid one.

These are definitions worthy of the Old Gringo, Ambrose Bierce!

Further Reading

Bruce-Novoa, Juan. *Chicano Authors: Inquiry by Interview*. Austin: University of
    Texas Press, 1980.
————. "Chicano Wins Major Prize." *Hispania* 59:3 (September 1976).
Lomelí, Francisco A. "Entrevista con Rolando Hinojosa." *La Comunidad* 295 (16
    March 1986); 296 (23 March 1986); 313 (20 July 1986).
Lomelí, Francisco A., and Carl R. Shirley, eds. *Dictionary of Literary Biography:
    Chicano Writers, First Series*. Detroit: Gale Research, 1989.
Martínez, Julio A., and Francisco A. Lomelí. *Chicano Literature: A Reference Guide*.
    Westport, Conn.: Greenwood Press, 1985.
Saldívar, José D. *The Rolando Hinojosa Reader: Essays Historical and Cultural*. Hous-
    ton: Arte Público Press, 1985.

DOLORES FERNÁNDEZ HUERTA

(1930–   )

Mexican American Activist,
Professional Labor Leader

Dolores Huerta occupies a unique, nontraditional position among U.S.
Latino women. As one of the founders, a vice-president, and chief ne-
gotiator of the United Farm Workers union (UFW), she undoubtedly has
had greater influence in shaping and guiding that organization's development than anyone other than **César Chávez**. The UFW has been the
focus of her life. Her responsibility as first vice-president and her decision-making role have weighed heavily upon her at times. On the other
hand, she believes totally in unionism and the nonviolent strike tactic of
boycott. Despite her belief in nonviolence, she is no stranger to confrontation; she has been threatened numerous times, has been arrested a
score of times, and was seriously injured by police in a peaceful 1988
demonstration in San Francisco, California.

Dolores Fernández was born on 10 April 1930, at the beginning of the
Great Depression, to Alicia Chávez and Juan Fernández in the small New
Mexican coal mining town of Dawson about 20 miles from the Colorado
border. Both her parents had been born in Dawson, and her mother's
family had settled there when the area was still a part of Mexico. While
Dolores was a small child her parents divorced and her mother moved

with her three children to Stockton in California's great central valley, where she had relatives. Her mother, an enterprising and hard-working woman, got jobs in a cannery and as a waitress in a Stockton restaurant. She put some of her earnings aside and soon opened her own restaurant; later during World War II she bought a small hotel that catered to farm workers and working-class *mexicanos*.

Dolores grew up in Stockton, deeply influenced by her highly motivated mother and by her maternal grandfather, who was the principal male role model of her childhood. With her two brothers she worked in the restaurant and hotel when not attending school. During her formative years she took it for granted that women and men were equal and that success was the result of hard work. Her ambitious mother had high expectations for her children and pushed Dolores to take music and dancing lessons and to participate actively in Girl Scouts and other educational activities.

Dolores spent six years in Lafayette School; then she attended Jackson Junior High, and finally Stockton High School. Only at Stockton High does she recall being subject to discrimination from some of her teachers and fellow students. Her early years appear to have been largely unmarked by ethnic prejudice, as the Fernández family lived in a relatively integrated middle-class neighborhood with varied minority groups including Filipinos, Chinese, and Japanese.

After graduating from high school Dolores married her high school sweetheart; however, the marriage soon ended in divorce. During this time she operated a small grocery that her mother had bought. After the grocery stored failed she got a job as a secretary at the Stockton Naval Supply Base and later worked in the sheriff's office. Dissatisfied with her employment and strongly supported intellectually and emotionally by her mother, she decided to become a teacher. She returned to school and earned an Associate in Arts degree from the Stockton junior college, an unusual accomplishment for a Chicana at the beginning of the 1950s. With her degree she was able to obtain a provisional teaching credential.

Dolores's experience as a teacher, combined with the rising tide of social awareness developed by World War II veterans, soon led her to become a social activist and labor organizer. In the mid-1950s she made the acquaintance of Fred Ross Sr., who had come to Stockton to develop a Community Service Organization (CSO) among Mexican Americans there. At first she was wary and suspicious of Ross and the CSO, but soon she was won over and became active in registering voters and helping with citizenship classes. From Ross she learned how to organize people, how to maintain popular interest in an organization, how to make use of community pressure. During this time she also met Ventura Huerta, a fellow community activist, and they married. In 1962 she was sent to Sacramento, California, as the CSO lobbyist.

Meanwhile Dolores had met **César Chávez** in San Jose, California, where he headed the local CSO organization. She gradually became convinced that he was right in believing that it would be possible to organize field workers into a union to improve their lives. Since then their careers have run parallel courses. With other early farm worker leaders they discussed how the workers might be organized. When Chávez resigned from the CSO in 1962 to begin organizing agricultural workers in California's central valley, Huerta soon followed and was sent to the Modesto-Stockton area, assigned the traditionally male task of recruiting workers. Despite occasional differences with Chávez, in 1964 at his request she went to Delano to assume a more important decision-making role at the headquarters of what was to become the UFW.

A complex and combative woman, this forceful, nontraditional Chicana put her rhetorical and leadership skills to work for the union. When the Delano grape strike began in the following year, Dolores Huerta's initial assignment was as a picket captain. Later she organized membership records, laid the foundation of the union's bookkeeping system, and set up a hiring hall. In 1966 when the Schenley Corporation became the first large grape grower to sign up with the UFW, she was put in charge of negotiating the contract.

During the long five-year boycott of California table grapes, Huerta continued to play a leading role. In addition to directing the boycott on the East Coast, this highly articulate woman gained friends and raised money for the strike by speaking to sympathizers at numerous luncheons, dinners, and other meetings. In the 1970s she went back to the Atlantic coast to coordinate the UFW's various boycott activities. She also took on the responsibility of directing the union's Citizenship Participation Day program, an unsuccessful effort to use the union's political clout to ensure the enforcement of California's Agricultural Labor Relations Act of 1975.

In the following decade, while continuing her heavy schedule of speaking engagements, fund-raising, and overseeing renewed grape and lettuce boycotts, Huerta found time to organize KUFW, the union's new radio station. She also testified cogently before congressional committees against grower-supported proposals to bring temporary "guest workers" into the United States.

During the 1988 presidential election campaign, Huerta was severely injured in a peaceful San Francisco demonstration against Republican candidate George Bush. She was rushed to the hospital, where her spleen, ruptured from clubbing by police officers, was removed in emergency surgery. She recovered slowly but fully from the operation and from broken ribs and was awarded a large financial settlement. In the early 1990s she gradually resumed her role in the UFW, concerning herself with issues such as immigration reform, pesticide use, and general farm labor health conditions. The future role of Huerta in the union was put at question by the unexpected death of **César Chávez** in April 1993. Since then she has been less visible in UFW affairs and has recently been speaking out for Women's Majority Organization, a group that has as one of its principal goals to encourage women to run for public office, especially on the local level.

Further Reading

Coburn, Judith. "Dolores Huerta: La Pasionaria of the Farmworkers." *Ms* (November 1976): 11–16.

Day, Mark. *Forty Acres: César Chávez and the Farm Workers*. New York: Praeger, 1971.

Garcia, Richard A. "Dolores Huerta: Woman, Organizer, and Symbol." *California History* (Spring 1993): 57–71.

Huerta, Dolores. "Dolores Huerta Talks about Republicans, César, Children, and Her Home Town." In *An Awakened Minority: The Mexican-Americans*, 2nd ed., Manuel P. Servín, ed. Beverly Hills, Calif.: Glencoe Press, 1974.

———. "Reflections on the UFW Experience." *Center Magazine* (July–August 1985).

Jensen, Joan M., ed. *With These Hands: Women Working on the Land*. New York: McGraw-Hill, 1981.

Mirandé, Alfredo, and Evangelina Enríquez. *La Chicana: The Mexican-American Woman*. Chicago: University of Chicago Press, 1979.

Rose, Margaret. "Traditional and Nontraditional Patterns of Female Activism in the United Farm Workers of America, 1962 to 1980." *Frontiers* 11:1 (1990): 26–32.

Taylor, Ronald. *Chávez and the Farm Workers*. Boston: Beacon Press, 1975.

JOSÉ ITURBI

(1895–1980)

Spanish American Musical Prodigy, Pianist, Conductor, Actor

A child prodigy, José Iturbi began playing the piano professionally at age 7. He demonstrated his expertise later in numerous performances both as a soloist and as a conductor. At times he filled both roles at the same time, conducting the orchestra while he played the piano. His sometimes elitist and arrogant attitudes antagonized a few music critics. Active in various Hollywood musical films from 1942 to the 1950s, he usually played himself or a character very near himself. His unflagging energy led to a flamboyant, mildly bizarre life-style in Hollywood. He continued concert tours until the year he died at age 84.

José Iturbi was born in Valencia, a charming winter resort town on Spain's Mediterranean coast on 28 November 1895, the son of Teresa Bagueña and Ricardo Iturbi, a gashouse worker who tuned pianos on the side. From his earliest years José showed an aptitude for music and at age 5 was enrolled in a special music school. Two years later he was playing music for money at social events and providing piano accompaniment to the new (silent) motion pictures in the first movie theater of Valencia. In the following year at age 8 he was enrolled in Valencia's Conservatorio de Música and continued to take private lessons as well. At the conservatory he showed himself to be a talented student, and especially outstanding on the piano.

José's musical studies at the conservatory were frequently interrupted to enable him to fulfill his numerous playing engagements and his schedule of teaching adults in private classes. With the help of a purse raised by the local newspaper he was able to continue his piano studies abroad. He entered the Conservatoire de Musique in Paris, France, where he studied under some of the finest music teachers of Europe. At age 17 he graduated from the Conservatoire with highest honors and then accepted a lucrative job playing in an elegant café in Zurich, Switzerland. Here he came to the attention of the director of the Zurich Conservatory of Music and in 1919 was appointed by him to head the Conservatory's piano department.

After devoting two years exclusively to academic duties at the Conservatory, Iturbi began to accept concert engagements and to schedule tours. He was an immediate and great success on the tour circuits. As a result, in 1923 he left the Conservatory to devote himself full-time to concert performances in the many elegant capitals of post–World War I Europe. His virtuosity at the piano met with widespread acclaim from both critics and the musically knowledgeable public.

Soon Iturbi moved to the United States. In October 1929 he made his American debut playing with the Philadelphia Orchestra under the direction of Leopold Stokowski. From Philadelphia he went to New York City, where his initial concert appearance with the Philharmonic was also a rousing success; the critics praised his dynamic style and his mastery of an extensive repertoire. On his first American tour in 1930 he gave 77 recitals.

Three years later, in 1933, Iturbi made his debut as a conductor in Mexico City. His aplomb and success on the podium led to his employment being extended to 11 more concerts there and to an offer from the board of directors of the Lewisohn Stadium in New York City to conduct two special concerts. Their outstanding success led to more concerts at the Lewisohn Stadium during the next two years, and in addition he was invited to conduct the Philadelphia, Detroit, and Rochester (New York) orchestras. He also directed concerts in the Hollywood Bowl and the Robin Hood Dell in Philadelphia. In 1936 Iturbi was offered and accepted a permanent appointment as conductor of the Rochester Philharmonic Orchestra, a post he held for several seasons. However, he also continued to accept bids to be guest conductor of nearly all the top concert and symphonic orchestras in the United States. In addition, he undertook South American, African, East Indian, and European concert tours and conducted special orchestral programs on radio in the United States.

Iturbi's energetic activities did not sit well with all the critics, and the general public looked askance at his sometimes temperamental and occasionally erratic actions. His difficulty in accepting American music as having any value led to conflict at one point with the American Society of Composers, Authors, and Publishers (ASCAP), which threatened a boycott. Some saw his intemperate remarks merely as another expression of his flamboyant personality and desire for publicity. In mid-1941 his refusal to appear on the same program with the famous Benny Goodman sextet added additional fuel to the flames of controversy. Some critics began to subtract from their earlier high praise by pointing out that the ease and spontaneity that characterized his piano playing was noticeably absent from his conducting. As a conductor he seemed too often to be imposing himself consciously and calculatingly as a personality and to be allowing his sense of showmanship to take precedence over his musicianship.

José Iturbi had a mercurial and impulsive temperament combined with an engaging, childlike vivacity that led him to take pleasure in being different even though he knew his behavior antagonized some of his fellow musicians. In addition to his love for music, he found boxing, motorcycles, and airplanes intriguing and indulged his interest in all three. An experienced pilot, he had over 650 flying hours to his credit and flew his private plane to many of his concert engagements. In 1939 he flew all the way to Buenos Aires, Argentina, for a concert.

A few months before the Japanese attack on Pearl Harbor on 7 December 1941, Iturbi took out citizenship papers and following the disaster offered his considerable experience as a flyer to the United States by enlisting, despite his nearly 50 years, in the Civil Air Patrol. By the war's end he had a total of more than 1,500 flying hours to his credit. He also lent his musical skills to promote the sale of U.S. war bonds by performing at numerous rallies. He continued to give recitals and in late 1943 made his film debut in a lush musical ultimately titled *As Thousands Cheer*. Although he essentially played himself and spotlighted his music, his ability as an actor received considerable praise from the critics, and he was given a long-term contract by Metro-Goldwyn-Mayer.

Iturbi's colorful, ebullient personality stood him in good stead in Hollywood, where he spent the last decades of his life. In addition to his concert performances he had a very successful film career, playing classical, jazz, and popular musical compositions for the enjoyment of millions. Among his best-known films were *Music for Millions, That Midnight Kiss,* and *Anchors Aweigh.* His films won him thousands of new admirers who then bought his many piano recordings. In 1946 his semi-annual royalty check from RCA Victor came to an impressive $118,029, the largest amount earned by any recording artist up to that time.

After the war Iturbi continued his recording, movie, and concert careers. Never one to pamper himself, he continued a rigorous concert tour schedule for the next three and a half decades, despite experiencing heart trouble from the mid-1950s on. Finally in March 1980 he ended his traveling because of his extremely poor health. Less than three months later, on 20 June, he died of a heart attack in Cedars-Sinai Hospital in metropolitan Los Angeles.

Further Reading

Current Biography, 1943. New York: H. W. Wilson Co., 1944.

Current Biography Yearbook, 1980 [obit.]. New York: H. W. Wilson Co., 1980.

Etude 48 (May 1930): 321–322.

Reyes, Luis, and Peter Rubie. *Hispanics in Hollywood: An Encyclopedia of Film and Television.* New York: Garland Publishing, 1994.

Sadie, Stanley, ed. *The New Grove Dictionary of Music and Musicians.* London: Macmillan Publishers, 1980.

Smolowe, Jill. "José Iturbi, 84, Pianist, Had Roles in Pictures and Conducted Opera." *New York Times* [obit.] (21 June 1980): 20.

The World of Music, vol. 2. New York: Abradale Press, 1963.

MARÍ-LUCI JARAMILLO

(1928–   )

Mexican American Ambassador, Educator, Professor, Administrator

When Marí-Luci Jaramillo was appointed by President Jimmy Carter as U.S. ambassador to Honduras in 1977, she became the first Mexican

American woman to hold the position of U.S. representative to a foreign country. It is, perhaps, the most signal of the many honors she has received. For being the first Latina to be named ambassador, she was given the Primera Award by the Mexican American Women's National Association in 1990.

Marí-Luci Jaramillo was the second of three children born to Maurilio Antuna from the central Mexican state of Durango and his Mexican American wife, Elvira Ruiz. Marí-Luci was born on 19 June 1928 in the northern New Mexico town of Las Vegas, east of Santa Fe. She grew up there during the difficult days of the Great Depression and received her early education in the local public schools. Encouraged by parents who were concerned that their children got a good education, she did outstanding work in her studies and became a top student in her high school class. After graduation she entered New Mexico Highlands University in Las Vegas but dropped out after a year to get married.

Living in a small New Mexico town with her schoolteacher husband, Marí-Luci had three children, held part-time jobs, and resumed her college studies. In 1955 she received her B.A. in education from Highlands University, *magna cum laude*, even though she had to work during nearly all her college years. With an education major and a minor in Spanish she had no difficulty obtaining a job teaching in the Las Vegas (New Mexico) elementary school system. She continued her graduate studies at New Mexico Highlands and in 1959 obtained her master's degree. She was then promoted from classroom teacher to language arts supervisor for all the schools in San Miguel County. Having become completely convinced by this time that education was the way out of the poverty cycle, she also taught literacy and English classes in the Hispanic American community.

Marí-Luci started studying for her doctorate at the University of New Mexico (UNM) in Albuquerque and in 1965 began teaching English as a second language to the university's students from Latin America. Soon she was also teaching them other classes, lecturing in Spanish, and in 1969 was appointed assistant director of instructional services in the university's Minority Group Cultural Awareness Center. Her work became an increasingly important aspect of the university's Latin American education program as the Chicano *movimiento* led to greater student activism beginning in the late 1960s. In addition to her teaching and administrative work at the university, she was acting as a consultant in bilingual education for the New Mexico Department of Education, in workshops for Teaching English as a Second Language (TESL), and in Mexican American affairs for the federal government's Department of Health, Education, and Welfare.

In the summer of 1966 Marí-Luci gave a course in methods and techniques of teaching English as a second language in TESL's National Defense Education Act (NDEA) institute at the University of Texas, El Paso.

During her summers she also acted as a consultant to the U.S. Agency for International Development (AID). Because of her fluency in Spanish and her minor in Latin American Studies as well as her specialization in bilingual and bicultural education, in (1) elementary and secondary school curriculum, and (2) preparation of learning materials she was a natural for AID institutes in Latin American education. In her capacity as consultant she traveled extensively, working with local educators in Central and South America and the Caribbean, setting up workshops and making recommendations for modernizing teacher-training programs. Her experience in teaching and counseling Latin American students at the University of New Mexico served her well as background experience for her work as educational consultant in their home countries.

In 1970 Marí-Luci Jaramillo completed her program at the University of New Mexico and received her doctorate in education. She was then hired in a tenure track position in the UNM Department of Elementary Education and was later promoted, first to associate, then to full professor, and ultimately to department chair. Because of her extensive knowledge in the field of education, particularly bilingual education, and the numerous articles she had published in professional journals over the years, she was frequently an honored guest speaker making presentations at regional and national conferences, symposia, and workshops of civil rights, educational, and other professional organizations in the Southwest.

In 1977 Dr. Jaramillo's nomination to the post of ambassador to Honduras came as a surprise to her. Apparently the appointment was made largely because of her deep involvement in U.S. educational projects in Spanish America. An admitted workaholic, as ambassador from 1977 to 1980 she oversaw the Peace Corps program in Honduras and the management of six other U.S. agencies in addition to other ambassadorial concerns. In September 1980 she returned to Washington, D.C., to take up new State Department duties as deputy assistant secretary for Inter-American Affairs. After Republican Ronald Reagan took over the presidency, she resigned in March 1981 at least partly because of disagreement with policies of the new administration.

On her return to Albuquerque in the middle of the academic year, Jaramillo was immediately appointed to a position of special assistant to the president of the University of New Mexico. Two years later she was appointed dean of the College of Education, and in 1985 she became vice-president for student affairs. After two years in this last position she was offered a position as assistant vice-president of the Educational Testing Service of Princeton, New Jersey—which she accepted. She served for five years as regional director in northern California and then, in 1992, was promoted to vice-president for field services in the entire

United States. She continues to have deep concerns for improvement in the education of bilingual children.

As a result of her expertise and high profile in bilingual and bicultural education, Marí-Luci Jaramillo has been the recipient of numerous honors and awards. In 1973 McGraw-Hill (publishers and) Broadcasting Company named her Outstanding Chicana of the Year, and four years later she was given the New Mexico Distinguished Service award by the state legislature. When she stepped down as ambassador in 1980, Honduras conferred honorary Honduran citizenship on her and the Mexican American Women's National Association gave her its PRIMERA award. In 1985 the New Mexico Mortar Board Alumni Association named her Distinguished Woman of the Year, and in that same year she was appointed to the board of trustees of the Tomás Rivera Center at the Claremont colleges in Southern California. Three years later the magazine *Hispanic Business* listed her as one of the 100 most influential Hispanics in the United States, and in 1989 the Association of Mexican American Educators gave her its award for Endless Efforts for Education. Clearly she has been one of the outstanding Mexican American educators in recent memory.

Further Reading

Chacón, José. *Hispanic Notables in the United States of North America*. Albuquerque: Saguaro Publications, 1978.

Hispanic Affairs Newsletter [Washington, D.C.: Office of Hispanic Affairs] 1:3 (March–April 1980).

"Hispanic Portraits." *La Luz* 6:11 (November 1977).

Pérez, Theresa. *Portraits of Mexican Americans: Pathfinders in the Mexican American Communities*. Carthage, Ill.: Good Apple, 1991.

Rebolledo, Tey Diana, ed. *Nuestras mujeres*. Albuquerque: El Norte Publications, 1992.

Telgen, Diane, and Jim Kamp, eds. *Notable Hispanic American Women*. Detroit: Gale Research, 1993.

Who's Who in America, 1980–1981, 41st ed., vol. 1. Chicago: Marquis Who's Who, 1980.

FRANCISCO JIMÉNEZ

(1943–   )

Mexican American Short Story Writer, Teacher, Administrator

Dr. Francisco Jiménez, associate vice-president for academic affairs of Santa Clara University, is an unassuming, gentle, soft-spoken man enveloped with the subtle aura of charisma. He directs and oversees university academic programs in women's studies, ethnic studies, and international studies as well as the Honors Program and the Center for Applied Ethics. He also administers a million-dollar Irvine Foundation grant to improve the university's ethnic and racial diversity. The successful teacher and administrator of today was once a shy youth who worked in California's fields as an undocumented immigrant and ran to hide when *migra* (Immigration and Naturalization Service, or INS) agents descended to make a sweep of the fields.

Francisco Jiménez was born at the height of World War II on 29 June 1943 in the small village of San Pedro Tlaquepaque, today virtually a suburb of Guadalajara, in the state of Jalisco, Mexico. When he was 4 years old his parents, María Hernández and Francisco Jiménez, brought the family across the border at Nogales to seek work in the United States. Unable to afford the cost of visas, they dug a hole under the wire fence and crawled through. Settling in Santa Maria, California, as their base, the Jiménezes joined the migrant stream, following the crops in the Central Valley from Santa Rosa to Bakersfield. From the time he was 6 years old Francisco worked in the fields with his parents and siblings.

Because of the family's semi-nomadic life-style, young Francisco's attendance at school was irregular. Not until the harvests were completed early in winter each year did he begin his classroom studies. Because of his poor understanding of English, Francisco was held back in the first grade; the language of the Jiménez home was Spanish. Despite his intelligence, he was even labeled mentally retarded. But he persisted, overcame the tremendous obstacles, and graduated from the Santa Maria schools. Just as he entered high school his father's illness forced the family to abandon the harvest circuit, and Francisco was able to attend the full school term from then on.

When Francisco was 15 years old, INS officers entered his junior high school classroom and arrested him as an illegal alien, to his intense em-

Francisco Jiménez. Photo courtesy of Francisco Jiménez.

barrassment. The entire Jiménez family was forced to depart for Mexico, but soon thereafter returned with proper documentation. And Francisco returned to the classroom. To help with family finances he also worked with his older brother Roberto for a commercial janitorial service company.

At Santa Maria high school Francisco was an outstanding student. Encouraged by his English teacher, Audrey Bell, and by his counselor, Robert Penny, he graduated in 1962 with three college scholarships and entered Santa Clara University in the fall. While attending Santa Clara he became an American citizen and achieved an enviable scholastic record, graduating in 1966 with honors in Spanish and receiving a prestigious Woodrow Wilson fellowship for graduate school. For his graduate studies he selected Columbia University in New York. Despite limited financial resources, he earned his M.A. in 1969 and his doctorate in Spanish and Latin American literature three years later.

While working on his Ph.D. Francisco Jiménez taught Spanish at Columbia, first as associate in Spanish, during 1971–1972, and then as an assistant professor of Spanish, 1972–1973. In September 1973 he began his work-filled career at Santa Clara University: assistant professor of modern languages, 1973–1977; associate professor, 1977–1981; full professor, 1981–   ; holder of the Sanfilippo Chair, 1986–   ; director, Division of Arts and Humanities, 1981–1990; associate vice-president for academic affairs, 1990–   . He has also made presentations and given lectures at a number of prominent universities. An impressive professional record! But there is more.

In 1973 Jiménez co-founded the *Bilingual Review* and two years later was named to the editorial board of the Bilingual Review Press, a position he still holds. Three years later in recognition of his knowledge in teacher education and his administrative skills he received an appointment to the California Commission on Teacher Credentialing from Governor "Jerry" Brown. He was reappointed for two additional terms and was twice elected chairman of the commission. In 1987 he was the only Democrat named by Republican governor George Deukmejian to the California Council for the Humanities, affiliated with the National Endowment for the Humanities. He was later elected vice-chairman. Meanwhile in 1981 he was nominated and elected to the Santa Clara University Board of Trustees as faculty representative, a position he held until 1987. In 1989 he was appointed to the Western Association of Schools and Colleges accreditation commission (WASC) and three years later was elected to its board of directors.

In addition to these many appointments and awards, which are indicative of his high level of ability and his hard work, Francisco Jiménez has been the recipient of prestigious honors and laurels too numerous to list here in their entirety. Because of his outstanding classroom teaching, he was given a Special Recognition Award for Faculty by the president of Santa Clara University in 1978, and two years later he was named Outstanding Young Man of America by the U.S. Junior Chamber of Commerce. In November 1986 the California legislature passed a special resolution congratulating him on ten years of outstanding leadership in the state credentialing commission.

In the field of Hispanic literature, Professor Jiménez is best known for his literary criticism and for his appealing semi-autobiographical short stories. His first short story originated in Audrey Bell's English class from an assignment to write an essay on a life experience. His stories come out of his childhood migrant agricultural worker experience; most successful are "Muerte Fria," 1972; and "Cajas de Cartón," 1973, entitled "The Circuit" in English. The latter won the *Arizona Quarterly's* annual award for Best Short Story of 1973 and was recently made into a one-act play. His short stories have frequently been reprinted in anthologies of American literature; "The Circuit" has had 27 reprintings. His many articles of literary criticism have appeared in various scholarly journals. As a founding editor of the *Bilingual Review* and editorial advisor on the

Bilingual Press/Editorial Bilingüe he has made important contributions to encouraging and developing Chicano literature.

Professor Jiménez is also the author, co-author, or editor of a number of books ranging from literary criticism such as *The Identification and Analysis of Chicano Literature*, 1979, and *Los episodios nacionales de Victoriano Salado Alvarez*, 1974, to collections of contemporary Latino writing such as *Hispanics in the United States: An Anthology of Creative Literature*, 1980, a text for college literature classes; and *Mosaico de la vida: Prosa chicana, cubana, y puertorriqueña*, 1981, for Spanish-language and culture classes. The second edition of his book, *Viva la lengua! A Contemporary Reader*, 1975, came out in 1987. His most recent publication is *Poverty and Social Justice: Critical Perspectives*, 1987, which resulted from Santa Clara University's Institute on Poverty and Conscience (which he directed during the previous year).

Stepping down from his vice-presidency in 1994, Jiménez devoted the following sabbatical year to the completion of a collection of semi-autobiographical short stories about children in migrant agricultural life. Early in May 1996 he signed a contract with the University of New Mexico Press to publish his manuscript with the title *The Circuit: Life of a Migrant Child*. Houghton Mifflin is also publishing some of his work as a children's book, tentatively entitled *La mariposa* ("The Butterfly"). He continues his long-time project of editing the correspondence of the 19th-century Mexican writer Victoriano Salado Alvarez.

Further Reading

"AMAE Honors Dr. Francisco Jiménez." *Semanario Azteca* 7:314 (3 November 1986).

Busico, Michalene. "Fields of Endeavor." *San Jose Mercury News* (18 April 1993): L1, L5.

Cassidy, Jack, et al., eds. *Follow the Wind*. New York: Scribners, 1987.

Dillon, Pat. "A Teacher with a Mission." *San Jose Mercury News* (7 October 1986).

Farrell, Harry. "How Francisco Jiménez Became the Pick of the Crop." *California Today* (19 October 1980).

Martínez, Julio A. *Chicano Scholars and Writers: A Bio-Bibliographical Directory*. Metuchen, N.J.: Scarecrow Press, 1979.

"Que triunfa como escritor y literato." *Tiempo Latino* 4:102 (17 December 1980): 3, 31.

RAÚL JULIA

(1940–1994)

Puerto Rican Actor

Picture a tall, dark, handsome man who has sex appeal along with an exuberant delight in acting and also has a charming, courtly, debonair, and somewhat daffy personality. Raúl Julia was all that and more. He rolled his expressive eyes with the same vigorous emotion that he rolled his R's. On stage and on screen he had what some see as a physical presence that cannot be learned or taught.

Raúl Rafael Carlos Julia Arcelay was the first child of Olga Arcelay and Raúl Julia, born on 9 March 1940 in San Juan, the capital of Puerto Rico. His father, after studying electrical engineering, opened a gas station, which he later converted into a restaurant specializing in fast foods, chicken, and pizza. His family was middle class and reasonably well off. Julia recalled that his mother from time to time took in poor children to live in their home.

Raúl was enrolled in a private grade school operated by English-speaking nuns. At age 5 he had the role of the Devil in a class play. He recalled that when he jumped on stage he "let go" and began rolling on the floor as if possessed by Satan himself. Surprised by these antics of an otherwise shy boy, his mother and the nuns thought he was having some sort of seizure. But young Raúl was simply acting. Suddenly he stood up and recited his lines letter-perfect. This early theatrical debut set his acting course for life; as a youth he participated in every stage production he could find.

During his high school years Raúl attended the prestigious San Ignacio de Loyola High School. Feeling pressure from his parents to study law, he claimed that he asked himself, "Are you going to do what you enjoy, which is theater, or are you going to go to law school?" After serious consideration he decided to pursue an acting career, and his parents were supportive. While attending college he continued to participate in various local amateur dramatic productions. He graduated from the University of Puerto Rico with a degree in liberal arts at the beginning of the 1960s.

During one of Julia's nightclub performances he met and impressed actor Orson Bean, who recommended that he go to New York City to study acting at the American Palace Theater. Just as Julia was about to leave for New York his youngest, 17-year-old brother was killed in an auto accident. This tragic disaster was devastating for Julia and his family, but he transformed his devastation and depression into a learning experience. The pain, sorrow, and guilt of this personal tragedy aided him in understanding literary tragedy and helped prepare the aspiring actor for future roles.

Julia left for New York in 1964 to live on the Upper West Side, rooming with a fellow actor. His parents continued to support him, particularly with financial assistance. After a few weeks in New York City he made his debut in Calderón's *Life Is a Dream*, a Spanish-language production, at the Astor Place Playhouse. For the next two years he played in Phoebe Brand's Theater on the Street; he performed in ghetto neighborhoods in works ranging from Chekhov to musicals, in both English and Spanish. The audiences were not easygoing, and on stage Julia sometimes suffered a deep sense of hurt and humiliation.

Offstage Julia went through some hard times when he and his roommate survived on chicken-back meals—four backs for 25 cents. Between acting jobs he supported himself by teaching Spanish, selling pens in grocery stores, and peddling *Life* magazine subscriptions door to door.

In 1967 Julia began an association with the New York Shakespeare Festival and a friendship with Joseph Papp, its producer and director. He played Macduff in the New York Shakespeare Festival's mobile unit production of *Macbeth*, the Spanish-language version. Over the years he appeared in more than a dozen productions for Papp, including *Othello, Titus Andronicus, As You Like It, The Taming of the Shrew, King Lear, Two Gentlemen of Verona*, and *The Cherry Orchard*.

Julia made his Broadway debut in 1968 in *The Cuban Thing*, a drama about Fidel Castro's revolution. This performance was pivotal in Julia's career, as it brought him to the attention of producers and directors. He soon began to receive employment offers and also became noticed by theater critics, who found him talented and versatile, rising above ethnic typecasting perceptions.

In 1971 Julia played supporting roles in Hollywood movies but remained active on the stage. During that year his Broadway portrayal of Proteus in *Two Gentlemen of Verona* brought Julia his first Tony nomination as best actor. The next year he played two different characters within the space of a few hours—Osric in *Hamlet* and Proteus in *Two Gentlemen of Verona*. In *Hamlet* he shared the stage with such prominent actors as Stacy Keach and James Earl Jones. In the summer of 1973 he took on lead roles in *As You Like It* and *King Lear*, playing at the outdoor Delacorte Theater. That same year he participated in three off-Broadway productions: *The Emperor of Late Night Radio, The Robber Bridegroom*, and *St. Clement's Church*. His second Tony nomination came that year for his role in the musical *Where's Charley?* In 1976 he received his third Tony nomination in six years for his MacHeath in *The Threepenny Opera*. Among his television appearances in the early 1970s was one year as Raphael, the Fixit Man on PBS's *Sesame Street*.

Julia was well known for taking good care of his health, especially his throat. For many years he carried a briefcase of Chinese herbs that he used to soothe his throat. In 1974 he became acquainted with EST, the cultist organization founded by Werner Erhard. He and Erhard became good friends, later traveling to India together to seek spiritual knowledge. After 1974 he devoted much attention to humanitarian concerns such as Erhard's Hunger Project, which aims to end world hunger by the year 2000.

In 1978 Julia joined a road company production of *Dracula* and was chosen to take over the lead role when Frank Langella left the cast in 1979. That year proved to be very hectic yet successful for Julia. He found himself commuting several times a week between New York and Washington, D.C., performing as Dracula at Washington's John F. Kennedy Center for the Performing Arts and as Petruchio with Meryl Streep as Kate in *The Taming of the Shrew* at New York's Delacorte Theater. That summer he finally got to play Othello; the *New Yorker* magazine raved about his outstanding performance.

Meanwhile Julia began to study arduously for his role as Jerry, the British literary agent in *Betrayal*. To master the British accent he hired a speech coach, and to create a reality that went beyond his lines he developed a full life biography for Jerry. This painstaking work before stepping on stage helps explain Julia's perfection in his craft. His fourth Tony nomination came in 1982 for his role as Guido Contini in the musical *Nine*, which received 12 Tony nominations and won 5.

Julia appeared in several films but went unnoticed by the public and by movie critics until he appeared as Kalibanos in Mazurky's *Tempest* in 1982. That same year he got his first starring movie roles, in the *Escape Artist* and Coppola's *One from the Heart*. After acting in several films produced by the Puerto Rican production company Zaga Films, in 1985 he co-starred in *Kiss of the Spider Woman*, which achieved both critical and commercial success. Since then Julia has appeared in numerous films: among others, *Compromising Positions* (1985), *The Morning After* (1986), *Tequila Sunrise* (1988), and *The Penitent* (1988). In 1988 he was nominated for a Golden Globe Award for his role in *Moon over Parador*. Julia's most renowned film role was as Archbishop Oscar Romero of El Salvador in *Romero*, released in 1989. Julia personally felt very strongly about Romero's humanitarian activity, for which he was murdered. Most critics agreed this was the finest performance of Julia's career.

Julia appeared in four movies released in 1990: *Presumed Innocent, Frankenstein Unbound, The Rookie* and *Havana*. In the summer of 1991 he filmed Camus's *The Plague*; in the fall *The Addams Family*, in which he played Gomez, had great commercial success. The following spring Julia was back on Broadway as Cervantes/Quixote in *Man of La Mancha*, following a successful five-month tour. A year later he rejoined Angelica Huston and Christopher Lloyd for an Addams sequel, *Addams Family Values*.

Julia was a staunch supporter of Hispanic cultural organizations such as Miriam Colón's Puerto Rican Traveling Theater; he also donated his time and his name to causes such as the fight against AIDS. By portraying different characters regardless of ethnicity he served as a positive role model for Hispanics. Both Nosotros and La Raza organizations honored him for portraying Hispanic culture positively. In October 1992 he received the first Global Citizen Award given by the Hunger Project. The New York Shakespeare Festival in June 1993 awarded him the fourth annual Susan Stein Shiva Award for his ongoing work in the theater.

In 1993 Raúl Julia's health began to fail as he started a losing battle against cancer. In early October 1994 he suffered a massive stroke, and on 24 October he died from complications of the stroke and cancer.

Further Reading

"Acting on Commitment." *Sojourners* 10:10 (1 November 1989): 27.

Current Biography 1995 [obit.] (New York: H. W. Wilson Co., 1995).

Mooney, Louise, ed., *Newsmakers '95*. Detroit: Gale Research, 1995.

"Raul Julia: One of the Busiest Actors in America." *Hispanic Business* 14:7 (1 July 1992): 48.

"Tribute." *People Weekly* 42:19 (7 November 1994): 127.

Vellela, Tony. "Raul Julia: An Interview." *Dramatics* 62:1 (1 September 1990): 12.

JOSÉ ARCADIO LIMÓN
(1908–1972)
Mexican American Choreographer, Concert Dancer, Dance Teacher

José Limón was simply the greatest American choreographer and male dancer of the 1940s, 1950s, and early 1960s. Unanimously described as one of the outstanding male dancers in the entire world, he was so far above any competitors as to rule out comparison. In his obituary the

New York Times described him as having a commanding stage presence, a sincerity and dignity, and a talent for stunning, gracefully lithe, animal-like movements. He also had, said the *Times*, an instinctive understanding of the fusion of dance, drama, and music. As a dancer he was an eagle, wrote a leading dance critic.

José Arcadio Limón was born on 12 January 1908 in Culiacán, the capital of the state of Sinaloa on Mexico's western coast, almost directly opposite the tip of Baja California. His parents, Francisca Traslavina and Florencio Limón, were middle class and artistically inclined, his father being a musician and orchestra director. José spent his early years in Culiacán and then was uprooted by Mexico's great revolution of 1910. In 1915, in the midst of the bitter struggle between Francisco (Pancho) Villa and General Venustiano Carranza to dominate the revolution in northern Mexico, the Limón family crossed the border into Arizona.

Subsequently José and his parents moved to Los Angeles, California, where he grew up and received his high school education. Undoubtedly influenced by parental attitudes, he developed an interest in painting and enrolled in the University of California at Los Angeles (UCLA) as an art major. After a brief period at UCLA he moved to New York in 1928 to study painting at the New York School of Design. He soon found that his interest in painting, which leaned toward the baroque and mystic (he found El Greco especially attractive), was at odds with contemporary trends that strongly favored the French modernists. Severely bewildered and distressed, he thought his career as an artist was finished. He quit art school, gave away his paints and brushes, and drifted aimlessly for a while.

Then friends introduced him to modern dance at a New York recital by Harold Kreutzberg, a leading German modernist, and he became as enthusiastic about dance as he had formerly been about painting. He immediately began taking classes, enrolling the next day in the well-known Doris Humphrey–Charles Weidman dance studio. Although his size (6 feet, 1 inch) and angularity of body worked against him in the dance, he proved an intense, dedicated, and eventually successful pupil. He had found what he wanted to do with his life.

In 1930 José Limón danced in the chorus of a modernized version of the Greek play *Lysistrata*, his first of various performances on Broadway during the 1930s, including parts in *As Thousands Cheer* and *Roberta*. He also performed concert duets with Doris Humphrey and other partners and began writing. In the spring of 1931 his first choreographed work was showcased, with the help of Humphrey.

In 1937 Limón's choreographic promise was recognized with a fellowship at the Bennington School of Dance in Vermont. While studying there he decided to specialize in concert dance, group performances with or without soloists. Always concerned about the dignity and manliness of male dancers, in his choreographing he made heavy use of the Mexican and Spanish dances he had witnessed as a child in Culiacán. Moreover, these Hispanic dances, especially the *jota*, suited his large frame and limited fluidity.

In 1939 Limón premiered his *Danzas mexicanas*. Then, with Martha Graham's protégé May O'Donnell, he toured the West Coast, where his Hispanic dances were extremely well received. Upon his return to New York in 1942 he became the featured dancer in the Humphrey company and soloed in his *Chaconne in D Minor*. In the spring of 1943 his performances at the Humphrey-Weidman studio won him lavish praise from dance critics.

In April 1943 World War II interrupted Limón's career. Although still a Mexican citizen he was inducted into the U.S. army and assigned to Special Services, where he spent his two years of military service organizing and directing shows. Occasionally he danced, but he did nothing of a serious nature while in the army. Meanwhile, with the break-up of the Humphrey-Weidman company toward the end of the war, he prepared for his future as a concert dancer by persuading Doris Humphrey to become artistic director of a tiny company he had organized. Her strong guidance until her death in the late 1950s established a pattern of brilliant successes for Limón's choreography.

At Bennington College in July 1946 Limón premiered Humphrey's *Lament for Ignacio Sánchez Mejías* based on a 1935 poem by the Spanish poet and dramatist Federico García Lorca. It was an immense success. In January 1947 Limón's company made its Broadway debut at the Belasco Theatre, repeating the *Lament*—again to critical acclaim.

Although Limón was at his artistic peak during this period, to support himself and his wife he found it necessary to teach at a number of universities and colleges: University of California, University of Pittsburgh, Temple University, Mills College, Bennington College, and Sarah Lawrence. In 1948 he secured a long-term appointment as a teacher and a summer home for his company at the Connecticut College School of Dance. He also taught at the Juilliard School of Music from 1953 until just before his death.

In 1950 Limón was invited by the Mexican government to return to Mexico to be director of an Academia Nacional de la Danza on a permanent basis with the purpose of reviving and modernizing dance there. He turned down the offer (he had become an American citizen in 1946 as a result of his war service), but for a while he returned to Mexico for several months each year to perform, teach, and choreograph.

In the 1950s and early 1960s Limón's dance company was selected four times to tour abroad in the State Department's cultural exchange program. In 1954 the troupe toured South America, in 1957 it made a five-month tour of Europe and the Near East, in 1960 it spent three months in Central and South America, and in 1963 it visited the Far East. At home Limón was a repeat guest at White House functions, at the invitation of presidents John F. Kennedy and Lyndon Johnson.

After 1960 José Limón seldom danced in public, devoting his time and energies to choreography and teaching. He did give one last performance in 1969, just three years before his death from cancer. Limón was the recipient of many honorary degrees and numerous awards and honors, for both his dancing and his choreography. Among his 69 outstanding works he is best remembered for *La Malinche*, 1949, *The Moor's Pavane*, 1949, and *Missa Brevis*, 1958. About a dozen of his works could be described as inspired by Mexican themes. Today there is a Limón-based dance company on both East and West coasts.

Further Reading

Candee, Marjorie Dent, ed. *Current Biography, 1953*. New York: H. W. Wilson Co., 1954.
"José Limón Dance Company." *Dance Magazine* 54 (May 1980).
Martínez, Al. *Rising Voices: Profiles of Hispano-American Lives*. New York: New American Library, 1974.
Moritz, Charles, ed. *Current Biography Yearbook, 1968*. New York: H. W. Wilson Co., 1968.
Obituary. *New York Times* (3 December 1972): 1, 85.
Sinott, Susan. *Extraordinary Hispanic Americans*. Chicago: Children's Press, 1991.
Who Was Who in America, vol. 5, 1969–1973. Chicago: Marquis Who's Who, 1973.

NANCY LÓPEZ

(1957–)

Mexican American Professional Golfer

Fewer than a dozen women have been inducted into the Ladies Professional Golf Association (LPGA) Hall of Fame. One of them is Nancy López. She is also one of only a handful of women golfers who have earned over a million dollars in prize money during their careers. The youngest woman ever to be installed in the LPGA Hall of Fame, she has been the winner in more than 130 tournaments. Partly because of her extraordinary golfing skills and partly because of her sunny disposition and warm personality she is very popular on the tournament circuit, usually followed by a large and admiring group of often vociferous youthful supporters sometimes referred to by sportswriters as "Nancy's Navy." Her charisma has been a factor in increased tournament attendance and in greater importance for women's golf and the LPGA.

Nancy Marie López was born on 6 January 1957 to Marina Griego and Domingo López in the city of Torrance, a large southern suburb of Los Angeles, California. Soon thereafter the López family—Nancy, her mother and father, and her considerably older sister, Delma—moved to Roswell in southeastern New Mexico, where her father established an automobile repair shop. Nancy grew up in Roswell, joined the Girl Scouts, and attended public schools there. In most respects she had a very normal, fairly traditional *mexicano* upbringing.

Both of Nancy's parents played golf, and her father was a considerably better than average golfer. Nancy tagged along with her parents when they played, usually on weekends, and her dad let the 8-year-old hit an occasional ball to keep her from being bored out of all patience. She showed remarkable strength and accuracy in hitting the ball. Soon her father cut down a four wood to help her hit the ball more easily and develop a more relaxed stance. She learned her golfing skills by carefully observing how her father and other good golfers played the game.

Nancy's childhood was that of a normal sports-oriented youth. She was an all-around athlete, playing basketball and touch football and participating in gymnastics, track, and swimming as well as golf. When it soon became apparent that she had a greater-than-average degree of natural golfing ability, her father took her in hand and began coaching her seriously. He was the only coach she ever had. He firmly believed in her potential and trained her specifically to achieve championship, but as a happy champion. She credits her father for her serene mental game that enables her to play calmly even when under heavy pressure.

By the time she was 9 years old Nancy won her first Pee Wee tournament, at age 11 she was consistently getting a lower score than her father, and at age 12 she won the Women's State Amateur tournament. By the time she entered high school she and her parents were serious about professional golfing as a career for Nancy. At Roswell's Godard High School she played on the otherwise all-male golf squad, in which she was the number one player. She led her fellow team members to the state championship and in her senior year came in second in the Women's Open. Despite her well-known golfing abilities she sometimes encountered mild forms of discrimination, particularly at exclusive country clubs. However, she recalls no traumatic incidents. To send Nancy to tournaments and to finance her other golf expenses her parents scrimped, saved, and did without new clothes and new household furnishings.

After completing high school Nancy accepted an athletic scholarship at the University of Tulsa in Oklahoma, where she enrolled as an engineering major. Later she was awarded a four-year Colgate Golf Scholarship for $10,000. Her walking away with amateur and intercollegiate titles and her membership on the Curtis Cup team won her awards in her sophomore year at the university as Most Valuable Player and Female Athlete of the Year. Because golf practice, traveling, and tournaments took up so much of her time, she had fallen behind in her class work by the end of her second year at Tulsa despite being tutored. At the end of her sophomore year she weighed her academic performance against her potential achievements on the golf course. After an impressive career as an amateur, at age 19 she made the reasoned decision to withdraw from the university and turn professional by joining the Ladies Professional Golf Association.

In her first three tournaments on the professional circuit, Nancy placed second. Then she hit her stride. In February 1978 at Sarasota, Florida, she won the Bent Tree Classic and went on to win five consecutive LPGA tournaments, including the LPGA title with a score of 275 for 72 holes. By the end of the year she had won purses totaling more than $200,000, far outdistancing all other women golfers and surpassing the earning record for women golfers set two years earlier. Commercials and endorsements of various golf-related products added very substantially to her tournament earnings. She was named Rookie of the Year and Player of the Year by the LPGA, and Female Athlete of the Year by the Associated Press. Always an intense and spirited competitor, in the following year Nancy López entered 22 tournaments and, in a tour de force, won 8 and placed among the top 10 scorers in 18 of them.

In 1982, after a short-lived earlier marriage, Nancy married professional baseball player Ray Knight. In the following year she took maternity leave to have her first child, a daughter who was given the name Ashley. Within two months of Ashley's birth Nancy was back on the circuit, taking the baby with her. By 1985 she was back on top of her game and once again dominated professional women's golf. It was her best year, at least financially, although she played fewer tournaments. She won five events, set a record low scoring average that gained her the Vare Trophy and earned nearly half a million dollars in prize money, more than any other player. Two years later, having won over 35 official tournaments, including two major titles, she was inducted into the LPGA Hall of Fame in Sugarland, Texas, the youngest woman ever to win that accolade. A few years later she was installed in the PGA World Golf Hall of Fame as well.

All this, of course, has been of great significance to Nancy López. On the golf course she is known to be sweet and smiling, but a determined and fierce competitor. She readily admits to being very ambitious and determined about the game. But her family is more important to her, she has stressed. In 1986 she again took maternity leave to give birth to a second daughter, Erinn, who was followed by Torri Heather two years later. Motherhood slowed down her golf game for several years, as did the weight she gained. However, in 1996 she lost 33 pounds and complemented her diet with a conditioning and exercising program. In mid-May 1996 she was a leading contender for the annual LPGA Championship but did not win it.

Nancy López is the author of two books relating to golf and to her role in the sport: *The Education of a Woman Golfer*, 1979, and *Nancy López's The Complete Golfer*, 1987.

Further Reading

Armijo, Lamberto. "Women in Sports." *La Luz* 8:4 (November 1979).

Barnes, Jill. "The Winning Formula of Nancy Lopez." *Vista* 2:12 (1 August 1987): 6–9.

Bartlett, Mike. "Nancy with the Laughing Face." *Golf Magazine* (June 1978).

Chacón, José. *Hispanic Notables in the United States of North America*. Albuquerque: Saguaro Publications, 1978.

Chavira, Ricardo. "Three to Cheer." *Nuestro* 1:5 (August 1977).

"Lighter Lopez Leading at LPGA Championship." *San Jose Mercury News* (12 May 1996): 2D.

López, Nancy, with Peter Schwed. *The Education of a Woman Golfer*. New York: Simon and Schuster, 1979.

Mooney, Louise, ed. *Newsmakers: The People behind Today's Headlines*. Detroit: Gale Research, 1989.

Moritz, Charles, ed. *Current Biography, 1978*. New York: H. W. Wilson Co., 1979.

Phillips, Betty Lou. *The Picture Story of Nancy López*. New York: J. Messner, 1980.

Purkey, Mike. "At Home with Nancy López." *Golf Magazine* 32:5 (1 May 1990): 86.

MARISOL (ESCOBAR)

(1930–   )

Venezuelan American Sculptor, Painter

Marisol Escobar has achieved great success in a field sown with land mines of taste and artistic viewpoints. Her early art was described by critics as new and refreshing in its perspective and as developing interaction with the viewer. Demonstrating expertise in whimsy and satire, her paintings and sculptures intrigued and engaged a delighted audience that saw in her pieces a sly criticism of American society and a sharp ridicule of its political life, as well as occasional undefinable feelings of menace. Her noteworthiness was increased by her close friendship with Andy Warhol, who gave her a prominent place in his films, and she was soon taken up by magazines such as *Glamour* and *Vogue*. By the early 1990s she had received the great accolade of an exhibition at the National Portrait Gallery.

Marisol Escobar was born of Venezuelan parentage in Paris, France, on 22 May 1930. Her parents, Josefina Hernández and Gustavo Escobar, extremely wealthy through real estate, spent most of their time traveling with their son and daughter in Venezuela, the United States, and the countries of continental Europe. As a result her early schooling took place in Paris and Venezuela. Her mother died in early 1941, during World War II. At the end of the war her father took the family to Los Angeles, California, where he settled down.

The 16-year-old Marisol continued her studies there in the private Westlake School for Girls and soon began the serious study of art at the Jepson School. Gifted with considerable artistic talent, she decided to become a painter and in a few years had mastered all she could learn from her West Coast instructors. Strongly supported by her father, at age 19 she left Los Angeles for Paris, France, where she undertook studies at the Académie des Beaux Arts. After completing her coursework there she returned to the United States and enrolled in the Art Students League in New York City.

In the first half of the 1950s, from 1951 to 1954, Marisol studied at the New School where the dominant art style at the time was impressionism. She became deeply immersed in the New York art scene and followed the impressionist style of her teachers and of many of her artist friends. However, increasingly her interest in impressionism declined. In 1953 she quit painting and, turning to pre-Columbian and Latin American folk art for themes, style, and materials, she began to fashion sculptures in wood, clay, and metal without any formal training in the art of sculpture.

In the second half of the 1950s Marisol, now using only her first name to give herself distinction, emerged as a sculptor, showing her carved wooden, molded terra cotta, and welded metal sculptures in group shows at several New York galleries. In November 1957 she had her first solo exhibition, at the Leo Castelli Gallery; her pieces were praised by critics for their originality and inventiveness. Her unusual sculptures did much to enliven the contemporary New York art scene. Nearly all her work excited critical acclaim, and she began to acquire a reputation for the imaginative use in her sculptural works of common, everyday materials, often used or recycled items. Although she was buoyed by her success, she soon felt that she needed to distance herself from it for a while so she took a long sabbatical in Rome. After a year of introspection she returned to New York, where she resumed and soon redoubled her artistic output.

In the early 1960s, as her artistic reputation grew, Marisol became increasingly involved with other artists and the New York art sphere. She was one of the artists invited to participate in the Art of Assemblage show at the New York Museum of Modern Art in 1961. In the following year one of her large groups, *The Family*, a part of her exhibit at the Stable Gallery, was bought by the Museum and another was purchased by the Albright-Knox Art Gallery of Buffalo, New York. Having "arrived" on the art scene, in the next year she was allocated a room of her own in the Museum's show entitled *Americans 1963*, and more of her works were purchased by other museums for their permanent collections.

During the early 1960s Marisol was extremely productive. Among the figures and group tableaus she created were *The Family, Tea for 3, The Kennedys*, and *The Generals*. Her reputation spread so widely that in 1967 she was commissioned by the *London Telegraph Sunday Magazine* to fashion satiric sculptures of the British prime minister and the royal family. To these figures she added President Lyndon B. Johnson, French president Charles de Gaulle, and Generalissimo Francisco Franco of Spain—all the figures reflecting a much more critical attitude than that shown in her tolerant and amiable spoofing of the Kennedy family seven years earlier. In the same year, commissioned by *Time* magazine, she created a 6-foot sculpture of Hugh Hefner, publisher of *Playboy*, the piece to be photographed for *Time*'s cover.

Like most Americans, Marisol was strongly affected by the Vietnam conflict and America's role in the fighting. Inevitably her increased politicization was expressed in her art, clearly shown in her works for the *London Telegraph*. Her feelings about the conflict were so deeply held that she spent much of the time during the Vietnam era traveling outside the United States, especially in Latin America. She took up scuba diving and underwater photography, both of which were reflected in her new artistic period of fish sculptures with human faces, often her own. Her fish sculptures received reviews that were polite but less enthusiastic than those that had greeted her earlier work.

Although as a teenager she had been critical of her parents' rather unusual life-style, Marisol soon began to show an extravagant and baroque side that helped create a somewhat offbeat, unconventional public personality. Earlier her extensive use of self-portraits and casts of her own body parts in her works had aroused some comment. Some saw it as narcissism or an unusual aspect of a search for identity. One critic made reference to her "eccentric indulgences" that approached "mere trickiness." Her appearance on a panel of artists wearing a stark white Japanese mask, eventually removed to reveal her face painted white to resemble the mask, helped develop the image of a somewhat bizarre persona. Her efforts to maintain some privacy through a reclusive and secretive attitude in face of the media also led to the growing legend of a somewhat Garboesque personage.

In the mid-1970s Marisol developed a deep interest in the works of other artists, especially painters, and became enthralled with the paintings of Leonardo da Vinci. Using some of his famous paintings as a basis for her own work, in 1978 she showed a relief sculpture entitled *Madonna and Child with St. Anne and St. John* and six years later unveiled *The Last Supper*, based on da Vinci's famous masterpiece. The latter drew high praise from most critics. During the early 1990s her works continued their sometimes gentle but always probing criticism of American politics and society.

Marisol's works have been shown in numerous national and international group exhibitions. In addition to the Modern Museum of Art, her works have been purchased for permanent collections by the Whitney Museum of American Art and other leading art museums as well as by many private art collectors. In 1991 Marisol received two very different tributes to her artistry and fame. In Washington, D.C., she had the great honor of exhibiting her sculptural works in the National Portrait Gallery, and in New York City her portrait appeared in the subways in an advertisement in English and Spanish in the drive against the spread of Acquired Immune Deficiency Syndrome (AIDS).

Further Reading

Berman, Avis. "A Bold and Incisive Way of Portraying Movers and Shakers." *Smithsonian* 14 (February 1984): 54–63.

Current Biography, 1968. New York: H. W. Wilson Co., 1968.

Glueck, Grace. "It's Not Pop, It's Not Op—It's Marisol." *New York Times Magazine* (7 March 1965): 34–37, 48, 50.

Telgen, Diane, and Jim Kamp, eds. *Notable Hispanic American Women.* Detroit: Gale Research, 1993.

Unterburger, Amy, ed. *Who's Who among Hispanic Americans.* Detroit: Gale Research, 1992.

Who's Who of American Women, 1968–1969. Chicago: Marquis Who's Who, 1968.

JOSÉ MARTÍ

(1853–1895)

Cuban (American) Journalist, Essayist, Poet, Playwright, Teacher, Revolutionary Leader

There are those, probably including José Martí himself, who would not consider Martí a Cuban American. However, as literary critic Professor Rodolfo J. Cortina has pointed out in an article titled "Cuban Literature of the United States: 1824–1959," published in *Recovering the U.S. Hispanic Literary Heritage* (1993), "It seems to me that if José Martí lived in New York for fifteen years, he was to an extent a Cuban writer, an exile writer, but also a Cuban American writer." **Dolores Prida**, a leading Cuban American playwright and poet, has advanced much the same view, declaring in a lecture given at Rutgers University in 1987: "I define Hispanic American . . . literature as that written by Hispanics living and working in the United States whose subject matter . . . reflects their expressions in this country." Martí certainly fits both these descriptions. He spent the last 15 years of his life in the United States—principally in New York City, where he wrote hundreds of essays and newspaper articles on life in the republic, warmly praising its virtues but also aware of its shortcomings. For a generation of Latin Americans he was *the* interpreter of the American experiment in democracy.

José Julián Martí y Pérez was born on 28 January 1853 in Havana, Cuba, one of eight children of immigrant Spanish parents. In the course of his early youth in Havana he came under the influence of a teacher who was highly critical of the Spanish government in Cuba and who encouraged José's protest activities. When he was only 16 years old, Martí published his first of many anti-administration tracts, as well as his first poem. While he continued to write and publish anti-Spanish articles he also began editing *La Patria Libre*. In October 1869 he was arrested for treason and sentenced to six years in prison. After three years in jail he was deported to Spain to complete his sentence in exile. Soon thereafter he enrolled in the University of Madrid to study law and continued to write denunciations of Spanish policy in Cuba. When the first Spanish republic was declared in 1873, he urged its leaders to grant Cuba independence.

Two years later, with law degree in hand, Martí left Spain to join family members in Mexico, where he obtained a job on one of Mexico

City's major newspapers. While in Mexico he married his Cuban fiancée. During 1877 and 1878 he taught in Guatemala; in mid-1878, as the result of a general amnesty, they were able to return to Cuba. However, Martí's anti-government activities soon got him into trouble and he was again jailed and then deported to Spain. After a few months he managed to escape into France and after a brief stay there left for the United States. He was to spend virtually the rest of his life (15 years, forming the bulk of his adult life and of his literary activity) in semi-voluntary exile in the United States.

On 3 January 1880 Martí stepped off a ship from Spain onto a Manhattan dock. In New York City he soon became the heart and organizing spirit of the exile groups struggling for Cuban independence. He also had to survive; after some difficult months he obtained employment partly through friendship with Charles Dana, an important figure in the world of American journalism. He was soon writing popular articles for Dana's *Sun*, a New York daily, and discussing more artistic topics in the magazine *The Hour*, both in English. Subsequently he also found employment as correspondent for a number of major newspapers throughout Hispanic America for whose readers he interpreted his new home. Through him they were able to understand better the principal literary, social, and political trends developing in the Colossus of the North.

Every aspect of American life was grist to the young Cuban's literary mill. One day he would write about the happy people enjoying a day at Coney Island; the next day he would describe his observations as one of the thousands attending the dedication of the Brooklyn Bridge; and then he would lament the death of the great American poet, essayist, and philosopher Ralph Waldo Emerson, with whose ideas he identified so completely. Walt Whitman, the great poet of the masses, the celebrator of freedom and democracy, was another of his heroes and models about whose death he wrote movingly. In addition, he discussed the writings of Whittier, Longfellow, Hawthorne, the Alcotts, and other lesser giants of 19th-century American literature, as well as the ideas of prominent political figures of the time and of the early days of the republic.

In his penetrating moral interpretation of the United States, Martí was not an indiscriminate lauder of things American. He was aware of the defects as well as the virtues of late 19th-century American society. Critical but not unsympathetic, he felt uncomfortable with some of the cruder, more materialistic aspects of American popular culture, but he praised the pervasive atmosphere of individual liberty. He wrote: "I am at last in a country where everyone appears to be his own master. One is able to breathe freely, to possess here freedom, [which is] the basis, emblem, and essence of life. Here one can feel proud of one's species." Martí understood and admired what was American as opposed to European, which he viewed as decadent. He saw that the United States with its Anglo-Saxon sources of Western civilization had something to offer to the Indo-Hispanic peoples of Latin America, and he envisioned an ultimate synthesis from which both might gain. He accepted "Our America" as including the United States, for better or worse.

Setting to one side his reputation as the hero of the revolution of 1895 that finally led to Cuban independence, José Martí is best known for his literary work. His reputation as a writer rests principally on his essays and extensive journalistic output while in the United States, as well as on his poetry and short stories. The three plays he wrote are considered lightweight, and his only novel, *Amistad funesta*, also written during his American exile period, has garnered little praise. On the other hand, his unaffectedly simple and touching poetry has long found laudatory critics, and he is credited with being a principal founder of the Modernism movement in Hispanic American poetry at the end of the 19th century. His most popular and undoubtedly best poems are contained in *Versos sencillos*, published in 1891. He was an immensely productive writer; the *Obras completas de Martí*, published in Havana between 1936 and 1949, number 74 volumes. His literary output has been exceeded only by the writings about him. To date there have been more than 200 book-length biographies of Martí.

On 31 January 1895 José Martí left the United States to take his place as one of the leaders of the independence uprising he had proclaimed in Cuba. Less than four months later, on 19 May, he was killed while observing a clash with Spanish forces, thereby becoming the only Latin American independence movement hero to die in battle. New York City remembers "The Martyr" with a large equestrian statue at the Avenue of the Americas entrance to Central Park.

Further Reading

Ardura, Ernesto. "José Martí: Latin America's U.S. Correspondent." *Américas* 32: 11–12 (1980): 38–42.

Baralt, Luis A., ed. *Martí on the U.S.A.* Carbondale: Southern Illinois University Press, 1966.

Delpar, Helen, ed. *Encyclopedia of Latin America*. New York: McGraw-Hill, 1974.

Foner, Philip S., ed. *Our America*. New York: Monthly Review Press, 1977.

Martí, José. *The America of José Martí: Selected Writings*, trans. Juan de Onís. New York: Noonday Press, 1953.

Ripoll, Carlos. *José Martí, the United States, and the Marxist Interpretation of Cuban History*. New Brunswick, N.J.: Transaction Books, 1984.

Antonio José Martínez

(1793–1867)

Mexican American Priest, Politician, Educator, Civic Leader

The Reverend Antonio José Martínez is still today, as he was during his lifetime, a controversial figure. In addition to experiencing Anglo prejudice while he lived, his historical image has been distorted by Willa Cather's classic novel, *Death Comes for the Archbishop*, in which he is cast as the villain, modeled on his least attractive qualities. His most recent biographer, Fray Angélico Chávez, conceding Martínez's egotism and overweening pride, still calls him New Mexico's major genius and its most prominent historical personage. Which he was.

Antonio José Martínez was born into an extensive, landed, and politically powerful family in the village of Abiquiú on the Rio Chama in north central New Mexico in January 1793, the eldest of six children of Antonio Severino Martín (as his father spelled the family name) and María del Carmen Santisteban. He received his early education from his parents and possibly from an occasional tutor. When he was 12 years old the family moved eastward to Taos, where he matured in an atmosphere of expanding family prestige and power. His daily routine as a lad included herding cattle and learning the rudiments of farming. In 1812 he was married to a young girl selected by his parents and also began to participate actively in the management of the family's ranches. The death of his young wife in childbirth the following year appears to have changed the course of his life.

In 1817, at age 24, he began to study for the priesthood at the Tridentine Seminary in Durango, where for the next five years he enjoyed an outstanding scholastic career. In February 1822 the young man with the eager mind and more than a little ambition was ordained to the priesthood, the first *nuevomexicano* to take the vows in nearly 100 years. Apparently in part because of his health he was sent back to New Mexico, serving at Tomé, Abiquiú, and Taos. In 1826 he was appointed rector of the parish at Taos, and there he remained for the rest of his life.

A staunch patriot of the recently independent Mexican republic, Father Martínez had great hopes for his homeland and his people and equally great ambitions for himself in both the church and the government. In keeping with new republican ideals he instituted a coeducational school in his rectory. In 1833 he expanded it to include a preparatory school for potential seminarians. His students became the *nuevomexicano* religious, political, and economic leaders for the next half-century. Twenty became priests. Martínez was also active in Mexican politics, serving as a deputy in the territorial legislature in 1830 and 1831.

Following the death of his father in 1827 Martínez inherited considerable property, which he increased through his astute management. He used this patrimony to help poor but able youths to continue their studies, to support various charities, and particularly to bring in the first printing press west of the Mississippi in 1838. All these activities served to ensure his role as premier leader of his people.

In 1837 Martínez was selected to serve in the new Departmental Council. During the late 1830s and early 1840s he became an important Mexican nationalist leader in the anti-American faction. Soon after his appointment as pastor at Taos, he began a long and serious study of civil law, both Spanish and Mexican. He was accused, although no proof exists, of encouraging the 1837 revolt against centralist Mexican control that led to the death of Governor Albino Pérez. Pérez's successor, Governor Manuel Armijo, accused him of being implicated in an uprising by Apache and Ute Indians in the following year. He is likewise accused, again without evidence, of involvement in the 1846 Taos conspiracy and the subsequent 1847 revolt in which the new American governor, Charles Bent, and others were killed.

Since the late 1830s Martínez had been warning the authorities of a potential threat from the Americans. His opposition did not completely end with the U.S. takeover in 1847. He did have expectations from American republican ideals and tried to make use of those aspects of the new government that he saw as being favorable to his people. He participated actively in the statehood convention that met after the Treaty of Guadalupe Hidalgo, and in 1849 he presided over a convention called to consider problems in government. He continued to be deeply involved in New Mexican politics during the 1850s, serving in the Legislative Council for three terms. In 1851 he was elected its president.

Father Martínez's quarrel with his new bishop, Jean Baptiste Lamy, an immigrant Frenchman, was compounded by his republican beliefs as well as his inordinate pride. He had strongly supported the termination of tithing by Mexican liberal legislation in the 1830s and was opposed to Lamy's reintroduction of the practice. He was especially irate at the bishop's orders that the sacraments be refused to those who failed to tithe. But more fundamental to the quarrel was Lamy's Jansenist and ethnic prejudices against the *nuevomexicano* clergy (even before he knew them) and his exclusive reliance on the French priests he recruited. The strong-willed bishop and the equally unyielding priest parried and fenced. Their prolonged struggle came to a climax in 1856 when Lamy appointed an anti-Mexican Spaniard to replace Martínez, who had declared his intent to retire in the proximate future because of poor health and his advanced age.

Disagreements between Lamy's appointee and Martínez soon led to the latter's assertion that he was still pastor, and he began using his private chapel as his parish church. Although warned by the bishop against this canonically unlawful practice, the Taos priest, who seems to have become mildly senile by this time, persisted and was suspended by Lamy. Sometime between 1858 and 1860, after further public admonitions that he ignored, Father Martínez was quietly excommunicated by the bishop. Convinced from his studies of canon law that Lamy had acted extralegally, Martínez continued his defiance of hierarchic control. He was supported by some *nuevomexicanos* (mostly his numerous relatives or close friends) and headed a schismatic (as Lamy called it) church until his death a decade later.

The intensifying issue of slavery aroused Father Martínez's concern, and during the Civil War he joined with a group of prominent *nuevomexicanos* who pledged support for President Abraham Lincoln's policies. But he left the political expression of those views to Santa Fe and Washington. Displaying the same concern for the plight of nomadic Indians that he had evinced two decades earlier in a report to the Mexican government, in 1865 he sent his views to the Doolittle Committee set up by the U.S. government, commenting that under the United States the Indians were, if anything, worse off than under Mexico.

On 27 July 1867 Antonio José Martínez, the intransigent old firebrand, succumbed to the ravages of age, dying quietly in his bed after receiving the last rites of the Catholic Church. More than 2,000 persons, *nuevomexicano* and Anglo, attended his funeral in Taos. Within a year nearly all his followers had become reconciled to the ecclesiastic authorities.

Further Reading

Bernard, Jacqueline. *Voices from the Southwest*. New York: Scholastic Book Services, 1972.

Chávez, Fray Angélico. *But Time and Chance: The Story of Padre Martínez of Taos, 1793–1867*. Santa Fe, N.M.: Sunstone Press, 1981.

Francis, E. K. "Padre Martínez: A New Mexican Myth." *New Mexico Historical Review* 31:4 (October 1956): 265–289.

Perrigo, Lynn I. *Hispanos: Historic Leaders in New Mexico*. Santa Fe, N.M.: Sunstone Press, 1985.

Romero, Cecil V. "Apologia of Presbyter Antonio J. Martínez." *New Mexico Historical Review* 3 (1928).

Sánchez, Pedro. *Memories of Antonio José Martínez*. Santa Fe, N.M.: Rydal Press, 1978.

Vigil, Maurilio E. *Los Patrones: Profiles of Hispanic Political Leaders in New Mexico History.* Washington, D.C.: University Press of America, 1980.

Vigil, Ralph H. "Willa Cather and Historical Reality." *New Mexico Historical Review* 50:2 (April 1975): 123–138.

VILMA SOCORRO MARTÍNEZ

(1944–)

Mexican American Attorney, Civil Rights Activist

Most of Vilma Martínez's adult life has been spent contending against discriminatory treatment and working for civil rights. She has served actively on a dozen or more influential boards, commissions, and committees. In 1976 she was appointed a member of the University of California Board of Regents and eight years later was elected chairman of the board for a two-year term. She served until 1990. From 1980 to 1989 she also was on the board of the Southwest Voter Registration and Education Project (SVREP) and in 1984 was appointed to the board of the Edward W. Hazen Foundation, concerned with educational opportunity for minorities and the disadvantaged. In 1985 she accepted appointment to the board of the Tomás Rivera Center at Claremont Graduate School. Among her numerous honors are the Jefferson Award from the American Institute for Public Service in 1976, the University Medal of Excellence from Columbia University in 1978, the Lex Award from the Mexican American Bar Association in 1983, and a Distinguished Alumnus Award from the University of Texas in 1988.

Vilma Socorro Martínez was born on 17 October 1944 in San Antonio, Texas, the oldest of five children born to Marina Piña and Salvador Martínez. As a small child she was raised partly by her grandmother, who taught her to read and write in Spanish at an early age. Although she grew up in a lower middle-class integrated neighborhood, she spoke only Spanish when she entered the first grade; but since she could already both read and write Spanish, she had relatively little difficulty learning English. She excelled in school and enjoyed it. She also enjoyed reading—especially biographies, which provided her with admirable, if sometimes inapplicable, male role models.

Although Vilma was an officer in the National Honor Society, her junior high school counselor urged her to go on to a vocational or tech-

Vilma Socorro Martínez. Photo courtesy of Vilma Martínez.

nical high school because she was Mexican American. However, in spite of this discouraging stereotyping and the prejudiced attitude it represented, she firmly resisted efforts to counsel her away from an academic career. While still in high school she worked one summer for Alonso Perales, a friend of her father and a well-known lawyer, author, and civil rights activist who had served as a diplomat in Latin America and as advisor to President Franklin D. Roosevelt. He became her hero and role model, and she decided that she too would become a lawyer. When her counselor would not help her apply for admission to college, she did it entirely on her own.

In 1961 Vilma graduated from Jefferson High School with a small scholarship that she had obtained for the University of Texas at Austin. When she announced to her parents her decision to go on to college, her mother was supportive and encouraging but her father was less certain that she would be able to persevere. To help finance her undergraduate education she got a student job working for the university. With her father's misgivings as a goad she worked extra hard, completing four years of college in less than three. In 1964 she graduated with a B.A. in political science as preparation for law school.

Feeling discriminated against in Texas both as a Mexican American and as a woman, Vilma decided, on the advice of a professor, to go east to Columbia University for her legal training. Although she found the atmosphere at Columbia less restrictive than in Texas, she also found it was not entirely devoid of prejudice, particularly against a woman who wanted to become a lawyer. With the help of scholarships she obtained her Bachelor in Laws degree in 1967 and then passed her New York state bar exams.

Interested in using her legal education to help others, as she had seen Alonso Perales do, Vilma Martínez (now married to Stuart Singer) took a position as staff attorney with the National Association for the Advancement of Colored People (NAACP) Legal Defense Fund. While working for the Legal Defense Fund she helped organize the Mexican American Legal Defense and Educational Fund (MALDEF) and acted as liaison between the two organizations. After three years with the NAACP she went to work in 1970 as a counselor for the New York State Division of Human Rights, Equal Employment Opportunity Council, and then for the major Wall Street firm of Cahill, Gordon & Reindel as a litigation associate.

Vilma Martínez had been a member of MALDEF since its inception in the late 1960s; in September 1973 she was selected to be president and chief legal counsel of this premier Chicano civil rights organization. As president her principal goals were to broaden and make more secure MALDEF's funding base, to train civil rights litigators, and to secure for Mexican Americans greater access to education, employment, and political power. During the nine years of her presidency, 1973–1982, MALDEF's budget rose from less than $1 million to more than $2.5 million. Programs that she inaugurated such as the Education Litigation Project, the Chicana Rights Project, the Employment Litigation Project, and an intern training program produced skilled civil rights litigators. Carefully selected court cases whittled away at adverse legal precedent in areas such as bilingual education, exclusion of undocumented children from schools in Texas, and at-large elections. One of the areas of great success for Martínez was in bringing Mexican Americans under the protective umbrella of the Voting Rights Act.

By the time Martínez left MALDEF's presidency in 1982, she had put her imprint deep upon that organization. In September 1982 she became a partner in Munger, Tolles, & Olson, a large private law firm in Los Angeles. She has given lectures at a number of top-flight law schools and is a sought-after speaker for academic and business groups. Although she is now in private practice, her lifelong activism in community affairs and public service enables her to continue her efforts to provide greater opportunities for minorities. She returned to MALDEF at the beginning of the 1990s as a member of its board of directors. In mid-1994 she was rumored to be on President Bill Clinton's short list for appointment to the U.S. Supreme Court, but she was not selected. She continues to have three important public concerns: equality before the law, access to education, and elimination of continuing discriminatory practices.

Further Reading

"An Angeleno on the Short List." *Los Angeles Times* 113 (6 May 1994): B6.
Benavides, Max. "Vilma Martínez, Pulling No Punches." *Forum* (March 1982).
Evangelista, Mario. "Advocate for La Raza." *Nuestro* 1:7 (October 1977): 38–40.
Hernández, Al Carlos. "Vilma Martínez, una chicana ejemplar." *Nuestro* 5:6 (September 1981).
Johnson, Dean. "Chair of the Board." *Nuestro* 9:7 (September 1985): 34–36.
Lichtenstein, Grace. "Chicana with a Backbone of Steel." *Quest* (February–March 1980).
Loper, Mary Lou. "Motherhood for Two Career Women." *Los Angeles Times* (13 May 1984).
Morey, Janet, and Wendy Dunn. *Famous Mexican Americans*. New York: E. P. Dutton, 1989.
O'Connor, Karen, and Lee Epstein. "A Legal Voice for the Chicano Community." In *The Mexican American Experience*, Rodolfo O. de la Garza, et al., eds. Austin: University of Texas Press, 1985.

JORGE MAS CANOSA

(1939–)

Cuban American Businessman, Politician

By all accounts Jorge Mas Canosa is the most politically influential Cuban American today, although he has never been elected to any government office. Most of his power derives from the Cuban American National Foundation (CANF), a well-financed conservative political action organization of which he was the principal founder in 1980 and remains chairman of the board. A charismatic and controversial figure, in Washington he can be the amiable if overly intense and persistent lobbyist; but in Miami he is more likely to act like the typical domineering, autocratic Latin American *caudillo* who brooks no opposition. Although well acquainted with the subtleties of American politics, he often seems to prefer what some observers describe as the Cuban way:

personal hostility, vindictive adversarial attacks, and organized vendet-
tas—all exemplified in his long feud with the *Miami Herald*, which he
has accused of harassing him and being the voice of communism. He
once challenged to a duel a Dade County commissioner who opposed a
$130 million real estate deal of his; the latter defused the worrisome
situation by selecting water pistols as weapons.

Jorge Mas Canosa was born on 21 September 1939 to Carmen and
Ramón Mas in Santiago de Cuba, the island's second-largest city, located
on its eastern coast. His father was a Cuban army veterinarian. Jorge
grew up in Santiago, where he attended primary and secondary school
and then studied for two years at the University of Oriente and for two
years at Presbyterian Junior College. He capped his educational career
with four years at the Instituto Santiago de Cuba.

After the revolution led by Fidel Castro overthrew the dictator Fulgencio Batista and took over the government, Mas Canosa fled Cuba in
1960 and ended up as an exile in Miami, Florida. A penniless refugee,
he obtained a job as a stevedore and lived in a one-bedroom flat with
nearly a dozen other Cubans. When the Central Intelligence Agency began recruiting young Cubans for the U.S.–sponsored Bay of Pigs invasion, he joined the approximately 2,000-man volunteer force. He was one
of the lucky few who were uninjured in the April 1961 Playa Girón
landing and who did not wind up in a Cuban jail. Like others in the
failed invasion he then enlisted in the U.S. army, where he served as a
second lieutenant. Returning to Miami after his service, he found employment as a shoe salesman and later worked as a milkman.

Mas Canosa's opportunity came at the end of the 1960s when he went
to work for a small, struggling construction firm. After having learned
the construction business, he was later able to buy the company from
the discouraged owner with a small loan from a bank. As owner and
president of Church and Tower of Florida, Inc., his hard work and aggressive management quickly paid off; by the mid-1970s the company
had 400 employees and a gross income of $20 million a year. A decade
later his efforts led to an associate directorship in Latin Builders and his
membership in the Industrial Association of Dade County. Today
Church and Tower, enjoying construction contracts with Dade County
and Southern Bell, has brought Mas a fortune he has estimated at more
than $9 million and has enabled him to finance an active role in conser-
vative American politics.

In 1982 Mas became an American citizen and quickly stepped up his
political activities. Two years earlier he had founded, with some other
conservative Cuban American businessmen, an organization that they
named the Cuban American National Foundation. Its initial objective
was to support the presidential candidacy of Republican Ronald Reagan,
but it soon developed a broad political agenda that had as its prime

objective the overthrow of the Castro dictatorship. CANF and Mas pursue their common goal by contributing funds to help elect congressmen in both parties who will vote in favor of legislation they advocate. Their largest successes were the Cuban Democracy Act of 1992, signed by President George Bush while Mas looked on, and the creation of Radio Martí and TV Martí.

Radio and TV Martí were the brainchildren of Jorge Mas. In the mid-1970s he began to develop the idea of a U.S.–based radio station that would beam uncensored news to listeners in Cuba. After winning the support of Florida congressman Claude Pepper early on, he spent time and money writing to senators and representatives and roaming the halls of the U.S. Congress buttonholing anyone who would listen to his ideas. When Ronald Reagan took over the presidency in 1981, Mas got the payback for his support in the elections; Reagan created a commission to study the idea and named Mas as one of its members. On 20 May 1985, the anniversary of Cuban independence, Radio Martí went on the air.

With Radio Martí in operation it was perhaps natural for Mas Canosa to turn his attention to television. He broached the idea as early as 1987, obtained federal funds for a feasibility study, and used the CANF and its very effective lobbying arm, the Cuban American Foundation, to promote the idea. His position on the Advisory Board of Radio Martí gave Mas additional leverage. Amid a good deal of controversy and concern about its effectiveness, TV Martí began transmitting in late March 1990. Mas was appointed chairman of the Presidential Advisory Board on Broadcasting to Cuba, the agency that oversees both Radio and TV Martí. Soon charges that he was using his position to further his own political ambitions were being heard. He was accused of systematically interfering with the operation of Radio and TV Martí, of slanting news coverage, and of influencing personnel decisions for his own ends. Looking into charges of alleged abuse, mismanagement, and fraud, a federal investigation in the inspector general's office of the U.S. Information Agency found in mid-1995 that he had meddled in the daily operations.

Although Mas Canosa has widespread support in the community, not all Cuban Americans support him and his cause. His motives in his fierce anti-communist crusade are suspect to some moderates, who question whether his efforts are intended to help all Cubans or to further his own political future. They have misgivings about the motivation of the autocratic power broker and fear that ultimately he hopes to succeed Castro—something he has not completely ruled out. Some of his followers have taken to addressing him as Señor Presidente as he strolls about Miami's Little Havana neighborhood. The fact that anyone who dares question Mas, his motives, or CANF runs the very real risk of becoming the object of his explosive temper and persistent persecution has tended to muffle opposition. Today Mas rides in a bulletproof Mercedes-Benz and employs bodyguards because, he says, he fears assassination at the hands of Fidel Castro.

In addition to the presidency of his first company, Church and Tower, Mas is president of M. P. Equipment Rentals, chairman of the board of Neff Machinery, and president of the Mas Group. He has served in the Industrial Association of Dade County, Latin Builders (associate director), the Latin Chamber of Commerce, and the Hispanic American Builders Association (director). He has also been active in civic groups such as the YMCA International José Martí, United Way of Dade County, and the Latin Chamber of Commerce. Among the honors he has received are the Lincoln-Martí Award from the U.S. Department of Health, Education, and Welfare, and an honorary doctorate from Mercy College in Dobbs Ferry, New York.

Further Reading

Bender, Lynn Darrell. "The Cuban Exiles: An Analytical Sketch." *Journal of Latin American Studies* 5:2 (1973): 271–278.

"Cuban American Lobby Grows in Influence." *Congressional Quarterly Weekly Researcher* (23 June 1990).

Forment, Carlos A. "Political Practice and the Rise of an Ethnic Enclave." *Theory and Society* (1 January 1989): 47–81.

Greenhouse, Steven. "Top Cuban-American Misuses U.S. Broadcast, Officials Say." *New York Times* 144 (23 July 1995): 4(N), 10(L).

"Jorge Mas Responds to Critics." *Broadcasting* (16 April 1990): 67–69.

Olson, James S., and Judith E. Olson. *Cuban Americans: From Trauma to Triumph*. New York: Twayne Publishers, 1995.

Palmer, Elizabeth A. "Exiles Talk of PACs and Power, Not Another Bay of Pigs." *Congressional Quarterly* (23 June 1990): 1929–1933.

Rohter, Larry. "A Rising Cuban American Leader: Statesman to Some, Bully to Others." *New York Times* 142 (29 October 1992): A8(N), A18(L).

Sleek, Scott. "Mr. Mas Goes to Washington." *Common Cause Magazine* 17 (January/February 1991): 37–41.

Harold Medina

(1888–1990)

Mexican American Federal Judge, Legal Scholar, Author, Teacher

"Harold Medina, U.S. Judge, Dies at 102," said the headline in the *New York Times* on Friday, 16 March 1990. At the time of his death he was the oldest federal judge in the United States and the oldest Princeton University alumnus. But a long life was not Medina's claim to fame. That long life had been dedicated to the law. In 1949 he was a central figure in the nine-month trial of 11 American communist leaders for conspiracy to teach and advocate the overthrow of the U.S. government by force. As the trial judge he was subjected to frequent name-calling, insults, and threats of bodily harm. The trial and his daily abuse both exhausted and exhilarated him. It also made his name a household word.

Harold Medina was born on 16 February 1888, the son of a Dutch American mother, Elizabeth Fash, and a Mexican American father, Joaquín A. Medina. His mother was from a New Jersey family that had come to America early in the colonial period. His father had come to the United States from Yucatán as a 12-year-old fleeing from a long, bitter civil and racial war that kept the peninsula in turmoil and chaos throughout most of the second half of the 19th century. His father started an import-export business in which Harold became, much later, a vice-president and director.

Harold Medina grew up in Brooklyn and attended Public School 44, where, he later averred, anybody named Harold had to be tough. After P.S. 44 he went to a private military academy and preparatory school. He then enrolled at Princeton University, majored in French, graduated Phi Beta Kappa in 1909, and was offered a job teaching in the Princeton University modern language department. However, he did not accept the position; instead he entered law school at Columbia University. In 1912 he graduated from Columbia, winner of the prestigious Ordronaux Prize for the third-year law student with the best scholastic record. He had gotten all A's, except for a single B.

On leaving law school Medina took a job as a clerk in the firm of Davies, Auerbach, & Cornell, having passed his New York bar examination before graduation. To supplement his $8 a week salary he began teaching a six-week coaching course to prepare law school graduates for the state bar exam. During the next three decades he "prepped" nearly 40,000 law students with a high rate of success. In 1915 he also began a long career teaching at Columbia Law School, first as lecturer in law, then as associate in law, and finally as associate professor of law, 1925–1947. In 1918 he joined with a colleague to begin his own law firm specializing in appeals; in the 1930s he devoted more time to original trial work.

During World War II Harold Medina first came to public notice when he was appointed by the court to defend Anthony Cramer, who was charged with treason for befriending two German spies. In this position Medina was reviled and spat upon as a Nazi sympathizer; even his mother scolded him. In the lower courts he lost the case—his first loss in 14 years—but then appealed it to the U.S. Supreme Court. In this first treason case to come before it, the Supreme Court reversed Cramer's conviction and dismissed the indictment.

On 1 July 1947 Medina was appointed by President Harry Truman as judge in the U.S. District Court for southern New York. He gave up a lucrative private practice, about $100,000 a year, to accept the appointment at $15,000 per year, saying, "I've made plenty of money. Now I'd like to do something for my country."

Eighteen months later the luck of the draw assigned Medina to preside over the trial of 11 members of the national committee of the American Communist Party charged with conspiracy under the Smith Act. It took eight weeks between January and mid-March 1949 just to impanel the jury. The rowdy and sensationalized trial itself took another 26 weeks and, after five million words of testimony, ended in the conviction of all 11. The five defense lawyers were also convicted of contempt of court by Judge Medina for their abusive, intimidating, and obstructive conduct. Both convictions were upheld by the U.S. Supreme Court. Although the dissenting justices chided Medina for the contempt of court convictions, most people felt he had comported himself with rare patience, great courage, and a deeply felt sense of the dignity of the law. To many he embodied the finest spirit of American jurisprudence. To his considerable discomfort and occasional embarrassment, he found that the trial had made him the darling of the anti-communist extreme right.

In 1951 Judge Medina succeeded his mentor, Judge Learned Hand, on the U.S. Court of Appeals for the Second Circuit and took up Hand's crusade as champion of First Amendment rights, a matter of deep concern to him, especially as it was related to the press. In the 1960s and 1970s he traveled extensively throughout the United States speaking out fervently against attacks on the First Amendment. In 1958 he "retired" from the circuit court to the position of senior judge, and in 1980, at age 92, he finally stepped down from the bench. Many of the opinions he handed down as a senior judge broke new ground in arbitration and legal procedures, establishing legal precedents. He died in his sleep at Westwood, New Jersey, on 14 March 1990.

In addition to being one of the outstanding jurists of this century, Judge Medina was an author of note. In addition to his many articles in law reviews, between 1922 and 1959 he wrote more than a dozen books on jurisprudence and the American legal system. In the 1950s he wrote in a more personal vein about the law. *Judge Medina Speaks Out*, 1954, and *Anatomy of Freedom*, 1959, combined his deep concern for free speech rights and freedom of the press with his personal involvement in the issues. He not only wrote, he also read. His 15,000-volume library of French, Latin, and Greek literature, which he read in the original, was testimony to his abiding interest in language.

Throughout his long life Harold Medina was the recipient of awards and honors too numerous to list. He was awarded 25 honorary degrees by universities and colleges and was honored by Columbia University Law School by the establishment of a new chair, the Harold R. Medina Professorship. Among the many organizations that singled him out for gold medals and distinguished service awards were the Freedom Foundation, Veterans of Foreign Wars, Federal Bar Association, National Society of Colonial Dames, National Education Association, New York Board of Trade, and Ohio Newspaper Association. He was prominent on numerous commissions and committees, was a fellow of the American Academy of Arts and Sciences, and was a member (sometimes officer) of various professional associations. On the occasion of his 90th birthday in 1978, the *Brooklyn Law Review* dedicated its annual Second Circuit Review to Judge Harold Medina.

Further Reading

American Bench: Judges of the Nation. Minneapolis: Reginald Bishop Forster & Associates, 1979.

Hawthorne, Daniel. *Judge Medina: A Biography*. New York: W. Funk, 1952.

Martínez, Al. *Rising Voices: Profiles of Hispano-American Lives*. New York: New American Library, 1974.

Moore, Leonard P., "Dedication to Judge Harold R. Medina on the Occasion of His Ninetieth Birthday." *Brooklyn Law Review* 44:4 (1978): xiii–xiv.

New Yorker 24:16 (29 January 1949): 16–17.

Rothe, Anne, ed. *Current Biography Yearbook, 1949*. New York: H. W. Wilson Co., 1950.

Who's Who in American Law, 2nd ed. Chicago: Marquis Who's Who, 1979.

LYDIA MENDOZA

(1916–   )

Mexican American Singer, Songwriter, Musician

Lydia Mendoza has long been known as the "Lark of the Border." Her career extended from the early 1930s to the late 1980s—more than 50 years, a remarkable achievement for any musician. When she was 18 years old she recorded "Mal Hombre," which became her "signature" song and has remained her most popular record. As the number one interpreter of border, particularly *tejano*, music, she was responsible more than anyone else for making this music known all over the Southwest and in Latin America. Her name became known all over Spanish-speaking America, an instrumentalist and singer with an international reputation, an institution. She has recorded more than 1,200 songs. And she does not read a note!

Lydia Mendoza was born in 1916 in Houston, Texas, the second child of Leonor Zamarripa Reyna and Francisco Mendoza, both from the central Mexican state of San Luis Potosí. During the early, uncertain days of the revolution of 1910 both the Mendoza family and the Zamarripa family had moved to the large northern city of Monterrey in Nuevo León, where her parents met and married. Soon after their marriage they crossed over the border into Texas because of continuing revolutionary turmoil and violence. After several years in Texas the family returned to Monterrey, but in 1920 again returned to the United States. Lydia's father worked as a railroad mechanic and for Cervecería Cuauhtémoc in Monterrey and was a bit of a vagrant spirit. In 1924 he again took the family back to Monterrey, where the Mendozas remained until 1927 when they again moved across the border into Texas. This time Lydia's mother made a definite family commitment to remain in the United States.

As one result of the constant moving and of her father's objections to educating girls, Lydia and her older sister did not attend school although both parents had at least a modest education. Lydia could neither speak nor write English. Her mother wanted to send the children to school but her father objected, seeing no reason to educate girls. A heavy drinker who was always argumentative and became ill-tempered and mean when intoxicated, her father argued that he had not gone to school, so why should they? Lydia received some education from her mother and was exposed to music.

By the time Lydia was 12 years old she had learned to play the guitar and mandolin and was studying the violin. When her father left his railroad job, the Mendoza family, led by her dauntless mother, began to do the only thing its members knew how: to play and sing. They toured the Mexican barrios in the lower Rio Grande valley, playing on street-corners, in front of shops and cantinas, and in restaurants, earning what-ever people were willing to give them. Lydia played the mandolin, her mother played the guitar and sang, her father shook the tambourine, and her younger sister Francisca beat time on the triangle. They played and sang in a simple, self-taught rural style that their campesino audiences found highly enjoyable.

In 1928 Lydia's father responded to an Okeh Phonograph Corporation advertisement in San Antonio for Mexican singers, leading to a contract to record 20 songs for which they were paid $140 plus expenses. They were known as the Cuarteto Carta Blanca, named by her father after the Cuauhtémoc beer. Soon thereafter, hearing that musicians could make good money in the North, he signed up the family with a labor contrac-tor to work in the Michigan sugar beet fields. Unused to strenuous field work, the Mendozas soon were back at the music game in Pontiac and, later, Detroit. Then came the Depression, and in 1930 the Mendozas re-turned to Texas, living at first on the outskirts of Austin.

Lydia's father wanted to go back to Mexico, but her mother and the older children refused to go. Her father finally decided to stay but re-fused or was unable to work for the rest of his life. Times were hard; sometimes they were evicted for nonpayment of rent, and often they were forced to accept relief to survive. In 1932 the family settled in San Antonio. Here, in addition to playing in year-around tent shows called *carpas*, they continued to play for tips in restaurants, cafés, and bars during the day and in the evening at the produce market, Plaza de Za-cate, where the musical groups-for-hire gathered every day.

At the Plaza de Zacate Lydia for the first time began singing solo. A local Spanish-language radio announcer heard her and persuaded her to enter his amateur contest on radio. She won first prize and soon began to sing regularly on radio; as a result she became widely known in the south Texas border region by 1934. From there it was only a short step to a contract with Blue Bird Record Company, for whom she made about 100 records between 1934 and 1939. At the same time, as a member of the family quartet she continued extensive tours of the Southwest, some-times encountering racial discrimination in motels and restaurants.

During the World War II years of the early 1940s, gasoline rationing and the drafting of Lydia's brother and her husband brought an end to most of the family touring. Lydia, now married and a mother, went into retirement and was on her way to becoming a dim, legendary figure by the war's end. Many of her ardent fans, confusing her with a younger sister, thought she had died. In 1947 the family returned to touring, now with a new variety-comedy format. During the late 1940s and early 1950s the Mendozas toured all over the United States, and Lydia was persuaded by a California empresario to reactivate her career.

During the 1950s and 1960s Lydia recorded extensively for Aguila, Alamo, Azteca, Columbia of Mexico, Corona, Falcon, Ideal, RCA Victor of Mexico, and many other record companies. She played and sang a wide variety of music, including corridos, canciones, rancheras, polkas, waltzes, boleros, tangos, and schottisches. Many of the songs she had learned from her mother; others she had picked up as a child from gum wrappers. She also wrote some herself. She continued to take part in family tours of Mexico and the Southwest, especially California, until her mother's death in 1952 when the group broke up. After her mother died she performed solo, accompanying herself on guitar.

In the 1970s Lydia Mendoza began a third musical career as her extensive knowledge of folk music began to be recognized. In 1971 she was invited to appear in the Smithsonian Festival of American Folklife at the World's Fair in Montreal, Canada. Five years later she was featured in *Chulas Fronteras*, a border music film that has become a classic. In January 1977 she was a featured participant at the American Folk Life Center, where she played guitar and sang for the Library of Congress Ethnic Recordings in America conference. In the following year she sang at the John F. Kennedy Center in Washington, D.C., for President Jimmy Carter.

Because of her outstanding contributions to the folk heritage of the United States, in 1982 Lydia Mendoza was one of the first people to be given a National Heritage Fellowship by the National Endowment for the Arts. During the 1980s she performed at numerous folk music festivals and made several tours of Latin America. In 1984 she was inducted into the Tejano Music Hall of Fame and in the following year into the Texas Women's Hall of Fame. In 1991 she was inducted into the Conjunto Music Hall of Fame.

Further Reading

Cavazos, David. "Entrevista con Lydia Mendoza." *Tejidos* 4:4 (Winter 1977).

Gil, Carlos B. "Lydia Mendoza: Houstonian and First Lady of Mexican American Song." *Houston Review* 3:2 (Summer 1981): 250–260.

Miller, Dale. "Lydia Mendoza: The Lark of the Border." *Guitar Player* 22:8 (August 1988): 38–41.

Strachwitz, Chris, and James Nicolopulos. *Lydia Mendoza: A Family Autobiography*. Houston: Arte Público Press, 1993.

Telgen, Diane, and Jim Kamp, eds. *Notable Hispanic American Women*. Detroit: Gale Research, 1993.

NICHOLASA MOHR

(1935–)

Puerto Rican Writer, Graphic Artist

Developing a craft to perfection and attaining recognition for it is not easy. Becoming an expert in a selected area takes ability, practice, and time. Despite obstacles, Nicholasa Mohr has been able to attain wide recognition in two important and distinct creative fields: graphics and literature. Mohr was the first Puerto Rican woman on the mainland to write in English about the vicissitudes of Puerto Rican family and community life in New York City's Lower East Side.

Nicholasa Rivera-Golpe was born to Pedro Golpe and Nicolasa Rivera on 1 November 1935 in New York City. Early in the Great Depression of the 1930s her parents had left Puerto Rico, migrating with their four children to a Manhattan barrio. Later three more children were born to the Rivera-Golpe family; Nicholasa was the only girl. As a young child Nicholasa had to overcome harsh realities; her father died when she was 8 years old and her mother was frequently ill, requiring her help at home. In spite of difficulties and limitations, her mother encouraged the children to develop their talents as much as possible. Her mother's early recognition of Nicholasa's artistic abilities encouraged her to develop her interest in drawing and painting. Nicholasa learned to believe that she could make magic with paper, pencil, and crayons—she could create her own world by drawing pictures.

While Nicholasa was in high school her mother died, but her influence remained. Nicholasa moved in with a guardian aunt who seemed neither to recognize her talents nor to provide much emotional support for her educational efforts. Nevertheless, Nicholasa excelled as a student and strengthened her art skills. In retrospect she thinks that art provided her with an escape from the bigotry and discrimination that Puerto Rican children frequently encountered in school.

During this period of many adjustments in her life, Nicholasa became unhappy when her guidance counselor, with typical bias about the abilities of minority children, recommended that she take sewing rather than academic classes. Fortunately she enrolled in a school that taught fashion illustration, so she was able to further develop her drawing skills. Upon high school graduation in 1953 she attended the Art Students League in

New York. While going to school she worked part-time as a waitress, a clerical worker, and a translator.

During her early years as a graphic artist Nicholasa saved money to visit Mexico City, where she attended the Taller de Gráfica Popular. She studied and was deeply impressed by the art of the great Mexican painters, particularly Clemente Orozco, Diego Rivera, and his wife, Frida Kahlo, whose paintings embodied their culture. Their works provided new insights and motivated her to look into her own ethnic origins. Upon returning to New York City she studied at the recently established New School for Social Research, where she met her future husband. Later, in 1959, she continued her fine arts studies at the Brooklyn Museum Art School and the Pratt Center for Contemporary Printmaking. By the end of the 1960s Mohr had begun to acquire recognition for her painting among people in New York City art circles.

In 1970 Mohr moved to New Jersey with her husband and their two sons. She became an instructor at the Art Center of Northern New Jersey from 1971 to 1973 and at the MacDonald Colony in Peterborough, New Hampshire, in 1976. From 1973 to 1974 she was artist-in-residence with New York City public schools. At this time she also began to develop an interest in writing.

As an illustrator Mohr had a vivid imagination and sharpened communication skills. Both abilities had aided in her development as a graphic artist; her drawings communicated her message through shape, texture, and color. She found the transition from drawing to writing not difficult. She discovered that many of her artistic skills were transferable, that she could also draw a picture with words. Her literary style was strongly shaped by recollections of her mother's storytelling.

During this period a publisher asked Mohr to write about her life as a young Puerto Rican. She wrote about 50 pages in autobiographical form; the publisher, expecting a stereotypical tale of drug abuse, rape, and crime, was unimpressed. So Mohr set her tame autobiographical vignettes aside. Soon thereafter she received an offer from Harper and Row to illustrate a bookcover. Not interested, instead of accepting she took her 50 pages to Harper and was encouraged to turn them into a novel. The result was her first book, *Nilda*, published in 1973.

Nilda was basically a third-person account of Mohr's growing up in Spanish Harlem. Ever the artist, she also designed the book's cover and did eight illustrations for it. For *Nilda*, Mohr received several prestigious awards: Outstanding Book Award in Juvenile Fiction from the *New York Times* (1973), Jane Addams Children's Book Award (1974), McDowell Colony writing fellowship for the 1974 summer, Society of Illustrators citation of merit for her book jacket design, and in 1979 a place on the *School Library Journal*'s Best of the Best, 1966–1978, list.

With this resounding success, Mohr published a second book in 1975. *El Bronx Remembered* is a collection of short stories in which she addressed once-taboo topics in a frank, matter-of-fact fashion. For this book she garnered the following accolades: Outstanding Book Award in Teenage Fiction from the *New York Times* (1975), Best Book Award from *School Library Journal* (1975). Also, she was a National Book Award finalist for the most distinguished book in children's literature (1976).

In 1977 Mohr published *In Nueva York*, similar in many ways to *El Bronx Remembered*. Again she was showered with awards: Best Book Award from the *School Library Journal*, Best Book Award in Young Literature from the American Library Association, and Notable Trade Book in the Field of Social Studies from the joint committee of the National Council for the Social Studies and the Children's Book Council. It was also selected as one of ten "Paperbacks: New and Noteworthy" by the *New York Times* (1980). Mohr also illustrated *In Nueva York*.

Felita, published in 1979, was another author-illustrated novel, the story of a small Puerto Rican girl whose parents move from the barrio to a better part of town but still encounter discrimination, prompting the family's return to the old neighborhood. *Felita* was another juvenile literature success, winning Mohr the American Book Award from the Before Columbus Foundation in 1981 and her second Notable Trade Book in the Field of Social Studies award.

With these fulfilling experiences as a writer, Mohr turned to teaching. In 1977 she became a lecturer in Puerto Rican studies at the State University of New York at Stony Brook. She also was the head writer and co-producer of the television series *Aquí y Ahora* ("Here and Now") and undertook brief engagements as a consultant. After the deaths of her husband and a brother she published *Rituals of Survival: A Woman's Portfolio* (1985), a collection of short stories and a novella written for adults. As a sequel to *Felita* Mohr wrote *Going Home* (1986), another tale for juveniles, the story of Felita's visit to Puerto Rico for a summer. It is filled with emotional and bittersweet memories of the island. In 1995 her latest book for children, *The Magic Shell*, was published by Scholastic Press. The story of young Jaime who uses his uncle's magic conch shell in New York to bring up happy memories of his earlier life in the Dominican Republic, it has met with the same positive reception as her previous works. Also in 1995 Viking Press issued her *Song of the Coquí and Other Tales of Puerto Rico*, a collection of three diverse folk stories for children.

Because of the realism of her writing and its psychological veracity, Mohr is highly regarded as a chronicler of life in the barrio. From 1988 to 1990 she was a distinguished visiting professor at Queens College in New York City. Mohr has also been awarded an honorary doctorate from the State University of New York at Albany. In addition she was honored by a New York State legislative resolution praising her for her "valuable contributions to the world of literature."

Further Reading

Gunton, Sharon, and Jean C. Stine, eds. *Contemporary Literary Criticism*, vol. 12. Detroit: Gale Research, 1983.

Kanellos, Nicolás. *Biographical Dictionary of Hispanic Literature in the United States*. New York: Greenwood Press, 1989.

Miller, John. "The Emigrant and New York City: A Consideration of 4 Puerto Rican Writers." *Melus* (Fall 1978): 94–99.

Ryan, Bryan, ed. *Hispanic Writers: A Selection of Sketches from Contemporary Authors*. Detroit: Gale Research, 1991.

Telgen, Diane, and Jim Kamp, eds. *Notable Hispanic American Women*. Detroit: Gale Research, 1993.

Weiss, Jerry M., ed. *From Writers to Students: The Pleasures and Pains of Writing*. Newark, Del.: International Reading Association, 1979.

GLORIA MOLINA

(1948–)

Mexican American Political Activist, Politician, Administrator

In 1982, after a tough campaign in which she defied Eastside political broker Richard Alatorre and his chosen candidate, Gloria Molina won at the polls, becoming the first Mexican American woman to be elected to the lower house of the California legislature, the Assembly. As a result she became an instant celebrity. In that same year she was selected by *Caminos* magazine as Hispanic of the Year. One year later she was named Woman of the Year by the Mexican American Opportunity Foundation and Democrat of the Year by the Los Angeles County Democratic Central Committee. In 1984 she was voted Woman of the Year by *Ms* magazine, and the Mexican American Legal Defense and Education Fund (MALDEF) gave her its Woman of Achievement award. In 1987 she added another first: the first Chicana elected to the Los Angeles city council; and four years later she became the first woman elected to the county Board of Supervisors.

Gloria Molina was born in Los Angeles, California, on 31 May 1948, the first of ten children born to Concepción and Leonardo Molina, who had emigrated from the northern Mexican state of Chihuahua a year earlier. She grew up in a strongly disciplined family atmosphere in nearby Pico Rivera, where she attended elementary and high school. When she began school she spoke and understood only Spanish, the language of home; she recalls being punished for speaking Spanish at school. School seemed to her shy child's perception to be the Anglo world; it was something outside her field of experience.

After graduating from El Rancho High School, Gloria entered East Los Angeles City College with intentions of becoming a fashion designer. However, in college she began to become politically active, joining the Mexican American Student Association (MASA), serving as a volunteer in Robert Kennedy's 1968 presidential nomination campaign, and participating in the National Chicano Moratorium march two years later. Then her father had an almost fatal on-the-job accident that left her the breadwinner in the family for two years.

As de facto head of the household Gloria Molina had to talk to her father's doctors, consult with her siblings' teachers, and interpret and make decisions for her mother. The shy young woman learned to be more forceful in order to get things done. Undaunted by her new role, she got a job working as a legal assistant during the day and completed her undergraduate college degree by attending classes in the evening. At the same time she volunteered to work with disturbed teenagers; this work led her to attend school board meetings and broadened her interest in community concerns. In 1970 she received her A.B. from California State University, Los Angeles. With her college degree she obtained a position as a job counselor for a Latino development agency, The East Los Angeles Community Union (TELACU).

Strongly influenced by the Chicano student *movimiento* of the late 1960s, after college Gloria redoubled her interest in politics and community affairs. She participated actively in the Latin American Law Enforcement Association and served on the board of United Way of Los Angeles. In 1973 she became the founding president of the Comisión Femenil de Los Angeles and served as national president from 1974 to 1976. As president and a driving force in the commission, she was influential in developing various social service programs to help Mexican American women avoid exploitation, especially in employment and housing. Always concerned about the rights of the poor and children, she was co-founder of the Centro de Niños in Los Angeles.

Gloria Molina also assisted in the organizing of two Latino political groups in the Los Angeles area: Hispanic American Democrats and the local chapter of the National Association of Latino Elected and Appointed Officials (NALEO). Her extensive networking and widespread activity in community affairs and organizations made her a natural in the political field and later became the vital base for her development as a Chicana political leader.

In 1972 Gloria volunteered to work on the state Assembly campaign of a young Eastside firebrand, Richard Alatorre. He was elected. Two years later her work in the successful Assembly campaign of Democrat Art Torres led to a position as one of his administrative assistants. After Jimmy Carter became president by defeating Republican Gerald Ford in 1976, she received an appointment to the Department of Health, Education, and Welfare as regional director of intergovernmental and congressional affairs with headquarters in San Francisco. When the Republican Party returned to power in 1980 with Ronald Reagan in the presidency, she received a position as a chief deputy to Willie Brown, the powerful Speaker of the California State Assembly.

As the 1982 elections approached, Gloria Molina, after discussing her chances with friends, decided to run for the California Assembly seat vacated by Art Torres, strongly convinced that she had the experience to qualify her for the job. Undeterred by opposition from the Alatorre-Torres clique, which tried to discourage her by arguing that it was not her time and that the community would not vote for a woman, she mounted an aggressive campaign based on her networking connections. She presented herself as an outsider and confronted her "insider" opponents with demands for answers to difficult questions of government. Despite disapproval from the clique and **César Chávez**, her grassroots confrontational approach and bulldog tactics paid off, bringing her widespread voter support. She won election to the Assembly. In 1984 she helped register thousands of new voters in East Los Angeles, working in the Southwest Voter Registration Education Project and the Woman to Woman Campaign '84.

In the California Assembly Gloria Molina found that to get legislation she wanted passed, it was necessary to compromise. She found compromise always difficult and often unacceptable to her. In 1987, after four years in the Assembly, Molina made up her mind to run for a position on the Los Angeles city council created to settle a gerrymandering suit filed by the Mexican American Legal Defense and Education Fund. In the special election that was held she ran a textbook campaign against three opponents. Despite the considerable likelihood of a runoff election because none of the four candidates might get a majority, she won, garnering 57 percent of the votes and thereby becoming the first Chicana to sit on the city council. In that position she continued her "more open politics" assertive and combative approach to representing the community.

Four years later, on 19 February 1991, with help and support from Congressman **Edward Roybal** and endorsement by the *Los Angeles Times*, Gloria Molina was elected to the five-member Los Angeles County Board of Supervisors. She was the first Mexican American in this century and the first woman ever to be elected to this most important and most powerful local governing body in the United States. She achieved this by decisively defeating, 55 to 44 percent, her political mentor and friend, Art Torres, although he outspent her two to one in the campaign. She promised to continue to be a grassroots activist who would shake up the board. And she has. In July 1995 she went to Washington, D.C., to plead for payment of $226 million due Medi-Cal for reimbursements in order to ease Los Angeles County's acute budget problem. In January 1996 she continued her pressure on officials to obtain a clearer picture of the county's budgetary shortfall.

Unrelenting and always direct, in the Tuesday meetings of the Board of Supervisors Molina can be very abrasive and at times even rude as she pugnaciously questions county officials in her quest for greater accountability from them. Her exposure of bureaucratic waste and inefficiency in county government has had greater success than her efforts to get positive programs passed by the board. Her critics accuse her of practicing politics of anger and recrimination and say that as a result she is less effective than she might otherwise be. Although she realizes her style can be counterproductive at times, she defends herself by responding that the board treats her in a patronizing and condescending manner that limits her political effectiveness.

In December 1992 Mexican president Carlos Salinas de Gotari presented Gloria Molina with the Aztec Eagle award, the highest Mexican honor given to a foreigner.

Further Reading

Díaz, Katherine. "Hispanic of the Year: Gloria Molina." *Caminos* 4:1–2 (January–February 1983).

Fiore, Faye. "Supervisors Plead for Aid in Washington." *Los Angeles Times* 114 (20 July 1995): B1.

"Galaxy of Rising Stars." *Time* 138:20 (18 November 1991): 73.

Mills, Kay. "Gloria Molina." *Ms* 13 (January 1985): 80–81, 114.

Olivera, Mercedes. "The New Hispanic Woman." *Vista* 2:11 (5 July 1987): 6–8.

Skerry, Peter. *Mexican Americans: The Ambivalent Minority*. New York: Free Press, 1993.

Telgen, Diane, and Jim Kamp, eds. *Notable Hispanic American Women*. Detroit: Gale Research, 1993.

"3 Supervisors Giving Raises to Charity." *Los Angeles Times* 114 (16 December 1994): B3.

Tobar, Héctor. "Gloria Molina and the Politics of Anger." *Los Angeles Times Magazine* (3 January 1993): 10–13, 32–34.

RICARDO MONTALBÁN

(1920–)

Mexican American Actor, Social Activist

Ricardo Montalbán has played a wide variety of nationalities in his theater and film career, everything from a Japanese in the film *Sayonara*, 1957, through **Joaquín Murieta** in a television film, to Mr. Roarke in the television series *Fantasy Island*, 1978 to 1985. Unquestionably he is most widely known for his role as Mr. Roarke and as spokesman for the Chrysler Corporation, his rich baritone extolling the luxurious appointments of its Córdoba automobile.

Ricardo Montalbán was born in Mexico City on 25 November 1920 in the last months of the great revolution, the youngest of four children born to Ricarda and Genaro Montalbán, who had come to Mexico as immigrants from Spain 14 years earlier. He spent the first years of his life in Mexico City, where his father had opened a shop selling men's clothing and personal articles. When he was 5 years old his father suffered financial reverses partly because of the revolution, and the family moved to Torreón, a large city on the western edge of the northern Mexican state of Coahuila, where his father accepted an offer to manage a dry goods store.

When the time came for Ricardo to begin his formal education, he was sent back to Mexico City to attend a school operated by the Marist Brothers, a Catholic teaching order. When the Mexican government closed down church-related schools a year later, he returned to Torreón. There he continued his education at the Alfonso XIII grammar school and at Colegio de la Paz. Perhaps because all his siblings were considerably older, Ricardo read a great deal, mostly adventure novels. He was not, however, unathletic; he became a good soccer and squash player and dreamed, like every Mexican boy, of becoming a bullfighter. After the Colegio he enrolled in the Academia Comercial Treviño to study accounting, but he did not complete the training. At age 17 he began working in his father's store.

Unenthusiastic about a career in dry goods, Ricardo soon left for California to join his brother Carlos, older by 15 years, and to continue his education. Carlos lived in Los Angeles pursuing a career as a dancer and, being an economic realist, was also the local sales representative for Carta Blanca beer. In Los Angeles Ricardo first enrolled in Belmont High

School to improve his English and, after passing his language test three months later, then entered Fairfax High.

At Fairfax High School Ricardo became interested in drama, appeared in several plays, was noticed by film scouts on the lookout for Latino types to succeed to Rudolph Valentino, and decided he wanted to follow more closely in Carlos's footsteps by becoming an actor. In 1940 Carlos and Ricardo made a trip to New York City courtesy of Carta Blanca beer. There followed days of making the rounds to the offices of producers and actors' agents, of tryouts and readings. Finally Ricardo got his big break when he tried out for a small part in Tallulah Bankhead's play *Her Cardboard Lover* and was hired for the role. The play was a big hit, and his Broadway experience soon enabled him to begin a film career in Mexico—to which he had returned in 1941 because of his mother's serious illness.

In 1942 Montalbán made his Mexican film debut. During the rest of the World War II years he remained in Mexico, making a dozen films and being nominated for the Mexican equivalent of an Oscar. His successful acting career in Mexico in turn led to a long-term contract with Metro-Goldwyn-Mayer studios (MGM) after the war. During his eight years with MGM he was usually cast as the suave Latin lover, but he made two pictures in the 1950s about Hispanic socioeconomic problems, *My Man and I* and *Right Cross*. Although Ricardo's skills and reputation as an actor increased, the demand for suave Latin lovers had declined and he found himself saddled with a succession of insipid roles. After a one-year extension of his contract, he was finally dropped by MGM in 1953.

After *Her Cardboard Lover* Ricardo Montalbán had continued his stage work by participating in summer stock. Now he returned to the stage. Acting in George Bernard Shaw's *Don Juan in Hell*, he won acclaim from the critics for his interpretation in a demanding role. Subsequently he acted in about a dozen plays, including *The King and I* and *Accent on Youth*. His touring the United States in these plays made him better known to the play-going public and helped lead to his selection to do the Córdoba commercials on television for Chrysler.

The decade of the 1960s was the low point in Ricardo Montalbán's career. The new visual medium, television, had made heavy inroads into the film industry. Yet Montalbán's distinguished good looks and his distinct, slightly accented English got him an occasional guest part in television specials, and he acted in a number of potboilers made in Italy and in Hollywood. His best part was as an Indian in *Cheyenne Autumn* with Dolores Del Rio and **Gilbert Roland**, 1964; critics praised him for a sensitive and sympathetic portrayal. He also made a satiric *Latin Lovers*, 1954; *Let No Man Write My Epitaph*, 1960; an early 1960s made-in-Italy movie, *Pirate Warrior*; *The Money Trap*, 1965; *Sweet Charity*, 1968; *Escape* *from the Planet of the Apes*, 1972; *The Train Robbers*, 1972; and others less memorable.

With the rising tide of ethnic awareness in the mid-1960s, Montalbán became increasingly concerned about the depiction of Latinos by Hollywood and the continuing reluctance to hire Latinos except for very limited roles. Although not a social activist, he joined a few fellow Hispanic actors and businessmen early in 1969 in founding Nosotros, an organization dedicated to increasing opportunities for *raza* actors and technicians and, especially later, to improving the image of Latinos as depicted in films. He was elected Nosotros's first president.

Although the moderate views of Nosotros and the more aggressive stance of other Latino organizations combined to achieve some improvements, Montalbán believed his role in Nosotros caused him to be the victim of Hollywood backlash. He did make some unmemorable films such as *Joe Panther*, 1976, and *Won Ton Ton*, also 1976; but the end of his lean years was approaching. In 1978 he was selected to play the part of Mr. Roarke in a weekly television series entitled *Fantasy Island*. The series was tremendously successful, running until 1985 and bringing him new eminence and fame. It was followed by a leading role in another popular television series, *Dynasty*.

Meanwhile, in 1979 Ricardo Montalbán received an Emmy award for his portrayal of an Indian leader in the television miniseries *How the West Was Won*. A decade later, in 1988, in recognition of his contributions to the cultural and social improvement of Mexican Americans, he received the Golden Aztec Award from the Mexican American Opportunity Foundation, an organization established in 1952 to provide a wide variety of social services to the community.

Further Reading

Duarte, Patricia. "Welcome to Ricardo's Reality." *Nosotros* 3:9 (October 1979).

Montalbán, Ricardo, with Bob Thomas. *Reflections: A Life in Two Worlds*. Garden City, N.Y.: Doubleday, 1980.

Newlon, Clarke. *Famous Mexican Americans*. New York: Dodd, Mead, 1972.

Reyes, Luis, and Peter Rubie. *Hispanics in Hollywood*. New York: Garland Publishing, 1994.

"Ricardo Montalbán." *La Luz* 1:9 (January 1973): 42–45.

RITA MORENO
(ROSA DOLORES ALVERIO)
(1931–)

Puerto Rican Actress, Singer, Dancer, Comedian

The Guiness Book of World Records lists Rita Moreno as the only entertainer in the world who has won all four of the most prestigious awards in show business. In the 1962 Academy Awards she won an Oscar as best supporting actress for her performance as Anita in the movie-musical *West Side Story*. In 1972 she won a Grammy from the recording industry for her participation in the soundtrack album of her popular children's television series *The Electric Company*. Three years later she won a Tony for her hilarious impersonation of Googie Gomez in Terrence McNally's Broadway comedy *The Ritz*. She also won two Emmy awards for her television guest appearances on *The Muppet Show* in 1977, and the series *The Rockford Files* in 1978. Her versatility is matched only by the tenacious spirit that has kept her struggling for international stardom despite adversity.

Rita Moreno was born Rosa Dolores Alverio in the small town of Humacao, on the southeastern side of Puerto Rico, on 11 December 1931. Not long thereafter her parents divorced; her mother left the island for New York City, where she worked as a seamstress. When Rosa Dolores was 5 years old her mother returned to Puerto Rico for her and subsequently moved back to the mainland, taking her daughter with her. Although they lived in a Manhattan tenement, soon after her arrival in New York Rosa began to take dancing lessons from Paco Cansino, dance teacher and uncle of Latina actress and dancer **Rita Hayworth**. Soon she supplemented the family income by performing in the children's theater at Macy's department store and also entertained at weddings and bar mitzvahs.

Later Rosa found employment in various small and usually seedy nightclubs. Unable to find work in a better-off, more refined environment because of her age, she was nevertheless challenged artistically by performances that required her to wear unusual and colorful costumes. With a headpiece of bananas and other fruit, she sang and danced like Carmen Miranda, the popular Brazilian singer and comedian who was at the height of her career at the time. Rosa also found employment dubbing Spanish in American films destined for Spanish-speaking audiences.

Rosa Alverio at first used the stage name Rosita Cosio, later changed it to Rosita Moreno, then finally became Rita Moreno at the behest of Metro-Goldwyn-Mayer (MGM) officials. MGM had given her a contract after her earlier film debut as a delinquent in a reform school melodrama, *So Young, So Bad* (United Artists, 1950). After appearing in two mediocre films for MGM, she was released by the studio. She was crushed by this rejection. She believed her much-publicized eight-year relationship with Marlon Brando had exacerbated the image of her as a Spanish spitfire, "Rita the Cheetah." This was an image that she fought hard to keep clear of and that resulted in her being typecast.

During the early 1950s Moreno suffered the humiliation of being out of work, having to collect unemployment checks, and dealing with the harassment of being asked for sexual favors in return for casting selection. Further, when she did get a role it was usually as a Latina, an Arab, or an Indian. At this time in the movie industry being typecast as an Indian, Hispanic, or Arab was considered humiliating as well as a clear badge of inferiority.

In 1954 her appearance on the cover of *Life* magazine helped her to obtain a contract with Twentieth Century Fox. The parts that followed were more substantial but still were the same stereotypical roles she was trying so hard to break away from. In the western film *Seven Cities of Gold*, she played a Mexican woman who asks a U.S. soldier, "Why joo no lub Oola no more?" After she gets his answer she jumps to her death off a cliff. The absurdity of this scene illustrates the condescending and demeaning way in which Latina actresses were often required to portray *la raza*.

Not being treated as a serious actress made Moreno feel both professionally unchallenged and emotionally frustrated. Although she finally found somewhat more satisfying roles in the 1956 hit musical *The King & I* (as a Burmese slave girl) and in Arthur Miller's *A View from the Bridge*, emotionally she hit rock bottom. She swallowed a bottle of sleeping pills in a suicide attempt. Her recovery was aided by the realization that she had alternatives and, as she said, that things would change, that they would get better.

For Moreno, things did improve. With her new attitude she landed the role of Anita in the 1961 film version of *West Side Story*. She did all her own singing for the part, and her rendition of "America" captivated audiences everywhere. Moreno won an Oscar for best supporting actress, one of ten Academy Awards given to the film.

Receiving an Academy Award paved the way for other career successes for Moreno. After *West Side Story* she returned to Broadway to perform in non-Latina parts, breaking out of the Hispana stereotype. One of her favorite roles was that of Googie Gomez in the Broadway play *The Ritz*. The character, which Moreno helped create, poked fun at characters of the sort that she so frequently played. During the late 1960s she went back to Hollywood, where she was cast in major motion pictures such as *Marlowe* and *Carnal Knowledge*.

Moreno's ability to move easily from screen to stage to television expanded her growing popularity, especially within the Hispanic community, and helped her garner a Grammy, a Tony, and two Emmy awards in the 1970s. Her artistic success meant recognition as an actress as well as financial benefits from commercial endorsements and from being spokesperson for major products such as Campbell's soups. Recently, Rita Moreno premiered a new NBC television sitcom in which she was allotted the starring role as Angie, the "holistic housekeeper."

In 1989 Moreno received a Hispanic Woman of the Year award. Her commitment to the Latino community remains strong, and she continues to combine it with her love for the theater. Moreno's work in movies in which women are depicted as intelligent, sophisticated, well spoken, and politically minded has provided inspiration to Hispanic women. She stresses the importance of developing a sense of self-esteem as a Latina. Her biggest professional accomplishment was proving to Hollywood that she could play a wide variety of roles. In an interview with *Nuestro* in March 1986 she said: "I crossed that enormous chasm and still maintain . . . my integrity and my dignity as an Hispanic person."

Further Reading

Bustillos, Javier, and Anthony Chase. "Rita." *Hispanic* (1 October 1989): 30–33.

Mirandé, Alfredo, and Evangelina Enríquez. *La Chicana: The Mexican-American Woman*. Chicago: University of Chicago Press, 1979.

Moritz, Charles, ed. *Current Biography Yearbook, 1985*. New York: H. W. Wilson Co., 1985.

Reyes, Luis, and Peter Rubie. *Hispanics in Hollywood*. New York: Garland Publishing, 1994.

Sinnott, Susan. *Extraordinary Hispanic Americans*. Chicago: Children's Press, 1991.

Telgen, Diane, and Jim Kamp, eds. *Notable Hispanic American Women*. Detroit: Gale Research, 1993.

LUIS MUÑOZ MARÍN

(1898–1980)

Puerto Rican Patriot, Statesman, Politician, Poet, Editor

Puerto Rico's best-known personality and best-loved governor was Luis Muñoz Marín. While still a youth, Marín declared his intent to become "the agitator of God," a man to meet challenges and perform nearly impossible tasks, a man to transform reality. His wish came true. For many people worldwide, Luis Muñoz Marín became that political genius. For many poor Puerto Rican *jíbaros* (country people), he became a symbol of freedom from oppression.

In the eyes and lives of grateful and adoring *jíbaros*, his wish became true. Many built shrines in his honor in their homes. His picture, surrounded by flowers and candles, had a place alongside images of saints, the Virgin Mary, and Jesus Christ. He was bigger than life. He earned the respect, trust, and admiration of those who suffered from poverty, malnutrition, and apathy. He brought dignity, hope, and purpose into the lives of poor Puerto Ricans.

Luis Muñoz Marín was born toward the very end of the last century, in 1898. He was the son of Luis Muñoz Rivera, a leading political figure before and after the U.S. occupation of Puerto Rico in that year, and his wife, Sra. Monserrate Marín de Rivera. Luis spent most of his youth with his mother in Barranquitas, Puerto Rico, and Washington, D.C., where his father was resident commissioner for the island. After grade school he attended Georgetown Prep School, and following his father's death in 1916 he applied for a job with the new resident commissioner.

Always interested in poetry, Muñoz Marín started a literary journal called *La Revista de Indias* ("Review of the Indies") in 1918. During this period his poems were published in various poetry magazines and in *La Democracia*, a newspaper his father founded in 1890 in Puerto Rico. Later he published a book, *Madre haraposa* ("Mother in Rags") and wrote essays for highly respected magazines such as the *Nation, New Republic, Smart Set*, and *American Mercury*.

In 1920 Luis returned to Puerto Rico to help his father's friend, Antonio Barceló, campaign in the elections of that year. Barceló was the head of the Partido Unión de Puerto Rico, which Muñoz Marín's father had helped found. Luis soon realized that this party represented wealthy

Puerto Ricans and the American sugar barons who bought the votes of the *jíbaros* for $2.00 at election time. Against all advice he decided to join the Socialist Party because it spoke out for the poor. He took to the mountains to discuss the many problems that faced the island—and particularly the poor—and urged them not to sell their votes. In order to understand the *jíbaros'* reality and their dreams, he listened to their stories. His approachability, humble demeanor, and sincerity won the hearts of the poor. These qualities, along with the memory of his father's leadership, established his political appeal. However, despite his efforts, which helped double the party's votes, the elections were lost. Luis then chose to return to the mainland.

The Depression years of the late 1920s and early 1930s were very hard on Muñoz Marín and on Puerto Rico. In Washington, D.C., Luis was out of work and for weeks lived in his car. Finally he decided to return to the island and took over *La Democracia* as editor. He agreed to support Antonio Barceló and the latter's new Liberal Party. In the 1934 elections Luis Muñoz Marín gained his first political office, becoming senator at large.

Using his political office advantageously, Muñoz Marín expanded his official duties by visiting the mainland to lobby for the island's needs. Through a friend he met the first lady, Eleanor Roosevelt, and later also met the president, Franklin Delano Roosevelt. Informally he told the president that his appointee as governor lacked the qualities Puerto Rico needed. F.D.R. accepted his assessment and shortly thereafter obtained the governor's resignation. Upon Muñoz's return to the island, he was met at the airport by a crowd that cheered its new hero and applauded the governor's departure.

Mrs. Roosevelt visited the island a few months later. Muñoz Marín toured her around the island's beautiful historic sites and also showed her the poverty-ridden areas of the capital, San Juan. Following her visit, three island leaders were invited to Washington to serve on a commission to study major issues affecting the island's citizens: health, education, and jobs. As senator, Muñoz took it upon himself to educate the U.S. Congress about his vision of the island's future. As a result the Puerto Rico Reconstruction Administration was created to develop new jobs, to stimulate industrial development, to bring electricity to all homes on the island, and, at least indirectly, to end the sugar barons' economic dominance.

Notwithstanding his achievements, Muñoz Marín underwent a severe political crisis in 1936. His controversial statements in relation to the assassination of the American chief of police in Puerto Rico affected negatively his political influence in Washington, D.C. As a result he was ousted by his own party. Also, his marriage fell apart and he quickly found himself with neither political influence nor family support. The following two years were times of introspection and soul-searching. He reexamined and refined his vision of Puerto Rico's political, social, and economic transformation and conscientiously sorted out his economic and political ideas.

In 1938 Luis Muñoz Marín organized the Partido Popular Democrático (PPD). He envisioned its principal mission as championing the needs of the Puerto Rican people rather than concerning itself with the island's political status, as all other parties had done. The message that appeared on the party flag read "Pan-Tierra-Libertad," and Muñoz's slogan was "Halda Arriba" ("Up the Hill").

In the 1940 elections Muñoz Marín's efforts paid off; his party won a close victory that marked the beginning of many election successes during the next two and a half decades. Muñoz Marín became the politically powerful president of Puerto Rico's senate. Along with his close friend, Governor Rexford Tugwell, he began to transform Puerto Rico. A Land Authority was created to purchase and redistribute land to the poor. Housing projects were developed, medical centers created, an electric power authority established, a minimum wage set, and a free school lunch program begun. The 1944 election results were predictable; the PPD won in a landslide.

After World War II, Muñoz Marín's efforts were dedicated principally to industrializing the island. The creation of Fomento Industrial Development Agency and the Industrial Incentives Act of 1947 helped to establish a modern economy. The famous "Operation Bootstrap" became a worldwide model of social and economic development for third world countries.

In 1947 the U.S. Congress passed legislation allowing Puerto Ricans to elect their governor. In the next year Luis Muñoz Marín became the first governor elected by Puerto Ricans. His major political contribution as governor was the design and passage of Public Law 600, which allowed Puerto Rico to become an Estado Libre with its own constitution in 1952. In 1960 Muñoz created a furor on the island by raising the birth control issue. Despite energetic opposition from the Catholic Church, which used the threat of excommunication, the PPD won the elections with nearly 60 percent of the vote.

After repeated re-election to the governorship of Puerto Rico, Luis Muñoz Marín decided to step down in 1964 and ran for senator at large. However, two years later he left the Senate because he felt that his overwhelming influence unduly affected his role as senator. He departed for Rome, where he lived for eight years. His return to Puerto Rico in 1972 was a phenomenal event. Thousands of Puerto Ricans gathered at the San Juan International Airport to welcome him home.

Following the 1972 elections, Muñoz Marín stayed in Puerto Rico but remained aloof from the local political scene. He served on an ad hoc committee named by the U.S. president to make recommendations for improving political relations between Puerto Rico and the mainland. He died in 1980, survived by his second wife, Inés Mendoza de Muñoz, and children. Puerto Rico has since not encountered a more beloved and admired political leader.

Further Reading

Ameringer, Charles D. "The Tradition of Democracy in the Caribbean: Betancourt, Figueres, Muñoz and the Democratic Left." *Caribbean Review* 11:2 (Spring 1982): 28–31.

Johnson, Roberta A. "An Interview with Luis Muñoz Marín." *Revista Interamericana* 9:2 (1979): 232–250.

Lopez Springfield, Consuelo. "The Memorias of Luis Muñoz Marín: An Intertextual Reading of Autobiography." *Caribbean Quarterly* 37:4 (December 1991): 23–39.

Mann, Peggy. *Luis Muñoz Marín: The Man Who Remade Puerto Rico.* New York: Coward, McCann & Geoghegan, 1976.

Mathews, Thomas G. *1925—Luis Muñoz Marín: A Concise Biography.* New York: American R.D.M. Corp., 1967.

Sterling, Philip, and Maria Bran. *The Quiet Rebels.* New York: Doubleday, 1968.

JOAQUÍN MURIETA

(mid-19th century)

Mexican American Folk Hero, Social Bandit(?)

Almost nothing is known for certain about Joaquín Murieta. Indeed, some historians suggest that as an individual he never existed, that he was the figment of fevered Anglo imaginations during the California gold rush and of creative authors later. The discovery of gold in California in 1848 led to a rapid influx of over 250,000 gold-seekers, of whom some 5,000 were experienced Mexican miners from Sonora. Also among the newly arrived were many of society's misfits, including confidence men, thieves, bandits, rustlers, and murderers. It should surprise no one that considerable crime occurred in the goldfields.

By the early 1850s the mining region of the new American state, lacking organized local government, was plagued with lawlessness and violence. Among Anglo miners, vigilantism became the accepted order of the day. The lynching of a Mexican woman named Juanita at Downie-ville in 1851 was an extreme but not isolated case. More common was the ousting of Mexican miners from their gold claims and the killing of accused cattle, horse, and mule thieves whose activities increased as the availability of placer gold decreased. Although some of the desperados were Mexicans, that group had no monopoly on crime but tended to be singled out by the Anglo majority and considered unquestionably guilty. Increasingly in the early 1850s, persons who were robbed on the road claimed the notoriety of having been robbed by a Mexican bandit they identified as Joaquín, even though their descriptions varied and their identifications seemed to give him the preternatural ability to be in two widely separated places at the same time.

It was in this highly charged atmosphere in the late spring of 1853 that the California legislature debated the creation of a ranger force to hunt down the "Five Joaquíns," identified as Joaquín Carrillo, Joaquín Valenzuela, Joaquín Ocomorenia, Joaquín Botellier/Botilleras/Botello, and Joaquín Muriati/Murieta—who might all be the same person, or might not. Many Spanish-speaking Californians, including two members of the legislature, protested that this proposed government action granted a virtual license to hunt Mexicans because identification was so extremely vague. Despite these objections the overwhelmingly Anglo legislature voted in favor of the rangers, the only concession being to limit their commission to a three-month period. Governor John Bigler offered a $1,000 reward for the capture of Joaquín and appointed a for-mer army officer, Texan Harry S. Love, to head a 20-man ranger force.

For nearly three months in 1853 Love's rangers unsuccessfully inves-tigated reports of Murieta's presence in isolated regions of the state. Fi-nally in July, with only days remaining in their mandate, the rangers encountered a small group of Hispanics. A shoot-out ensued. When the shooting ended and the gunsmoke cleared there were two corpses, which Love later identified as Murieta and his lieutenant, Three-Fingered Jack García. The head of the former and the hand of the latter were preserved in jars of alcohol, and Love claimed the reward. From the beginning there was considerable doubt about the casual identification, even some sly remarks about the alcohol probably being whiskey; but the public wanted a success, not a debate. The legislature confirmed the identifi-cation by awarding Love and his rangers $5,000.

The alleged head of Murieta became a San Francisco "museum" piece, then a successful touring curiosity, and finally a saloon display item for the rest of the nineteenth century. It finally disappeared in the great San Francisco earthquake and fire of 1906. One version of the Murieta legend not only denied that this was the head of Joaquín; it alleged that in fact Murieta had returned to Sonora, where he died peacefully in bed during the 1870s.

Out of this incident, whatever truth it may have contained, grew the myth. In the year following 1853 a half-Cherokee journalist named John Rollin Ridge published a romantic novel titled *The Life and Adventures of Joaquín Murieta, the Celebrated California Bandit*. Sensitive to racial prejudice, he presented Murieta as a peace-loving miner who was driven to vow vengeance on Anglos because they stole his claim, hanged his brother, raped his wife, and left him beaten almost to death. The legend was on its way. Ridge's tale was later pirated both in the United States and abroad, in English and in several other languages. It was elaborated into a Robin Hood theme in numerous half-dime novels that used the Ridge story as a framework.

In 1869 the eccentric western poet Cincinnatus Miller published a slender volume of verse in defense of his hero titled *Joaquín et al.* and took to labeling himself Joaquín Miller. Toward the end of the century the legend was given a further degree of sanction by being included in the California histories of Hubert Howe Bancroft and Theodore Hittell. It has since been made into a biography, an epic poem, and a movie scenario; most recently it was dramatized by the Nobel Prize–winning Chilean poet Pablo Neruda, who claimed to have proof that Murieta was not a Sonoran at all, but a Chilean. So much for indisputable historical facts.

It was almost inevitable that among Chicano students of the 1960s and 1970s Murieta would become one of the icons of the *movimiento*, along with Emiliano Zapata, Fidel Castro, and Ernesto "Che" Guevara. Kept alive by youthful romantic zeal as well as by moth-eaten, timeworn nationalism and the popular taste for romantic heroes, the historical Joaquín, such as he may have been, has been overwhelmed and completely obscured by the enduring fame of the vigorous and dynamic, larger-than-life myth.

Further Reading

Castillo, Pedro, and Albert Camarillo, eds. *Furia y Muerte: Los Bandidos Chicanos*. Los Angeles: Chicano Studies Center, University of California, 1973.

Farquhar, Francis P. *Joaquín Murieta, the Brigand Chief of California*. San Francisco: Grabhorn Press, 1932.

Jackson, Joseph H. *Bad Company*. New York: Harcourt, Brace, 1939.

Latta, Frank. *Joaquín Murieta and His Horse Gang*. Santa Cruz, Calif.: Bear State Books, 1980.

Nadeau, Remi. *The Real Joaquín Murieta*. Corona del Mar, Calif.: Trans-Anglo Books, 1974.

Neruda, Pablo. *Fulgor y Muerte de Joaquín Murieta*. New York: Farrar, Straus and Giroux, 1972.

Pitt, Leonard. *The Decline of the Californios*. Berkeley: University of California Press, 1966.

Ridge, John Rollin. *The Life and Adventures of Joaquín Murieta, the Celebrated California Bandit*, 3rd ed. San Francisco: F. MacCrellish, 1871.

Rodríguez, Richard. "The Head of Joaquín Murrieta." *Nuestro* 9 (November 1985): 30–36.

JULIAN NAVA

(1927–)

Mexican American Ambassador, Historian, Professor

Julian Nava is perhaps most widely known as the first Mexican American to be appointed U.S. ambassador to Mexico. Under presidents Jimmy Carter and Ronald Reagan he represented the United States to our southern neighbor, directing the State Department's largest embassy with over 1,200 staff members. Always concerned about education, during his tenure as ambassador in 1980 and 1981 his initiatives with Mexican leaders were responsible for the organizing of several binational programs in academic and cultural areas. Among them were a collaborative research program between Harvard University and Mexican experts; MEXUS, a joint program of Mexican universities and the University of California; and a people-to-people self-help program between northwestern Mexicans and southern Californians.

Julian Nava was born on 19 June 1927 in East Los Angeles, California, the second son in a family of eight children born to Ruth Flores and Julian Nava. His parents, like many other Mexicans, had fled from their native country during the chaotic days of the 1910 revolution and had settled in southern California. An attempt by his parents to return to Mexico in 1935 (because of the Depression) was aborted because Julian's appendix ruptured at the last minute, but they continued to talk about going back. Julian was a teenager before he realized that it was only talk and that the family would remain in Los Angeles.

As a youngster growing up in the Boyle Heights neighborhood of East Los Angeles, Julian attended Bridge Street Elementary School and then went on to Hollenbeck Junior High School and Roosevelt High. During summer vacations he, his brothers and sisters, and their parents followed the fruit harvests. Tired after a long day in the orchards, in the evening

Julian Nava. Photo courtesy of Julian Nava.

he absorbed Mexican culture through the *corridos, rancheras,* and folk tales that were sung and told around the embers of the cooking fires.

Although Julian was an excellent student, he had no expectations of going to college and was counseled in high school to take shop courses rather than college preparatory classes. Before graduating from Roosevelt High School during World War II he volunteered for service in the navy and served in the last year of the fighting as an aircrewman. On returning to civilian life he joined an older brother working in auto repair.

However, wartime military service gave Julian a new sense of self-worth and expanded his horizons. When East Los Angeles Community College opened its doors on the edge of the barrio, he decided to take advantage of the G.I. Bill and enrolled. As a student he excelled and was elected student body president. In 1949 he received his A.A. degree and went on to Pomona College, where he earned his B.A. degree two years later. From Pomona two fellowships took him to graduate studies at Harvard University, to an M.A., and ultimately to a Ph.D. in Latin American history in 1955. Upon receiving his doctorate he took a position as an instructor in the humanities at La Universidad de Puerto Rico in Rio

Piedras. After two years in Puerto Rico he accepted an appointment to the history department at California State University, Northridge, where he remained until 1990, except for leaves of absence to undertake other academic activities.

Julian Nava has lived, taught, and worked abroad for a total of seven years. In 1953–1954, while still working on his doctorate, he taught English at the U.S. Information Services Center in Caracas, Venezuela; from 1963 to 1964 he took a leave to accept a Fulbright fellowship teaching at the ancient and famous Universidad de Valladolid in north central Spain. A year later he again took a leave to establish and administer the Centro de Estudios Universitarios Colombo-Americano from 1964 to 1965 in Bogotá, Colombia, for a consortium of 12 institutions constituting the Great Lakes Colleges Association. In 1980 and 1981 he was again on leave, having been appointed U.S. ambassador to Mexico by President Jimmy Carter.

After he returned from Colombia in 1965 to his position as professor of Latin American history at Northridge, Nava became deeply involved in the rising concern—especially among students—about *raza* problems, particularly in the field of education. As part of that involvement in 1967 he ran for a position on the seven-member governing board of the Los Angeles Unified School District and won. By the end of his first term he had been elected president of the board and was easily elected to subsequent four-year terms on the board in 1971 and 1975. As part of his civic involvement he also served on the boards of the Plaza de la Raza and the Hispanic Urban Center and was a member of the advisory committee for the Mexican American Legal Defense and Education Fund, MALDEF. He has served—often as a founder, organizer, or director—on various educational and professional committees, boards, and councils far too numerous to list.

In addition to his role as a civic leader, Professor Nava has been one of the pioneers in writing the history of Mexican Americans. In 1969 he published one of the first ethnic-oriented textbooks for high schools, titled *Mexican Americans: Past, Present, and Future*. In the early 1970s he wrote a short pamphlet for the Anti-Defamation League of the B'nai B'rith, *Mexican Americans: A Brief Look at Their History*, and edited two books of readings: *The Mexican American in American History* and *Viva La Raza! Readings on Mexican Americans*. In 1974 he published *Our Hispanic Heritage* and two years later co-authored *California: Five Centuries of Cultural Contrast*. He has also authored a series of five short bilingual books on tracing family history, entitled *Discovering My Past*, 1989. More recently *A Social and Cultural History of Venezuela under Guzmán Blanco*, based on his doctoral dissertation, was published in Caracas. In addition, since 1985 he has been writing a column that appears regularly in several newspapers in Los Angeles and in Mexico. In 1993 he ran for mayor of

Los Angeles but lost. He continues to enjoy teaching his classes in U.S. Latino and Latin American history.

Dr. Julian Nava has been the recipient of various honors in addition to his Fulbright appointment and his ambassadorship. In the early 1980s he was awarded honorary doctorates by Pomona College and Whittier College. In 1987 he was named U.S. liaison for the new Universidad Pública de Navarra at Pamplona and three years later was appointed the Thompson Distinguished Visiting Professor at Pomona College. In the 1990s his contacts with Spain, Mexico, and Latin America continue. He continues to combine academic achievement with civic involvement.

Further Reading

Alford, Harold J. *The Proud Peoples: The Heritage and Culture of Spanish-Speaking Peoples in the United States*. New York: David McKay, 1972.

Chacón, José. *Hispanic Notables in the United States of North America*. Albuquerque: Saguaro Publications, 1978.

Martínez, Al. *Rising Voices: Profiles of Hispano-American Lives*. New York: New American Library, 1974.

Nieto, Jess G. "Julian Nava, Our Voice in Mexico." *Caminos* 1:7 (November 1980).

Antonia Novello

(1944–)

Puerto Rican Physician, U.S. Surgeon General

During her three-year tenure in Washington, D.C., Antonia Novello wore the gold braid—a vice-admiral's stripes—on her Public Health Service uniform. As U.S. surgeon general her job was to monitor the nation's public health. Her primary responsibility was to issue warnings about threats to the nation's health. Dr. Novello was both the first woman and the first Hispanic in U.S. history to hold the position of surgeon general. In that role she led the battle against disease, smoking, teenage drinking, drug abuse, AIDS, domestic violence, and other health-related problems.

Antonia Flores was born on 23 August 1944 to Antonio and Delia Flores in Fajardo, a beautiful coastal town on the eastern side of Puerto Rico. She was the oldest of three children. When she was 8 years old her father died; her mother later married Ramón Flores, an electrician. As a small child Antonia suffered from a malfunctioning colon and became seriously ill every summer. Although she was scheduled to have an operation to correct the defect when she reached the age of 8, she was not operated on until after she turned 18 because of an oversight by her doctors. Medical complications necessitated further corrective surgery.

Antonia was inspired to become a doctor by the example of her kindly pediatrician; her caring gastroenterologist; her favorite aunt, who was a nurse; and her mother, who was the principal of a junior high school. Her mother felt strongly that educational attainment was the road to a successful life.

At the beginning of the 1960s Antonia entered the University of Puerto Rico in San Juan and graduated in 1965 with a Bachelor of Science degree. She applied and was accepted to medical school, completing her M.D. degree work in 1970. She then married Joseph Novello, a naval flight surgeon. The couple moved to Ann Arbor, Michigan, where they both continued their medical training. She specialized in pediatrics and he specialized in psychiatry. In 1971 Antonia earned the University of Michigan Medical Center award as intern of the year.

Because her favorite aunt had died of kidney failure, she decided to pursue a subspecialty in pediatric nephrology (kidney disease) at the University of Michigan Medical Center from 1973 to 1974 and later at Georgetown University Hospital in Washington, D.C., from 1974 to 1975.

In the following year Dr. Antonia Novello began a private practice in pediatrics and nephrology in which she worked for two years before applying for a position in the U.S. Public Health Service. She was hired in 1978 as project officer in the artificial kidney and chronic uremia program at the National Institutes of Health (NIH). During this period she also continued her formal education, and in 1982 she received a master's degree in public health from the Johns Hopkins University School of Public Health in Baltimore, Maryland.

In 1986 Novello was named deputy director of the National Institute of Child Health and Human Development, one of the top positions at the NIH. She held this position for four years. With a desire to learn more about management, in 1987 she entered a program for senior managers in government at the John F. Kennedy School of Government at Harvard University, earning a certificate on completion. In that same year she also became clinical professor of pediatrics at Georgetown University School of Medicine in Washington, D.C.

While at NIH Novello made major contributions in the areas of pediatric AIDS research and women's health issues. As a legislative fellow, she played a large role in drafting national organ transplant legislation as well as the warning label required on cigarette packages. On 17 October 1989 President George Bush nominated her to be surgeon general. Her nomination and confirmation hearings were without controversy— in contrast with those of the previous nominee, Dr. C. Everett Koop.

Antonia Novello shared his opposition to abortion, but she preferred not to stress her position. She was of the opinion that other women's medical issues such as spousal abuse deserved equal if not greater attention.

As surgeon general Novello focused her efforts mainly on health care for minorities, women, and children, on domestic violence, alcohol abuse, nicotine issues, and accident injury prevention. On these topics she was very outspoken. In March 1992 she and James S. Todd, executive vice-president of the American Medical Association (AMA), held a news conference at which they denounced the R. J. Reynolds Tobacco Company's advertisements featuring the cartoon character Joe Camel, because research showed that it appealed to young children. Referring to government projections that by the second half of the 1990s women might be smoking at a higher rate than men, Novello told an interviewer that she considered it a tragedy that lung cancer had surpassed breast cancer as the number one cause of cancer death in women.

Novello also attacked alcohol advertising. At a 1991 press conference she admonished ad agencies against sending "the wrong message about alcohol" by featuring sports heroes and physically attractive people having fun drinking as part of a desirable and carefree life-style. Novello held this advertising to be reprehensible and found particularly irresponsible the liquor advertisements that featured hazardous sports such as skiing, surfing, and mountain climbing because they suggest it is safe for people to drink while engaging in these activities.

Novello gave significant attention to familial violence. At a January 1992 American Medical Association Press Conference she called domestic violence a "cancer that gnaws at the body and soul of the American family" and added that it was "the second most common cause of injury among women overall, and the leading cause of injuries to women ages fifteen to forty-four, more common than automobile accidents, muggings and rapes combined."

Novello labeled as critical the increasing failure to vaccinate children against common diseases as well as the widespread lack of proper prenatal care, resulting in unnecessarily high infant mortality rates. She also believed injury prevention should be viewed as a public health concern. In 1991 she convened a conference, entitled Farm Safe 2000, to impress safety specialists and health-care professionals with the numerous health risks faced by children of rural families. During her tenure as surgeon general she continued working on issues related to children with AIDS, and on other aspects of AIDS such as its spread in the heterosexual population.

At the end of June 1993 Dr. Novello, the Bush appointee, methodically filled cardboard cartons with the evidence of four years of hard work and quiet leadership, leaving her office to the new Clinton appointee, Dr. Joycelyn Elders. However, Novello was not departing from public service. She accepted a new post as special representative to UNICEF, where she continues her concern for women and children.

Over the years Novello has received many honors and awards, including the following: Life Achievement Award, National Puerto Rican Coalition, 1990; Outstanding Achievement Award, National Association of Cuban American Women USA, 1991; Award for Service to Humanity, Puerto Rican Chamber of Commerce in the United States, 1990; Simón Bolívar National Award, 1991; also honorary degrees from the Medical College of Ohio in Toledo, College of Notre Dame of Maryland in Baltimore, Meharry Medical College in Nashville, University of Notre Dame in Indiana, and Universidad del Caribe in Puerto Rico.

Antonia Novello's ethnic pride was clearly evident during her first official trip to Puerto Rico, where she received a hero's welcome. She decorated the walls of her Washington office with gifts she received in Puerto Rico. She is highly regarded by colleagues as bright, sharp, and practical, as a person who cares about women, minorities, and the poor. Her husband fondly characterizes her as "where Mother Teresa meets Margaret Thatcher."

Further Reading

Cohn, Victor. "Novello: I Intend to Be Like Dr. Koop." *Washington Post* (8 May 1990): PWH 17.

Easterbrook, Gregg. "Antonia Novello, United States Surgeon General, Monitors Nation's Public Health." *Los Angeles Times* (12 May 1992): M3.

Graham, Judith, ed. *Current Biography Yearbook, 1992*. New York: H. W. Wilson Co., 1992.

"La mujer de hoy." *Imagen* [San Juan, Puerto Rico] (June 1990): 106–113.

"Profile: Dr. Antonia Novello: The Right Stuff." *Hispanic* (January–February 1990): 20.

Schwartz, John. "Dr. Novello's Steady Pulse." *Washington Post* 116 (2 July 1993): B1.

Telgen, Diane, and Jim Kamp, eds. *Notable Hispanic American Women*. Detroit: Gale Research, 1993.

ELLEN OCHOA

(1958–   )

Mexican American NASA Astronaut, Engineer

When she blasted off in the space shuttle *Discovery* in April 1993, Ellen Ochoa became the first Latina to be part of a space mission crew. It was a fitting pinnacle to the notable scientific career of the energetic 34-year-old Chicana. In 1989 she had been selected for the Hispanic Engineer National Achievement Award as Most Promising Engineer in Government, and in the following year just before beginning her astronaut training she received the Pride Award from the National Hispanic Quincentennial Commission.

Ellen Ochoa was born on 10 May 1958 in Los Angeles but considers La Mesa, California, a suburb of San Diego, to be her home town. One of two girls and three boys born to Rosanne Deardorff and Joseph Ochoa, she grew up in an atmosphere in which education was esteemed, and she and her siblings were encouraged to follow their individual intellectual bent. Her mother, who had completed high school before her marriage, enrolled in college after Ellen's birth, took courses when she was able to, and finally graduated from San Diego State University 23 years later.

With this background Ellen Ochoa worked hard in school and was an outstanding student in the sciences and mathematics. But she excelled in her other studies as well. In high school she was regularly the top person in her classes. A hard-working and persevering student, she won the San Diego County spelling bee at age 13 and was an outstanding music student, specializing in the flute. In 1975 she graduated with honors from Grossmont High School in La Mesa and was selected to represent her fellow students as class valedictorian.

From Grossmont High Ellen Ochoa followed her mother to San Diego State University, where she enrolled as a music major. Interested in many subjects, she changed her major several times, from music to business to journalism to computer science, and finally settled on physics, perhaps the most demanding field of study at the university. In 1980 she received her Bachelor of Science degree in physics and again was class valedictorian.

From San Diego State Ellen Ochoa went north to Stanford University, where she obtained her Master of Science degree in electrical engineering in 1981. A Stanford Engineering Fellowship for 1980–1981 and an IBM Predoctoral Fellowship for 1982–1984 helped to finance her graduate education. Her doctoral dissertation centered on the use of photorefractive crystals to filter images from space and resulted in a patent in this very specialized field. While a graduate student at Stanford she also continued her interest in music, playing the flute in the Stanford Symphony Orchestra and winning the student soloist award in 1983. In 1985 she received her doctorate in electrical engineering.

Upon obtaining her Ph.D., Dr. Ochoa accepted a position as a researcher in the imaging technology section of Sandia National Laboratories at Livermore, California. As a research engineer for Sandia she continued her work in developing optical methods for filtering noise and other distortion from space images. In the course of her work at Sandia she was credited as co-inventor in two patents in this field.

After three years at Sandia Laboratories Dr. Ochoa moved to the National Aeronautics and Space Administration (NASA) Ames Research Center at Moffett Field Naval Air Station in Mountain View, California, as part of a research team in optical recognition systems. Her research group's principal concern was optical processing as applied to space images. Six months later she was named head of the Intelligent Systems Technology Branch, becoming both technical and administrative leader of a research team of 35 engineers and scientists. In her new position she had responsibility for NASA's research and development of computational systems for aerospace missions.

While she was a student at Stanford University, Ellen Ochoa first became interested in the U.S. astronaut program. But at that time NASA was not accepting women candidates, so she had little or no hope of getting into the program. NASA's exclusionary policy changed in the late 1970s, and in 1985 Ochoa was one of more than 2,000 candidates who applied for admission to the NASA astronaut school. Two years later she made it to the top 100 finalists, and in January 1990 she was one of 5 women and 18 men selected to begin astronaut training at the Lyndon B. Johnson Space Center in Houston, Texas. In July 1991, after one year of training, she became a full-fledged astronaut and qualified for assignment as a mission specialist.

Ochoa was selected as a member of the five-person crew in the 55th flight in the space shuttle program. On 8 April 1993 she blasted off at Cape Canaveral in the 16th flight of the space shuttle *Discovery*. During the nine-day mission she was responsible for experiments examining the effects of variations in solar activity on the earth's climate and environment. As part of a long-term study of the impact of solar energy on the earth's middle-atmosphere, she gathered data on the relationship between the sun's energy and chemicals in the ozone layer, especially those that might deplete it. She reported the experience of the flight as hard work but enjoyable and inspiring.

Ellen Ochoa finds that being an astronaut keeps her very busy, but she manages to find some time for her hobbies. First and foremost, of course, is playing the flute, which she once considered as a possible career goal and which she finds relaxing as well as enjoyable. Since 1988 she has had a pilot's license for small planes and continues to fly occasionally when she can find the time. She also enjoys more physical sports, especially bicycling and volleyball.

In addition to the patents that she holds, Ochoa has published numerous papers in professional journals and presented scientific papers at technical conferences. Through her persistence and hard work she continues to open frontiers for all women and especially for young Chicanas. She takes her responsibilities as a role model very seriously and has been active traveling about the country ever since her selection as an astronaut, giving talks about her experience to groups of young people.

Further Reading

"Biographical Data." Houston, Tex.: Lyndon B. Johnson Space Center, 1993.

"New Astronaut's Higher Profile an Opportunity." *Houston Post* (23 July 1990): A9–A10.

Sinnott, Susan. *Extraordinary Hispanic Americans*. Chicago: Children's Press, 1991.

Telgen, Diane, and Jim Kamp, eds. *Notable Hispanic American Women*. Detroit: Gale Research, 1993.

Yuen, Mike. "New Astronauts Ready Despite NASA Problems." *Houston Post* (17 July 1990): A9–A10.

ESTEBAN OCHOA

(1831–1888)

Mexican American Entrepreneur, Civic Leader

When the army of the Confederate States of America invaded the Southwest during the Civil War, volunteer Southern troops seized Tucson in late February 1862. This event created a crisis for Esteban Ochoa, a prominent merchant of Tucson and a fervent and vocal supporter of Abraham Lincoln's Union. Given the alternatives of taking an oath of allegiance to the Confederacy or of having his property confiscated, he showed no hesitation. He not only gave up everything he had worked so many years for but also was forced to leave Tucson. Despite the potential danger from Apache Indians he mounted his horse and rode out of town alone, leaving his entire life's work behind. He journeyed eastward for several days across the mountains, eventually arriving at Mesilla on the Rio Grande River. Fortunately for him, the arrival of Northern forces a few months later compelled the Confederates to withdraw from Tucson, and by midyear he was able to return and recover most of his property.

This staunch Unionist was an immigrant. Esteban Ochoa was born on 17 March 1831 into a prominent *norteño* (northern Mexican) mining and ranching family in tiny Ambamen, Chihuahua. Because of the rapid development of the Santa Fe trade at this time, his father, Jesús Ochoa, decided to move to Nuevo México, the southern axis of that trade. As Esteban grew up he was sent, like other *norteños*, to the American end of the trade route in order to complete his classroom education and to gain hands-on experience in the trade.

In Kansas City and Independence, Missouri, young Ochoa learned merchandising and freighting skills and mastered the English language. Having completed his northern apprenticeship, he returned to New Mexico, now part of the United States as a result of the war with Mexico and the 1848 Treaty of Guadalupe Hidalgo. Barely out of his teens, he began to put his training and education into practice while he acquired further business experience. At Las Cruces, New Mexico, he formed a freighting partnership and also opened a general store in nearby Mesilla. Because Mesilla was becoming an important local trade center and stopover on the route westward to Tucson, Yuma, and the southern California goldfields, he succeeded handsomely. He used his profits to establish a flour mill in Las Cruces and small general stores in several nearby towns.

At the end of the 1850s, while still in his twenties, Ochoa was unanimously elected to head a Las Cruces committee to seek the establishment of the area west of the Rio Grande as a territory separate from New Mexico. In 1859 he dissolved his freighting partnership but kept his New Mexico businesses and moved his headquarters to Tucson, prompted by his perception that it was becoming an important hub for trade in both Arizona and the adjoining Mexican state of Sonora. When the Civil War broke out in 1861, this businessman who had just turned 30 years old was considered one of the leading entrepreneurs of the Arizona border region.

A year later, as already related, Ochoa had lost everything and languished in New Mexican exile. With the retaking of Tucson by Northern forces he was able to return and resume his business career. He quickly became an important U.S. army contractor, buying grain, cattle, and sheep in Sonora to feed Union troops. The presence of Northern soldiers ended the Confederate threat to Arizona and greatly reduced depredations by nomadic Indians and bandit gangs. With greater security, the frontier economy began expanding rapidly and mining boomed because of new discoveries and the reopening of old mining areas. Ochoa was in a position to provide the miners with food, hardware, equipment, and other supplies.

Needing more capital for his expanding operations, in early 1864 Ochoa entered a partnership with Pinckney R. Tully, a prominent Anglo entrepreneur. Later they added a third partner, creating Tully, Ochoa, and Company with headquarters at first in Tubac, Arizona, and then in Tucson. For more than a decade it was by far the largest freighting and mercantile firm in the Southwest. Not only did it supply miners and the inhabitants of the many small towns; it also held contracts with the U.S. government to deliver food and other supplies to Indian reservations and the numerous post–Civil War army posts in the Southwest.

Tully, Ochoa, and Company prospered mightily and made the partners leading citizens. In his far-ranging business interests Ochoa made several trips to the East investigating woolen mills, which, he was convinced, could become a very profitable southwestern business once the Apaches were subdued and sheep-raising could be expanded. The mill he subsequently built was initially a great success but later languished. He also promoted cotton culture half a century before its time, making experimental plantings. In order to irrigate the many trial plantings around his home, he was one of the first *tucsonenses* to erect a windmill to pump water.

Ochoa added to his economic and political stature by playing an active role in civic affairs. In April 1871 he was one of a number of prominent Tucson businessmen who petitioned for municipal status. Four years later he was elected mayor over his Anglo opponent by a vote of 187 to 40, having earlier served in two territorial legislatures, on the Board of Supervisors, and on the school board. As mayor and head of the Tucson school trustees he was, more than anyone else, responsible for Arizona's first public school, in Tucson. He also donated the land on which it was built.

In the late 1870s Esteban Ochoa was without question one of the leading citizens of Tucson and the Arizona Territory, if not the whole Southwest. He was involved not only in civic service but also in the most extensive and widest variety of business enterprises and agricultural experiments. Yet he somehow found time in 1877 to woo and marry Altagracia Salazar.

Meanwhile the tracks of the Southern Pacific Railroad were rapidly approaching southern Arizona. On 25 March 1880 Ochoa and about 1,200 other Arizona citizens officially celebrated the railroad's arrival. Ochoa made a short congratulatory speech and presented the railroad officials with a welcoming silver spike. Although Tully, Ochoa, and Company had been strong supporters of the railroad, its arrival unsettled the company and brought irreversible economic changes to the Arizona Territory. It greatly weakened the longtime economic and social ties between Arizona and Sonora and strengthened east-west links. Also, it was now much cheaper and quicker to ship goods and equipment from the East via the railroad than by sea and through the Mexican state of Sonora.

The price of goods dropped precipitously and Tully, Ochoa, and Company was caught by the change, as were other southwestern firms. Many of their customers were forced to sell some in-stock merchandise below cost to compete with cheaper goods arriving by rail. Some were unable to pay for merchandise already received, or paid in Mexican pesos, now depreciated by a decline in the price of silver. Some went bankrupt. The railroad did not cause the collapse of Tully, Ochoa, and Company, but it did end Ochoa's preeminent financial position. The company hung on in a reduced position as a feeder line to the railroad. Along with many other Tucson wholesale houses, it finally was forced to close down in the mid-1880s and liquidate its assets to satisfy creditors.

Despite this severe setback, Ochoa continued his various entrepreneurial activities but was unable to adapt to the new economic conditions as Arizona became more and more an integral part of the national business scene. He lived quietly with his wife and young son in their large home in Tucson. In the fall of 1888, while visiting his mother in Las Cruces, he caught pneumonia and died there on 27 October. He was 57 years old. His obituary succinctly summed up his life: "For many years Mr. Ochoa . . . was among the leading merchants in the territory and made and lost many hundreds of thousands of dollars. . . . That he was financially unfortunate detracts none from the good name he leaves behind. He was a courageous and enterprising citizen and will be long remembered for his good works."

Further Reading

Alford, Harold J. *The Proud People: The Heritage and Culture of Spanish-Speaking Peoples in the United States*. New York: David McKay, 1972.

Lockwood, Frank C. *Pioneer Portraits*. Tucson: University of Arizona Press, 1968.

Meier, Matt S. "Esteban Ochoa, Enterpriser." *Journal of the West* 25:1 (January 1986): 15–21.

Officer, James E., and Adela A. Stewart. *Arizona's Hispanic Perspective*. Phoenix: Arizona Academy, 1981.

Sheridan, Thomas E. "Peacock in the Parlor: Frontier Tucson's Mexican Elite." *Journal of Arizona History* 25 (Autumn 1984).

SEVERO OCHOA

(1905–1993)

Spanish American Nobel Prize–Winning Biochemist, Pharmacologist, Professor

An authority in the field of enzyme chemistry, in 1959 Dr. Severo Ochoa was awarded the Nobel Prize in Medicine along with his former graduate student, Dr. Arthur Kornberg of Stanford University. The courtly, unassuming Ochoa received the Nobel for his discovery of a bacterial enzyme able to synthesize ribonucleic acid (RNA) and his outstanding pioneering work in understanding RNA. His research has been basic to deciphering the genetic code and to comprehending more clearly the basic chemistry of all living things. In addition to his work on enzymes, he pioneered in studies of vitamin B-1 in the late 1930s.

Severo Ochoa was born in the north of Spain on 24 September 1905 to Carmen Albornoz and Severo Ochoa of the small fishing port of Luarca on the Bay of Biscay. Here he spent his early years and attended grade school. He received the greater part of his education in the south of Spain to which his family moved, graduating in 1921 from the *colegio* in Málaga on the Mediterranean coast. One of his teachers had aroused his interest in chemistry, and that interest led him to study medicine as a foundation for the life sciences. Encouraged by his parents, he enrolled in the University of Madrid for his medical studies. He was a hardworking and achieving student, pushing himself industriously and indefatigably toward his goals. He was awarded his doctorate in medicine with honors eight years later in 1929. However, his interest remained organic chemistry and he never practiced medicine.

While still a student at the university in Madrid, Severo began what was to be several years of medical research training outside of Spain. He spent the summer of 1927 working as a research assistant with physiologists at the University of Glasgow in Scotland, and after graduating from the University of Madrid in 1929 he spent two postgraduate years in Germany: the year 1929–1930 in Berlin at the Kaiser Wilhelm Institute for Biology, and 1930–1931 at the University of Heidelberg's institute for medical research. Upon his return to Spain he secured a position as lecturer in physiology and biochemistry in the school of medicine at the University of Madrid. Four years later he was named head of the physiology section in the university's institute for medical research. Then in

1936 he returned to the University of Heidelberg as guest research assistant to Nobel laureate Otto Meyerhoff. From Heidelberg Ochoa went to England. He spent six months as the Ray Lankester investigator in the Marine Biology Laboratory at Plymouth and then accepted an appointment as Neufield research assistant in biochemistry at the Oxford University Medical School. He remained there for a little over two years.

In Spain the victory of General Francisco Franco and the Falangists in 1939 brought an end to the Civil War and also persuaded Severo Ochoa that research would be circumscribed in Spain for the near future. Deciding that his future in scientific research would be best served in the United States, he left England for America in 1940 instead of returning to Spain. In the United States he first secured a position as lecturer and research assistant in pharmacology in the medical school of Washington University in St. Louis. One year later he received an appointment as research assistant in the College of Medicine at the New York University Bellevue Medical Center. In 1945 he was promoted to assistant professor of biochemistry; in the following year he was advanced to professor of pharmacology and became chairman of that department. He remained in these positions until 1954, when he was named professor and chairman of the Department of Biochemistry. He was sworn in as a U.S. citizen two years later. New York University remained his academic "home" until 1986.

At New York University, in addition to his teaching and administrative duties, Ochoa continued the research on enzymes that he had begun earlier in Europe. During the early 1950s he advanced a theory that NADP, a nucleotide present in both plant and animal tissue, plays a key role in the pathway by which foods are converted into the energy needed by living organisms. In 1955 he announced a discovery that cast new light on the basic chemistry of life and forever changed biochemical research. His research concerned the synthesis of ribonucleic acid (RNA), a chemical essential to instruct all living organisms on their production of proteins.

This momentous achievement was crucial to an understanding of how the genetic code is used by organisms to produce proteins and to control cell reproduction. It also was important to a better conceptualization of viral replication and was seen by some scientists as a first step toward a clearer perception of the nature of abnormal cell growth in some cancers. In addition, it was basic to genetic engineering—the introduction into plants and animals, including humans, of genetic materials that specify desirable characteristics.

As a result of his discovery, in 1959 Dr. Ochoa and one of his former students, Dr. Arthur Kornberg, then chairman of the biochemistry department at Stanford University in California, shared the Nobel Prize in Medicine. In addition to the Nobel award, Severo Ochoa has been the recipient of numerous other honors both before and since his Nobel. In 1951 he received the Neuberg Medal in Biochemistry and four years later was given the Price Award by the Société de Chemie Biologique of France. In 1958 he was honored with the Borden Award in the Medical Sciences by the Association of American Medical Colleges. In addition, he received honorary degrees from Washington University in 1957 and from Oxford University four years later. His expertise has also been recognized by professorships at various universities in the United States and Latin America.

Ochoa was the author of numerous publications in his fields of interest in biochemistry. He was a fellow of the American Association for the Advancement of Science and of the American Academy of Arts and Sciences. Very active in professional organizations, he served on and later chaired the biochemistry panel in the U.S. Office of Naval Research in the 1950s, while at the same time serving as a member of the science advisory committee of the Massachusetts General Hospital. In 1953–1954 he was president of the Harvey Society and four years later was president of the Society of Biological Chemists. Because of his outstanding contributions in the fields of organic chemistry, he was also singled out for honorary memberships in numerous academies and scientific societies in the United States, Latin America, and Europe.

Possibly because of the death of his wife in 1986, Severo Ochoa retired from New York University that year and returned to the Spain he had left exactly half a century earlier. He died of pneumonia in a Madrid hospital on the first day of November 1993 and was buried in his home town, Luarca. He was characterized by colleagues and many world-famous scientists as a warm-hearted, modest man of subtle and lucid mind with unlimited enthusiasm for pure research. A staunch democrat, he believed in an open, pluralistic society and spoke out boldly against the Franco regime in Spain.

Further Reading

American Men of Science: A Biographical Dictionary, 10th ed. New York: R. R. Bowker Co., 1962.

Current Biography Yearbook, 1962. New York: H. W. Wilson Co., 1962.

International Who's Who. London: Europa Publications, 1993.

"Severo Ochoa, Biochemist, a Nobel Winner, 66, Dies." *New York Times* [obit.] 143 (3 November 1993): G23(N), D25(L).

Who's Who in America, 1962–1963. Chicago: Marquis Who's Who, 1962.

World Biography. Bethpage, N.Y.: Institute for Research in Biography, 1954.

EDWARD JAMES OLMOS

(1947–)

Mexican American Actor, Director, Producer, Singer

Edward James Olmos is a man with a mission. His objective is to portray Latinos who can be role models for youth. He believes in portraying characters that have meaning and truth. In the script for the film *American Me*, he rewrote his character, Santana, to deglamourize gang leaders and gangs, which he has referred to as a cancer on society. He recognizes that films are entertainment and business, but he holds the opinion that they can also be something more. He believes that his success brings with it an obligation. For over two decades he has criss-crossed the United States, giving as many as 150 talks a year in schools, halfway houses, juvenile detention centers, and prisons. His message: set goals, develop self-discipline, and persevere.

Born on 24 February 1947 in East Los Angeles, California, Edward James Olmos was the second of three children of Pedro Olmos, who emigrated from Mexico as a youth, and Eleanor Huizar, a third-generation Mexican American. He spent his early years in the ethnically mixed Boyle Heights section of Los Angeles. After his parents divorced in the mid-1950s, Olmos lived with his mother in Montebello. He became an avid baseball fan and player, observing professionals and practicing nearly every day. In Little League he won the Golden State batting championship and was skilled enough as a 13-year-old to catch for practicing major league pitchers in a Dodger farm club. Olmos credits baseball with teaching him the importance of discipline, patience, and perseverance—all qualities that later became important in his professional career.

Having been a singer as a young boy, at Montebello High School Olmos became absorbed in music and his baseball days ended. He taught himself to play the piano; and from his father, who remained an important part of his children's life, he learned to dance. In the mid-1960s with several young friends he formed a band called Eddie and the Pacific Ocean, which played at weddings, bar mitzvahs, and nightclubs. During the day Olmos attended East Los Angeles Junior College, graduating with an Associate of Arts degree in sociology. Later he studied at California State University at Los Angeles. Drama and dance classes that he took to improve his stage presence led him to move from music to acting. Eddie and the Pacific Ocean was dissolved.

Using the band's van, Olmos started a furniture delivery business to support himself, and soon a wife as well, while he studied, practiced, and learned to be an actor. With the same self-discipline and determination he had shown in baseball and music, he worked in local experimental theaters to get experience and sought bit parts in television shows. After much hustling and a number of walk-on parts as an extra, Olmos got the part of a Puerto Rican bartender in the television series *Kojak* and later small parts in *Hawaii Five-0* and *Medical Center* and in a television documentary about undocumented Mexicans titled *Alambrista*, directed by Robert Young.

Early in 1978 Olmos and some 300 other actors tried out for the part of El Pachuco in *Zoot Suit*, a play by **Luis Valdez** based on the famous murder trial of Chicano youths in Los Angeles during World War II. He got the part of the flamboyant, strutting, supermacho spirit of the barrio, El Pachuco, the narrator in the musical. It was his first paid stage role. *Zoot Suit* opened in Los Angeles at the Mark Taper Forum, where it ran for 18 weeks. A great success, it then moved to the Aquarius Theater for a nine-month run and finally went to Broadway for nearly two months. Later the play was also filmed. For his portrayal of El Pachuco, Olmos won the Los Angeles Critics Circle Award as well as a Theater World award, and was nominated for a Tony award.

At the beginning of the 1980s Olmos got supporting roles in the movies *Wolfen* and *Blade Runner* and in 1982 played the lead in the PBS American Playhouse presentation, *The Ballad of Gregorio Cortez*. In *Gregorio Cortez* he portrayed the real-life story of a border *tejano* accused of murder, finally captured after a long chase, convicted, and ultimately pardoned by the governor of Texas. Largely as a result of Olmos's persistent efforts, the television film about this *mexicano* folk hero was later released to theaters and copies were donated to schools, libraries, and other institutions. *Gregorio Cortez* was a breakthrough film for Mexican Americans; for Olmos it was a major step in his career.

Olmos appeared in some early episodes of the popular television series *Hill Street Blues* but rejected a regular part because it involved an exclusive contract. In 1984 he finally got what he wanted: a nonexclusive contract to play police lieutenant Martin Castillo in the television series *Miami Vice*. His characterization won him an Emmy for best supporting actor in the following year and a Golden Globe award in 1986. In 1988 he co-starred in *The Fortunate Pilgrim*, a television miniseries. He has also made numerous guest appearances on television.

Meanwhile, because of his nonexclusive contract Olmos was able to devote himself to a project to portray **Jaime Escalante**, a Bolivian-born calculus teacher at Garfield High School in Los Angeles. Olmos's portrayal of Escalante in the film *Stand and Deliver* illustrates the qualities in which he so strongly believes. For that role he was nominated for Best Actor award in 1989. Olmos considers it his most important piece of acting because it provides Latino youths a lesson and a role model.

In 1992 Olmos had his first opportunity to direct a film. He rewrote the script to *American Me*, a story about Chicano gangs that had been floating around Hollywood for nearly two decades; he co-produced, directed, and played the lead in the film. Some reviewers saw his harshly realistic portrayal as an effort to offset the glamour he had given El Pachuco earlier. As with *Gregorio Cortez*, Olmos hopes to get copies distributed widely to bring home to young people the sordid realities of gang life. In April 1994 Olmos's documentary *Lives in Hazard*, a follow-up to the semi-fictional *American Me*, was the latest in his continuing efforts to convince young people how self-destructive gang involvement can be.

After *Stand and Deliver* Olmos played leading roles in *Triumph of the Spirit*, 1989, a story about Auschwitz concentration camp life, and in *Talent for the Game*, 1991, in which he played a baseball catcher. His film *My Family/Mi Familia*, 1994, brought him further praise; his current film project is entitled *Caught*, due to be released late in 1996. Among his television films are *The Burning Season, Menéndez: A Killing in Beverly Hills*, both in 1994, and *Dead Man's Walk*, 1996. With longtime friend Robert Young he formed a company, YOY Productions, that has a number of films in various planning stages. Among them is an adaptation of Miguel Cervantes's *Don Quixote*, a role Olmos has coveted for years. He has won numerous honors and awards, and in 1988 he was the subject of a *Time* cover story.

Further Reading

Aufderheide, Pat. "An Actor Turns Activist." *Mother Jones* 8:9 (November 1983): 60.

———. "Reel Life." *Mother Jones* 13:3 (April 1988).

Brady, James. *Parade, San Jose Mercury News* (5 May 1996): 30.

Breiter, Tom. "Edward James Olmos." *Nuestro* (May 1983).

Current Biography, 1992, vol. 53:8. New York: H. W. Wilson Co., 1992.

Díaz, Katherine A. "Edward James Olmos—You Ain't Seen Nothing Yet." *Caminos* 1:7 (November 1980).

"Emmy Award Winner Inspires Young Chicanos." *Forum* (October 1985).

Meyers, Jeff. "Keeping Close to the Street." *Los Angeles Times Magazine* (22 June 1986).

Montane, Diana. "Edward James Olmos." *Vista* 1:1 (8 September 1985): 8–12.

Mooney, Louise, ed. *Newsmakers: The People behind Today's Headlines*. Detroit: Gale Research, 1990.

Stayton, Richard. "The Ballad of Edward James Olmos." *L.A. Style* [Los Angeles, California] 5 (March 1990).

MIGUEL ANTONIO OTERO JR.

(1859–1944)

Mexican American Political Leader, Governor, Businessman, Banker

Today Miguel Otero Jr. is probably best remembered for the three-volume biography that he wrote after his retirement and published between 1935 and 1940. In it he tells not only about his experiences growing up on the western frontier and his acquaintance with many of its leading figures but also about frontier problems, territorial politics, and land grant issues. He paints a picture of a nonconformist West—rough and energetic, the stuff on which much myth of the West has been based. His warm, vivid biography is still one of the important primary sources for the history of the southwestern frontier during an exciting and important period.

Miguel Antonio Otero was born on 17 October 1859 in St. Louis, Missouri, the second of four children born to Mary Blackwood from Charleston, South Carolina, and Miguel A. Otero Sr. of New Mexico. His father, who had been a college professor and lawyer, was an important Democratic politician in the Territory of New Mexico as well as a leading landowner and businessman of the southwestern frontier with interests in freight forwarding, merchandising, mining, ranching, railroading, and banking. Because of his father's widespread business interests, the Otero family moved a lot; when Miguel was 7 years old, just after the end of the Civil War, he was sent, with his older brother, to a boarding school in Topeka for a short time and then to a private school in Leavenworth, Kansas. He also gained much practical education in the streets and business establishments of post–Civil War frontier railroad towns and trade centers in Kansas, Colorado, and New Mexico, where his father's presence was required as an officer in the Santa Fe Railroad and in Otero, Sellar, and Company. His autobiography tells of his acquaintance with frontier celebrities such as Billy the Kid (William H. Bonney), Jesse James, Buffalo Bill Cody, Wild Bill Hickok, and George Armstrong Custer.

As a young man Miguel was sent by his father "back East" for his higher education. He attended St. Louis University (1869–1870); received an appointment to the U.S. Naval Academy in Annapolis, Maryland, but left; and in 1877 studied business administration at the University of Notre Dame in Indiana. In part his moves were the result of bouts of ill health in addition to a certain lack of enthusiasm for academia. He never

Miguel Antonio Otero Jr. Photo courtesy of the Center for
Southwest Research, General Library, University of New
Mexico.

did complete his degree, much preferring the excitement of the West.
Upon his return to the Kansas frontier he worked as a cashier and bookkeeper in his father's firm, Otero, Sellar, and Company, at age 18. In 1881
he was elected cashier of the San Miguel National Bank, and Otero, Sellar, and Company was liquidated as the culmination of longtime es-
trangement of the principals.

When his father died of pneumonia in 1882, 22-year-old Miguel Jr.
assumed a leading role in the family's many business interests, making
good use of his earlier training and experience. In addition to replacing
his father in mining, ranching, banking, real estate, and merchandising,
he took his place in politics—but in the Republican rather than the Democratic Party. A year after his father's death he was city treasurer of Las
Vegas, New Mexico, where Otero, Sellar, and Company had had its
headquarters. Elected San Miguel County probate court clerk in 1886,
three years later he became county clerk, and from 1890 to 1893 he was
clerk of the Fourth District Federal Court. He was extremely popular
socially and active in community service; for a while he played semi-
professional baseball.

Meanwhile as the New Mexican delegate to the Republican national convention Otero met Ohio delegate William McKinley. In the election of 1896 Otero was one of the Republicans mentioned as a potential vice-presidential candidate. He was not selected, but McKinley was elected president of the United States. Despite some heavy opposition within the Republican Party, Otero was named governor of the New Mexico Territory by the new president. The Senate confirmed his appointment, and at age 37 Otero became the youngest and first Mexican American territorial governor since Donaciano Vigil in 1847.

A consummate politician and man of action rather than an intellectual, Otero gave the Territory vigorous business-oriented leadership during his two terms as governor and developed an effective political organization, particularly among elite *nuevomexicanos* whose aspirations he supported. By obtaining control over some federal appointments in the territory, he considerably increased his powers as governor. During the Spanish American War in 1898 he was responsible, more than anyone else, for originating, recruiting, and organizing the regiment known as the Rough Riders, led by Assistant Secretary of the Navy Theodore "Teddy" Roosevelt. Roosevelt acknowledged his indebtedness to Otero and pledged to support his fight for New Mexican statehood.

At the beginning of the 20th century, statehood became a red-hot issue dominating Otero's second term. A man of strong convictions who never hesitated to express them and to fight vigorously anyone who opposed them, he vociferously supported separate statehood for New Mexico and for the Arizona Territory. In 1901 he called a statehood convention to meet in Albuquerque and appeared before it, giving a forceful and eloquent speech in support of New Mexican statehood. Despite his vigorous efforts, New Mexico was not admitted as a state until 1912, after he had left office.

As a leader in New Mexico's business community, Otero actively fought against President Teddy Roosevelt's policy of setting aside timber lands as National Forests. His opposition antagonized a large segment of the Republican Party known as the Progressives, who now opposed his appointment to a third term. As his second term came to a close, Roosevelt, who belonged to the Progressive wing, was persuaded not to reappoint him. On 1 January 1907 Otero stepped down as governor; he also switched his allegiance to the Democratic Party.

After a protracted tour of Europe and England with his son Miguel IV, Otero returned to New Mexico and to politics. In 1909 he was appointed territorial treasurer and president of the board of penitentiary commissioners. From 1913 to 1917 he served as president of the new state's parole board. In the presidential elections of 1912 and 1916 he headed the New Mexico delegation to the Democratic national conventions, and from 1920 to 1924 he was a member of the Democratic National Committee. With the Democrats in power in Washington, he was appointed by President Woodrow Wilson as marshall of the Panama Canal Zone and served from 1917 to 1921.

During the 1920s Otero began to write, publishing *Conquistadors of Spain and Buccaneers of England, France and Holland* in 1924. At the suggestion of friends that he set down his memoirs, he also began writing his autobiography, the first volume of which appeared in 1935. In the following year he published *The Real Billy the Kid*, whom he both knew and greatly admired, saying that he was more sinned against than sinning.

During World War II Miguel Otero Jr. died at the age of 84 on 7 August 1944, ending a productive and richly filled public career of over 50 years.

Further Reading

Crocchiola, Stanley. *The Otero, New Mexico, Story*. Pantex, Tex.: Pampa Print Shop, 1962.

Lamar, Howard. *The Reader's Encyclopedia of the American West*. New York: Thomas Y. Crowell, 1977.

Lomelí, Francisco, and Carl R. Shirley, eds. *Dictionary of Literary Biography*, vol. 82, Chicano Writers, First Series. Detroit: Gale Research, 1989.

"Miguel Otero Dies; Leader in West, 84." *New York Times* (8 August 1944): 17.

Otero, Miguel A., Jr. *My Life on the Frontier, 1864–1882*. New York: Press of the Pioneers, 1935.

———. *My Life on the Frontier, 1882–1897*. Albuquerque: University of New Mexico Press, 1939.

———. *My Nine Years as Governor of the Territory of New Mexico, 1897–1906*. Albuquerque: University of New Mexico Press, 1940.

———. *Otero: An Autobiographical Trilogy*. New York: Arno Press, 1974.

Twitchell, Ralph Emerson. *The Leading Facts of New Mexican History*, 5 vols. Cedar Rapids, Iowa: Torch Press, 1911–1917.

EDUARDO PADRÓN

(1945–   )

Cuban American Educator, Administrator

Eduardo Padrón's professional career has been characterized by a long record of notable accomplishments. As president of the Wolfson campus

Eduardo Padrón. Photo courtesy of Eduardo Padrón.

of Miami-Dade Community College, he has achieved an enviable reputation in educational circles as an initiator of innovative academic programs as well as a staunch defender of the basic rights of all students to
access to higher education. Most recently his qualities of academic leadership were again confirmed when he was given the prestigious Chief
Executive Officer Award by the Association of Community Colleges
Trustees in 1995.

Eduardo Padrón was born in Cuba in 1945. Born into a middle-class
urban family, he received his primary and most of his secondary education on the island. In 1961, less than two years after the revolution led
by Fidel Castro had succeeded in ousting Fulgencio Batista, he and his
family came to the United States. The family settled in the rapidly growing Cuban refugee community in Miami, Florida, and Eduardo attended
Miami Senior High School. After graduating from high school he entered
Miami-Dade Community College and completed his bachelor's degree
four years later at Florida Atlantic University, *summa cum laude*. Subsequently he earned a master's degree and in 1970 a Ph.D. in economics
at the University of Florida in Gainesville.

Even before he completed his doctorate, Padrón had a long history of leadership in the community as well as in academia. During the early 1970s he was instrumental in the founding of the first two Hispanic social service agencies in Miami and chaired their boards of directors. Later in the 1970s he also served on the boards of the Urban League, Miami Mental Health Center, Community Relations Board, and a half-dozen other important local civic agencies. He was named a "lifetime leader" in an editorial by the *Miami Herald*.

In the aftermath of the disturbances and rioting in Miami following the Mariel landings in 1980, Padrón was one of the city's business and civic pacesetters who joined together to found an organization of concerned leaders, the Greater Miami United. During the 1980s he also gave active service on the boards of various city and regional councils and commissions, including the Greater Miami Chamber of Commerce, the Eleventh District Judicial Nominating Commission, and the Fair Elections Campaign Practices Commission. In the 1990s his involvement with numerous civic groups has not diminished.

In addition to these varied civic involvements, Padrón has had a long history of effective and successful working relationships with local, state, and national government officials who have made use of his expertise in education by appointing him to numerous trusteeships and chairmanships. He has cultivated the support of county and state legislators for his institution as well as that of federal agencies and has testified before Florida and federal legislatures on numerous occasions.

Three Florida governors have entrusted him with positions on important statewide councils and political agencies, and three American presidents have called upon his extensive educational experience. President Jimmy Carter named him to the very important 12-member panel whose job it was to design the president's educational program; later he served in several other capacities at the appointment of President Carter. President George Bush appointed him chairman of the National Columbus Scholars Commission in connection with the quincentennial celebration in 1992 of the European encounter with the New World. In the following year President Bill Clinton publicly recognized his experience and expertise by proclaiming him "one of America's most outstanding educators." Earlier the president had called upon him for advice in formulating a national educational policy and appointed him to the White House Commission on Educational Excellence. In addition to the advice he has given directly to the president, he is often called upon for consultation by both the U.S. Department of Education and the National Science Foundation.

As an educator, Padrón is noted for his ideas and his action. He rose from classroom teacher to vice-president and then president of the Wolfson Campus in just a decade. His 15 years as educational leader of the campus have been characterized by the introduction of numerous innovative programs that have made the Wolfson campus not only one of the most successful community colleges in the country but also a downtown Miami center for a wide variety of cultural and civic events. In various forums he has brought to campus such divergent leaders and personalities as former president Gerald Ford, Congresswoman Shirley Chisholm, businessman Malcolm Forbes Jr., scientist Carl Sagan, sports figure Duke Snider, and astronaut **Ellen Ochoa.**

Dr. Padrón's more academic-oriented innovations include the development of an English as a second language curriculum, the creation of the first U.S. bilingual instructional program, a Council for the Continuing Education of Women, the South Florida Thinking Skills Institute, and the Environmental Demonstration Center with programs in the areas of nutrition and vegetarian studies, among others. To promote greater literacy he founded Miami Book Fair International, which annually attracts many thousands of visitors to the campus but which also provides special literacy-oriented programs for over 20,000 children in the greater Miami area. He has consistently encouraged the adoption of new technology in the classroom and urged his faculty to develop expertise in this area.

Padrón has been the recipient of more than 100 awards and honors. He has made presentations at a number of important international educational conferences and has been invited to give guest lectures at several universities in Europe and Latin America. He has received honorific awards from the governments of Mexico, Colombia, Argentina, and Israel. The king of Spain, Juan Carlos, gave him that country's most prestigious award, Order of Queen Isabel La Católica; and in 1990 France honored him with its highest award to a foreign national, L'Officier des Palmes Académiques, a distinction established by Napoleon Bonaparte in the early 1800s. Domestically, among many honors he has been given the Distinguished Leadership Award by the United Negro College Fund, the Leonard Abbess Human Relations Award by the B'nai B'rith, and the Silver Medallion from the National Conference of Christians and Jews. In 1994 he represented the president of the United States at the inauguration of Ernesto Samper-Pizano, the new president of Colombia.

Further Reading

Boswell, Thomas, and James R. Curtis. *The Cuban-American Experience: Culture, Images and Perspectives.* Totowa, N.J.: Rowman & Allanheld, 1984.

Fradd, Sandra. "Cubans to Cuban Americans: Assimilation in the United States." *Migration Today* 11:4–5 (1983):34–42.

Gilder, George. "Miami's Cuban Miracle." *Reason* 16:6 (1984):21–28.

Unterburger, Amy, ed. *Who's Who among Hispanic Americans, 1994–1995.* Detroit: Gale Research, 1994.

AMÉRICO PAREDES

(1915–)

Mexican American Folklorist, Teacher, Writer, Poet

Cited by his colleagues as one of the seminal Mexican American scholars of the 20th century, soft-spoken Américo Paredes usually kept his strong feelings about racial discrimination and bias deep within himself. But his gentle, dignified demeanor obscured a deep-seated indignation and anger that caused him to be considered a flaming radical by many during his youthful activism in Brownsville, Texas. Following in the impressive footsteps of **Carlos Castañeda** and **George I. Sánchez**, he fought racism as he made imposing intellectual contributions to Chicano scholarship from the 1950s onward in his studies of *corridos*, machismo, folk medicine, and border stereotypes of *mexicanos*. He also trained a whole school of southwestern folklorists.

Américo Paredes was born on 3 September 1915 in Brownsville, Texas, at the height of the border disorder and violence brought on by the great Mexican revolution of 1910. His rancher father, Justo Paredes, came from a family that had settled in the lower Rio Grande valley, on both sides of the river, in the mid-1700s after nearly 200 years in a Nuevo León Sephardic colony. The family of his mother, Clotilde Manzano-Vidal, had emigrated from Spain around 1850. She gave him the name Américo after the great 16th-century navigator and geographer Amerigo Vespucci, as the result of a promise to an aunt and her Italian sailor husband.

Américo grew up in a family of eight children and received his early education in the Brownsville public schools. After school hours he worked at various jobs and in the summers listened, in the ranches on the Mexican side of the river, to *corridos*, oral traditions, and old folk stories. In high school he recalls first encountering anti-Mexican prejudice; among several incidents the most traumatic was his school counselor's racist presumption that he would not go on to college. It nearly deterred him. However, with the active encouragement of one of his teachers and a first prize from Trinity University in a statewide poetry contest, upon graduation from high school in 1934 he enrolled in Brownsville Junior College. He received his Associate of Arts degree two years later. While attending college he also began working for the Brownsville *Herald* as a translator, proofreader, and staff writer. On the *Herald* he again faced discrimination, and the experience led to his life-long energetic fight against racism and ethnic bias.

Américo Paredes. Photo courtesy of Américo Paredes.

At age 20 Américo began seeing his poetry in print in the literary supplement to San Antonio's *La Prensa*, and in 1937 he had his first book published, a collection of his poems titled *Cantos de adolescencia*. While continuing his job with the *Herald*, in 1940 he began to do war-related work at Pan American Airways, a position he resigned to enter the U.S. army in 1944. In the army he was assigned to the staff of the *Stars and Stripes* and at the war's end was sent to the Far East as a correspondent to cover the war crimes trials in Tokyo. During his last year in the army he was political editor of the Pacific edition of the *Stars and Stripes*. Taking his discharge in Japan, whose culture he found very appealing, he worked there for two years as a public relations specialist in the American Red Cross. He also married Amelia Nagamine, a young woman of Uruguayan-Japanese heritage.

Following his return to the United States in 1950 Américo set about to fulfill a longtime dream—to become a professor of English. He enrolled in the University of Texas at Austin (UTA) and graduated with an A.B. in English in one year, *summa cum laude*. Two years later he completed his Master of Arts degree in English and folklore and in 1956 was awarded his Ph.D. in those same fields. He wrote his doctoral dissertation on **Gregorio Cortez**, the *tejano* hero of a border *corrido* and a towering figure in Mexican American folklore. In 1956 he secured a job on the faculty of the University of Texas, El Paso, which he left in the following year to accept a tenure track position teaching folklore and creative writing at his alma mater in Austin.

During his first year in Austin, Paredes's doctoral dissertation was published by the university press under the title *With His Pistol in His Hand: A Border Ballad and Its Hero*. It met with an enthusiastic reception and was to remain his most widely acclaimed work. Paredes taught at the University of Texas in Austin for the remainder of his academic career, becoming a giant in the anthropology and English departments. In 1967 he founded UTA's interdisciplinary folklore program. At the beginning of the 1980s he was named the Ashbel Smith Professor of English and anthropology, and in 1983 he was appointed the Dickson, Allen, and Anderson Centennial Professor, to which title was added Emeritus when he retired two years later.

An outstanding teacher, Paredes often brought his guitar to class, giving what he called singing lectures based on ballads he had learned as a youth both in Brownsville and across the Rio Grande in Mexico. In his anthropology classes he trained an entire generation of folklorists concerned with understanding and appreciating the complex culture of the southwestern border region.

Always an activist, at Austin Paredes fought doggedly in the 1960s for the creation of a Mexican American studies program at the university despite obstacles and opposition. Finally in 1970 he succeeded, becoming founder and first director of UTA's Center for Mexican-American Studies. Twice in the early 1970s he handed in his resignation when his suggestions were not given serious consideration by university administrators.

Recognized from early on for his exceptional folklorist skills and contributions, in 1962 Paredes was the recipient of a Guggenheim fellowship and five years later was invited to the University of California at Berkeley as a distinguished visiting scholar. He was also singled out by appointment as editor of the *Journal of American Folklore* from 1968 to 1973. In 1989 he was awarded the $5,000 Charles Frankel Prize by the National Endowment for the Humanities for his work in creating greater understanding of the humanities.

In 1990 Américo Paredes was decorated by the Mexican government with the Aguila Azteca, Mexico's highest award to a foreigner, for his defense of human rights and preservation of northern Mexican culture. In the following year he also received the Order of José de Escandón from Mexico. In October 1993 the University of Texas at Austin paid homage to his extensive and impeccable scholarship by dedicating to him a two-day symposium entitled "Regional Identity and Cultural Tradition: The Tejano Contribution." It included, properly, a folkloric concert in his honor.

In addition to *With His Pistol in His Hand*, which has had at least eight reprints, Américo Paredes has written two other very important folkloric works—*Folktales of Mexico*, 1970, and *A Texas Mexican Cancionero: Folksongs of the Lower Border*, 1976—as well as some 60 articles in scholarly journals. He is also the author of *George Washington Gómez: A Mexicotexan Novel*, 1990; a book of poetry, *Between Two Worlds*, 1991; a collection of Mexican American border jokes, *Uncle Remus con chile*, 1993; and a collection of scholarly articles, *Folklore and Culture on the Texas-Mexican Border*, 1993. A collection of his short stories is currently in press with the title *The Hammon and the Beans and Other Stories*.

Further Reading

"Américo Paredes, a Man from the Border." *Revista Chicano-Riqueña* 8:3 (Fall 1980).

García, Kimberly. "Author Battles Racist Views." *Brownsville Herald* (4 August 1991).

Limón, José. "With a Corrido in His Heart." *Nuestro* 3:7 (Fall Special 1979).

Martínez, Julio A. *Chicano Scholars and Writers: A Bio-Bibliographical Directory*. Metuchen, N.J.: Scarecrow Press, 1979.

Martínez, Julio A., and Francisco Lomelí. *Chicano Literature: A Reference Guide*. Westport, Conn.: Greenwood Press, 1985.

The Mexican Texans. San Antonio: Institute of Texas Culture, 1971.

Palacios, Arturo, ed. *Mexican American Directory*, 1969–1970 ed. Washington, D.C.: Executive Systems Corp., 1969.

Simmen, Edward, ed. *New Voices in Literature: The Mexican American*. Edinburg, Tex.: Pan American University, 1971.

ESTELA PORTILLO TRAMBLEY

(1936–)

Mexican American Playwright, Author, Poet, Teacher

Portillo Trambley has described herself as Chicana who has become much Anglicized. Born into a middle-class Mexican American family, she seemingly had little personal experience with social discrimination while growing up. As an author and schoolteacher, married to an Anglo, she says that she finds herself at times torn between a strong feeling for Mexican culture and the Mexican American community and an uncompromising feminist criticism of some of its negative cultural attitudes such as machismo. She is aware of some internal conflict.

Estela Portillo was born on 16 January 1936 in El Paso, Texas, to Delfina Fierro and Francisco Portillo, one of four children. Her mother was from the state of Chihuahua and her upwardly mobile father was from Jalisco; he was a diesel mechanic and her mother taught piano. Unlike some Mexican American writers of the 1970s, she grew up in middle-class comfort; at no time did she experience the hardships of working in agriculture. She has no recollection of traumatic racial or other discrimination as a schoolgirl and teenager. She grew up living mostly with her grandparents until their deaths when she was 12 years old. She then returned to her El Paso home to live with her parents.

As a child Estela spoke mostly Spanish in the home and English outside, and she learned to read and write in English. At her El Paso high school she worked on the school paper and won a prize for her poetry. During her formative years her favorite authors were romantic novelists such as Kathleen Norris and Gene Stratton-Porter. Later in college she enjoyed reading a wider spectrum of authors from world literature, including the Mexican philosophers José Vasconcelos and Octavio Paz.

Upon graduating from high school Estela Portillo married at a very young age, kept house, and began a family. She also continued her formal education at the University of Texas in El Paso (UTEP), where she earned her undergraduate degree in English in 1957. Upon graduating from UTEP she took a job teaching at the El Paso Technical High School and from 1965 to 1969 chaired the English department there. She also continued her studies for a Master of Arts degree in English at UTEP, finally completing her degree work in 1978. She credits the English department faculty at UTEP with much of her success in writing creative fiction.

When the youngest of her six children, 9-month-old Robert Kieth, died of a rare gland infection at the end of the 1960s, Portillo Trambley turned to writing in part as therapy for her grief. After intensive reading in the European philosophers she wrote her first book, which was roundly rejected by publishers. However, she did not give up, and in 1972 her play *Days of the Swallows* won the Quinto Sol Award given each year by the Berkeley, California, publishing company Quinto Sol. In the same year she took a leave of absence from her teaching position to produce a two-hour radio talk show on El Paso station KIZZ. After two years as hostess of stimulating and challenging programs there, she was invited to direct a semiweekly cultural television program called "Cumbres" at local station KROD. By the time the financing for "Cumbres" dried up, her experience in writing for television had convinced her that she wanted more than anything else to be a writer. In order to give herself more time for writing she worked for the school district's Department of Special Services starting in 1979, teaching in the high school's Homebound and Hospital programs.

As a result of her communications experience as well as her dramatic talents, Estela Portillo received an appointment as resident dramatist at the El Paso Community College. She was also one of the founders of bilingual theater in El Paso. These activities gave her the opportunity to revise, direct, and stage some of the five plays she had written in the meantime. In addition to *Days of the Swallows*, she wrote *Blacklight* in 1973 and *Hombre cósmico* in the following year. In 1976 she completed a musical comedy called *Sun Images*, the first musical authored by a Chicana. She also composed most of its songs.

Meanwhile, in 1975 Portillo Trambley became the first Chicana to publish a collection of short fictional pieces, titled *Rain of Scorpions and Other Writings* after its main novella. The thought-provoking themes in these tales added both a female voice and feminist foci of concerns to Chicano literature. Because of her literary success Portillo Trambley has enjoyed considerable popularity as a guest lecturer at various universities, particularly where her plays have been presented.

Portillo Trambley's writings present a hopeful view of the human spirit overcoming the self-evident wretchedness and suffering of the barrio. They center mostly on women and show a deep concern for their full equality and right to control themselves and their roles in life. Deriving in large measure from Portillo's Mexican American background, they assert without qualification the right of women to liberate themselves from traditional social norms that may be outmoded. They deal sensitively and sometimes lyrically, if at times somewhat melodramatically, with the emancipation of women who rebel against societal oppression, and they ponder the philosophic questions of life. They therefore often transcend their ethnic setting and have universal application.

Many literary critics and other readers regard Portillo Trambley as a feminist writer, but she says that she does not see herself in this role. However, she readily admits to writing from a feminine viewpoint about women and their personal crises in a society that assigns them subservient roles. They therefore are at the center of her narratives, and through her description of their life experiences of thwarted aspirations and exploitation she expresses her views about the role she believes women should play in society. As a result, she has been charged by some critics with being more concerned with moral lessons than with artistic creativity.

At the beginning of the 1980s Portillo Trambley was involved in writing a number of scripts on Hispanic history and culture for National Public Radio. In 1983 she published a new play about Sor Juana Inés de 9la Cruz (the famous colonial feminist nun of 18th-century Mexico) entitled *Sor Juana and Other Plays*, and three years later she brought out a novel entitled *Trini*. At the beginning of the 1990s the Bilingual Press published a new edition of *The Rain of Scorpions*, which Portillo Trambley had considerably revised and to which she added four new stories.

She clearly has made substantial contributions to Chicano literature and remains one of the foremost contemporary Chicana writers as well as the outstanding Chicana dramatist.

Further Reading

Bruce-Novoa, Juan. *Chicano Authors: Inquiry by Interview.* Austin: University of Texas Press, 1980.

Fem 8:34 (June–July 1984): 37–40.

Martínez, Julio A., and Francisco A. Lomelí. *Chicano Literature: A Reference Guide.* Westport, Conn.: Greenwood Press, 1985.

Ryan, Bryan, ed. *Hispanic Writers.* Detroit: Gale Research, 1991.

Tatum, Charles. *Chicano Literature.* Boston: Twayne Publishers, 1982.

Vallejos, Tomás. "Estela Portillo Trambley's Fictive Search for Paradise." *Frontiers: A Journal of Women Studies* 5:2 (Summer 1980): 54–58.

DOLORES PRIDA

(1943–)

Cuban American Playwright, Actress, Director, Novelist, Journalist, Poet

The Cuban American theater has deep roots in the United States, going back to the activities of groups like El Club Lírico Dramático Cubano in the early years of the 1900s. Following in the footsteps of pioneering Cuban American playwright **María Irene Fornés**, Dolores Prida burst upon the theatrical scene in the 1980s. She has been ranked by critics as one of the most important dramatists of the contemporary Latino American theater. Multifaceted expressions of the cultural duality experienced by recent immigrants and their children, her plays have been performed in the United States, Venezuela, Puerto Rico, and the Dominican Republic. In seeking the broadest possible audience she skillfully weaves into her works music, humor, and various embodiments of popular culture from *santeriá* to *telenovelas*. She makes reference to favorite foods, popular songs, and courting customs and incorporates common, everyday expressions in her dialogue. In addition to her plays she writes about problems of social injustice, especially those suffered by women, as well as the Latino American search for identity.

Dolores Prida was born on 5 September 1943 in the small town of Caibarién on the northern coast of Las Villas province in central Cuba. Her parents, Dolores Prieta and Manuel Prida, belonged to the Cuban middle class. Dolores received her elementary education in Caibarién and later attended business school there. While still a teenager in Cuba she began writing poetry and short stories, which she kept to herself. Shortly after Fidel Castro took power at the beginning of 1959 her father fled the island to the United States, and the rest of the family followed him to New York City two years later, a part of the first exile wave. In the mid-1960s Dolores entered New York City's Hunter College, where she majored in Spanish American literature for four years but did not complete her degree requirements. While at Hunter she also worked as the company magazine editor for Schraffts Restaurants and published her first work, a book of poetry entitled *Treinta y un poemas*, 1967.

Prida left Schraffts in 1969 to take a one-year position with Collier-MacMillan International as a foreign correspondent. There followed a series of short-term jobs in which she gathered a wide variety of writing experience: 1970–1971, assistant editor for Simon and Schuster's *International Dictionary*; 1971–1973, director of Information Services for the National Puerto Rican Forum; 1973–1974, managing editor at the Spanish-language daily *El Tiempo*; 1975–1976, arts and science editor in London and later New York correspondent for the magazine *Visión*; 1977–1980, senior editor of *Nuestro* magazine; and 1980–1983, consultant, translator, and literary manager for International Arts Relations, Inc. (INTAR). In 1983 she accepted the position of director of publications for the Association of Hispanic Arts. In all these jobs her bilingualism was of prime importance. Although her varied experiences are not unusual among Latina writers, her versatility and success are.

Meanwhile Prida was doing some of her own writing. In 1976 she received the Cintas Fellowship award for literature, and in the following year her first play, *Beautiful Señoritas*, was performed in New York. It was extremely well received and subsequently was performed all over the United States. In 1979 her musical *The Beggars Soap Opera*, based on Brecht's *The Threepenny Opera*, was produced, also in New York. In the next year she was given the Creative Artistic Public Service Award for Playwriting and also saw her third play, *La era latina* (a bilingual musical comedy co-authored with Victor Fragoso), produced. It won a special award in 1981 at the International Third World Theatre Competition in Caracas, Venezuela. In 1981 three more of her plays were performed for the public. In 1985 her *Pantallas* was staged at the Duo Theatre in New York and in the following August was staged at the 1986 Festival Latino de New York. It was her first play written wholly in Spanish; but in 1992 an English-language version appeared. Prida's principal language is English and most of her characters are New Yorkers. *Botánica* is her most recent work, dating from 1990. In all Prida has written at least ten plays, a number of which have merited international prizes.

As member of a group of young Cuban American intellectuals who were interested in "normalizing" relations with Fidel Castro's government, Prida made trips to Havana in 1978 and 1979 to take part in talks that eventually enabled exiles to come back to visit relatives. Her role in this undertaking led to boycotting of her plays by single-minded anti-Castroite exiles in New Jersey and Florida, who denounced them as "insidious." In some cases advertised performances were canceled because of this pressure, as in 1986 in Miami. Prida's 1989 visit to Miami caused widespread protest gatherings. Periodically she has received death threats from extreme right-wing Cuban refugees—not something to be taken lightly, because two of the youths who accompanied her to Cuba were murdered.

Prida's plays form a part of what is sometimes referred to as the theater of protest. At the beginning of the 1970s she began to feel that she had things to say about various issues. While covering the International Theatre Festival in Venezuela for *Visión* in 1976, she was struck by the fact that not one of the plays presented concerned itself with feminist problems that were so prominent at the time, and she determined to fill that void. She did, with *Beautiful Señoritas*, and went on to poke fun at anti-poverty agencies, gentrification, cultural assimilation, the nuclear threat, *telenovelas*, and the Latino theater itself. As her writing evolved she has turned to more universal human problems. These topics are presented with a fine sense of irony and humor, and there is little sense of nostalgia common in the writings of earlier Cuban exiles.

Prida has written scripts for documentary films and published two volumes of her poetry. In 1985 she taught a workshop in playwriting at Eugenio María de Hostos Community College in New York. In 1987 she received the Excellence in the Arts Award from the Manhattan Borough president and two years later was the recipient of an honorary Doctorate of Humane Letters from Mt. Holyoke College in Massachusetts.

Further Reading

Cortina, Rodolfo J., ed. *Cuban American Theater*. Houston: Arte Público Press, 1991.

González-Cruz, Luis, and Francesca Colecchia, eds. *Cuban Theater in the United States*. Tempe, Ariz.: Bilingual Press, 1992.

Kanellos, Nicolás, and Claudio Esteva-Fabregat, eds. *Handbook of Hispanic Cultures in the United States*, vols. 1 and 4. Houston: Arte Público Press, 1993.

The Oxford Companion to Women's Writing in the United States. New York: Oxford University Press, 1995.

Prida, Dolores. "The Show Does Go On." In *Breaking Boundaries*, Eliana Ortega et al., eds. Amherst: University of Massachusetts Press, 1989.

Weiss, Judith, ed. *Beautiful Señoritas and Other Plays.* Houston: Arte Público Press, 1991.

TITO (ERNEST ANTHONY) PUENTE

(1923–   )

Puerto Rican Musician, Composer, Band Leader

Tito Puente once proudly said: "I am one of the pioneers [of Latin jazz]. . . . I've been around a long time. If people aren't into me, they're left out. Where have you been? In jail? In the hospital?" Timbalist and band-leader Puente is a four-time Grammy award winner whose fiery musical style has prompted crowds to burst into dance—even in theaters. He is truly a legend who at age 73 still tours the world with as much energy as he did when he was a young musician.

Tito Puente, son of Ercilia Ortiz and Ernesto Puente, was born Ernest Anthony Puente on 20 April 1923 in New York City. As a young child Ernestito learned to play the piano and percussion instruments, sang in a neighborhood barbershop quartet, and studied dance along with his sister Anna. The two children performed together as a juvenile song and dance team.

Before he reached his teen years Tito was performing with local Latin and society bands. He regularly played matinees with Los Happy Boys at the Park Palace Hotel. By age 13 he was widely considered a musical prodigy in Spanish Harlem. As a teenager Puente attended Central Commercial High School during the week and performed with Noro Morales and the Machito Orchestra on weekends. He credits Montesino, a black Cuban musician who showed him the fundamentals of playing the timbals, or kettledrum, as the earliest influence on his Latin drumming style.

Tito soon became interested in the saxophone, clarinet, woodwinds, vibes, and marimba. He distinguished himself in his earliest recordings by being one of the first drummers in Latin music to use a combination of timbal, bass drum, and cymbals to "kick" big band figures, often without bongo or conga accompaniment. He gradually began to play the timbals as a soloist by standing at the front of the stage, rather than in a sitting position in the rear.

During World War II, after Puente turned 19 years old, he was drafted into the U.S. navy and was assigned to an aircraft carrier. Important among his duties were loading ammunition into the planes and playing drums and alto saxophone in the ship's band. He also blew reveille in the morning to wake up the crew. Once, as a warm-up he accidentally played general quarters, the signal to man battle stations, causing the crew to think the ship was under attack. During his wartime years in the U.S. navy Puente was greatly influenced by an experienced fellow musician from whom he learned the fundamentals of composing: how to write a good chart, how to lay out voicing, and how to get the desired sounds out of the brass and reeds.

After his discharge from the navy in 1945 with a presidential commendation for participating in nine sea battles, Puente enrolled in the Juilliard School of Music. Making use of the G.I. Bill, he studied conducting, orchestration, and music theory. Between 1945 and 1948 Puente also played regularly with several bands at the famous Copacabana nightclub and the Alma Dance Studios, later known as the Palladium. In 1948 he formed his own *conjunto* and in the next year recorded both his first hit, "Abaniquito," and his second hit, "Ran Kan Kan."

By the early 1950s mambo had become a national rage and Tito Puente was in the forefront and in an ecstasy, exploring Afro-Cuban jazz sounds and straight jazz as well. Big band sound and Puente's Latin flavor maintained the band's versatility and he soon released "Puente Goes Jazz," an instrumental album that received instant recognition from critics. In two weeks it sold 28,000 copies. In 1957 he released "Top Percussion," which featured African religious musical themes and showed their influence on Latin American music.

In that same year Puente was recognized by the Cuban government in a ceremony honoring the great Cuban musicians of the past half-century. Puente was the only non-Cuban among the musicians so honored. In the following year his recording "Dance Mania" was issued, becoming a favorite of dance instructors almost overnight and continuing in its popularity today. Puente's visit to Japan early in the 1960s gave rise to a cultural phenomenon. It changed the musical tastes of Japan, as Japanese musicians created their own Latin rhythms after having been exposed to the sounds of Puente.

Back in New York City, Tito Puente became the host of his own television show on Hispanic television, performed his compositions at the Metropolitan Opera House, and was given the key to the city by Mayor

John Lindsay. In 1963 Tico Records released his classic tune "Oye Como Va," later popularized by Carlos Santana and his band.

During the early 1970s Puente's style became widely known as "salsa," but he has never liked the salsa denomination for his music. He argues that salsa means sauce, which you can taste but hardly listen to. Because he combines jazz melodies with Latin rhythms, he prefers the term "Latin jazz" to "salsa." He points out that his music is firmly rooted in the jazz tradition of improvisation with certain rhythms like the mambo and the cha-cha as a backdrop.

In 1979 Puente and his ensemble again toured Japan, where their overwhelming reception caused him to fully realize the worldwide popularity of his music. In the same year he played for President Jimmy Carter at the White House and won the first of his four Grammies. He has been nominated for a Grammy eight times—more than any other Latino American musician. In the early 1980s Puente established the Tito Puente Scholarship Foundation to provide financial assistance to musically talented youths.

Among other recognitions and awards, in 1980 Puente was given an honorary doctorate by the College at Old Westbury and in August 1990 was unanimously voted to receive a Hollywood Star. In addition, Puente was honored by the National Academy of Recording Arts and Sciences with its Eubie Award, a lifetime achievement tribute recognizing his 50 years of contributions to the recording industry. In 1994 he was singled out by the American Society of Composers, Authors, and Publishers for his contributions to the music world.

The King of Mambo is indeed one of the most prominent Latin jazz band leaders and percussionists in the United States. He has composed over 400 songs and made some 2,000 musical arrangements. He launched his 103rd LP release in 1993, marking 50 years of recording. His music has been featured in such varied films as *Carlito's Way*, Woody Allen's *Radio Days, Armed and Dangerous* with John Candy, *The Mambo Kings Play Songs of Love* with Armand Assante, and *Dick Tracy* starring Warren Beatty. His busy performing schedule includes more than 380 engagements every year and has taken him abroad to Japan, Finland, Expo '92 in Seville, and Barcelona just before the Olympic Games. Domestically he has played at the White House, Carnegie Hall, New York's Central Park's Summer Stage, and many other places including cruise ships. He has entranced three generations with his music.

Tito Puente says his enduring success comes from knowing jazz, stressing basic rhythms, doing good combinations, and playing harmonies and counterpoint. All his life he has been equally proud of his music and his Puerto Rican heritage, so evident in his music. His family, which includes two grandchildren, plays a central role in his life.

Further Reading

About Tito Puente. Garfield, N.J.: Latin Percussion, 1990.

Bouchard, Fred. "Tito Puente: King of the Middle World." *Down Beat* 58:5 (1 May 1991): 20.

Fernández, Enrique. "Hot to Trot." *Harper's Bazaar* 3378 (June 1993): 154.

Flores, Aurora. *Tito Puente: Celebrating Life, the Mambo King 100th LP*. New York: Ralph Mercado Management, 1991.

Gordon, Diana. "Tito Puente." *Modern Drummer* 14:4 (1 April 1990): 24.

Pérez Firmat, Gustavo. "Qué rico el mambo." *Más* (November–December 1991): 78–81.

Soergel, Brian. "Tito Puente." *Inland Valley Daily Bulletin* (14 May 1993).

ANTHONY QUINN

(1915–)

Mexican-American Actor, Writer, Sculptor, Painter

Few actors have been successful in as many artistic fields as Anthony Quinn, and none has portrayed so many different ethnic types on stage and screen. Over a period of six decades he has played American Indians, Mexicans, Spaniards, Frenchmen, Italians, Greeks, Englishmen, a Russian, Eskimo, Berber, Arab, Hun, Roman, Jew, Irishman, Portuguese, Panamanian, Dominican, Malaysian, Madagascan, Hawaiian, Filipino, Chinese, Japanese, and even a Mexican American. He won two Oscars for best supporting actor, was nominated several times for best actor, and helped make many films successful. He has appeared in over 200 motion pictures as well as television films and a considerable number of stage plays. In 1986 the Foreign Press Association of Hollywood gave him the Cecil B. DeMille Award for Lifetime Achievement.

Anthony Quinn was born on 21 April 1915 in Chihuahua, Mexico, during the throes of the Great Revolution, the son of Manuela Oaxaca and Francisco Quinn, who fought with the bandit-revolutionary leader Pancho Villa. His Irish grandfather had ended up in Mexico, where he married and raised a family. His idealistic son Francisco and the latter's wife joined the forces of Pancho Villa to help instigate the 1910 Mexican revolution. When Anthony was a few months old his mother fled the revolution and Mexico, taking him to Ciudad Juárez and then across to El Paso, where his father joined them some months later. In 1919 the family moved to East Los Angeles, and his father obtained employment in the Selig film studio. His father's tragic death in an automobile accident when Anthony was 11 years old caused a severe trauma in his early life.

As a result of his father's untimely end, Quinn knew abject poverty, worked at various jobs to help support his mother and younger sister, Stella, and sporadically attended Los Angeles public schools. When his mother later remarried, he and Stella lived with his paternal grandmother. He read voraciously and widely and had an early encounter with the stage as boy evangelist at Aimee Semple McPherson's tabernacle. Further interest in the theater at that time was inhibited by a speech defect, corrected in his late teens by an operation he paid for on the installment plan.

Leaving high school in the middle of the Depression of the early 1930s, Quinn worked at a wide variety of jobs including boxer, tango contestant, band leader, fruit picker, butcher, construction worker, ditch digger, and ranch foreman. He also participated in Franklin D. Roosevelt's New Deal Federal Theater Project. After playing with an amateur acting group in Noel Coward's *Hay Fever*, Quinn was hired early in 1936 for a role in Mae West's production of *Clean Beds*, his first commercial play. There followed a succession of small film roles, usually as a gangster or an Indian. His selection by Cecil B. DeMille to play a Cheyenne leader in *The Plainsman*, 1936, brought him Hollywood recognition and also led to his marrying DeMille's adopted daughter, Katherine. Their marriage lasted nearly 30 years and resulted in five children.

From 1937 to 1947 Quinn played supporting roles in a large number of notable Hollywood films including *The Last Train from Madrid*, 1937; *Blood and Sand*, 1941; *The Oxbow Incident*, 1943; *Guadalcanal Diary*, 1943; *Irish Eyes Are Smiling*, 1944; and *Back to Bataan*, 1945. In 1947 he became a naturalized U.S. citizen and left Hollywood to escape the often undemanding parts he was being offered. He turned to the legitimate theater, opening on Broadway in *The Gentleman from Athens*, which closed after one week. A year later he took to the road, successfully replacing Marlon Brando for two years as Stanley Kowalski in Tennessee Williams's *A Streetcar Named Desire*. He also played in other stage productions and on television as well as in summer stock on the East Coast.

In 1950 Quinn returned to films, continuing to play supporting roles to leading men like Brando, Kirk Douglas, and Gregory Peck in action-packed films. Although there had been an early interest in him as a Latin lover in the mold of Rudolph Valentino, he was usually cast as the swarthy villain or less-than-noble savage.

In 1952 his portrayal of Emiliano Zapata's (Marlon Brando) older brother Eufemio in *Viva Zapata* won him his first Academy Award. In the early 1950s he also began a new phase of his career, making films in

Italy; many of these were so-called "spaghetti westerns"; but *La Strada*, in which he played a brutal circus strongman, gave Quinn an international reputation and won an Oscar as the best foreign language film in 1956. In that same year he won a second Oscar for his supporting role as Paul Gauguin in *Lust for Life*. He also had several nominations for best actor.

At his father-in-law's instigation Quinn directed a number of films in the late 1950s, with indifferent success. In 1961 he returned to Broadway as King Henry II opposite Lawrence Olivier in *Becket*. The 1960s saw Quinn reaching his cinematographic peak, with outstanding performances in *Guns of Navarrone*, 1961; *Requiem for a Heavyweight*, 1962 (which many critics thought should have won him an Oscar); *Lawrence of Arabia*, 1963; *Zorba the Greek*, 1964; and *Shoes of the Fisherman*, 1968.

Quinn's resounding triumph in *Zorba* led him back to the theater in an equally successful stage version, and in 1970 he also returned to television after an absence of 15 years. Although he had some success in television films, his series *The City* was canceled after 13 weeks. Despite his age, he continued to accept parts in action films in Europe and Mexico as well as in Hollywood. His best films of the next two decades were ones in which he played strong ethnic characters, for example, *The Greek Tycoon*, 1978; *The Children of Sánchez*, 1978; *Lion of the Desert*, 1981; *The Salamander*, 1984; *Onassis: The Richest Man in the World*, 1988; and *Revenge*, 1990. Four years later he appeared in the television movie *This Can't Be Love* opposite Katherine Hepburn. In early 1994, approaching age 80, Quinn agreed to appear in 100 one-hour installments of the Spanish-language *telenovela Rubirosa*, playing the part of the Dominican dictator Rafael Trujillo. His latest film is *Gotti*, which made its television premiere in August 1996.

In addition to being an actor of international fame, Quinn is a talented painter who has had a number of one-man exhibitions, a sculptor, playwright, and author, and he has dabbled in architecture and music. As a boy he decided he wanted to be an artist, and becoming an architect was his great dream. Fluent in Spanish and Italian as well as in English, he relentlessly pursues self-improvement in his acting and in his life. He once told an interviewer that rather than being exceptionally talented he was simply very hard-working and persevering.

Like the character he played in *Zorba*, Anthony Quinn lusts after life and believes in living every day to the fullest. He has fathered at least 12 children—ranging in age from 2 years to 56 years—by various wives and lovers. During the past few years he has devoted much time to mending fences with his children and to seeking to understand himself. His early autobiography, *The Original Sin*, is closer to St. Augustine's *Confessions* than to a typical Hollywood biography. Both it and his second autobiography, *One Man Tango*, 1995, convey a strong feeling of machismo. Quinn reads extensively in American novels and philosophy and owns a library of several thousand volumes. A painter and sculptor of considerable ability, he also has assembled a small but impressive collection of the works of modern painters, mostly French and including Degas and Renoir.

Further Reading

Current Biography, 1957. New York: H. W. Wilson Co., 1957.

Marill, Alvin H. *The Films of Anthony Quinn*. Secaucus, N.J.: Citadel Press, 1975.

Martínez, Julio A., and Francisco A. Lomelí, eds. *Chicano Literature: A Reference Guide*. Westport, Conn.: Greenwood Press, 1985.

Quinn, Anthony. *One Man Tango*. New York: HarperCollins, 1995.

———. *The Original Sin: A Self-Portrait*. Boston: Little, Brown, 1972.

Randolph, Donald A. "Autobiography as Pain: Anthony Quinn's *The Original Sin*." *Americas Review* 16:3–4 (Fall–Winter 1988): 144–164.

Reyes, Luis, and Peter Rubie. *Hispanics in Hollywood*. New York: Garland Publishing, 1994.

Villanueva, Tino. "Autobiographical Disclosures: Tino Villanueva Interviews Anthony Quinn." *Americas Review* 16:3–4 (Fall–Winter 1988): 111–143.

FELISA RINCÓN DE GAUTIER

(1897–1994)

Puerto Rican Political Leader, Activist

Snow in Puerto Rico? Imagine! Felisa Rincón de Gautier wished that Puerto Rican children might be able to experience snow. During her tenure as mayor of San Juan she had given children toys, roller skates, bats, balls, gloves, dolls, and many other gifts but always felt that island children would enjoy a good snowball fight, as she had seen children do in New York City's Central Park. She was able to realize her wish when she was named Woman of the Americas in 1954. To honor her for the award Captain Eddie Rickenbacker, former president and chief executive officer of Eastern Airlines, asked her to name her prize. This was her chance to bring a most unusual present to the children of Puerto Rico. Collected by Puerto Rican children in New Hampshire, snow was transported to Parque Sixto Escobar, where island children had a snowball fight under the hot tropical sun. It was a heart-warming goodwill offering.

This dynamic political leader was born in Ceiba, Puerto Rico, on 9 January 1897 to attorney Enrique Rincón and schoolteacher Rita Marrero. Her childhood was filled with joy and experiences that she recalled as the best part of her life. A tomboy, she played baseball with her brothers and got her nose broken in the process. As the eldest daughter in a family of nine children, when she was 12 years old Felisa assumed the household duties upon her mother's death.

Felisa learned to cook, sew, and play hostess to her father's distinguished friends after her mother died. The impressionable young girl enjoyed listening to her father's guests discuss politics, recite poetry, and argue philosophical topics. Among the highlights of her young life were attending lectures and listening to her father recite from *Don Quixote* and the Bible. She also loved to dance; her father was a social man who enjoyed taking his children to dances.

As a child Felisa wanted to become a doctor, but she was never able to achieve that dream. Stepping into her mother's shoes, she had the responsibility of caring for her siblings' needs, particularly when they fell ill. Then she became the family's problem solver. On occasion she also came to the aid of the household servants, buying medicines for their sick children.

Although Rincón's childhood was sprinkled with positive experiences, she was aware of discrimination. There was the time she planned to attend a carnival celebration at the Casino social club with a friend. Her friend was the cook's daughter. Felisa refused to go to the party when she learned that her friend could not attend because blacks were not allowed in the Casino. Looking back on this incident, she felt she was taking after her father, a staunch egalitarian who fought to end racism and class distinctions.

Rincón de Gautier also credited her elementary teachers as being influential in developing her character and talents. A very good student with a photographic memory, she attended public schools in Fajardo, Humacao, and Sunturce, up to the third year of high school. When she was a young woman the family moved to a farm in the Vega Baja. With the exception of attending school, the children were not allowed to leave the premises. Her father was a very strict man, but on occasion he allowed Felisa and her sisters to attend evening galas and dances with a chaperone. During this period Rincón's father appointed her *mayordomo* (foreman) of the farm, making her boss of the tobacco plantation and fruit farm. She and her sister worked in the fields along with the *jíbaros* in their daily work. Although rigorous, this experience gave Rincón insights into the *jíbaros'* basic goodness and fostered great admiration for their humble demeanor and quiet resignation.

In 1934 Rincón went to New York City, where she worked as a seamstress for a while. Upon her return to Puerto Rico she opened a dress boutique called Felisa's Style Shop. Her business gave her considerable visibility among the elite of San Juan, but she also became involved with the poor, especially families in La Perla, the worst slum in San Juan.

Although Felisa's informal exposure to politics as a child had been intense, her early participation in politics was limited. In deference to her old-fashioned father's wishes, she restricted her participation in public life. Her early goal was to sign up women to take the census in San Juan and to compile electoral lists. When Puerto Rican women were given the vote in 1932, a goal she had campaigned for, Rincón openly initiated her political career. She began her partisan involvement by joining the Liberal Party, which she then headed for several years. Later she switched to **Luis Muñoz Marín**'s Popular Democratic Party, assisting in its formation at the end of the 1930s.

In 1940 she married Jenaro Gautier, a lawyer, who was the perfect husband for Felisa; he encouraged her to participate in politics in any way she desired. After a fierce campaign she was elected mayor of San Juan in December 1946, becoming the first woman mayor of one of the larger cities in the Americas. She served in that capacity until January 1969, nearly a quarter of a century. Her administration was distinguished for its probity and its progressive leadership. Her long tenure enabled her to transform San Juan into one of the most modern and attractive capitals in the western hemisphere. In 1959 it was awarded the "All American City" prize for its pleasing appearance and cleanliness.

During Rincón de Gautier's tenure the mayor's office became known as a place where citizens could obtain help for local needs. People flocked to her office day and night. Some were hungry, others had no jobs, some needed house repairs, others wanted first aid or just advice. Rincón was always there for them. She held Open House every Wednesday at city hall, opening her door to everyone. She was like no mayor San Juan had ever seen.

Rincón Gautier launched a series of very successful campaigns and programs, creating a network of neighborhood medical dispensaries, building day-care centers, improving hospitals, finding jobs for the poor and care for the sick, providing scholarships for medical students to attend schools on the U.S. mainland. During Rincón's tenure Puerto Rico went through "Operation Bootstrap," a period of rebuilding the island's infrastructure. Factories were built, roads were constructed, taxes were lowered, and work became available to the poor. Rincón became known as the "Slums Lady" because she frequently visited La Perla to investigate firsthand the many problems affecting the very poor. Once, on her way to attend a reception at the governor's mansion in a formal silver gown, she stopped to help persuade a family in La Perla to leave their home because the tide was about to wash it away.

Rincón was always concerned with the impact of her work on the poor and their children. Among her major victories affecting San Juan's poor was the accreditation of the Municipal Hospital Association in 1948 and the establishment of the School of Medicine at the University of Puerto Rico two years later. She was responsible also for the modernization of the Municipal Medical Center in Rio Piedras and the construction of eight new diagnostic treatment centers.

The dynamic Felisa was seen everywhere, cutting ribbons at new buildings and starting engines at power stations. Her fame was not limited to Puerto Rico; she came to be the best-known female political figure in Latin America in this century. She traveled to many foreign countries to receive honors and awards. Among the 131 commendations she received from governments and institutions throughout the world are: the Lazo (ribbon) de Isabel La Católica from Spain; the Cross of the Order of the Holy Sepulcher of Jerusalem in 1959 from the Vatican; the Jeanne d'Arc Medal from France; the Merit Order from Israel; the Medal for Distinguished Public Services from the U.S. navy in 1957; and the Certificate for Patriotic Services from the U.S. army in 1959. She was also the recipient of seven honorary doctorates. The mayor's highest honor was being named Woman of the Americas in 1954.

In 1987 the Felisa Rincón de Gautier Foundation opened the doors to the Felisa Rincón de Gautier Museum, which housed all historical documents and important belongings that reflect her life. The museum includes a school that strongly stresses the value and importance of public service. In 1992, at age 95, Gautier was the oldest delegate attending the Democratic National Convention in New York. Two years later she died in San Juan, Puerto Rico.

Further Reading

Current Biography. New York: H. W. Wilson, October 1956.

Gerber, Irving. *Felisa Rincon: Woman of the Americas.* New York: Book Lab, 1979.

Obituary. *New York Times* (19 September 1994): 9D.

Olivera, Annette. "Doña Fela, The Great Lady of Puerto Rican Politics." *Americas* 33:1 (January 1981): 49–53.

Ortiz, Altagracia. *The Lives of Pioneras. Centro Bulletin* 2:7 (Winter 1989–1990).

Ramos, Josean. *Palabras de mujer.* San Juan, P. R.: Editorial Universidad de América, 1988.

Una Nueva Colección Documental en el Archivo General de Puerto Rico, Colección Felisa Rincón de Gautier, No. 2. San Juan, P.R., 1986–1987.

CHITA RIVERA
(DOLORES CONCHITA FIGUERO DE RIVERA)
(1933–)

Puerto Rican Dancer, Singer, Actress

"Dancing is one way of merging with something greater than the dancer," says Chita Rivera in an uncharacteristically mystical comment about her art. The 1994 Antoinette Perry (Tony) Award winner for outstanding performance by an actress in a musical (*Kiss of the Spider Woman*) continues active in her theatrical career. Her memorable musical roles in *West Side Story, Bye Bye Birdie*, and *Kiss of the Spider Woman* have brought her peer appreciation and popular fame. She is known both as an energetic and explosive dancer and as a performer with serious theatric skills as well as a powerful voice and outstanding comedic skills.

Rivera was born Dolores Conchita Figuero de Rivera on 23 January 1933 in Washington, D.C. Her father was a Puerto Rican musician who played various wind instruments in the U.S. navy band; he died when Rivera was only 7 years old. Her mother, who worked as a government clerk, was of Puerto Rican and Scotch-Irish descent. Rivera remembers her parents as being very strict with her as a young girl. Her mother's influence was instrumental in Conchita's choice of a career in dance. She enrolled Conchita in singing, ballet, and piano lessons. As children, Chita and her brother improvised a theater in the basement of their home, where she performed the arabesques and splits she was learning in dance class. Even as a child she had a passion for dance.

As a youthful dancer Rivera was well coordinated, but she remembers herself also as a feisty tomboy who regularly challenged the boys in the neighborhood. Her physical strength and talents eventually paid off when she was noticed and encouraged by her ballet teacher to audition for the noted ballet director George Balanchine. As a result she won a scholarship to Balanchine's School of American Ballet in New York City. To attend the school she was forced to move from Washington, D.C., to the Bronx, where she lived with her uncle's family during her ballet training.

Rivera graduated from Taft High School in New York City in 1951; in the following year she accompanied a girlfriend to an open call for dancers for the national touring company of the Irving Berlin musical *Call Me Madam*. She was hired, but her friend was not. This role marked the beginning of her career as a professional dancer. By mid-decade Chita Rivera began to acquire recognition, appearing as a guest on television variety shows including two very popular programs, the *Ed Sullivan Show* and the *Dinah Shore Show*. In 1956 she performed one of the outstanding dance roles of her career as Anita in the Broadway musical *West Side Story*. The musical play ran for 732 performances, and Chita garnered a Tony nomination. For her performance as Rosie in *Bye Bye Birdie*, which ran in 1960–1961, she was again nominated for a Tony.

In 1964 Rivera appeared in England in a television benefit with the world-famous British rock group, the Beatles. During the same year her performance as Anyaka in *Bajour* brought her a third Tony nomination. Two years later, now an internationally known stage star, Chita toured the United States and Canada in a cabaret act.

In 1969 Rivera appeared in the motion picture version of *Sweet Charity*. However, her experience with Hollywood was less than satisfying. She felt out of place and complained of the Hollywood mentality about working in the theater, which she characterized as "really a job . . . out of which sometimes comes fame," as opposed to the Broadway attitude, which she saw as centering on "dedication, hard work, and the development of a craft."

During 1973 she appeared as neighbor Connie Richardson in the situation comedy series *The Dick Van Dyke Show*, which ran on the CBS television network. In that same year she also resumed her cabaret act called *Chita Plus Two*, which was widely acclaimed by critics. Two years later she turned in an outstanding performance in *Chicago* as sassy Velma Kelly, "the second most famous murderess in Cook County jail," and was extended her fourth Tony nomination.

Rivera spent the latter part of the 1970s and early 1980s on tour and in 1980 received recognition from the National Academy of Concert and Cabaret Arts for best variety performance. Although *Bring Back Birdie*, the show she starred in during 1981, closed after several performances, Rivera's dance numbers in the production earned her a fifth Tony nomination. Later, for her portrayal of the queen in *Merlin*, she won yet another Tony nomination.

In 1984, after six nominations, Chita Rivera finally won a Tony Award for outstanding actress in a musical for her performance as Anka in *The Rink*. After 32 years of hard work she finally received the accolade her exceptional dancing warranted—a Tony. In describing the energetic dancer's stage presence, *Time* magazine critic Richard Corliss commented: "she commands the audience like a lion tamer with a whip snap in her walk; and, by the forces of magnetism and sheer will, she eats co-stars for breakfast."

In 1985 Chita Rivera was inducted into the Television Academy Hall of Fame. During the following year she broke her left leg in 12 places as the result of an automobile accident, but after hospitalization, recovery, and 11 months of intensive therapy she resumed her dancing routines. Seven years later at the New York State Theater in Lincoln Center she was honored with a Lifetime Achievement Award from her alma mater, the School of American Ballet. For her role in *Kiss of the Spider Woman* Rivera won a second Tony Award for best actress in 1994. Early in May 1996 she took time out from touring with *Kiss* to accept the Tiffany-designed American Express Tribute at the Helen Hayes Awards in Washington, D.C. Even in her sixth decade this exuberant dancer, singer, and actress entertains, amuses, and delights everyone. As one critic put it succinctly, she continues to wow her audiences.

Further Reading

Contemporary Theater, Film, and Television, vol. 8. Detroit: Gale Research, 1990.
Moritz, Charles, ed. *Current Biography Yearbook, 1984*. New York: H. W. Wilson Co., 1984.
New York Times (26 November 1989): Sec. 1, p. 71.
Telgen, Diane, and Jim Kamp, eds. *Notable Hispanic Women*. Detroit: Gale Research, 1993.
Who's Who in the Theater. London: Pittman, 1981.

GERALDO RIVERA

(1943–)

Puerto Rican Television Personality, Journalist, Lawyer

"A junkyard dog—a greasy, banged-up old German shepherd with a limp, but nobody will mess with," responded talk show host Geraldo Rivera when asked what kind of animal he would want to be. However, during his years on television the aggressive Geraldo has never been as bleary as a junkyard dog. His heavily mustachioed face is known worldwide in the media. An experienced advocacy journalist, the flamboyant reporter was named top television newsperson in New York at age 28. The state's Associated Press Broadcasters Association called him "a special kind of individualist in a medium which too often breeds plastic newsmen."

Geraldo (*Hair-awl-dough*, the Spanish pronunciation, which he insists on) Miguel Rivera was born on 4 July 1943 in New York City. His father, Cruz Rivera, a native of San Juan, Puerto Rico, and his mother, Lillian Freedman, of East European Jewish descent, at first raised their children in a dilapidated neighborhood of Brooklyn. When Geraldo was 7 years old they moved to Long Island.

During his youth Rivera was more interested in athletics and street gang activities than in school. He suffered an identity crisis because of his Brooklyn Latino accent. He wanted so much to be mainstream American that he even took to calling himself Jerry Rivers for a time. He soon realized that despite his efforts, he was not accepted. When he became of age he joined the merchant marine and after this experience enrolled at the University of Arizona, where he obtained his undergraduate degree in 1965. Rivera then attended Brooklyn Law School and obtained his J.D. four years later. He then pursued postgraduate studies at Columbia University and the University of Pennsylvania on a Smith fellowship.

After attaining membership in the New York State Bar Association in 1970, Rivera joined the Legal Service Program of the Office of Economic Opportunity in New York City to practice poverty law. He quickly sensed that he was virtually powerless in the face of insurmountable difficulties within the system. Feeling that his efforts to help individuals were pointless, he decided to provide assistance to youth groups like the Young Lords, a militant Puerto Rican grassroots organization. As spokesperson for the group he was interviewed for three consecutive days on television's *Today Show*. As a result he was "discovered" by WABC-TV executives. Under pressure to hire more minority journalists and impressed by Rivera's credentials as well as his on-camera appeal, ABC persuaded him to join the WABC-TV Eyewitness News team in September 1970. The intensive grooming of Rivera for the job included a crash course in journalism.

In 1972 he made a "commando raid" on the Willowbrook State School on Staten Island, a treatment facility for the retarded. Forcing his way into the building, he filmed the atrocious conditions of the children, many of whom lay naked in their own filth. His report filled an unprecedented seven minutes of air time, although news stories seldom exceed two minutes. He made a follow-up visit the next day and vowed to return to the facility "again and again until somebody changes things." Outraged viewers responded, and within seven days the governor restored $25 million to New York's mental health budget.

Rivera loved his new vocation. Sometimes he felt so moved by the plight of people he was interviewing that he burst into tears on camera. Some of his critics said he had a penchant for self-indulgent behavior; it was even suggested that given his ego, he might wind up interviewing

himself on his television show. He was doing exactly what he had envisioned in his earlier years as an attorney: helping the powerless. Now
he saw the possibility of bringing about meaningful change on a large
scale through the medium of television.

Later, in 1972, an ABC News television special based on Rivera's reports won him the George Foster Peabody Broadcasting Award for public service. It was the first of his 10 (3 national and 7 local) Emmy awards
for excellence in individual reporting. Geraldo's career as an investigative journalist had taken off. In 1973 his camera crew filmed the visible
suffering of babies born of drug-addicted mothers at New York City
hospitals. This 30-minute documentary, "The Littlest Junkie: A Children's Story," attracted an unprecedented 47 percent of the television
audience.

After four years of intensive investigative reporting, Rivera became
the host of *Good Night America*, a 90-minute magazine format, for three
years. In 1978 Rivera became producer and reporter for *20/20*, a highly
respected news show. After 15 years Rivera left ABC-TV in 1985, motivated by a felt sense of scorn from his peers and by an incident in the
Israeli-Palestinian conflict. Rivera's rescue of a young Palestinian soldier
at considerable personal risk, filmed by his crew, was excluded from the
television news that night when *World News Tonight* aired the story. Rivera was deeply aggrieved by the editing.

Soon thereafter he was offered a job hosting a live special, "The Mystery of Al Capone's Vault." It turned into a total fiasco when, after breaking through a brick wall and seeing the dust settle, he found no loot, no
cash, no bodies, and no Mafia secrets. He felt humiliated, although the
special obtained the best ratings in the history of syndicated television.

In 1987 Rivera began hosting his own talk show, *Geraldo*, filmed before
a studio audience in New York. His shows allowed him to continue his
investigative reporting, thereby sustaining his image of fearlessness and
bravery. His most dramatic show took place in November 1988 when a
brawl involving about 50 audience members developed on the set during
the taping of "Young Hatemongers." Rivera emerged from the scuffle to
pose for pictures with his nose broken, bloody and swollen. As a former
boxer, Rivera proudly showed his wounds as red badges of his courage.

Among his more controversial topics, Rivera once presented an
alarming, horror-filled show on Satanism, which was widely criticized.
Another show, "Murder: Live from Death Row," included views of dead
bodies and other gruesome prison scenes. As a topic Rivera even discussed on the air the personal infertility problems he and his wife had
experienced. Sensational real-life death scenes, discussion of kinky sex
practices, and voodoo topics helped spread his notoriety for a tabloid-
like journalistic style and aroused much criticism. Rivera's response was

that although he presented tabloid and soap opera themes, he raised them above mere titillation.

In 1993 Rivera's show *Geraldo* competed with about 19 talk shows for its audience. Rivera then complained that his afternoon audiences were not interested in the serious subjects he wished to discuss. In the following year he started broadcasting *Rivera Live*, a late-night call-in show in which he felt he was able to attract more serious viewers and provide a higher caliber of journalism. In 1995 the show's popularity soared when the decision was made to focus on the O.J. Simpson trial. Rivera also turned away from so-called ambush journalism to the earlier aggressive but intelligent style that had made him so popular during the second half of the 1970s and early 1980s.

In spite of his often controversial career, Geraldo has been the recipient of many prestigious awards. Among them are the George Foster Peabody Award for distinguished achievement in broadcast journalism, two Robert F. Kennedy awards, two Columbia-DuPont awards, ten Emmy awards already mentioned, and three honorary doctorates. He also has received more than 150 additional awards for achievements in broadcast journalism. The U.S. Information Agency has acknowledged his importance by producing a biographical documentary about him. Geraldo Rivera is also the author of five books, including two for children.

Further Reading

Frymer, Murry. "Next—On Geraldo." *San Jose Mercury News* (16 November 1993).

Moritz, Charles, ed. *Current Biography Yearbook, 1975.* New York: H. W. Wilson Co., 1975.

Sheehan, Neil A. "Geraldo Bursts into Print." *Washington Journalism Review* (December 1991): 31–34.

"Small Paper Solves Big Mystery," *Hispanic Link Weekly Report*, 14:17 (12 Feb. 1996), 4.

TV Guide (18 April 1987), (26 March 1988).

TOMÁS RIVERA

(1935–1984)

Mexican American Author, Teacher, Administrator

Because he felt that he could improve higher education and help fellow Mexican Americans most as a university administrator, Tomás Rivera spent the last decade of his short life in that sometimes difficult role. Given the time-consuming realities of his administrative positions, his literary output was understandably limited. However, the quality of his writing, especially of his novel "*. . . y no se lo tragó la tierra*", set new high standards for Mexican American authors and has greatly influenced Chicano creative writers ever since its publication. Indeed, he has been called the father of Chicano literature. Widely respected as a leader in the Chicano literary renaissance of the 1970s, Rivera is arguably still the most influential voice among Mexican American writers. His legacy will undoubtedly be felt into the next century.

Tomás Rivera was born in Crystal City, Texas, on 22 December 1935 to Josefa Hernández Rivera and Florencio Rivera. Both parents had limited formal education. Both had immigrated to the United States from Mexico (his mother from the border state of Coahuila as a very small child with her family, and his father from Aguascalientes as a teenager), so Tomás grew up speaking Spanish in the home. Not until he was in the fifth grade did he speak English without mentally translating first. The Riveras were migrant farm workers, and from childhood Tomás annually followed the harvests from Texas to Michigan and Minnesota with his parents, usually leaving sometime in mid-April and returning to Crystal City early in November. His early instruction was in Spanish in the Crystal City barrio school. He obtained his later education where he could and when he could, always ending up in the segregated schools of his native Texas, where he typically had to make up schooling missed because of following the crops.

His father—and especially his maternal grandfather, who had received some schooling at the Colegio Militar de México—placed a high value on literacy and education. As a result Tomás, despite the difficulties and sacrifices involved, despite alternating between field work and school, managed to complete high school. After he enrolled in Southwest Texas Junior College in 1954, his parents limited his migratory work to school vacation time. Four years later he graduated from Southwest Texas State Teachers College (now University) at San Marcos with a degree in English education and began his academic career.

At first Rivera taught English, then Spanish in Texas high schools in San Antonio, Crystal City, and League City. In 1964 he got his M.Ed., specializing in administration with minors in English and Spanish, also from Southwest Texas State. In the second half of the 1960s he taught in the modern language department of the Southwest Texas Junior College at Uvalde. Continuing his studies, he obtained his master's degree in Spanish literature and in 1969 his Ph.D. in Romance languages and literature from the University of Oklahoma at Norman.

After receiving his doctorate Rivera went to Huntsville in eastern Texas to teach at Sam Houston State University. He moved with extraordinary rapidity and ease up the academic and administrative ladder. In 1971 he accepted a full professorship in Spanish and chairmanship of the foreign languages division at the University of Texas, San Antonio (UTSA). Five years later, after serving as associate dean for several years, his administrative ability was recognized by appointment as vice-president for administration, a position he left in 1978 to become executive vice-president for academic affairs at the University of Texas in El Paso. Two years later he accepted appointment as chancellor of the University of California at Riverside, the youngest of the university system's chancellors and the first Mexican American in that position. Even more notable in academia was the fact that he was named chancellor less than a decade after receiving his doctoral degree. As an administrator who believed strongly in quality education for everyone, his most immediate concern was the educational problems faced by minority students.

Despite his rapid rise and the accompanying task of learning various administrative duties at three different universities, Tomás Rivera also found time for literary creativity. Encouraged by his parents and grandfather, he began writing at an early age but did not publish until the advent of ethnic periodicals as part of the Chicano literary renaissance. He published some of his poetry toward the end of the 1960s in these new Chicano journals. In 1970 his novel about Mexican American migrant life, "... y no se lo tragó la tierra," won the first Quinto Sol National Literary Prize awarded by that newly founded publishing house in Berkeley, California. The story of the plight and heroism of migrant workers as seen through the eyes of a young boy, it was published in a bilingual edition in the following year. A second translation, by **Rolando Hinojosa-Smith**, was published by Arte Público Press in 1985 under the title *This Migrant Earth*. Widely hailed as a benchmark, "*tierra*" reflects both Rivera's literary artistry and his deep respect and empathy for farm worker migrants who endure despite brutal socioeconomic conditions. It stresses their simplicity and dogged determination in a search for self and an understanding of their existence. Also, it responded to Rivera's belief that he ought to document, to fix forever, the life of the migratory *mexicano* worker.

In addition to "*tierra*," Rivera published a collection of his poetry in English entitled *Always and Other Poems* in 1973. After the publication of "*tierra*" he had time to publish five short stories, some essays, and poetry. Many of his poems and short stories have appeared in journals and literary collections. When he died unexpectedly of a heart attack at age 48, he had been working for several years on a second novel, tentatively entitled *La casa grande del pueblo*. He also left behind some unpublished poems.

Because of his administrative abilities and his dedication to meeting the educational needs of students, Tomás Rivera received various honors in his all-too-short academic career. Among them were memberships on numerous prestigious boards and important national committees. In 1976 he was appointed to the board of the Carnegie Foundation for the Advancement of Teaching; later in the 1970s he was named by President Jimmy Carter to the Board of Foreign Scholarships (Fulbright Program) and then became a member of the National Chicano Council on Higher Education. He was on the Ford Foundation's board of directors and served on a presidential commission to identify educational problems the United States would face in the 1980s. He also was awarded several honorary doctoral degrees.

Further Reading

Bruce-Novoa, Juan. *Chicano Authors: Inquiry by Interview*. Austin: University of Texas Press, 1980.
Hinojosa-Smith, Rolando, et al. *Tomás Rivera, 1935–1984: The Man and His Work*. Tempe, Ariz.: Bilingual Review/Press, 1988.
Kanellos, Nicolás. "Tomás Rivera." *Magazín* 1:8 (1973).
Lomelí, Francisco, and Carl R. Shirley, eds. *Dictionary of Literary Biography*. Detroit: Gale Research, 1989.
Olivares, Julián, ed. *Tomás Rivera: The Complete Works*. Houston, Tex.: Arte Público Press, 1992.
"Riverside Chancellor Tomás Rivera Called an Inspiration to Chicanos." *Chronicle of Higher Education* (15 February 1984).
"Tomás Rivera, 1935–1984." *Caminos* 5:6 (June 1984).

ARNALDO ROCHE-RABELL

(1955–   )

Puerto Rican Painter

Arnaldo Roche-Rabell believes that we can live two lives: one when we are awake and the other while we are asleep and dreaming. His dreamborn experiences are very real to him, as real as those he has when he is awake. These experiences the artist brings to his works. As a neoexpressionist, Roche-Rabell maintains that his paintings are a medium for self-communication. He once said to an interviewer, "I always try to just find something to touch, something that tells me I'm still alive, that I can still move, that I can still change." The artist, then, apprehends the reality of a dream, an idea, a sentiment, and makes it a human, moving, and feeling entity expressed in his work.

Arnaldo Roche-Rabell was born to María Rabell and Félix Roche Díaz on 5 December 1955 in Santurce, a barrio in the greater metropolitan area of San Juan, Puerto Rico. Arnaldo was the youngest of six children, one of two boys. His early childhood was spent in Vega Alta, a small town on the periphery of San Juan. His formative experiences were shaped mainly by his mother's special spiritual sensibilities and strength of character and by his policeman father's sense of order and creative talents. His childhood and adolescence were disturbed by painful, sometimes emotional family traumas, which Roche-Rabell prefers not to discuss.

As a child he felt that his opinions were ignored, perhaps because he was the youngest child. Yet his creative talents and academic strengths helped him develop a confidence that aided him in overcoming his feelings of neglect. Today he realizes that he combined the best of his father's creative talents with his mother's sensitive nature to create the person and artist he has become.

Arnaldo first attended Lucchetti High School, where art education, heavily emphasized, provided him with fertile ground for his artistic inclinations. In 1970 his family moved to Rio Piedras, another section of San Juan, in order to reside near the University of Puerto Rico. Later he graduated from Central High in San Juan, where he was yearbook photographer. During much of this period Roche-Rabell suffered unexplained mood swings; at age 26 he was found to be hypoglycemic.

In late adolescence Arnaldo remained uncertain about his future career. He was aware that he possessed an instinctive and extraordinary feeling for color and texture. He loved painting but was not sure how and where to channel his talents. This state of confusion and an existential despair lasted for many years and later greatly influenced his art.

After high school Roche-Rabell enrolled in the School of Architecture at the University of Puerto Rico, where he completed three years of the six-year program. While there he entered and won a painting contest. Following a significative dream in 1976 Roche-Rabell left for Illinois to attend the Art Institute of Chicago, where he completed both his B.A. and his master of fine arts in painting. His work was greatly influenced by neo-expressionism, the school that prevailed in the Chicago art scene of the early 1980s.

Upon arriving in Chicago, Arnaldo was shocked to encounter considerable cultural difference as well as language problems. His confusion and discomfiture, combined with his hypoglycemia, provoked severe feelings of anxiety. As a student with a tight financial budget, he often experienced hunger and unwittingly exacerbated his hypoglycemic condition.

When his illness was finally diagnosed, the awareness of his physical condition triggered in Roche-Rabell a desire to take control of his body's responses and, in turn, his life as a person and as an artist. In an effort to understand himself fully, he began to search inwardly to find the real Roche-Rabell. This search motivated the artist to begin a series of introspective self-portraits in which his face, instead of being a mere physical semblance, reflected his intense emotional moods. The facial expressions conjured up disturbing phantoms, images of ethnic, personal, and cultural demons. This introspective style characterized his early works. When his critics concentrated on his audiences' response to his paintings, which often were perceived as bizarre and violent, Roche-Rabell countered that his work was not violent but merely intense.

Roche-Rabell's highly personal style is based on the traditional technique of "frottage," which consists of covering the model with a canvas and then rubbing it with a spoon or spatula. After completing this stage, Roche-Rabell alters the image projected into the canvas by adding or removing elements. His technique involves a highly ritualistic process by which he transforms reality into art. His painting, therefore, is a transformation rather than a depiction of reality. In this way he reveals his inner self to the viewer.

Yet his art also serves Roche-Rabell. As he explains, "My work is a mirror of myself where others can look into and find me. But it is also a mirror *for* myself that I can come back to and find things that talk about me, how I think and how I perceive the world." Roche-Rabell often goes back to study his finished works at his leisure and at great length in order to better understand himself. Just as in a dream the mind is not fully conscious of its creation until after it has been completed, so too Roche-Rabell is not fully conscious of himself as revealed in his paintings until he has studied the completed product. Just as one cannot interpret a dream at the time of its creation, Roche-Rabell can fully understand and interpret his paintings more fully only upon reflection, after completion. The technique of frottage serves him well psychologically/therapeutically, providing liberation and exorcism. His art is a metamorphosis of his inner self.

Much of the encouragement Roche-Rabell received early in his career was provided by his mentor Ray Yoshida, who urged him to ignore artistic convention and to experiment with forms and techniques. Not long after his self-discovery stage, Roche-Rabell's development as an artist entered a new period when he discovered that to find himself he needed also to look into others. He realized that his relationship to others was a key element in his happiness and self-realization both as an artist and as a human being.

Roche-Rabell sees himself as a person whose dreams of fulfillment have come true. He continues searching to rediscover the world and himself in his art. Roche-Rabell humbly says, "The thing I most cherish is that God gave me the opportunity not only to find myself, but to find myself through my art." Referring to one of his paintings depicting yellow flowers, Roche-Rabell has said, "The flowers are devouring entities, they are intense, they are there, they jump at your face, you have no choice but to look at them." This description also applies to the artist, ready to engulf others with his energy, aura of mystery, enigmatic hazel eyes, thunderous laughter, and large hands flapping in the air as he talks.

Among the prizes, recognitions, and honors Roche-Rabell has received are the James Nelson Raymond Fellowship as an outstanding Art Institute student in 1982; Third Prize in the Bienal Internacional de Pintura at Cuenca, Equador, in 1989; Award in the Visual Arts 10, Southeastern Center for Contemporary Art, Hirshorn Museum, Washington, D.C., in 1990; and Premio de Pintura, Muestra Nacional, Museo de Arte Contemporáneo de Puerto Rico, in 1991.

Further Reading

Beardsley, John. *Hispanic Art in the United States: Thirty Contemporary Painters and Sculptors*. New York: Abbeville Press, 1987.

García Gutiérrez, Enrique. "The Island Man." *Fuegos* [Museo de Arte Contemporáneo de Puerto Rico] (August 1993).

―――. *The Rebellious Icon Espiritus, Works by Arnaldo Roche-Rabell*. Hato Rey, Puerto Rico; Galería Botello, 1990.

Orgállez, Oscar R. "El mundo compulsivo e intenso de Arnaldo Roche-Rabell, hombre del mundo." *Editorial América, S.A.* 15:12 (1990): 62–65.

Routte-Gómez, Eneid. "Puerto Rico, Arnaldo Roche-Rabell." *Art News* 92:6 (Summer 1993): 138.

Venegas, Haydee. *Arnaldo Roche-Rabell: Compulsive Acts*. Ponce, Puerto Rico: Museo de Arte de Ponce, 1984.

Chi Chi (Juan) Rodríguez

(1935–   )

Puerto Rican Professional Golfer

"I am a mental millionaire. When you have peace of mind, you have everything." Such was the reflection on his life by Chi Chi Rodríguez, one of the world's great golfers, whose personal philosophy has always been to help those in need, to lend a hand to those who suffer, and to assist the poor.

The fifth child in a poor Puerto Rican family of six children in Río Piedras, Rodríguez often experienced hunger and as a lad suffered from crippling vitamin deficiency diseases. He nearly died at age 4 after suffering from rickets and contracting sprue, a chronic tropical disease characterized by intestinal disorders and anemia. His diet was completely inadequate.

When Chi Chi was 7 years old his parents separated; to help support his mother and siblings he got a job plowing sugarcane fields under the fierce tropical sun for a dollar a day. Two years later he became a caddie at a nearby golf course. As a caddie he made 25 cents for assisting golfers as they played 18 holes. While he caddied he also began to learn the game, often arriving at the course early in the morning to practice and staying until sunset. His first golf club was a guava tree branch with which he hit tin cans rolled tightly into balls.

Because of family financial reasons, Chi Chi was forced to drop out of República de Colombia High School in San Juan, Puerto Rico. Briefly he tried careers as a boxer and as a baseball player for the Santurce Red Sox. While playing baseball he adopted the nickname of Chi Chi from an unexceptional player who aroused his admiration by trying harder than everyone else on the team. Rodríguez played at the semi-professional level as a pitcher with or against such players as **Roberto Clemente**, Orlando Cepeda, and Juan Pizarro.

In 1955, at age 20 Chi Chi entered his first golf tournament, the Puerto Rican Open; he placed second. That year he also entered the U.S. army and continued playing golf for two years at Fort Sill (Oklahoma) Country Club. Upon his discharge from the army in 1957 he was hired as an assistant to the golf professional at the famed Dorado Beach Hotel in Dorado, Puerto Rico. With the help of the older pro, Rodríguez continued to practice and improve his game; he started winning local tournaments. Soon his mentor felt he was ready for the big time.

Sponsored by the owner of the Dorado Beach Hotel, and others, in 1960 Chi Chi set out at age 25 to play in the U.S. Tour. He showed up at his first event, the Buick Open, in a long-sleeve white shirt with cuff links and a necktie! In addition to his unusual and perhaps inappropriate golf attire, his preference for using women's clubs because they were lighter than men's tended to set him apart. He played in 12 tournaments that year, finishing fourth in the Eastern Open and winning $2,262.

In 1963 Rodríguez won his first PGA title, the Denver Open. The next year he played even better. He finished ninth in the money list, winning two tournaments: the Western Open and the Lucky Strike International Open. In the latter he defeated Don January, and in the Western Open he beat out Arnold Palmer by one stroke. He attributed his improvement to changes in his stance and grip and to his new set of men's clubs. By this time he claimed to have discovered a great golf secret, which he calls the "solid left wall," described in his book, *Secrets of Power Golf*.

However, soon after these victories Chi Chi, never a consistent tournament winner, suddenly lost his touch on the green. The death of his father at this time deeply affected him, and he felt a need to stop, to examine his life with this new void. After much introspection he took a lesson from the experience, recovered from his depression, and began to recover his game. Yet he did not make a splashy comeback. His only big victory came in the 1979 Tallahassee Open. His best finish in a championship tournament was a tie for sixth place in the 1981 U.S. Open. Despite this professional setback he continued to be a money maker and to feel positive about life, asserting that there was more to life than golf.

In tournament golf Rodríguez often felt isolated and sometimes deeply hurt when colleagues expressed displeasure or annoyance at his playing to the crowd or when sports critics disparaged his sometimes flamboyant antics. Among his "pieces" Rodríguez performed a celebratory bull-fighter dance after a birdie; in this he attacked the hole with his putter, cleaned the imaginary blood off his club, thrust it into his imaginary scabbard, and limped off the green. (This seemingly violent act was done by a person who was unable to dissect a frog in the 11th grade.) Some golf fans loved these antics; others found them distasteful.

For many years Chi Chi Rodríguez has delighted his dedicated fans, known as Chi Chi's Bandidos, by joking with the gallery, whistling as he walks between holes, and performing playful rituals like the bull-fighter dance. He is known for placing his hat over the hole after sinking a long putt, and doing a tango around it. This trademark sight gag dates back to a 5-cent bet on a 40-foot putt when he was a youngster. He lost his nickel when a toad that was in the hole hopped out along with his golf ball. Ever since, Rodríguez has been throwing his hat over the hole to keep the ball down, toad and all.

At the beginning of the 1980s Rodríguez continued to participate in golf tournaments, but with limited success. In 1984 his game was still in the doldrums when his friend, golf pro Jack Nicklaus, who had just bought the MacGregor Golf Company, asked him to endorse a line of clubs. The offer was a mark of confidence that lifted Chi Chi's spirits. It represented psychological as well as financial backing, which he badly needed at the time. In its wake came other endorsement offers. Later he entered into discussions with Toyota, the Japanese automobile manufacturer, to become its spokesman. The psychic lift from these deals revived Rodríguez's belief in himself, negating feelings of failure on the golf course.

After a 26-year career on the regular PGA tours, in late 1985 Rodríguez joined the Senior tour, winning three tournaments in the following year.

He improved his putting and as a senior began playing some of the best golf of his life. In 1987 he set a money-winning record for seniors. Partly as a result of his new star status Chi Chi became Choice Hotels International's television "celebrity in a suitcase," popping out of luggage to promote senior discount rates. By late 1994 his senior circuit playing had brought him more than $335,000 in prize money. Happier than ever before, he and his wife of 29 years, Iwalani, divide their time between their home in Puerto Rico and one in Florida. He continues to appear on the senior circuit.

Chi Chi Rodríguez has always wanted to spread well-being and happiness. He believes that the only way to achieve peace of mind is through compassion, so he shares his good fortune with those less fortunate. Motivated by these sentiments, in 1979 he established the Chi Chi Rodríguez Youth Foundation, to provide educational and counseling services to troubled, abused, and disadvantaged children. Rodríguez takes a personal interest in these youths, calls 15 to 20 of them each week with words of encouragement, and visits the foundation several times a year. He has often declared that he loves children because he was never one himself. "I was too poor," he once said.

Further Reading

Díaz, Jaime. "Chi Chi Has a Last Laugh." *Sports Illustrated* 67:23 (23 November 1987): 38–40, 61–63.

Friedman, Jack. "At 51, Chi Chi's Still Laughing, Now It's on His Way to the Bank." *People* 28:2 (21 September 1987): 51–57.

Kelly, Colleen Bernadette. "For Chi Chi the White Hat Means God, Country, Family." *Spectrum* 12:3 (March 1993): 6.

Moritz, Charles, ed. *Current Biography Yearbook, 1970*. New York: H. W. Wilson Co., 1970.

Newlon, Clarke. *Famous Puerto Ricans*. New York: Dodd, Mead, 1989.

RICHARD RODRÍGUEZ

(1944–)

Mexican American Author, Journalist, Television Commentator

Richard Rodríguez became an instant celebrity and a center of controversy following the 1981 publication of his book *Hunger of Memory: The*

Education of Richard Rodríguez: An Autobiography. If Richard Rodríguez's second book, *Days of Obligation: An Argument with my Mexican Father*, 1993, aroused less controversy among reviewers and other readers than had *Hunger of Memory*, it was perhaps because he covered much the same ground, albeit on a more personal level at times. Both books were essentially collections of interrelated essays, some published earlier in various journals, all candidly scrutinizing and reporting Rodríguez's long journey of self-discovery.

Ricardo Rodríguez was born on 31 July 1944 in San Francisco, California, one of four children of office worker Victoria Morán and dental technician Leopoldo Rodríguez. His parents were middle-class Mexicans who had immigrated to the United States only a few years earlier. When Ricardo was 3 years old the family moved to the state capital, Sacramento, where his parents bought a small house on the edge of a white-collar neighborhood. He grew up in Sacramento learning English on the street and in the Catholic parochial school that he attended. After his teachers recommended it, his parents were persuaded to replace Spanish in the home with English. And Ricardo became Richard. As a teenager he worked at a number of part-time jobs to help with family finances and attended Bishop Armstrong High School, where he developed a reputation as a markedly able student.

In 1963 Rodríguez entered Stanford University and graduated four years later with a B.A. in English. From Palo Alto, California, he went to New York, completed a master's program at Columbia University, and in 1969 with M.A. in hand returned to California. At Berkeley he entered a University of California doctoral program in English language and literature. Notably he did not take an active part in Chicano student politics on campus.

Rodríguez worked on his doctorate for four years at Berkeley and then obtained a Fulbright scholarship, which enabled him to spend a year at the Warburg Institute in London. As he worked year after year at his dissertation on English Renaissance literature, he became more and more conscious of a growing separation from his cultural roots and of a diminishing sense of ethnicity. Increasingly he felt ambiguity in his personal identity. He became aware that his education, which was pushing him toward amalgamation, was an important factor in his developing alienation from his Mexican roots and from his family, especially from his Mexican-born parents. On the other hand, his dark complexion kept him isolated in mainstream Anglo society. He never did turn in his completed dissertation to obtain his Ph.D.

As a minority graduate student Richard Rodríguez enjoyed the academic and economic benefits of a fellowship from the National Endowment for the Humanities in 1976. However, he chose not to accept any of several university teaching positions offered to him. He believed these jobs were proffered to him because he was a Mexican American, yet he felt definitely separated from his ethnic roots. He turned instead to free-lance writing and began to be published in a number of prestigious journals while he worked on what he viewed as his "educational" auto-biography.

As Rodríguez thought about his life experiences, his education in a broad sense as he saw it, he came to a number of conclusions. Chief among these were the shortcomings and undesirability of affirmative action and bilingual and bicultural education as they were being imple-mented. His objections were not so much to the programs themselves as they were to the targeted group; he felt that middle-class Mexican Amer-icans like himself were the chief beneficiaries, instead of barrio Chicanos who had much greater need of programs to bring them within the Amer-ican mainstream. He argued that minority children should be taught in the "public language" and believed that affirmative action should be based on class rather than ethnic considerations. He expounded on these ideas in various magazines and journal articles.

In 1981 *Hunger of Memory*, Rodríguez's description of his "educa-tional" journey, was published. Reviewers—some 50 of them—varied widely in their reactions to the work, its message, and its author. In the book he revealed himself and his reaction to the American educational system with a perceptiveness and candor that not all reviewers, partic-ularly Latinos, viewed positively. Although most praised him for a clear and graceful style, some viewed his criticism of affirmative action and bilingual education as a betrayal of *la raza*.

Rodríguez's viewpoints made him the instant darling of right-wing conservatives who opposed bilingual education and affirmative action, and his writing skills won him immediate recognition as an articulate and able language stylist. The Commonwealth Club of California awarded him a gold medal for nonfiction writing. In 1982 he won the Christopher prize for autobiography and the Cleveland Foundation's Anisfield-Wolf Award for Race Relations for his defense of civil rights. He also went on a U.S. tour for the English Speaking Union, giving talks at a number of colleges and universities. In 1984 he accepted a one-year appointment as the Perlman Lecturer at the University of Chicago.

A decade later Rodríguez published his second work, *Days of Obliga-tion*. As in his first book, he seems to be primarily concerned with lan-guage as a carrier of culture. *Days* has been described as more autobiographical polemic than polemical autobiography. As with his first work, many reviewers disagreed with his views. One reviewer saw him as meditating on what it means to be a Mexican American in the 1990s, whereas another saw him as lamenting the erosion and dismantling of ethnic cultures in the United States, especially Mexican culture. The re-views may tell us more about the reviewers than about Rodríguez and his *Days of Obligation*.

In 1981 Richard Rodríguez attacked the liberal sacred cows of bilingual and bicultural education and of affirmative action in his first book. Today, while still embracing Anglo assimilation with fervor, at the same time he laments the loss of Latino culture both within and outside the United States. He presents his views in the *Los Angeles Times* and the Pacific News Service. He has also been a frequent commentator on the Public Broadcasting System's *MacNeil-Lehrer News Hour*. He has spoken out clearly in the media, defending the North American Free Trade Agreement (NAFTA) when it was being hotly debated and bringing out into the open the issue of popular American resentment and fear of immigrants. Currently he is working on a book about Mexican migrants.

Further Reading

Christopher, Michael. "A Hispanic Horatio Alger." *U.S. Catholic* 47:8 (August 1982).

Holt, Patricia. "Richard Rodríguez." *Publishers Weekly* (26 March 1982): 6–8.

Lomelí, Francisco, and Carl R. Shirley, eds. *Dictionary of Literary Biography*, Vol. 82: Chicano Writers, First Series. Detroit: Gale Research, 1989.

Magill, Frank N. *Masterpieces of Latino Literature.* New York: HarperCollins, 1994.

Rodríguez, Richard. *Days of Obligation: An Argument with My Mexican Father.* New York: Viking, 1993.

———. *Hunger of Memory: The Education of Richard Rodríguez: An Autobiography.* Boston: David R. Godine, 1981.

Zweig, Paul. "The Child of Two Cultures." *New York Times Book Review* (28 February 1982).

GILBERT ROLAND
(LUIS ANTONIO DAMASO ALONSO)
(1905–1994)

Mexican American Actor, Writer

Gilbert Roland could boast of one of the longest acting careers in Hollywood, a career that spanned nearly 70 years and included over 60 films as well as numerous television appearances. Throughout most of his career he played a sophisticated romantic hero. Sometimes he might be just a bit of a rascal and sometimes even a charming rogue, but he was always likeable. He was especially remembered by many fans for his characterization of the Cisco Kid in a half-dozen films just after World War II. An early advocate of racial equality and nondiscrimination, he spoke out against ethnic bias in the film industry long before the Chicano movement of the late 1960s and was known, despite his complete professionalism, to threaten to walk off a set rather than portray *la raza* negatively or stereotypically.

Luis Antonio Alonso was born on 11 December 1905 in the northern Mexican border town of Ciudad Juárez, Chihuahua, where his parents, Consuelo Damaso and Francisco Alonso, operated a bullring. The third son in a family of six children, he was christened Luis Antonio by his parents, who had recently emigrated from Spain. He spent his early childhood years in Juárez. In May 1911 when he was 5 and a half years old, Villista forces attacked the federal troops of General Victoriano Huerta who held Juárez, and the Alonso family joined thousands of Mexicans who sought safety across the Rio Grande in El Paso, Texas. As the Mexican revolution continued year after year for a decade the Alonso family remained in El Paso, and Luis began his schooling, learned English, and sold newspapers on barrio streetcorners to help the family finances. In his pre-teen years he also learned the rudiments of bullfighting from his father, who was a matador.

In the west Texas border town of El Paso, Luis Alonso first became acquainted with the wonders of the new miracle, motion pictures, and soon developed an intense passion for the infant movie industry. The silver screen and its stars became his obsession. At age 13 with only $2.60 in his pocket he hopped a freight train to California with the goal of becoming a movie star. But the road to stardom was slow and torturous. Close to broke most of the time, at first he worked at whatever jobs he could get, went hungry, and sometimes slept on park benches; but he remained determined to break into films.

Finally Luis Alonso's determination paid off, and soon he found fairly regular employment as an extra in silent films at $2.00 a day plus lunch. After years of extra work and bit parts, Luis was selected for one of the principal roles opposite Clara Bow in the 1925 film *Plastic Age*. However, the role brought the 19-year-old actor no further jobs as a principal, and he continued playing bit parts and supporting roles while he struggled to break into the leading man circuit dominated by Douglas Fairbanks, Ramón Novarro, Rudolph Valentino, and John Gilbert. At this point he adopted a professional name made from two of his silver screen favorites: John Gilbert and the serial queen Ruth Roland.

In 1927 Gilbert Roland came to the attention of screen star Norma Talmadge, who selected him to play the lead male role opposite her in the United Artists film *Camille. Camille* made Roland a leading man much in demand, and he soon starred in various silent films with other leading ladies such as Billie Dove and Mary Astor. He quickly became part of a Hollywood era that included the Barrymores, the Talmadges, Mary Pickford, Gloria Swanson, Dolores Del Rio, and Lupe Velez.

The advent of talking pictures at the end of the 1920s brought Roland a temporary career setback because of his accent. As his career continued to wane somewhat in the early 1930s, he took whatever film roles he was offered including some leads as a Latin lover. In 1931 he played opposite Lupe Velez in *Resurrection*, the next year opposite Clara Bow in *Call Her Savage*, and in 1933 with Mae West in *She Done Him Wrong*. He also was selected for supporting parts in other Hollywood films and made some Spanish-language pictures as well.

In 1937 Gilbert Roland had one of the leading roles in *The Last Train from Madrid*; his performance received high praise from the critics. It was followed by outstanding portrayals in a Columbia Studios Spanish-language film, *La vida bohemia*, in the same year; in *Gateway*, 1938; in *Juarez*, 1939; and in *The Sea Hawk*, 1940. After the United States entered World War II in December 1941, Roland, who became a U.S. citizen in 1942, enlisted and served in Army Air Corps Intelligence. His army service was to be the only interruption to his 60-some-year career in films; as soon as he was mustered out he returned to Hollywood, where he then starred in six Cisco Kid films.

At the end of the 1940s Gilbert Roland was selected by John Huston as the lead in *We Were Strangers*, 1949. Although the film itself was only moderately successful, the critics were enthusiastic about Roland's performance and he was again in demand for more meaningful roles. His outstanding performance in *The Bullfighter and the Lady*, 1951, was followed in the next year by leads in *My Six Convicts*, *The Miracle of Our Lady of Fatima*, and *The Bad and the Beautiful*. In 1953 he made *Beneath the 12-Mile Reef* and *Thunderbay*, followed two years later by *Underwater* and *The Treasure of Pancho Villa* as well as *That Lady* and *The Racers*. In some of these and many of the other films that he made in the 1950s and 1960s, he was typecast as the smooth Latin lover.

In addition to his Hollywood activity, Roland appeared in a large number of television series including *Zorro, Bonanza, High Chaparral, Gunsmoke, Wagon Train, Medical Center, Playhouse 90*, and many others. He was also a successful writer, author of the autobiographical novel *Wine of Yesterday*, of numerous short stories (three of which won national prizes), and of some television scripts. He had a deep interest in history, especially the history of the 1910 Mexican revolution that he had experienced firsthand. Among his less intellectual pursuits were tennis, which he played with great skill and verve, and bullfighting. He counted most contemporary bullfighters among his close friends.

Along with **Ricardo Montalbán**, Roland had a leading part in *Cheyenne Autumn*, 1964, which brought him further critical acclaim. Like **Anthony Quinn** he also made some so-called spaghetti westerns in Italy during this period. In the 1960s and 1970s he had important supporting roles in a large number of not overly memorable films; during the early 1980s he continued to appear on television, mostly in Westerns, and made an occasional film appearance.

Although not an active member of any *raza* organizations, Gilbert Roland was noted for speaking out against discrimination and bias. In 1969 he was awarded a commendation for his sympathetic portrayals of Mexicans and for his positive work toward the bettering of Mexican–U.S. relations by both the California state legislature and the city of Los Angeles. In that same year the League of United Latin American Citizens (LULAC) gave him its Entertainment Favorite Award.

Gilbert Roland died in 1994 shortly before his 89th birthday.

Further Reading

"Gilbert Roland." *Hollywood Close-Up* 2:26 (16 July 1959).

Kanellos, Nicolás, ed. *Hispanic-American Almanac.* Detroit: Gale Research, 1993.

Martínez, Al. *Rising Voices: Profiles of Hispano-American Lives.* New York: New American Library, 1974.

Reyes, Luis, and Peter Rubie. *Hispanics in Hollywood.* New York: Garland Publishing, 1994.

Unterberger, Amy L., ed., *Who's Who among Hispanic Americans.* Detroit: Gale Research, 1992.

Who's Who in America, 1980–1981, 41st ed. Chicago: Marquis Who's Who, 1980.

CÉSAR ROMERO

(1907–1994)

Cuban American Actor

After one of the longest careers in the entertainment field, the suave, sophisticated César Romero died in 1994 at the age of 86. On his mother's side he was a grandson of the great leader of Cuban's struggle for independence, **José Martí**. Always very proud of his descent from his Cuban patriot grandfather, Romero was the guest of honor in 1965 at the unveiling of Martí's statue in New York's Central Park. He liked to refer to himself as a Latin from Manhattan. Because of his dark Latino good looks, dancing skill, and debonair manners, the actor had little difficulty in moving smoothly from the New York stage to Hollywood films, to television, to dinner theater in a career that lasted nearly seven decades. A perennial bachelor, congenial and elegant, of impeccable manners and dress, he was seen by many observers as the last of a more elegant Hollywood era. He himself on occasion said that he felt somewhat of an anachronism in today's Hollywood.

César Romero was born in New York City on 15 February 1907 into a distinguished Cuban American family. His mother, María Mantilla, a daughter of José Martí, was a concert pianist and singer; his father, César Julio Romero, was a well-to-do exporter of sugar machinery to Cuba. Educated in private Catholic schools, he developed a yen for acting after playing in his boarding school's rendition of *The Merchant of Venice*. While he was still a teenager his father's business went to pieces when the sugar market collapsed, and the Romeros fell on difficult times financially. "We had plenty of clothes and no money," he once told a reporter in explaining how he became an elegant gate-crasher at fancy dinner dances.

After high school, in spite of the daytime banking job his father got for him, young César began working on his future career in show business by becoming a ballroom dancer in nightclubs and theaters. In 1927 he made his stage debut as a dancer in a New York show, *Lady Do*, and by the beginning of the 1930s had switched his interest to acting. Five years later he made his Broadway debut with a part in the immensely successful *Dinner at Eight*. There followed roles in a number of other plays in New York, including *All Points West* and *Mr. Barry's Etchings*; he also toured the United States after replacing the lead in *Strictly Dishonorable*.

By the mid-1930s Romero heard the call of Hollywood, which viewed him as a possible successor to Rudolph Valentino. Whereas some other Latino Americans suffered with the advent of talking pictures, the changes probably helped Romero's career. In 1934 he had a small role in his first film, the slick MGM comedy *The Thin Man*, starring William Powell and Myrna Loy. He followed that with leading roles in a number of popular films, including *Cardinal Richelieu*, 1935; *Love before Breakfast*, 1936; and *My Lucky Star*, 1938. His urbane good looks made him a natural for the Latin lover in sophisticated comedies, and his dancing likewise recommended him for musicals with such partners as Carole Lombard, Alice Faye, and Betty Grable.

Between 1939 and 1941 Romero also did six Cisco Kid films, firmly establishing himself in the role with the assistance of Chris-Pin Martin as his sidekick, Pancho. Definitely not the cowboy type, he played Cisco as a showy dandy. His Cisco was very well received by Anglo audiences but offended some sensibilities in Latin America, resulting in complaints to Washington at a time when the United States was courting Latin American support in the struggle against Hitler and fascism. As a result

Darryl Zanuck, head of Twentieth Century Fox Studios, decided to discontinue the series when Washington put on the pressure. Romero is still remembered as the actor who established the early personality of Cisco.

Although Romero was in his mid-thirties when the United States entered World War II, he interrupted his career to join the armed services. He enlisted at the Long Beach office of the Coast Guard, where he spent three years, ending up as a chief boatswain's mate. He left the service at the end of the war in 1946 to resume his Hollywood career.

Out of the service, Romero was sent by Fox on an eminently successful goodwill tour of Latin America in 1946. In the following year he appeared in one of his best roles, and his personal favorite, as Hernán Cortés in *Captain from Castile*. This high-water mark was followed by *That Lady in Ermine* and *Deep Waters*, both in 1948. After 15 years with Fox, during which he often made five or six films a year, Romero severed the relationship when his contract came to an end. Nevertheless he remained extremely busy in Hollywood during the 1950s as a freelance actor, making such films as *The Story of Mankind* and the classic *Around the World in 80 Days*; but he also turned to the new entertainment medium, television.

Romero began his television career as a guest star on series such as *Bonanza* and *Zorro* and played guest roles in drama series such as *Playhouse 90*, *The Zane Grey Theater*, and *Passport to Danger*. He also appeared frequently on variety shows headed by figures such as Milton Berle, Dinah Shore, and Red Skelton, among many others. On television he made his biggest impact on viewers as the comically evil punster, the Joker, in the *Batman* series of the mid-1960s. Always pragmatic in seeking the medium that could use his talents, in the 1970s and 1980s he turned to regional theater and traveled the dinner theater circuit. He made no effort to resurrect his earlier career as a nightclub dancer, claiming he was too old "for that kind of stuff." Not that his television career had ended. He celebrated his 80th birthday while playing Greek shipping magnate Nick Stavros in the long-running soap opera *Falconcrest*.

Romero developed a certain fame for keeping himself ever youthful and always ready to party. But in late December 1993 he was hospitalized in Santa Monica with a severe case of bronchitis and pneumonia, and as the new year was ushered in he died of complications from a blood clot.

In honor of his half-century in films, Romero was given a lifetime achievement award at the Hollywood International Celebrity Awards Banquet in 1984 and also received a Golden Eagle Award that year from Nosotros, the Hispanic actors association, for his long, versatile, and successful career in entertainment. In 1991 he was given the Imagen Hispanic Media award for his lifetime of portraying Latino characters, and in the following year he was honored with the Will Rogers Memorial Award from the Beverly Hills Chamber of Commerce.

Further Reading

"Cesar Romero, Actor, Dies at 86." *New York Times* 142 (3 January 1994): A9(N), A24(L).
"Hail, Cesar." *People Weekly* 41:2 (17 January 1994): 49.
Kanellos, Nicolás, ed. *The Hispanic Almanac*. Detroit: Visible Ink Press, 1994.
Oliver, Myrna. "Cesar Romero, Suave Star for over 60 Years, Dies at 86." *Los Angeles Times* 113 (3 January 1994): A3, A16.
Reyes, Luis, and Peter Rubie, eds. *Hispanics in Hollywood*. New York: Garland Publishing, 1994.

LINDA RONSTADT

(1946–)

Mexican American Singer

Holder of awards for more than a dozen platinum (sales of over one million) and at least 17 gold albums, Linda Ronstadt began her musical career in the 1960s, became a superstar in the 1970s, and was the number one female vocalist of the 1980s. A remarkably versatile song stylist, by the 1990s she was an outstanding pop, rock, jazz, and blues singer, Mexican folk song interpreter, operatic performer, and Broadway attraction. She is seen by many as the elder stateswoman of pop culture. She has won numerous music awards, including four Grammies, and has become one of the top concert attractions worldwide. Up to 1990 she had cut 26 albums and 38 singles in addition to appearing on two dozen albums of other singers. She has also graced the covers of various magazines, including *Time, Rolling Stone, People*, and *Us*.

Linda Marie Ronstadt was born on 15 July 1946 not far from the Mexican border in Tucson, Arizona, the third of four children of Ruthmary Copeman and Gilbert Ronstadt. Her mother came from a family in Michigan; her father, owner of a large hardware store in Tucson, was the grandson of a German-Mexican mining engineer and his Mexican wife. Linda grew up in a musical environment, listening to the music of her grandfather and father, who were both *mexicano* musicians of considerable ability, and to the country and western records of her older sister

Susie. She was also exposed to a wide variety of jazz, blues, and semi-classical music by her father. As a teenager her favorite musical models were **Joan Báez**, the Beatles, Elvis Presley, and *norteña* balladeer Lola Beltrán. She began her public musical career at age 14, singing at parties and in small eateries around Tucson in a trio composed of Susie, her older brother Peter, and herself.

Ronstadt remembers the years of her early education in St. Peter and Paul parochial school in Tucson as not pleasant. She regarded the discipline as too strict and recalls the nuns as constantly irritated by her prepubescent interest in boys. At public Catalina High School she continued to be an uncomfortable rebel and insecure teenager. She found high school intimidating and claims she got through only by immersing herself completely in music. Singing semi-professionally with her siblings helped. In the fall of 1964 she entered the University of Arizona but dropped out after one semester.

At age 18, after dreaming about the move for several years, Linda Ronstadt left Tucson for the music scene in Los Angeles, California. In the mid-1960s musical Los Angeles was a jangling mélange of rock and roll, off-the-wall philosophies, and drugs. Through friends Linda joined with two other young musicians to form a singing group that called itself The Stone Poneys. Her remarkable (though untrained) voice quickly attracted attention, but she was too lacking in confidence to go solo. For three years the Poneys stumbled around searching for a distinctive musical style. After three albums for Capitol Records and several tentative splits, they broke up for good.

In the late 1960s and early 1970s Linda Ronstadt spent eight years mostly on the road, opening concerts for more established singers. In these hectic years the professionally uncertain and personally insecure singer allowed managers and producers with whom she was emotionally involved to dominate her musically. She coped with the hectic, ragged tour pace by resorting, at times, to amphetamines and other drugs. For a while in the mid-1970s she underwent psychiatric counseling about her self-doubts. Today she finds that jogging brings her the needed tranquillity.

Only when Peter Asher became her manager and producer and she decided to move from Capitol to Asylum Records did Linda begin to find herself musically. Synthesizing rock and roll with country music, she laid the groundwork for a spectacular leap to the top of the charts. Her last album for Capitol, "Heart Like a Wheel," 1974, was her first to sell over a million copies. It was followed by eight consecutive platinum albums, including "Prisoner of Disguise," 1975; "Linda Ronstadt's Greatest Hits," 1976; "Hasten Down the Wind," 1976; and "Simple Dreams," 1977.

Despite the magnitude of her accomplishments, Ronstadt remained unsure of her talent and went around apologizing for her success. Her friendship with singers Emmylou Harris and Dolly Parton, both of whom she greatly admires, along with Asher's musical direction, increased her self-confidence. In 1976 the young woman who earlier viewed having her own washing machine as a mark of affluence had an income of over $3 million from record sales.

In January 1977 Linda Ronstadt, a staunch Democrat and fund-raiser for the party, sang at President Jimmy Carter's inaugural concert. A few months later she was selected to sing at the World Series opening game. In between she won her second Grammy for Best Female Vocalist. In the following year she made her motion picture debut in *FM*, a rock and roll comedy in which she played herself. The film was no howling success, but the soundtrack album became a top ten hit.

Although the press tended to exaggerate the numbers and degree of involvement, Ronstadt has been romantically linked with a number of men, including George Lukas, Steve Martin, Mick Jagger, Chip Carter, and most notably "Jerry" Brown, the bachelor former governor of California, whom she accompanied on a trip to Africa in 1979. Trailed closely and sometimes badgered by the press, Ronstadt and Brown often reacted negatively to the publicity.

In 1980 Linda Ronstadt moved from her Malibu beach home to New York City, where she began rehearsing for *The Pirates of Penzance* in a newly launched theatrical career. After a summer run in Central Park, *Pirates* officially opened on Broadway in January 1981 to rave reviews from the critics. Linda's singing got a Tony Award nomination and greatly boosted her self-confidence. *Pirates* was then made into a film, which debuted in mid-February 1983. During the next year Linda was equally successful doing *La Bohème* as a pop opera.

In the 1980s Linda Ronstadt moved in several directions. She was greatly influenced by Nelson Riddle, who did many of her arrangements, until his death in 1985. She performed live with ballet dancer Cynthia Gregory, sang with Dolly Parton and Emmylou Harris, and did a duet in Spanish with Panamanian singer **Rubén Blades** for his album "Escenas." Although not fluent in spoken Spanish, in 1985 she agreed to sing in the Tucson Mariachi Festival. This led to her 1987 album, "Canciones de mi Padre," in which she sang Mexican songs that she had learned as a child, and to a second album, "Más Canciones," 1991, followed by an album entitled "Frenesí" in the next year. "Canciones" also became the basis for a successful concert tour.

In 1995 Ronstadt came out with one of her strongest albums yet, "Feels Like Home," an eclectic pop mix of folk, rock, and country in which she is joined by Emmylou Harris. "Home" was originally developed as a follow-up to "Trio," the platinum record she made in 1987 with Harris and Parton. Still on the boards is a possible album with Harris and the

McGarrigle sisters. In mid-1996 Ronstadt, who has explored so many varieties of music, issued an album titled "Dedicated to the One I Love," a collection of rock classics sung as lullabies for her newly adopted baby who appears on the cover.

Linda Ronstadt has an open, winning manner, a face that easily breaks into a gamine grin, and a stupendous voice. *Rolling Stone* magazine once said she owed her success to her looks, her charm, and above all her voice. She is so bright and articulate as to appear at times to some people as flippant. Despite her early dependence on men, she is a good example of a woman who made it in the male world of rock and roll. In doing so she has opened doors wider for other female singers. She has won special awards far too numerous to list here. Never married, recently she adopted a second child, a baby named Carlos, as a sibling for her earlier adoptee, Mary Clementine. In a move still further away from show business, she now spends most of her time back in Tucson. Here, with her two children, her parents, her brothers, and their families, she embraces Ronstadt family life.

Further Reading

Appleford, Steve. "Ronstadt Spans Generations." *Los Angeles Times* (26 August 1996): F7–F12.

Bego, Mark. *Linda Ronstadt: It's So Easy*. Austin, Tex.: Eakin Publications, 1990.

Berman, Connie. *Linda Ronstadt*. Carson City, Nev.: Proteus Publishing Group, 1980.

Burciaga, José Antonio. "Linda Ronstadt: My Mexican Soul." *Vista* 2:10 (July 1987): 6–8.

Claire, Vivian. *Ronstadt*. New York: Flash Books, 1978.

Current Biography, 1978. New York: H. W. Wilson Co., 1978.

Holden, Stephen. "And This Is What 48 Looks Like." *New York Times* 144 (19 April 1995): B1(N), C1(L).

Katz, Susan. *Superwomen of Rock*. New York: Grosset & Dunlap, 1978.

Moore, Mary Ellen. *The Linda Ronstadt Scrapbook*. New York: Sunridge Press, 1978.

ILEANA ROS-LEHTINEN

(1952–   )

Cuban American Politician, Entrepreneur, Teacher

Ileana Ros-Lehtinen is an energetic woman with a large number of political firsts. She was the first Latina elected to the Florida state House

Ileana Ros-Lehtinen.

of Representatives, the youngest person and the first person of Hispanic descent to be elected to the state Senate, the first Latina elected to the U.S. Congress, as well as the first Cuban American elected to the U.S. House of Representatives. When she and Florida state representative Dexter Lehtinen married in 1983, they became the first and only legislator couple in the entire United States. In Congress she became the first Latina to chair a subcommittee, the first Republican member of the Hispanic Caucus, and the first woman to be elected its secretary-treasurer.

Ileana Ros was born on 15 July 1952 in Havana, Cuba. The daughter of Armanda Adato and Enrique Emilio Ros, prominent members of the Havana educational community, she received her early education in Cuba. When she was 7 years old her family joined the first refugee exodus to the United States, leaving Cuba as the leftward turn of Fidel Castro's revolution became evident. Like the overwhelming majority of the first wave of Cuban exiles, the Ros family was unyieldingly anticommunist and, like most, settled in Miami, Florida.

In Miami Ileana completed her grade and high school education and entered Miami-Dade Community College, from which she graduated with an Associate in Arts degree in 1972. Three years later she earned her B.A. in English with honors at Florida International University, and in 1987 she completed requirements for a Master of Science degree, again with honors, at the same institution. She specialized in educational leadership. Meanwhile, in South Hialeah she started a private elementary school called Eastern Academy, which she directed and at which she taught. She is currently a candidate for a doctorate in education at the University of Miami.

Running a victorious campaign for a newly created seat in the Florida House of Representatives, in 1982 Ros began a very successful political career. She was the first Latina to be elected to that body. By the mid-1980s Cuban Americans had made themselves a formidable force in south Florida politics; and in 1986 she ran a winning race for the state Senate, again becoming the first Latina elected to that more select group. A staunchly conservative Republican, she distinguished herself in the Florida legislature by introducing and getting passed an amendment to the state constitution creating a Victim's Bill of Rights. She also introduced and championed legislation concerning young people: a Prepaid College Tuition Program, School-Area Drug Law, and Missing Children Identification Act.

When longtime U.S. representative Claude Pepper, a Democrat, died in May 1989 at age 88, Ros-Lehtinen decided to run for his seat in the special election that was held in August. One of 11 candidates for the position representing the large Florida 18th congressional district, which includes Dade County and part of Miami, she ran a strong ethnic campaign and defeated her ten competitors to capture the seat for the Republican Party. On 6 September 1989 she was sworn in, becoming the first Cuban American and the first Latina in the U.S. Congress. Her committee assignments were to Government Operations (Government Justice, Information, Transportation, and Agriculture) and Foreign Affairs (Western Hemisphere Affairs). Later she was twice elected secretary-treasurer of the congressional Hispanic Caucus, both the only woman and the only Republican in that loose association.

In Congress Ros-Lehtinen has tried to avoid a specialization in women's issues, although she recognizes a special interest in family and education topics arising from her background. Understandably she has a legitimate special concern about Latin America because of her committee assignment. A die-hard Republican in foreign policy, she has consistently voted the party line there but has differed with party leaders at times by straying on educational issues. In 1990 and 1992 she was reelected by extremely comfortable margins in a district that is 67 percent Latino, and in the 1994 election she ran unopposed. She has a firm hold on the Cuban American vote, without which a candidate cannot win in Dade County, as political scientists have repeatedly pointed out.

Currently Ileana serves on the House International Relations Committee and the Government Reform and Oversight Committee. Her seat on the former is of particular interest to her Cuban American supporters, most of whom are adamantly in favor of a hard-line policy toward Castro's Cuba (to which many still hope to return some day). She played a strong role in the discussions on the Cuban Democracy Act, which prohibits subsidiaries of U.S. corporations from trading with Cuba. She has strongly and vocally opposed any softening of the U.S. embargo policy toward Cuba despite arguments that it hurts the common citizen more than the Cuban government or Fidel Castro.

Although it is true that Ros-Lehtinen has encountered some opposition to her political career from ultra-conservative Cuban males, she represents their viewpoints well enough to blunt most of their criticism. Moreover, exile in the United States with the need to earn a living has tended to dilute Cuban prejudice against upper-class women working outside the home, as well as to blur class distinctions. Also, Ros-Lehtinen is the darling of the majority of Cuban American community, especially the women, their beloved "Ilianita," living proof that the exiles are doing well in their new home.

Further Reading

Bonillo-Santiago, Gloria. *Breaking Ground and Barriers: Hispanic Women Developing Effective Leadership*. San Diego, Calif.: Marin Publications, 1992.

Congress A to Z: A Ready Reference Encyclopedia. Washington, D.C.: Congressional Quarterly, 1993.

de la Garza, Rodolfo O., et al., eds. *Barrio Ballots: Latino Politics in the 1990 Elections*. Boulder, Colo.: Westview Press, 1994.

Kanellos, Nicolás, ed. *The Hispanic Almanac*. Detroit: Visible Ink Press, 1994.

Kanellos, Nicolás, and Claudio Esteva-Fabregat, eds. *Handbook of Hispanic Cultures in the United States*, vol. 4. Houston: Arte Público Press, 1993.

"Language as a Factor in Florida Debates." *Washington Post* 115 (1 November 1992): A10.

Women in Congress, 1917–1990. Office of the Historian, U.S. House of Representatives. Washington, D.C.: Government Printing Office, 1991.

EDWARD ROYBAL

(1916–)

Mexican American Congressman, Educator

In January 1993 Edward R. Roybal retired from the U.S. House of Representatives, after having served his California district for 30 years. Dur-

Edward Roybal. Photo courtesy of the Center for
Southwest Research, General Library, University
of New Mexico.

ing his congressional service he enhanced his reputation as a champion
of elderly Americans by chairing the House Select Committee on Aging
for 12 years. At his retirement he announced a parting thank-you gift to
his constituents—the Roybal Institute for Applied Gerontology at California State University, Los Angeles. It was his dream for the past half-
dozen years, an institute that would both undertake research and
provide training in health care for the elderly.

Edward Roybal was born on 10 February 1916 in Albuquerque, New
Mexico, the first of eight children born to Eloisa Tafoya and Baudilio
Roybal. His father worked on the railroad, as many other Mexican Americans did in that era, but lost his job when the strike that he had joined
failed. The family then moved to California when Edward was 4 years
old, settling in Boyle Heights, a Mexican barrio of Los Angeles.

Roybal's parents stressed the importance of education, and his mother
especially motivated him strongly in his schooling. He grew up attending public school in East Los Angeles and working after school part-time
as a newsboy and later in a laundry. In 1933 he graduated from
Roosevelt High School and, because of widespread unemployment dur-

ing the Great Depression, entered the Civilian Conservation Corps (CCC), which had just been created by the Franklin D. Roosevelt administration to provide work for young males. In the CCC, which was under the U.S. army, Roybal found that excellence was generally rewarded, with ethnicity having little or no relevance. The CCC created an atmosphere in which he learned to do the best he possibly could, an attitude he carried with him all his life.

After his stint in the CCC, Roybal entered the University of California in Los Angeles as an accounting major in the School of Business Administration. Later he attended Southwestern College in Chula Vista, California, near San Diego. Upon graduation he took a job with 20th Century Fox Studios in Los Angeles. While working for Fox he became aware of the high incidence of tuberculosis among Mexican Americans and the importance of testing for the contagious disease, especially among children. He volunteered to help the Tuberculosis Association in its task of testing schoolchildren. When the association purchased mobile X-ray units, he was given a job operating one. Later he was promoted to the position of public health educator for the Los Angeles County Tuberculosis and Health Association.

Roybal's career in public health was interrupted by World War II, during which he served for two years in the U.S. army. Upon his discharge he resumed his career in public health as a director of health education for the county tuberculosis association. In his new position he quickly perceived the political aspects of public health service. Encouraged by some of the people he worked with in public health and backed by a number of Mexican Americans concerned about the lack of *raza* political representation, in the late 1940s he decided to file for political office.

In 1947 Roybal ran for a seat on the Los Angeles City Council and lost by less than 500 votes. Two years later, with the help of Fred Ross Sr. and the backing of the Community Service Organization (CSO) that Ross developed, he won the election, becoming the first Mexican American to serve on the council since 1882. In 1954 he ran for lieutenant governor of California and lost; four years later he was equally unsuccessful in his bid for a seat on the Los Angeles Board of Supervisors. However, he regularly won re-election to the City Council, twice without opposition. A member of the council from 1949 until the end of 1962, he served on many important committees and for 13 years was chairman of the Public Health and Welfare Committee. In 1961 he was elected president pro tem of the council. As a councilman his principal emphasis was on community health and the development of programs for child care.

In November 1962 Edward Roybal ran for the U.S. House of Representatives in California's 25th district and, with the help and support of the CSO, won. For the next 30 years he was re-elected every two years, usually by more than two-thirds of the votes cast. As a congressman he continued his concern for health care and social reform and had his interests broadened by appointment to various committees. During his 30 years in the House he served on the Foreign Affairs Committee, the Subcommittee on Inter-American Affairs, the Appropriations Committee, the Select Committee on Aging, the Committee on Veterans Affairs, and the Subcommittee on Education and Training, as well as other committees and subcommittees. In committee work he was always carefully prepared, sharply focused, and a quiet but persistent advocate of his views.

As a congressman Roybal was a strong supporter of bilingual education; in 1967 he introduced a federal bilingual education act and pushed it through the House. In succeeding years, especially during the Reagan administration, he fought opposition efforts to cripple the act through inadequate funding. He also introduced and won approval of a bill to create a cabinet-level Committee on Opportunities for Spanish Speaking People.

During his almost 50 years of public service, Edward Roybal always advocated greater citizen participation in the political process at all levels, especially by minority peoples. He was the inspiration behind and a founder of the National Association of Latino Elected and Appointed Officials (NALEO) in 1975 and two years later was instrumental in establishing the congressional Hispanic Caucus. During the early 1980s, as chairman of the Caucus, he led the opposition to what later became the Simpson-Rodino Immigration Reform and Control Act of 1986 (IRCA). In addition to his participation in these groups he was active in the Democratic National Committee, the CSO, the American Legion, the Knights of Columbus, the Boy Scouts, and other organizations.

Roybal has been honored with a number of awards. In 1973 Yale University appointed him a Visiting Chubb Fellow, and three years later he was given the Excellence in Public Service Award by the American Academy of Pediatrics. In the early 1980s his strong advocacy of better Jewish-Latino relations brought him the Joshua Award. He was also the recipient of two honorary Doctor of Laws degrees. Honors aside, he once said, "I want to be remembered as an advocate of good health, good education, and good nursing." The Roybal Institute for Applied Gerontology may achieve that objective.

Further Reading

Alford, Harold. *The Proud Peoples: The Heritage and Culture of Spanish-Speaking Peoples in the United States.* New York: David McKay, 1972.

Chacón, José A. *Hispanic Notables in the United States of North America.* Albuquerque: Saguaro Publications, 1978.

Díaz, Katherine A. "Congressman Edward Roybal: Los Angeles before the 1960s." *Caminos* 4:7 (July–August 1983).

Ehrenhalt, Alan, ed. *Politics in America.* Washington, D.C.: Congressional Quarterly, 1983.

Martínez, Al. *Rising Voices: Profiles of Hispano-American Lives.* New York: New American Library, 1974.

Morey, Janet, and Wendy Dunn. *Famous Mexican Americans.* New York: E. P. Dutton, 1989.

RUBÉN SALAZAR

(1928–1970)

Mexican American Print and Television Journalist

It was a pleasant, warm August day in 1970. The National Chicano Moratorium's six-mile march to Laguna Park in East Los Angeles to protest the Vietnam War, and especially the high percentage of Mexican American casualties, had gotten under way just before noon. At 3 o'clock some minor violence caused the police to decide that the situation was out of hand, and the 500 police began to sweep the park with billy clubs upraised and hurling tear gas grenades. Panic and riot ensued. Two hours later many businesses on Whittier Boulevard had been vandalized, nearly 200 marchers had been jailed, hundreds were injured, and three were killed. Among the dead was Rubén Salazar, who had attended the rally to report the story for Spanish-language television station KMEX. The never adequately explained tragic killing of the prominent, controversial, and popular Salazar made him an instant martyr of the Chicano movement and a symbol of police abuse of Mexican Americans.

Rubén Salazar was born in Ciudad Juárez, Chihuahua, across the Rio Grande from El Paso on 3 March 1928. A year later his parents, Luz Chávez and Salvador Salazar, a watch repairman, moved across the river, and Rubén grew up in El Paso. He attended primary and secondary schools there and learned to practice the Boy Scout virtues. After high school he entered the U.S. army, where he served a two-year hitch just before the Korean conflict.

Out of the service and now an American citizen, Salazar entered the University of Texas at El Paso (UTEP) and received his B.A. in journalism four years later in 1954. During his last two years as a student at UTEP he worked as a reporter for Ed Pooley on the El Paso *Herald Post*, where he demonstrated both great interest and skill in investigative reporting. Under Pooley's tutelage he became deeply aware of police mistreatment of *mexicanos* and once got himself arrested on a fake drunkenness charge in order to do an exposé of conditions in El Paso's jail.

After graduation Salazar took a job with the *Press Democrat* in Santa Rosa, a small town in northern California; three years later he left the staff of the *Press Democrat* for a reportorial position on a big city newspaper, the *San Francisco News*. Having served his seven years of apprenticeship, in 1959 he moved south as a reporter on the city staff of the *Los Angeles Times*. During his six years there in the city room he persuaded his superiors to allow him to write a column, sometimes troublesome for the *Times*, in which he gave voice to the problems and concerns of eastside Chicanos. He continued to give evidence of his ability as reporter, writing an award-winning series of articles on the Los Angeles Latino community that earned him a well-deserved reputation for conscientious and objective reporting.

In 1965 Salazar was sent by the *Times* to Vietnam as a foreign correspondent to cover the rapidly escalating American involvement there, of special interest to the Latino community because of the proportionately large number of Mexican Americans in the U.S. forces and among the casualties. After nearly two years in Vietnam Rubén Salazar was called back by the *Times* to take over the job of bureau chief in Mexico City. Two years later, while reporting on the election of Arnulfo Arias as president of Panama, he was captured and briefly held by terrorists who accused him of being a CIA agent or a puppet of the U.S. State Department. At the end of 1968 Salazar was returned to Los Angeles with a special assignment to cover the Mexican American community, in which the Chicano movement was beginning to move into high gear. Aware of the increasing importance and rising militancy of Mexican Americans, in the following year the *Times* took steps, involving Salazar, to focus more sharply on the Chicano community.

Meanwhile, in late 1969 Salazar decided to accept a position as news director of station KMEX-TV and planned to leave the *Times*. The response of the *Times* was to suggest that in his new position Salazar continue writing a weekly column explaining and interpreting Chicano life and culture to the greater Los Angeles community. He decided he could handle both jobs and subsequently used both forums to articulate the many grievances that Mexican Americans had nursed for so long. A political moderate, he nevertheless spoke out fearlessly, condemning racism, prejudice, and segregation. Abuses by the police became the special target of his hard-hitting weekly essays, and he repeatedly pointed out in his column the much higher than average Mexican American casualty rate in the Vietnam War. He was under investigation by the Los Angeles

Police Department and the FBI, and pressure was put on him to tone down his language.

When the National Chicano Moratorium called a march for late August 1970 in Los Angeles, Rubén Salazar naturally was present at the event in his dual capacity. With his crew from KMEX he covered the march from Belvedere Park to Laguna Park. While relaxing with a beer in the Silver Dollar Café on Whittier Boulevard after the rampage, he was killed instantly by a high-velocity 10-inch tear gas projectile that hit him in the head. The subsequent 16-day coroner's inquest, which was televised and carried live by all seven Los Angeles television stations, did not indict the deputy sheriff who fired the projectile. Many Mexican Americans and Anglos felt that the inquest was flawed.

Salazar's tragic death became an immediate symbol of police abuse and the failure of the American justice system to provide Mexican Americans with equality of treatment. Rubén Salazar's funeral was a quiet testimonial to his belief that Chicano grievances could be resolved within the system and to his efforts to bring about that resolution. His informed, articulate, and level-headed voice for social change was sorely missed in the Los Angeles area. In 1971 he was posthumously awarded a special Robert F. Kennedy Journalism Award, and after the hurt of his death had subsided, Laguna Park was renamed Salazar Park in his honor. Later he received the supreme *mexicano* tribute, a *corrido* describing his contributions to *la raza*. On the tenth anniversary of his death his widow, Sally Salazar, was the guest of honor at the dedication of the Rubén Salazar Library in Santa Rosa, California.

Further Reading

Chacón, José. *Hispanic Notables in the United States of North America*. Albuquerque: Saguaro Publications, 1978.

"Death in the Barrio." *Newsweek* (14 September 1970).

Gómez, David. "The Story of Rubén Salazar." In *Introduction to Chicano Studies*, 2nd ed., Livie I. Durán and H. Russell Bernard, eds., New York: Macmillan, 1982.

Herrera, Albert. "The National Chicano Moratorium and the Death of Ruben Salazar." In *The Chicanos: Mexican American Voices*, Ed Ludwig and James Santibañez, eds. Baltimore: Penguin Books, 1971.

Martínez, Al. *Rising Voices: Profiles of Hispano-American Lives*. New York: New American Library, 1974.

Salazar, Rubén. *Border Correspondent: Selected Writings, 1955–1970*, Mario T. García, ed. Berkeley: University of California Press, 1995.

Salazar, Sally. "Rubén Salazar: The Man Not the Myth." *Press Democrat* [Santa Rosa, California] (29 August 1980).

Shorris, Earl. *Latinos: A Biography of the People*. New York: W. W. Norton Co., 1992.

Sifuentes, Frank. "La muerte de Rubén Salazar." *Regeneración* 1:6 (1970): 8–9, 12.

Weingarten, Steve. "The Life and Curious Death of Rubén Salazar." *Reader* 3:44
    (26 August 1981).

GEORGE I. SÁNCHEZ

(1906–1972)

Mexican American Educational Psychologist, Sociologist, Professor

George I. Sánchez spent a lifetime as an activist who advocated greater
social justice for Mexican Americans. Both as an individual and as a
professional he constantly concerned himself with the interests and
rights of his fellow Chicanos, especially the educational rights of the
young. In his research he questioned the applicability of standard IQ
tests to measuring the intelligence of Mexican American schoolchildren,
and through his writings he sought to correct common misconceptions
about their intellectual capacities and academic performance. He was an
early champion of bilingual education to improve educational opportunities for the Spanish-speaking, and he wrote enthusiastically and zeal-
ously in its support. He viewed education as the key to effecting social
changes and to wider participation by Mexican Americans in the American dream.

    Jorge Isidro Sánchez y Sánchez was born on 4 October 1906 in the tiny
town of Barela, New Mexico. His parents, Juliana Sánchez and Telesfor
Sánchez, came from families whose ancestors had pioneered in the very
early settlement of New Mexico during the Spanish colonial period.
When he was 7 years old the family moved to Jerome in central Arizona,
where his father, a hard rock miner, found employment in the copper
boom that had developed there. Jorge grew up and received his early
education in Jerome. In school his liking for mathematics and his writing
ability caught the attention of his teachers.

    With money he had earned from scavenging copper, Jorge bought a
coronet on which he then took lessons at school. The copper boom collapsed at the end of World War I, and the family moved back to New
Mexico when he was 15 years old. During the postwar Depression of the
early 1920s he was able to contribute to the family's support by providing music with his coronet at local parties, dances, and weddings. He

George I. Sánchez. Photo courtesy of the University of Texas at Austin.

also played in a jazz combo, was a dance promoter, and briefly boxed professionally under the name "Kid Féliz."

After graduating from Albuquerque High School at age 16, Jorge began teaching at the one-room school in a small settlement east of Albuquerque. In 1926 he entered the University of New Mexico in Albuquerque, majoring in education and modern languages. He combined taking classes at the university during the summers with teaching during the regular school year. In the late 1920s he was promoted to school principal and, upon receiving his A.B. degree, was offered the superintendency of his poor rural school district in eastern Bernalillo County in central New Mexico. His early educational experience strongly shaped his later intellectual and scholarly research interests.

Through a Rockefeller Foundation fellowship Sánchez was able to continue his studies at the University of Texas in Austin, and in 1931 he completed the requirements for a master's degree in educational psychology and Spanish. For his master's thesis he studied the test scores of Spanish-speaking children. Aided again with scholarship money, he went from Texas to Berkeley, California, where he studied courses leading to his Ed.D. in educational administration from the University of California in 1934. His doctoral dissertation was entitled "The Education of Bilinguals in a State School System." His first postdoctoral job was as a research associate of the Chicago-based Julius Rosenwald Fund, for which he did a survey of rural schools in the Southwest, South, and northern Mexico. This took him over much familiar ground. Three years later he went to Venezuela as director of that country's Instituto Pedagógico Nacional (National Teaching Institute) in Caracas.

After one year in Venezuela, Sánchez returned to the Southwest to accept an associate professorship at the University of New Mexico. Then in 1940 he moved to the University of Texas at Austin, where he remained for the rest of his life except for his service in World War II and shorter postwar trips to Washington, D.C., to share his sociological and educational experience and expertise with various government agencies and several occupants of the White House.

During World War II Sánchez took a leave of absence to work in Washington, D.C., in the Office of Coordinator of Inter-American Affairs, where he was influential in having **Carlos Castañeda** appointed to the Fair Employment Practices Commission. After the war he spent a quarter of a century researching, writing, consulting, teaching, and both organizing and directing numerous institutes, programs, and workshops centering on issues in the education of Spanish-speaking children. In 1951 he was the driving force in founding and directing the American Council of Spanish-Speaking People, which for nearly a decade focused attention on issues of segregation and discrimination. In addition, he chaired the Department of History and Philosophy of Education and headed the Latin American Studies Center at the university. During the last ten years of his life he was also director of the university's Center for International Education.

Outside the university, Sánchez was active in a number of organizations. He participated actively in various Mexican American groups, serving as director of education in the League of United Latin American Citizens (LULAC) for several years and as its president in 1941–1942. During the 1950s he was one of the leading organizers of the American Council of Spanish-Speaking People; in the following decade he firmly supported the Chicano movement, which he saw as an important step in righting the wrongs committed against Mexican Americans, particularly in education. Unfortunately, some of the young activists felt that he was not sufficiently militant and criticized him, partly because he failed to support their ideas of Chicano nationalism. On the other hand, it appears that he may have suffered both professionally and financially because of his clearly articulated, outspoken views in support of the movement.

In research and writing activities that extended over more than 40 years, Sánchez detailed his concerns and explained his ideas in more than 100 professional journal articles, bulletins, and reports as well as in a number of important books. Not content merely to criticize, over the years he made many proposals for educational reform in New Mexico. Today he remains best known for his 1940 book, *Forgotten People: A Study of New Mexicans*, a seminal work that came in part out of a Carnegie Foundation grant he received in the late 1930s. Important among his other books are *The Development of Higher Education in Mexico*, 1944; *The People: A Study of the Navajos*, 1948; *The Development of Education in Venezuela*, 1963; and *Mexico*, 1965.

A distinguished researcher, teacher, author, and editor, Sánchez was an outstanding scholar who lived a productive life on several levels. He served as spokesman for *la raza* for more than 40 years, championing the Spanish-speaking against educational and social segregation and arguing for greater equality of opportunity for them and for all Americans.

Further Reading

Chavarría, Jesús. "On Chicano History: In Memoriam, George I. Sánchez, 1906–1972." In *Humanitas: Essays in Honor of George I. Sánchez*, Américo Paredes, ed. Los Angeles: University of California, Chicano Studies Center, 1977.

García, Mario T. *Mexican Americans: Leadership, Ideology, and Identity, 1930–1960.* New Haven, Conn.: Yale University Press, 1989.

Murillo, Nathan. "The Works of George I. Sánchez: An Appreciation." In *Chicano Psychology*, 2nd ed., Joe L. Martínez Jr. and Richard H. Mendoza, eds. New York: Academic Press, 1984.

Paredes, Américo, ed. *Humanitas: Essays in Honor of George I. Sánchez*. Los Angeles: University of California, Chicano Studies Center, 1977.

Romo, Ricardo. "George I. Sánchez and the Civil Rights Movement: 1940–1960." *La Raza Law Journal* 1:3 (Fall 1986): 342–362.

Welsh, Michael. "A Prophet without Honor: George I. Sánchez and Bilingualism in New Mexico." *New Mexico Historical Review* 69:1 (January 1994): 19–34.

LUIS RAFAEL SÁNCHEZ

(1936–)

Puerto Rican Dramatist, Short Story Writer, Novelist

Although baseball fever, like the chicken pox or measles, is caught by just about every Puerto Rican child, for Luis Rafael Sánchez it never had great allure. A shy and introverted boy, Luis Rafael was not interested in joining a game of catch with his friends. As a result his early life was sometimes difficult. He has recollections of being uncomfortable with friends who preferred to play ball rather than make conversation. Sánchez has characterized his childhood as sad and often lonely, at times even tense. Because he changed schools repeatedly, for long periods of time he felt like an outsider. In adult life this very introverted boy became Puerto Rico's best-known dramatist, whose works have been included in half a dozen anthologies.

Luis Rafael Sánchez was born on 17 November 1936 in Humacao, Puerto Rico, where he spent his childhood. The small town of Humacao, located in the southeastern part of Puerto Rico, later served as the background in some of his short stories, for example, "En Cuerpo de Camisa." Luis Rafael was a very studious boy who spent much of his time with his homework and other scholastic activities. When he was 12 years old his family moved to the capital, San Juan. His memories of Old San Juan, its two fortresses, and its tourism greatly influenced his later writing and served as the setting for his play, *Sol 13, Interior*, 1987.

Luis Rafael broke out of his intense introversion while attending the ninth grade at Baldorioty School in San Juan. At this time he encountered Victoria Espinoza, the founder and director of the University of Puerto Rico drama department's La Commedieta Universitaria, a traveling troupe that brought plays to youthful audiences. She became Luis's theater teacher. As a result of her generous inspirational mentoring, Sánchez very early in life developed an extraordinary interest in and love of the theater.

From Baldorioty Sánchez entered the University of Puerto Rico to study drama. While still a teenager he and a friend founded the Juan Acosta Experimental Theater. Sánchez's next notable achievement came at age 19 when he went to Mexico to take part in the play *El boticario* at the National Mexican Youth Institute. More than 100 actors had entered this competition; Sánchez was selected and given recognition as the best young actor of the year. While visiting Mexico he participated in the filming of an educational film, *Comunidad universitaria* ("University Community"), for Mexico's Department of Education.

After Sánchez's visit to Mexico, he returned to the University of Puerto Rico. He became an active member of the theater group Tablado del Coquí, as well as La Commedieta Universitaria, participating in nearly a dozen plays. He also had the lead role as Don Cristóbal in Federico García Lorca's play *Títeres de Cachiporra*, which ran for over a year. For a period of time he gained additional experience as a dramatic actor in radio soap operas, working with several well-known Puerto Rican actresses.

Although Sánchez's goal during his years as a student at the University of Puerto Rico was to become an actor, his experiences in the theater sparked a strong interest in writing, particularly short stories. He found his friends very supportive of his new commitment, especially the writer Hugo Margenat, who was enthusiastic yet honest about Sánchez's talents. He persuaded Sánchez to enter a university literature contest. He did and he won.

In 1959 Sánchez graduated from the University of Puerto Rico with a bachelor's degree in drama and a minor in Hispanic literature. During this period the theater was an energizing political force among university students in Puerto Rico. Sánchez's first play, *La espera* ("The Waiting"), was presented in 1958 at the opening night of the University of Puerto Rico's Experimental Theater. In the following year Sánchez received an award for his *Cuento de la cucarachita viudita*, a short story for children based on the folk characters Cucarachita Martina and Ratoncito Pérez. *Farsa de amor compradito*, 1960, became his first significant play; in it he further developed themes explored in the children's story.

For Sánchez there were two major events in 1961. Two of his one-act plays were staged, and his collection of short stories, *En cuerpo de camisa*, was published. This short story collection is significant for his development as a literary figure because in it Sánchez for the first time made use of ornate language, which became a characteristic of his later work. This Antillean baroque, common with earlier Puerto Rican literary figures, is reflected in his use of highly literary language combined with popular urban speech patterns. He also used this unique style in his later novel, *Macho Camacho's Beat*.

In subsequent years Sánchez published two new plays: in 1965, *Y casi el alma*; and in 1968, *La pasión según Antígona Pérez*. The latter play, which premiered in the following year, was significant for its dramatic force. In it Sánchez portrayed a new political consciousness, expressing Puerto Rican feelings in the decade of the 1960s, particularly the rising sentiment for the island's independence. With a fellowship from his alma mater, Sánchez went to New York to study theater and creative writing at Columbia University, where he then obtained his Master's degree in Spanish literature. At Columbia he developed a deeper affinity for Spanish baroque literature, and his contact with New York City and its theater exerted a significant influence in developing his interests as a playwright. From Columbia he went to Spain to get his doctoral degree at the University of Madrid. He received his Ph.D. in 1973.

As a playwright, short story writer, novelist, and essayist, Sánchez has demonstrated an uncanny ability to use popular languages to depict comic situations that also convey a serious or tragic message. It is clear that he has considerable disdain for the characters he creates but loves their linguistic faults. The irony of the world Sánchez portrays is that his characters seem to relish the expressions he puts into their mouths, creating a false gaiety that wins out over their miserable human condition.

His most celebrated work is the novel *Macho Camacho's Beat*, first published in 1976 by Ediciones de la Flor in Buenos Aires, Argentina, as *La guaracha del macho Camacho*, and translated into English in 1980 as well as Portuguese in the following year. The novel's success is due primarily to its dialogue; the plot is relatively inconsequential. Sánchez presents a sardonic view of existence by contrasting life in modern Puerto Rico with its portrayal on Macho Camacho's radio hit, "Life Is a Phenomenal Thing." Because of its great popularity, *La guaracha* has gone through a dozen printings by various publishers, the most recent in 1993.

In 1979 Sánchez introduced a new play, *La parábola de Andarín*, and in 1984 *Quíntuples*. In San Juan *Quíntuples* was presented in Spanish, and in New York City in English. Both plays give evidence of the playwright's deep and abiding concern about the political future of the island. In 1986 Sánchez tackled a new issue, the problems of being a Puerto Rican writer, in his play *No llores por nosotros, Puerto Rico*, an obvious take-off on the song "Don't Cry for Me, Argentina" from the play *Evita*. His play *La guagua aérea* ("The Aerial Bus"), 1994, further explored the same difficulties. His second novel, *La importancia de lilamarse Daniel Santos*, was first published in 1988 and, although not as successful as *La guaracha*, has since gone through several printings.

As an author Sánchez is considered a traditionalist in that he shares the longstanding tradition of Puerto Rican writers who view the island's political relationship with the United States as a lingering vestige of colonial oppression. Rather than treating literature as art for art's sake, Sánchez, in accord with his feeling of political obligation as an author, examines the problems arising from dependency and the enervation of Puerto Rican identity and consciously develops these themes in an effort to bring about political and social reform.

Sánchez has been the recipient of a number of honors. In 1979 he was awarded a highly esteemed Guggenheim scholarship. In 1985 he visited Berlin and spent a year there after receiving a grant from the Deutscher Akademischer Austrauschdienst-Berliner Künstler Program. Sánchez also has taught on the U.S. mainland, in 1988 spending a year as a visiting professor at City College of New York and in 1989 teaching at Johns Hopkins University in Baltimore. He also has traveled throughout Latin America and Europe as a much sought after participant in conferences and as a judge in literary contests.

Sánchez has long been associated with the University of Puerto Rico as a professor of Spanish literature. He publicly claims that he does not enjoy being a professor, but that he has no choice since he needs to earn a living. He would like to become a theater director and believes he would make a good one. Sánchez feels that as a director he could make

use of his finely honed critical judgment to develop imaginative inter-
pretations of literary works.

Further Reading

Calaf de Agüera, Helen. "Entrevista: Luis Rafael Sánchez." *Hispanoamerica* 23–24
    (1979): 71–80.
Flores, Angel. *Spanish American Authors: The Twentieth Century*. New York: H. W.
    Wilson Co., 1992.
González, Rafael M. "La guagua aérea." *Library Journal* 120 (January 1995): 79.
Kanellos, Nicolás. *Biographical Dictionary of Hispanic Literature in the United States*.
    Westport, Conn.: Greenwood Press, 1989.
"Luis Rafael Sánchez." In *Gente importante*, Darcia Moretti, ed. New York: Plus
    Ultra, 1973.
Ryan, Bryan, ed. *Hispanic Writers*. Detroit: Gale Research, 1991.
Stein, Sharon R., and Jean C. Stine, eds. *Contemporary Literary Criticism*, vol. 23.
    Detroit: Gale Research Center, 1983.
Trosky, Susan M., ed. *Contemporary Authors*, vol. 128. Detroit: Gale Research,
    1990.
Waldman, Gloria F. "Luis Rafael Sánchez: An Interview." *Revi* 9 (1979): 9–23.

GEORGE SANTAYANA
(1863–1952)
Spanish American Philosopher, Novelist,
Poet, Essayist

George Santayana is one of the most important philosophers of the past
one hundred years. In intellectual circles he was, and is, most widely
known for his philosophical concepts. However, at age 72 he also became
known popularly as a result of the publication in 1936 of his semi-
autobiographical novel *The Last Puritan*. Readers found it appealing because of the beauty of Santayana's writing: his fluid, rhythmic prose and
his sometimes ironic style, best exemplified, perhaps, by his famous aph-
orism: "Those who cannot remember the past are condemned to repeat
it." *The Last Puritan* was an immediate and resounding success, winning
a place on best seller lists and being picked up by the Book of the Month
Club. It has gone through many editions, the most recent published by
the Massachusetts Institute of Technology Press in 1994.

George Santayana was born in Madrid, the capital of Spain, on 16 December 1863, the only child of widow Josefina Borrás Sturgis and her second husband, Agustín Ruiz de Santayana. When he was 3 years old the family moved to the nearby small medieval town of Ávila, where he later began his formal education in the tiny local school. His father, who was a retired civil servant with deep artistic and literary interests, had a profound effect on young George. The child thus spent his early years in an atmosphere of concern for art and literature.

While George was still a small child his parents separated and his mother immigrated to the United States with the children from her first marriage, leaving him in Spain with his father. At age 9 he left Spain to join his mother and half-siblings in Boston. Here he was first enrolled in a private kindergarten, where he began to learn English and American culture. He then entered a public grammar school and after two years there began eight years of highly disciplined study in the Boston Latin School, famous since colonial times for its scholastic excellence. Here he started his literary career by writing poetry; in 1881 he helped establish and became editor of the school paper, the *Boston Latin Register*.

In 1882 at age 18 Santayana was enrolled in Harvard University, where he became involved in various student organizations. During his four years there he wrote for the *Lampoon*, took a prominent role in Harvard theater productions, was elected president of the Harvard Philosophy Club, and in 1885 helped found the *Harvard Monthly*. In the following year he received his B.A. *summa cum laude* and accepted a fellowship that took him to Europe, to the University of Berlin at which he studied classical Greek philosophy. After two years of intense study in Germany he returned to Harvard for another year of graduate study and in 1889 was awarded both the master's degree and the doctorate in philosophy. His outstanding talents were recognized by Harvard, which hired him that same year to teach in the philosophy department.

Young Professor Santayana quickly gained a student following on campus. He soon became one of the most popular teachers in the philosophy department, during his career counting among his students future Supreme Court justice Felix Frankfurter, Nobel Prize–winner in literature T. S. Eliot, and syndicated newspaper pundit Walter Lippmann. It was not long before his reputation extended beyond the classroom and outside Harvard University environs. Santayana lived on campus, making frequent visits to his mother in Brookline, Massachusetts; during summer vacations he also regularly visited his father in Spain.

At age 30 Santayana published his first book of poems, *Sonnets and Other Verses*, 1894, which met with a polite but fairly lukewarm reception from both critics and the public. Despite the lack of rousing enthusiasm for his first publication, he continued to write and publish his poetry. Two years later his first book of philosophy, *The Sense of Beauty*, came out. In it he argued that the human mind was capable of developing an imaginative yet rational concept of physical beauty. It garnered high praise from critics and colleagues alike as one of the best philosophical works on aesthetics (the philosophical study of the abstract conception of beauty) written by an American. Its importance is indicated by the fact that it has been repeatedly reprinted; the most recent edition was issued in 1988.

In the ensuing years Santayana continued regularly to write and publish both his philosophical studies and his poetry, being deeply involved in criticism of poetry from a philosophic viewpoint. In 1905 he published *The Life of Reason*, which was to be the first of five volumes tracing the development of human rationality and expounding his broader philosophical views. These centered around his philosophic synthesis, which argued that the human spirit was able to rise above materialism. As a result of these ideas Santayana began to be perceived by colleagues, critics, and the public as an outstanding American philosopher. Continuing with his literary criticism from a philosophic viewpoint, in 1910 he published his most detailed critical work, *Three Philosophical Poets*, an in-depth study of Lucretius, Dante, and Goethe.

After nearly a quarter-century of teaching at Harvard, Santayana resigned in 1912 when he received a comfortable legacy. He left the United States and spent the rest of his life in England and continental Europe—particularly in Rome, where he settled in the early 1920s. Although he corresponded widely, he made no effort to meet or see people in his field of interest and had few visitors. He led a quiet, obscure life of withdrawal from the world, particularly the academic world, and rarely made public appearances. However, in 1932 because of a special request he presented lectures in England and Holland on the occasion of the 300th anniversary of the births of the famous philosophers John Locke and Benedict Spinoza. In the meantime he continued to write prolifically (in English) and published in both the United States and Great Britain. The four volumes of *The Realms of Being*, the distillation of his philosophical ideas, date from this period.

So does *The Last Puritan*, Santayana's only novel. Published by Scribners shortly after his 72nd birthday, it was based on his 40 years in the United States. He subtitled it "A Memoir in the Form of a Novel." It was extravagantly praised by many reviewers as one of the truly great American novels of all time, whereas others found it not so much a novel as a vehicle for Santayana's philosophic observations and insights. However it may be viewed, it became by far the most popular of his 40-some publications, going through numerous editions.

During World War II Santayana, now in his latter 70s and in failing health, continued to live in Rome, moved into a nursing home, and began writing his detailed autobiography. In a scenario reminiscent of a

James Bond thriller, Volume 1, entitled *Persons and Places: The Background of My Life*, was smuggled out of Italy with the help of the U.S. Department of State and was published in 1944. Because of the U.S. need for Latin American support during World War II, it was viewed by many officials in government as a timely and valuable bridge between Latino and Anglo cultures that would help in the war effort. The second volume of Santayana's autobiography was published at the end of the war, and the third came out posthumously in 1953.

After a long illness George Santayana, one of the outstanding philosophers of the 20th century, died in Rome on 26 September 1952. Although he never became an American citizen, Santayana's entire life and all his writings were dominated by the 40 years he lived in the United States. He once said of himself that he was an American by long association.

Further Reading

Arnett, Willard E. *George Santayana*. New York: Washington Square Press, 1968.
Butler, Richard. *The Life and World of George Santayana*. Chicago: H. Regnery Co., 1960.
Cory, Daniel. *Santayana: The Later Years*. New York: G. Braziller, 1963.
Current Biography, 1944. New York: H. W. Wilson Co., 1945.
Current Biography, 1952. New York: H. W. Wilson Co., 1953.
McCormick, John. *George Santayana: A Biography*. New York: Knopf/Random House, 1987.
Santayana, George. *Persons and Places: Fragments of Autobiography*. Cambridge, Mass.: MIT Press, 1986.
Stallknecht, Newton P. *George Santayana*. Minneapolis: University of Minnesota Press, 1971.

JUAN SEGUÍN

(1806–1889)

Mexican American/Texan Patriot, Political Leader, Soldier

Seguín, as he asserted, believed in "God, Mexico, and the Federal System" in that order, but came to support Texas independence from Mexico when all three failed him. He was an outstanding *tejano* and Texas leader. Juan Seguín served Texas faithfully and well and was repaid with unremitting and intense persecution by some Anglo Texans, although other leaders repeatedly demonstrated their confidence and faith in him. Many of his problems arose from the complex and confusing conditions on the Texas-Mexico border in the second half of the 1800s.

Juan Nepomuceno Seguín was born on 27 October 1806 at San Antonio, Texas, the first son of a prominent young civic leader of the town, Juan José María Erasmo Seguín. Of French and Spanish descent, he came from ancestors who had migrated from central Mexico to the Texas frontier just after the founding of the settlement at San Antonio de Béxar in 1718. A century later his father Erasmo, who owned extensive property in the area, was active politically and was one of the leaders in creating the first "public" school, which his first-born then attended. Given his father's political and economic prominence, it was perhaps inevitable that Juan should enter politics at an early age. Before he was out of his teens he had been elected *alcalde* on the San Antonio town council.

In his official position Juan Seguín came into frequent contact with the newest settlers in Texas, the Anglo Americans, whose principal leader, Stephen Austin, had become a close friend of father and son. Both, along with other prominent *tejanos* like José Antonio Navarro, joined with the Anglos in opposing Mexican president Antonio López de Santa Anna's efforts in the 1830s to impose a centralist government, which would have destroyed their local self-rule. In a convention that met at San Felipe in 1832 despite official opposition, Juan helped draw up a memorial to the government in Mexico City requesting a remedy for Texas and its concerns. As relations between Texas and the central government continued to deteriorate, Juan and his father were important in swinging *tejano* support behind the Austin faction.

When General Martín Perfecto de Cos was sent with an army to force the Texans to submit to the central government, Juan Seguín volunteered his services to the Texas dissidents and was placed in command of a small force. Although under surveillance, he visited ranches on the lower San Antonio river, effectively recruiting adherents. Austin appointed him captain over the troops he had recruited. In addition to reconnoitering for the Texans and engaging Mexican forces in skirmishes, Seguín led numerous foraging expeditions. He supplied the insurgents with valuable information about the Mexican troops, and both he and his father gave generously of their resources. One of his father's ranches was used as a rebel supply storage depot. In November 1835 Juan was appointed a Béxar district judge by the provisional Texas government and in the following January received a regular appointment as a cavalry captain.

Juan Seguín and the Second Company of Texas Volunteers, which he had recruited, provided valuable military intelligence prior to the siege of the Alamo by Santa Anna. At the Alamo he headed a small force of *tejanos*, but on the night before Santa Anna's final, and successful, attack he was sent through the tight Mexican lines to seek help. After the fall of the Alamo and the Texans' withdrawal eastward, Seguín was placed in command of the rear guard. In the battle of San Jacinto on 21 April he and his troops had a conspicuous role in the defeat and capture of Santa Anna. At the end of May, Seguín was promoted to lieutenant colonel and ordered to take possession of San Antonio from the Mexican forces. He did so. He remained military commandant of the city, which was threatened by various Mexican reconquest attempts, until civil government was finally restored in September 1837.

While on a three-month recuperative leave in New Orleans early in 1838, Seguín was elected to the Texas Senate. Obtaining his discharge from the Texas army, he took his seat in the Senate in May and immediately became an active participant in Texas government. In the autumn of 1840, after more than two years in the Senate, he resigned to lead a group of *tejano* volunteers into Mexico to support old-time federalist Antonio Canales in his continuing struggle against centralism from Mexico City. Returning to San Antonio in December, Seguín ran for mayor in the following January and was elected in a closely contested election. As mayor his defense of *tejano* rights earned him the bitter enmity of the horde of Anglo adventurers and social misfits who had descended on Texas to plunder well-to-do *tejano* families. Later that year he was unjustly accused of betraying the Texan Santa Fe expedition. His indignant denials failed to stop the slanderous rumors even after his re-election as mayor in January 1842.

When Mexican reconquest forces entered San Antonio in March 1842 after Seguín and the other defenders had been forced to withdraw, a new charge was made against him: that of being friendly to the invading army. Numerous threats to his life and increasing danger to his family compelled him to go into hiding. He finally bowed to Anglo pressure and stepped down as mayor. Fearing that neither he nor his family were safe anywhere in Texas because of widespread threats, he reluctantly decided to cross over the Rio Grande to live in the country against which he had fought in the Texas revolution. At Nuevo Laredo, Tamaulipas, he was jailed by local military authorities. At President Santa Anna's order he was given the choice of imprisonment or service in the Mexican army. Heavily in debt and with a large family to provide for, Seguín felt he had little choice. He accepted military service and served in the Mexican army during the war between Mexico and the United States. After the Treaty of Guadalupe Hidalgo in 1848 he requested permission to come back with his family to his native Texas. Through the influence of friends he was permitted to return despite anonymous accusations still made against him.

For the next two decades Seguín lived quietly on one of his father's

ranches just south of San Antonio. He continued his longstanding interest in politics but seems not to have taken an active part in the slavery
debates of the 1850s. After his father's death in 1857 he published his
memoirs, in which he defended his patriotism and conduct and described the hounding by his enemies. Sometime during the 1870s Seguín
again crossed the Rio Grande, apparently because some family members
were living in Mexico. He stayed on the border at Nuevo Laredo for a
while and in 1889 died at the home of one of his sons near Monterrey,
Nuevo León.

Further Reading

Chabot, Frederick C. *With the Makers of San Antonio*. San Antonio, Tex.: Artes
Gráficas, 1937.
Jackson, Jack. *Los Tejanos*. Stamford, Conn.: Fantagraphics Books, 1982.
Lindhelm, Milton. *The Republic of the Rio Grande: Texans in Mexico, 1839–1840*.
Waco, Tex.: W. M. Morrison, 1964.
Seguín, Juan. *Personal Memoirs of Juan N. Seguín from 1834 to . . . 1842*. San An-
tonio, Tex.: Ledger Book and Job Office, 1858.
———. *A Revolution Remembered: The Memoirs and Selected Correspondence of Juan
N. Seguín*. Austin: State House Press, 1991.
Vernon, Ida S. "Activities of the Seguíns in Early Texas History." *West Texas
Historical Association Year Book* 25 (October 1949): 11–38.
Weber, David J. *The Mexican Frontier, 1821–1846*. Albuquerque: University of
New Mexico Press, 1982.

MARTIN SHEEN
(RAMÓN ESTÉVEZ)
(1940–)

Spanish American Actor, Social Activist

For most actors, acting is a career; fantasy, fiction, and reality usually
blend to produce a hybrid—the actor. The world of acting generates
values of its own, relative values. Ironically, Martin Sheen, an actor of
the finest quality for over 30 years, does not subscribe to this world. "I
don't think of what I do as a career. My kids [actors Emilio Estévez,
Charlie Sheen, and Renee Sheen] have careers. I think of myself as a
journeyman actor, who has been fortunate to make his living at it most

of his life. I consider that a very great blessing and hope I will continue to do that the rest of my life. But it's only a part of my life. I'm a father, a husband, a grandfather, an activist, a Catholic. I'm all these things that make up the whole. Being an actor is just part of the whole!" For Martin Sheen, life orbits around his basic values of justice and equality, as well as his long-held belief in political commitment, his Christian faith, and his deep belief in family.

Martin Sheen was born Ramón Estévez in Dayton, Ohio, on 3 August 1940. He was one of ten children born to his Irish immigrant mother and Spanish immigrant father, Francisco Estévez. His mother died when he was 11 years old; his father, a drill-press operator, was left to raise the family. Independence with responsibility became a value central to Ramón's life. His father stressed these values, together with stringent Catholic morals and the basic tenets of work, honesty, and family. Helped by the people of the Holy Trinity Church in Dayton, Ramón and his siblings continued with their Catholic education and upbringing. "We went to a Catholic grade school and an all-boys [Chaminade] Catholic high school," Sheen recalls, "so there had to be tuition paid and you had to buy your own books and your own [uniform] clothes." The Reverend Alfred Dropp at Holy Trinity Church became a mentor for the youth.

Enveloped by a working-class environment and often not far from poverty, during most of the 1950s Ramón and his brothers, worked as caddies at the prestigious Dayton Country Club. Ramón earned from $1.25 to $2.75 plus tips for a golf game and turned this money over to his father. He caddied from the age of 9 to 18. For a while he hoped to become a professional golfer but was turned on to acting in high school. From his work at the country club he not only earned money to help support the family but also learned the discipline of the workplace and developed an awareness of class differences in society, as well as the existence of snobbery and prejudice.

Sheen remembers: "I got a pretty good look as a child at how the better half lived, and I wasn't impressed with these people." Sheen also became aware of the "silent world" of women and the "invisibility" of the poor. "People," he remembers, "with servants tend to forget their presence because they don't recognize servants as people very often, certainly not as equals. They thought I [as a caddie] was deaf or dumb or something. They'd say things in front of you that would be insulting anywhere else." Observing women playing golf, he noted that they depended heavily on their husbands and had little independence. Differences in gender roles and sexist behavior were quite apparent to him, especially since he tended to see the world from a strict religious perspective of equality and respect.

Seeing these value differences in his worlds of school, caddying, and family, Ramón began to link them through activism. He started developing a commitment to changing these realities of life. In 1955, at age 15, he led a strike of caddies for higher wages and better working conditions. "I understood," he said, "about labor relations at an early age. Anybody who works does." Sheen saw work as both enabling and dignifying. Holding this central belief, he supported **César Chávez** and the farm workers in the second half of the 1960s during their strike for humane conditions in California's fields. His sense of social justice caused him to stand behind Mitch Snyder's campaigns for the homeless, Mother Teresa's struggles in India for better treatment of untouchables, and Jesse Jackson's campaigns to equalize opportunity in America. He also helped raise funds for children wounded in Nicaragua's internal violence and campaigned against nuclear war and all war. Sheen's activism was fundamentally driven by his notion that "work for all" was a minimum requirement for equality and, ultimately, for a sense of dignity and spirituality among humans. "When I go on demonstrations and commit civil disobedience, I do it with a profound sense of spirituality. I pray. I don't know what else to do. My job," he says, "is to try to call attention and raise consciousness on the important issues."

However, if honest work, self-pride, spirituality, and family were always basic to Sheen's life, his concept of "risk" has been the catalyst to his achievement. He became imbued with the idea that taking chances was an American trait and particularly an Estévez family trait. During his high school years he began to think about the possibility of a career as an actor. In "risking" by appearing on a local Dayton television program called "The Rising Generation," and by going to New York for theatrical experience instead of to college, he felt little sense of caution or risk because he firmly believed in himself and what he was doing. While in New York as a winner of "The Rising Generation" program's trip, he constantly looked "for opportunities."

In New York Sheen supported himself as a car washer, soda jerk, busboy in a restaurant, and night stock boy at American Express. Later, while making the rounds of casting directors' offices, he became a janitor at the Living Theater. During this period in the 1960s he could not afford acting lessons, so he organized a performance company called the Actor's Co-op, to which aspiring actors (including Barbra Streisand, Al Pacino, and others) came to perform parts of plays and be critiqued. In order to avoid typecasting, at this time Sheen changed his name from Ramón Estévez to Martin Sheen. He took "Martin" from his second mentor, CBS's Robert Dale Martin, and "Sheen" from Bishop Fulton J. Sheen, a notable religious television personality of the day and a figure in the Catholic Church. However, he pointed out, "My name is still Ramón Estévez on my passport, my birth certificate, driver's license, everything, every official document. [Sheen's] just a stage name." However deeply immersed in the world of acting, he never forgot his basic self.

During this period Sheen met Janet Templeton, an art student, who became his wife and the mother of what has become known as the Sheen/Estévez acting dynasty of the 1990s: Emilio Estévez, Charlie Sheen, Renee Sheen, and Ramón Estévez. A strong sense of family, a commitment to humanitarianism, a reliance on the value of work, and a belief in Sheen's notion of "risk" permeates this "ethnic American" clan of Martin Sheen's.

In a 1991 interview Sheen cited several other influences on his personal and public life: the unique and quiet rebelliousness of actor James Dean, the multi-talentedness of Elvis Presley, and the combination of talent with activism of Bob Dylan. Sheen worked hard at his craft and was always his most severe critic, as he continues to be. He first rose to prominence in the Broadway hit *The Subject Was Roses* in 1964 and later played in various off Broadway productions. By the 1990s he had become a first-rate actor and a Tony winner, gaining plaudits for his outstanding performances in such films as *Apocalypse Now, The Execution of Private Slovick, Badlands, Rage*, and others. In addition to his many movie roles Sheen has done well in television, with numerous appearances (often as the villain) in many major television drama series and then as the lead in a number of television specials.

In 1977 Sheen suffered a massive heart attack and returned to practicing his Catholic faith, strengthened his family ties, and became even more active in political and humanitarian causes. By the mid-1980s he was firm in his conviction that his life should be centered on work, family, and activism. "It was one of the happiest days of my life, if not the happiest, because I was finally free to be everything I was and had become." His life, he realized, was more than just a hybrid of his acting and his activism, and acting was more than just a career. "Acting [and living] is fun," he says.

Further Reading

Boston Globe (11 March 1987): 78.
Boston Globe (8 May 1988): 29.
Detroit Free Press (13 June 1987): 10c.
Detroit Free Press (23 November 1989): 16a.
Hargrove, Jim. *Martin Sheen*. Chicago: Children's Press, 1991.
Hispanic 6:9 (October 1993): 14–22.
Hispanic 7:3 (May 1994): 14.
Omni 14:2 (November 1991): 10.
Rocky Mountain News (27 May 1989): 114.
Rocky Mountain News (9 June 1989): 190.

ROBERTO SUÁREZ

(1928–)

Cuban American Newspaper Editor

Cuban refugees to the United States have been characterized in numerous studies as typical members of the middle class who adapt most readily to their new life. Roberto Suárez certainly fits that description. In addition to his middle-class qualifications, he benefited from the fact that his family had pre-revolutionary social and business contacts on the mainland and that he himself had spent four years there in college. But he must be credited with both a willingness to repeatedly try out new paths of enterprise in three different countries and a persistence that at least warranted success, if it did not guarantee it. Success he did achieve, through intelligence and diligent application.

Roberto José Suárez was born on 5 March 1928 in the Havana suburb of Marinao, the second youngest of seven children of Esperanza de Cárdenas and Miguel A. Suárez. His father was a real estate developer who had business ties with North Americans. Like many Cuban businessmen he was also deeply involved in community political affairs, including opposition to the detested dictator of the early 1930s, Gerardo Machado. Partly because of his father's concern that all his children learn English, Roberto was enrolled in private American primary schools in Havana: first in Mrs. Phillips School and later in St. George School, at which he completed the eighth grade. His ability to speak English well was to serve him immensely later in life.

Roberto grew up in the middle-class Coronela and Miramar sections of Havana. After primary school he was enrolled by his parents in the Colegio de Belén, an all-boys school operated by the Society of Jesus (Jesuits) and at the time one of Cuba's most respected educational institutions. Among his fellow students was young Fidel Castro, who was in the class ahead of him. At Belén Roberto made a name for himself not only as a scholar but also as an athlete, particularly in baseball, basketball, and track. In his junior year he was awarded the first Capi Campusano (the school's athletic director) medal for the combination of his outstanding athletic record and equally distinguished scholarship. While still at Belén he also played centerfield on one of the city baseball teams and taught mathematics at the Escuela Electromecánica, a free trade school directed by the Jesuits.

Accepting the counsel of his father who had not finished high school,

Roberto Suárez.

after Roberto graduated from Belén in 1945 he entered the College of Commerce and Finance of Villanova University in Pennsylvania both to study finance and to perfect his English. The 17-year-old Roberto found the experience of attending college with many American veterans of World War II a very instructive one, since most of them were serious students interested in obtaining knowledge as well as in getting good grades. At Villanova, in addition to taking a full schedule of finance, accounting, and elective classes, he did a program on the college radio station, was active in sports and even played tackle on the football team, and played the part of Pocahontas in a Turf and Tinsel Club theatrical presentation. In 1949 he graduated from Villanova with a B.S. in finance and economics and returned to Cuba at age 21, eager to start his business career.

Upon his return Roberto took a job as a trainee in a commercial bank, the Trust Company of Cuba. After a year there he was promoted to assistant bookkeeper in a small branch office and a year later moved up to branch accountant. Having given some thought to his future and the financial possibilities outside of banking, he then quit his banking job to go into the real estate business. On the side he soon organized a construction company with an engineer friend, Ernesto Mestre, and $500 capital. It became a huge success. When Fulgencio Batista's coup d'état in 1952 had clearly turned into a dictatorship, Roberto joined with fellow Cubans to bring about his overthrow.

After the 26th of July Movement under the leadership of Castro ousted the dictator, Suárez experienced a brief period of hope but soon became disenchanted with the revolutionary government's turn to the left—especially its confiscation of private property, including his construction company. He soon sent his wife and eight children across the Florida Straits to Miami and six months later, in late March 1961, followed. His plan to return clandestinely with military supplies for the anti-Castro Movimiento Revolucionario del Pueblo was aborted partly as a result of the Bay of Pigs invasion in mid-April.

Faced with the necessity of finding a job, Suárez soon became aware that jobs were not easy to find. After several months of seeking work he finally took a part-time job in the mail room of the *Miami Herald*. Soon he was put on full-time, assembling and bundling newspapers. As a result of his work experience in Cuba he soon was assigned to preparing the mail room payroll, and after several months he was promoted to a position as mail room foreman. Four years after coming to the United States, he became controller of the subsidiary operations of the *Herald*.

In 1969 Suárez resigned his position with the *Miami Herald* to join Ernesto Mestre, his former partner in the construction business who had fled to Honduras and started a new company. But the relationship between the partners was not the same as it had been in Cuba, and during his second year in Tegucigalpa Roberto left the construction business and started a new company, selling and installing industrial equipment. Meanwhile he perceived a rising Cuban influence in Honduras and was, as a result, open to offers to return to the United States. Early in 1972 he accepted the position as controller of the Knight Publishing Company, publisher of two newspapers in Charlotte, North Carolina, and moved his family back to the States.

During 15 years in Charlotte Suárez was promoted from controller to treasurer, to business manager, to general manager and vice-president, and finally at the beginning of 1986 to president. In these years he also took an active role in the community. He accepted a position on the Charlotte Symphony board and soon was named treasurer; later he became a board member of the Charlotte Arts and Science Council and was elected its president for a one-year term. A founding member of the Urban League in Charlotte, he served as its treasurer as well as a board member; he also put in two years on the board of directors of the National Conference of Christians and Jews. In 1986 he was named chair of the committee organized to celebrate the 200th anniversary of the U.S.

Constitution. He fully expected to grow old and retire in Charlotte, but on 1 September 1987 the Suárez family returned to Miami.

Earlier that year Roberto had gone to Miami to contribute his views about a *Herald* project for a possible new Spanish-language paper. The *Miami Herald*, the Knight-Ridder company's flagship newspaper, was encountering serious readership problems in the large Cuban American community in greater Miami, and there was a growing and increasingly articulate Spanish-language press proffering competition. After two days of discussion and ultimately a decision to publish the paper, Suárez was offered the position of publisher. He accepted for a one-year period but later was persuaded to take the position for an indefinite period.

Suárez adjusted quickly to his new job and the new life, helped by many friends in the greatly enlarged Dade County Cuban American community, including many of his schoolmates from the Colegio de Belén. His role as publisher of *El Nuevo Heraldo* was a very satisfying one and brought him new respect and honors. In 1989 he was awarded the John S. Knight Gold Medal of Excellence by Knight-Ridder as the "most distinguished executive" of all its newspapers. In the following year he received the Hispanic Alliance Heritage Award in media and entertainment and in 1991 was given a leadership award by Washington, D.C.–based Aspira. He was also honored with the "Mariano Guastella 1993" award from the Association of Latin American Advertisers. Currently he heads the executive committee of the Inter American Press Association.

Further Reading

"A Cuban Success Story—In the United States." *U.S. News & World Report* (20 March 1967): 104–106.

"Flight from Cuba—Castro's Loss Is U.S. Gain." *U.S. News & World Report* (31 May 1971): 74–77.

Fradd, Sandra. "Cubans to Cuban Americans: Assimilation in the United States." *Migration Today* 11:4/5 (1983): 34–42.

Kanellos, Nicolás, ed. *The Hispanic Almanac*. Detroit: Visible Ink Press, 1994.

Linehan, Edward J. "Cuba's Exiles Bring New Life to Miami." *National Geographic* 144 (July 1973): 68–95.

"Roberto Suárez." *Selecta Magazine* (April 1990): 46–47.

Unterburger, Amy, ed. *Who's Who among Hispanic Americans, 1994–95*. Detroit: Gale Research, 1995.

age 17 she went to observe the Finck Cigar Company workers in their strike and wound up jailed with them. After graduation from high school she got a job as an elevator operator in the Gunter Hotel at a dollar a day and spent most of her free time helping to organize Mexican American workers into a militant, job-oriented, communist-supported union, the Workers Alliance. She later acted as secretary for Workers Alliance groups in San Antonio. She also helped organize a San Antonio chapter of the International Ladies Garment Workers Union, the ILGWU.

By the mid-1930s Emma had become convinced that to obtain change it was necessary to stand up to the power structure. In 1937 she led a sit-in of unemployed Mexican Americans at the San Antonio city hall to protest relief policies and to demand jobs. Her strong activist role during the unsettling days of the Great Depression and her widespread support within the Mexican American community soon made her the object of special monitoring by the police. She was frequently arrested and hauled off to jail, but she seldom spent more than a few hours in detention. From each such experience she emerged more determined than ever to continue to speak out for social justice and civil rights for the poor.

In late 1937 Emma married Homer Brooks, a Communist Party organizer in Houston and the party secretary for Texas. She kept her maiden name and remained in San Antonio. Convinced that only the Communists were interested in helping the poor and disenfranchised, she joined the party but remained a member for only a year and a half. In 1939 Brooks and Tenayuca published an article titled "The Mexican Question in the Southwest," an analysis of the position of *mexicanos* from the communist perspective. It suggested a course of action that included working for better education; for an end to political, economic, and social discrimination; and for bilingual schools.

When some 2,000 pecan-shellers struck spontaneously because of a 15 percent wage cut in late January 1938, they asked Emma Tenayuca to represent them. As the strike went on week after week she became a symbol of the radically led strike and became known as La Pasionaria, a comparison to Dolores Ibarruri, a leader of the anti-Franco forces in the contemporary Spanish Civil War (1936–1939). A strong local reaction to communist leadership in the strike caused her to be replaced, but the strikers responded by naming her honorary strike leader. She continued to support the strikers in less confrontational ways. In March the strike was settled by arbitration that granted the workers union recognition and a minimum wage.

With her fiery speeches and inflammatory personality, which made her a good organizer and leader, Emma also created many enemies. In 1939 she scheduled a Communist rally in August at San Antonio's city auditorium. A near-riot occurred when a fierce mob of over 5,000, incited by the Soviet-Nazi nonaggression pact of a week earlier and by a well-

EMMA TENAYUCA

(1917–   )

Mexican American Labor Organizer, Activist, Teacher

On 1 February 1938, at the height of the pecan-shelling season, several thousand Mexican American workers walked off the job at some 120 shelling plants in San Antonio, Texas. The strike, which lasted more than five weeks, called national attention to the extreme exploitation of pecan-shellers but had limited success. It was opposed, or at least denied support, by the Mexican Chamber of Commerce, the League of United Latin American Citizens (LULAC), the San Antonio Ministers' Association, and the Catholic archbishop of San Antonio, Arthur J. Drossaerts. Opposition to the strike was based on its alleged Communist Party leadership. Among the leaders accused of being Communists was 21-year-old Emma Tenayuca.

Emma Tenayuca was born on 21 December 1917 in San Antonio, Texas. Her mother was a descendant of the Cepeda family, which had helped establish the Spanish colony in Texas during the early 1700s; her father was a Native American. Hence the non-Spanish family name. The extended family was very close-knit, and Emma recalls growing up enveloped in the warmth and love of her parents and grandparents. She went fishing in the San Antonio River with her father, and on Saturdays and Sundays she accompanied both him and her maternal grandfather to the plaza at Milam Square. There they listened to the soapbox orators: pulpit thumpers, Mexican revolutionaries, and native-born and foreign radicals, both left and right, and she first became aware of social injustice.

From the tender age of 7 or 8 Emma Tenayuca was exposed to a wide variety of economic and political ideas. An inquisitive and serious student in school, she spent hours reading in the San Antonio library after school hours. At Brackenridge High School she belonged to a student book-discussion group and had begun to question whether America was the "best of all possible worlds" for minority peoples. Her reading in Charles Darwin, Thomas Paine, and later Karl Marx gradually led her from a theoretical reformist position to a more active stance.

In 1931, while still a student at Brackenridge High, Emma Tenayuca helped organize and lead a march of unemployed workers on the capitol in Austin to demand immediate relief and unemployment insurance. At orchestrated campaign against her, attacked and broke up the meeting. The ten-year friendship pact between the USSR and Germany caused her later to terminate her Communist affiliation, and a short time afterwards she ended her political activism. Blacklisted by the U.S. House of Representatives Un-American Activities Committee, she discovered she was unable to find employment and soon left San Antonio.

Emma Tenayuca first went to Los Angeles and in the early 1940s tried to find a place in the California Mexican American labor movement there, recruiting among laundry, cement, and garment workers. She subsequently moved to San Francisco, where she enrolled in San Francisco State College (now University) in 1949. She graduated with honors three years later with an A.B. in the liberal arts. In the 1960s she returned to Texas, got a master's degree, and obtained a job teaching in the San Antonio elementary schools. She quietly continued teaching until her retirement in 1982.

Further Reading

Blackwelder, Julia K. *Women in the Depression*. College Station: Texas A&M University Press, 1984.

Calderón, Roberto, and Emilio Zamora. "Manuela Solís Sager and Emma Tenayuca: A Tribute." In *Chicana Voices*, Teresa Córdova et al., eds. Austin: Center for Mexican American Studies, University of Texas, 1986.

Croxdale, Richard, and Melissa Hield, eds. *Women in the Texas Workforce: Yesterday and Today*. Austin: People's History in Texas, 1979.

Larralde, Carlos. *Mexican American Movements and Leaders*. Los Alamitos, Calif.: Hwong Publishing, 1976.

Menefee, Selden, and Orin Cassmore. *The Pecan Shellers of San Antonio*. Reprinted in *Mexican Labor in the United States*, Carlos Cortés, ed. New York: Arno Press, 1974.

Rips, Geoffrey, and Emma Tenayuca. "Living History: Emma Tenayuca Tells Her Story." *Texas Observer* (28 October 1983): 7–15.

PIRI (JOHN PETER) THOMAS
(1928–)
Puerto Rican Writer, Poet, Social Activist

"Every child is born a poet and every poet is a child, no child was born to be a minority. Words can be bullets or butterflies. Love is a sharing and a caring born of truth. Being called 'nigger' and 'spik' messes up the minds of children. Study words, they are incantations." With these pronouncements, often lyrical and sometimes rhyming, Piri Thomas likes to intrigue those who listen to him when he gives dramatic motivational speeches and lectures about his transformation from a drug addict, gang leader, and convict to a multifaceted artist. Speaking of this remarkable conversion, Thomas says, "I am a miracle, I am Matrus, born of light, I am my own truth. I am the good-will ambassador from 'El Barrio.' " The qualities that make the new Piri Thomas resulted from long soul-searching and painful transitions.

Piri Thomas was born John Peter Thomas on 30 September 1928 in Spanish Harlem to Dolores Montañez from Puerto Rico and Juan Thomas, a Cuban who had immigrated to Puerto Rico. The eldest of seven children, physically Piri Thomas was dark like his black father and felt that the latter favored his siblings, who were fair like his mother. Growing up in the barrio, he felt unsure of his identity because society labeled him black yet his family identified itself as Puerto Rican. He was deeply influenced by his mother, a strongly religious woman. His name Piri, he once said, comes from *espiritu* ("spirit"). He explained, "My mother is my inspiration. She called me 'Piri' but I was called Pete on the streets. I returned to my old name 'Piri' when I left the penitentiary. I am a spirit incarnate."

Referring to his formative years, Thomas has said, "I was raised . . . in a protective environment where my parents took time to read to me, help me with homework, where we talked about our history, about God and the Bible, about Puerto Rico, about the kind of people we are. Mami said to me that nobody was better than one, better-off, maybe. She said we were decent people, and my home was so clean you could eat from the floor."

Contradictory cultural values of home, school, and the streets caused Piri to feel alienated from the ethical and moral values as well as the traditions of his parents. His school experience with racism was particularly alienating. After the family moved to the Italian section of East Harlem, he became even more aware of societal attitudes. During his mid-teen years problems with self-identification as a Puerto Rican and society's perception of him as a black became an obsessive factor. Embittered by the racism he encountered, he adopted a street survival mode by turning to petty theft and gang membership. Thomas became convinced that the only way out of the barrio was to obtain money in any way one could.

After his family moved to Brooklyn, Piri became more convinced of his father's favoritism and completely alienated by the middle-class values of his new neighborhood. At age 16 he returned to Spanish Harlem, where he survived by means of petty theft and peddling drugs. His culturally driven machismo (male reputation for courage and cool) greatly affected his search as a young adult for a new value system.

In his quest for identity Piri traveled to the U.S. South and then joined the merchant marines for a time. Upon his return from overseas, he became addicted to heroin and became a pusher to support his addiction. In an effort to regain control over himself he quit his daily habit "cold turkey" but turned to armed robbery to solve the pressures of survival on the "mean" streets of the barrio. A 1950 Greenwich Village holdup turned into a shootout with police, which left him a wounded prisoner.

Convicted of attempted armed robbery and felony assault, Thomas was sentenced to 5 to 15 years in prison, of which he served 7, mainly in Comstock, New York. In jail he soon realized he had not left the "mean streets"; they existed everywhere—in the prison corridors, dining halls, workplace, and jailyard. He was still living on the fringe, and his longed-for escape from barrio hopelessness was still in the future. In his cell he escaped through introspection; daily he pondered his beliefs, his past, and his future. And he set about to create a new Piri Thomas.

While in prison Thomas spent a great deal of time in what he calls "memory trips": going back in time to re-live his early days. He has said that when the lights went out, he was able to recall and reexperience the love and tenderness that he knew as a small child. While serving time in jail he made his time in jail serve him. He obtained a high school equivalency diploma, studied the Black Muslim faith, learned brick masonry, read, and wrote. He was able to survive the seven years in prison with a feeling of quiet dignity. His gradual transformation led him to conclude that to attain self-esteem and respect he had to develop reliance on the power of his mind.

Upon Thomas's parole at age 28 he returned to his old neighborhood to live with an aunt and through her became involved in the Pentecostal church. He got work as a baker and soon married a young woman newly arrived from Puerto Rico. Their bliss was shattered when they lost their home in Long Island because of concerted hostility from racist neighbors. Although once again confronted with racism, Piri's transformation in prison now prompted him to seek a positive response. He began working in a church youth center as a counselor, helping youngsters avoid street violence and drug addiction. He also worked as a volunteer in a prison rehabilitation program. As a result of his activism he was given a Lever Brothers community service award a decade later. Strongly convinced of the importance of education, he became a staff associate in the Center for Urban Education in 1967.

While in his early thirties Thomas made his first visit to Puerto Rico, where he met a film editor who encouraged him to apply for a grant from the Louis M. Rabinowitz Foundation to complete the autobiography he had begun writing. With the help of the grant, in 1967 Thomas published *Down These Mean Streets*, a rough-hewn, gut-wrenching account of his maturing, of his education and search for a value system as well as racial identity. The book combined urban street talk, Spanish phrases, and sometimes poetic prose in a stream-of-consciousness technique that rendered the book both unique and spellbinding. Thomas's gutsy and luxuriant descriptions of how a black Puerto Rican boy grew up in a mean society characterized by racism, victimization, and hopelessness made the book extremely popular on college campuses, which were just beginning to accept multiculturalism. Many critics have praised his book as deeply moving and have embraced it as literature rather than sociology. After more than 25 years of reprintings it is now considered a classic.

Subsequently Piri Thomas completed his autobiographical trilogy with two other books: *Savior, Savior, Hold My Hand*, 1972, and *Seven Long Times*, 1974. In general all depict the problems of a black, working-class Puerto Rican in a racist environment, seeking to establish himself in society despite its unwillingness to accommodate him. Thomas details the love and inner strength of family, the power of friendship, and the support provided by community as well as his need to validate his machismo amid drugs, crime, and poverty, and the struggles to escape the mean streets. Thomas also refers to other themes: the sometimes hypocritical role of organized religion, the degrading nature of the penal system and its failure to rehabilitate, and society's racial and economic inequities. These themes also appear in his fictional *Stories from El Barrio*, 1978.

After the civil rights movement and interest in ethnic diversity and multiculturalism began to decline in the mid-1970s, Piri Thomas's books lost some of their earlier primacy. School districts considered them controversial; some even banned them from high school libraries. However, most of the bans were later rescinded, and *Down These Mean Streets* is still considered a powerful, passionate indictment of racism and discrimination.

Further Reading

Binder, Wolfgang, and Piri Thomas. "An Interview with Piri Thomas." *Minority Voices* 4:1 (Spring 1980): 63–78.

Gunton, Sharon R., and Jean C. Stine, eds. *Contemporary Literary Criticism*, vol. 17. Detroit: Gale Research, 1983.

Magill, Frank N., ed. *Masterpieces of Latino Literature*. New York: HarperCollins, 1994.

Mohr, Eugene. "Piri Thomas: Author and Persona." *Caribbean Studies* 20:2 (1980): 61–74.

New York Times Book Review (21 May 1967); (4 March 1979).

Ryan, Bryan, ed. *Hispanic Writers*. Detroit: Gale Research, 1991.
Zimmerman, Marc. *U.S. Latino Literature*. Chicago: MARCH/Abrazo Press, 1992.

REIES LÓPEZ TIJERINA

(1926–   )

Mexican American Social Activist

In his 1969 "Letter from Prison," Tijerina affirmed his strong commitment to Hispanic rights. From the New Mexico State Penitentiary he wrote: "Here in my prison I feel very content—I repeat very content and very happy because I know and understand well the cause I defend. My conscience has never been as tranquil as it has during these days in prison because, as I have said before and now repeat from prison: For the land, culture, and inheritance of my people I am ready not only to suffer imprisonment, but I would, with pleasure and pride, sacrifice my life to bring about the justice which is so much deserved by my people— the Spanish American people."

Reies López Tijerina occupies a unique position in the Latino experience. In large measure his leadership was based on his persuasive rhetorical skills. A fiery, compelling spellbinder, he was clearly the most dynamic Mexican American speaker of the 1960s. Unflagging in delivering his message, he appealed viscerally to people who lacked influence, power, and wealth. He had great resoluteness and a messianic conviction that God had singled him out to regain for Hispanos the lands they had lost.

Reies Tijerina was born on 21 September 1926 in a tiny adobe house near Falls City, Texas, about 40 miles southeast of San Antonio. He was one of ten children born to Herlinda and Antonio Tijerina. His strong-willed mother, who died when he was 6 years old, greatly influenced his young mind, reading her small son Bible stories and encouraging a precocious embracing of mystical experiences. His father made a precarious living as a sharecropper, and during the Depression of the 1930s the family was forced to go on the migratory harvest circuit, wintering in San Antonio. He grew up there in harsh social and economic conditions that included discrimination, extreme poverty, and at times gnawing hunger. By age 7 or 8 Reies was working at stoop labor in the fields

Reies López Tijerina. Photo courtesy of the Center for Southwest Research, General Library, University of New Mexico.

alongside his father and older brothers as they followed summer harvests from Texas to Michigan.

Because of this migratory life-style, Tijerina's early education was disjointed and limited. He became a serious reader of the Bible when he was 12 years old as a result of his mother's lingering influence and the gift of a New Testament from a passing Baptist minister. At age 18 he left the Catholic Church and entered an Assembly of God Bible institute at Ysleta, Texas. In this fundamentalist school he soon became known as a fiery, inspirational speaker who was intense and sincere but not always docile or tractable. In 1946 he was suspended for violating an institute rule against dating and left without graduating after three years of study.

A few months after leaving Ysleta he married and began the life of a circuit preacher in the Southwest for the Assembly of God. By 1950 his disagreement with the church over tithing caused the loss of his ministerial credentials, but he continued his itinerant ministry as a nondenominational preacher. Meanwhile he gradually moved from a purely religious concern about social justice to a more pragmatic and political consideration. In the mid-1950s with the families of 17 followers he founded a utopian community, La Valle de Paz, in southern Arizona midway between Tucson and Phoenix. Successful at first, the Valley of Peace soon faced severe hostility from the local community and, after harassment and violence (including arson), it was eventually abandoned.

In 1957 Tijerina was arrested for allegedly helping one of his brothers in a jailbreak. As the result of jumping bail he then became a fugitive from Arizona until 1962. He traveled to Mexico and then to California, where a messianic vision led him to northern New Mexico and a deep interest in the complex history of Spanish land grants. Gradually he came to believe that all *nuevomexicanos'* problems stemmed from loss of their lands. In 1960 with a few Valle de Paz settlers he moved to Albuquerque, where he quietly started recruiting followers. Convinced that it was his mission to regain lost grant lands, in 1963 he organized the Alianza Federal de Mercedes (Federal Alliance of [Land] Grants) and began openly to recruit supporters. With evangelistic fervor he lectured, explained, exhorted, wheedled, and scolded in a never-ending crusade. He stressed economic, political, educational, and cultural rights for his followers and all Hispanic Americans. As a result of his charisma and persuasiveness on radio and television and in the press, as well as in small meetings, the Alianza grew rapidly to 10,000 members.

To dramatize their land claims and to obtain the redress they sought, Tijerina and his followers drew attention to Hispanos' plight by a variety of aggressive actions. They undertook a motorcade to Mexico City in a futile effort to enlist Mexican government support, they filed lawsuits against both federal and state governments, they marched on Santa Fe to present their demands to the governor, they took over part of the Kit Carson National Forest and proclaimed it the Republic of San Joaquín del Río Chama. A confrontation with forest rangers resulted in the arrest of Tijerina and several *aliancistas* on federal charges.

In a running feud between the Alianza and district attorney Alfonso Sánchez, a dozen *aliancistas* were arrested in June 1967 on blank warrants and taken to the Tierra Amarilla courthouse. Fellow *aliancistas'* decision to free their comrades and make a citizen's arrest on Sánchez led to the famous Courthouse Raid in which two lawmen were wounded. Panic ensued. Many believed that Tijerina was beginning "the revolution" or at least a guerrilla war. In a massive manhunt the National Guard with tanks, artillery, and helicopters searched New Mexico's mountains for Tijerina and his close followers. A week later Tijerina was captured and charged with various offenses, state and federal, in connection with the raid.

Now a national front-page news personality and free on bail, Reies Tijerina took to the lecture circuit and public forum to promote the goals of the reorganized Alianza Federal de Pueblos Libres (Federal Alliance of Free Towns). He spoke to young Chicanos at colleges and universities, starred in national conferences, was an extremely vocal leader in the Poor Peoples March on Washington in mid-1968, announced his candidacy for the governorship of New Mexico and was declared ineligible, and in a 1969 upsurge of militancy attempted a citizen's arrest on New Mexico's governor David Cargo and U.S. Supreme Court nominee Warren Burger.

Despite some acquittals in court, Tijerina was eventually convicted on both state and federal indictments stemming from the Carson National Forest and Tierra Amarilla incidents and began serving his sentences. At the end of July 1971 he was released on parole on the condition that he hold no office in the Alianza. He told followers who greeted him on his release that he now advocated brotherhood rather than confrontation. Deprived of his leadership, the Alianza was languishing even before his release. It now split along militant and moderate lines; Reies lost the support of many of his earlier enthusiastic youthful followers.

A year later Tijerina spoke at the national La Raza Unida Party (LRUP) convention in El Paso, stressing brotherhood and dispensing elder states-man counsel to the young Chicano delegates. At a Tierra y Cultura con-gress he convened in the following October, he lost more followers after angrily sweeping from the hall upon being outvoted by youthful LRUP activists. When his parole ended in 1976 he resumed the presidency of a much diminished Alianza and devoted most of his time in the second half of the 1970s to vain efforts to persuade two Mexican presidents to champion the land grant issue at the United Nations. No longer in the media spotlight, in the mid-1980s he soft-pedaled the brotherhood theme but continued his moderate stance, weakly supported by a much reduced following, mostly older *nuevomexicano* land grantee descendants.

Interviewed in Mexico City in mid-1987, the Indohispanic (his term) activist promised to continue his fight against racial and religious dis-crimination. At the 20th anniversary celebration of the Tierra Amarilla raid he ranted and railed, blaming Jews for Mexican Americans' mis-treatment and loss of lands. His harangue attracted fewer than 100 peo-ple, and the national press scarcely noticed the event.

In his crusade Tijerina tapped into an underlying unity based on his-torical experience, ethnicity, and religion. Among Hispanic leaders in the 1960s he alone seemed to answer youthful activists' calls for action, sei-zure of lands, and creation of a Chicano nation of Aztlán in the South-west. Yet his legalistic approach and emphasis on family and cultural traditions also appealed to conservative rural *nuevomexicanos*. He re-awakened pride in ethnic identity, language, and culture.

Further Reading

Bernard, Jacqueline. *Voices from the Southwest*. New York: Scholastic Book Serv-ices, 1972.

Blawis, Patricia Bell. *Tijerina and the Land Grants*. New York: International Publishers, 1971.

Gardner, Richard. *¡Grito! Reies Tijerina and the New Mexico Land Grant War of 1967*. New York: Harper & Row, 1970.

Knowlton, Clark S. "Tijerina, Hero of the Militants." In *An Awakened Minority: The Mexican-Americans*, 2nd ed., Manuel P. Servín, ed. Beverly Hills: Glencoe Press, 1974.

Meier, Matt S. " 'King Tiger': Reies López Tijerina." *Journal of the West* 27:2 (April 1988): 60–68.

Tijerina, Reies López. *Mi lucha por la tierra*. Mexico City: Fondo de Cultura Económica, 1978.

MARÍA ELENA TORAÑO-PANTÍN

(1938–   )

Cuban American Businesswoman, Consultant, Social Activist

The need for Cuban refugee wives to help support their families enabled María Elena Toraño-Pantín to overcome a Cuban view that women working outside the home exhibited threatening indications of independence from male authority. Intelligence, hard work, and persistence enabled her to become a highly respected businesswoman and an ardent advocate of rights for Latinas. They also brought her many honors. In addition to being named associate director of the U.S. Community Service Administration in 1977 by President Jimmy Carter, a decade later she was given the Governor's Award by the state of Florida and was named Outstanding Woman of the Year by the U.S. Department of Transportation, also in 1989. In the following year she was appointed to the Commission on Minority Business by the White House. In 1991 she received the Minority Business Person of the Year Award from the South Florida Small Business Administration and was named Woman of the Year by the Coalition of Hispanic American Women.

María Elena Díaz Rousselot was born in Havana, Cuba, on 13 February 1938. She was the daughter of Sira Vidal and Julio C. Díaz Rousselot, who were upper middle-class urban Cubans. She grew up in Havana, where she received her primary education. Her parents sent her to the United States to continue her education at the School of the Sacred Heart in New Orleans, Louisiana, where she specialized in home economics. On her return to Cuba in 1957 she attended the University of Havana, where she earned a bachelor's degree in modern languages three years later.

Meanwhile, just days short of her 20th birthday she married Arturo Toraño and soon took a position teaching home economics at the university. However, the leftward turn of Fidel Castro's revolutionary government caused her and her husband to flee Cuba and to settle in Miami, Florida. There they fitted well into the early Cuban refugee community, whose members were over 90 percent white and well educated by Cuban standards. As part of the exile community the Torãnos were inevitably involved in the widespread plotting against Castro, and Arturo became a member of the CIA-backed Bay of Pigs (Playa Girón) invasion force in 1961. He survived the failed attempt but was incarcerated in a Cuban prison.

To support herself and two young sons while her husband was in prison, María Elena at first took whatever jobs she could get, mostly menial and short-term. Because of her educational background and her English-speaking ability she was soon able to obtain work that was more interesting as well as more remunerative. From 1961 to 1963 she taught home economics at a senior high school in Dade County, Florida, and then, partly because of her bilingualism, obtained a job as a case worker and later welfare supervisor for the Florida Department of Public Welfare, where she worked for five years.

In 1968 Toraño began a nearly decade-long association with Eastern Airlines. She began with Eastern in 1968 as a ticket agent but quickly moved up to more responsible positions. Eventually she was promoted to manager of Latin American Affairs, a position in which she developed programs to increase Eastern Airlines' share of Hispanic American customers. Her persisting interest in social problems of Latinos moved her in 1976 to take a position with Jackson Memorial Hospital in Miami, where she was director of Latin American Affairs. While working there she was recruited by the Carter administration.

As associate director for public affairs in the Community Service Administration, in 1977 Toraño became the first Cuban American of either sex to be appointed to a high federal office by the president of the United States. Among her achievements while in Washington, D.C., she counts the founding of the National Association of Spanish Broadcasters, in which she served as president from 1979 to 1980, and the National Hispana Leadership Institute, the latter having the goal of addressing the concerns and promoting the interests of Hispanic women. This was in addition to her job of making federal government agencies more aware of Latino, especially Cuban American, interests.

When the Republican administration of Ronald Reagan took over in

1981, the Community Service Administration was disbanded and Toraño found herself back in Miami not sure what to do. She had meanwhile divorced her first husband and in 1980 had married Leslie Pantín, a prosperous Miami businessman. Encouraged by her new husband who helped her learn the basics of operating a business, she began a public relations company, META, Inc. Although her hard work again paid off in obtaining contracts with clients like the Miami Dolphins football team and the Adolph Coors Brewing Company, she soon came to the conclusion that there was a social need and a fertile field for her talents in the field of management services. These services could be of great value to many of the more than 7,000 Cuban-owned businesses in the Miami Standard Metropolitan Statistical Area. This new emphasis of META enabled Toraño-Pantín to help fellow Cuban Americans by providing them with assistance in securing minority-owned small business contracts with federal agencies. When the savings and loan companies crisis developed in the late 1980s and the U.S. government created the Resolution Trust Corporation to solve it, she was awarded a contract to manage nearly $90 million worth of commercial and residential real estate in the Greater Miami area.

It is clear that Taraño-Pantín has become not only a very successful businesswoman but also a helping hand to the Cuban American community and an asset to the Greater Miami business community. In addition to being the president and chief executive officer of META, she has been involved with both the Greater Miami Chamber of Commerce and the Latin Chamber of Commerce. Among her community service roles she serves on the City of Miami International Trade Committee, the Florida Arts Council, and the International Health Council. She feels her service has been generously rewarded in the personal satisfaction and the power it has given her to help others. She is an excellent example of the many capable, hard-working Cuban Americans who have become assimilated and continue to make important contributions to American life.

Further Reading

"A Cuban Success Story—In the United States." *U.S. News & World Report* 62 (20 March 1967): 104–106.

Díaz-Briquets, Sergio. "Cuban-Owned Businesses in the United States." *Cuban Studies* 14:2 (1984): 57–64.

Ferree, Myra Marx. "Employment without Liberation: Cuban Women in the United States." *Social Science Quarterly* 60:1 (June 1979): 35–50.

"How the Immigrants Made It in Miami." *Business Week* (1 May 1977).

Linehan, Edward J. "Cuba's Exiles Bring New Life to Miami." *National Geographic* 144 (July 1973): 68–95.

Peterson, Mark F. "Success Patterns of Cuban-American Enterprises." *Human Relations* (1 August 1993).

Telgen, Diane, and Jim Kamp, eds. *Notable Hispanic American Women*. Detroit: Gale Research, 1993.

Unterburger, Amy, ed. *Who's Who among Hispanic Americans, 1993–94*. Detroit: Gale Research, 1993.

Edwin Torres

(1931–   )

Puerto Rican Jurist, Lawyer, Novelist

The Honorable Edwin Torres, justice of the New York State Supreme Court, has earned the reputation of being one of the sternest judges in New York City. His experiences growing up in Spanish Harlem and later working as an assistant district attorney, as a criminal lawyer in private practice, and finally as a judge have deepened his understanding of the criminal mindset and the criminal world. This grasp in turn has helped him bring a feeling of gritty realism to the three crime novels he has written. On the bench his style is reflected by his sentencing remarks, and in his novels it can be seen in the street language he puts in the mouths of his characters. This element of authenticity in his novels *Carlito's Way, Q and A*, and *After Hours* has brought him highly favorable reviews in many well-known publications, including the *New Yorker*. These extremely popular novels have gone through several reprintings and became the basis for two successful movies.

Edwin Torres was born in 1931 in a tenement bedroom in New York City to Ramona and Edelmiro Torres, Puerto Rican immigrants to the mainland. He grew up exposed to the Upper East Side's gang-ridden barrio streets as well as to the Mafia-dominated underworld. He endured beatings with garbage can lids and bicycle chains, but many of his peers, whose lives were ultimately claimed by drugs or bullets, were obviously not as lucky as he. Torres once said that he had lost so many of his contemporaries to gunfire that he felt as if he had grown up in the middle of a war.

The influence and authority of Edwin's strict father were sufficiently strong to steer him away from the insidious attraction of gangs and drugs. In fact, Torres attributes much of his success as a jurist to the stern views of his father, a Post Office security guard. His father provided a strong role model for young Edwin with his active involvement in their New York tenement neighborhood and his community leadership.

Edwin's appreciation and admiration of his father, combined with a fear of not "toeing the mark" for him, helped him excel in school. He attended Stuyvesant, one of New York City's prestigious magnet high schools, and then enrolled in Brooklyn City College, where, in his English class, he began to display considerable talent as a writer. Torres was considering becoming a teacher, but after serving in the navy during the Korean War he decided he wanted to be a court stenographer. Later, he was set on becoming a policeman. However, his father thought otherwise; he admits, "my father prevailed upon me. It was he who kept urging that I should be an attorney because the Hispanic community in New York . . . was bereft of legal representation."

Young Torres financed his way through Brooklyn Law School by waiting on tables and after his graduation went on to become the first Puerto Rican appointed to the Manhattan District Attorney's Office in New York City. In 1958 his ability to communicate in Spanish helped him obtain a coveted position in the Homicide Bureau. He was the only assistant district attorney who was able to interrogate Spanish-speaking witnesses. For three years he prosecuted some of New York's most heinous criminals. He switched sides in the judicial system by moving in 1961 to private practice as a criminal-defense attorney.

In 1977 Edwin Torres was nominated to the bench by Abraham D. Beame, then mayor of New York City. The move was a natural transition for Torres. Not known for his modesty, Torres has said that he was the most qualified candidate who has ever been appointed to the bench. He believes that because of his lack of privilege while growing up and his familiarity with the "low life," he makes a better judge than many who serve on the bench. He became acting State Supreme Court Justice in 1979, and later he was elected to a full 14-year term ending in 1993.

Having worked on both sides in the judicial system—first prosecuting criminals and then defending them—has helped him both as a judge and as a writer. The fascinating stories he related to friends about his legal experiences caused them to encourage him to put the tales on paper. Ultimately their coaxing and stimulation led to his literary career.

While in private practice Torres first began writing seriously, pushed by his wife Vicki and by his father who urged Torres to document the everyday lives of Puerto Ricans in Spanish Harlem. "No one's recording our lives," his father repeatedly pointed out. "Our history, our culture will just disappear." The writing did not come easily for Torres, who worked on his manuscripts in the middle of the night at the kitchen table.

He based his novels on people he had met over the years, using actual dialogue he remembered from dramatic occurrences in his life.

Torres attributes his success as a writer to quoting real people, to using the street language with which he is so familiar. *Carlito's Way*, written in the first person as an autobiographical life of crime, served as the inspiration for the movie of the same name, starring Al Pacino. The movie is a blend of two of his novels, *Carlito's Way* and *After Hours*. It is the story of Carlito Brigant, a Puerto Rican drug dealer who, returning to the barrio as an ex-convict, tries to extricate himself from the barrio's harmful influences and as a result runs afoul of the Mob. His third novel, *Q and A*, 1977, looks at crime and corruption in high places; it is a skillfully constructed story of a rogue policeman whose murder of a suspect is covered up by his department. It was the basis for the Sidney Lumet movie of the same title with Nick Nolte, **Rubén Blades**, and Timothy Hutton. *Carlito's Way* was translated into Spanish with the title *Atrapado por su pasado* and published in 1994.

As a jurist Torres often couches sentences in his court in an idiosyncratic and original manner that has gained him considerable notoriety. Known as the "Time Machine" for frequently giving maximum sentences, he once addressed a man convicted of murder by saying, "Your parole officer has not yet been born." Torres has a reputation for being unsympathetic to excuses for criminals and their crimes. In a case where the defendant stole $85,000 of drug money, then took an infant from his crib, sat him next to his father, and shot off the baby's head at close range, Torres unabashedly commented that he would not mind throwing the switch of the electric chair on a monster so ruthless in his disregard for human life.

Although Torres officiates in a state that has outlawed the death penalty, he is outspoken in his support of capital punishment. The reason for this position and his long sentences, he says, is that "rehabilitation is poppycock nonsense. I believe in high-end sentences, because the crime rate here is insane. [In New York City] we're up to 2,000 murders a year. I compare us to Beirut or Belfast. Cities at war. So if a guy's convicted and I can get him off the street for a long period of time, I'm doing something to stop the war."

Justice Torres's dedication and commitment to justice have assisted him in making the difficult transition from growing up in the middle of crime warfare to personally trying to stop it. His experiences in this transition have helped him become, as Howard Kaminisky, president of Heart Trade Books, asserts, "a talent that mingle[s] the sounds of the barrio with the insights of the baccalaureate."

Further Reading

Gelb, Barbara. "New York's Worst Finest." *New York Times Book Review* (5 June 1977): 16, 23.

Grimes, William. "His Honor Himself Is Counselor to Pacino." *New York Times*, "The Arts" (27 July 1993): C13.

Kauffmann, Stanley. "Q & A." *New Republic* 202:21 (21 May 1990): 26.

Schoene, Philipe P. "Justice Disrobed." *Sunspots* 8:4 (Fall 1991): 14–17.

Vázquez Zapata, Larissa. "Dos mundos, una justicia." *Imagen* (February 1994): 50–54.

Weber, Bruce. "Tough Phrases from the Bench." *New York Times* (30 November 1991): 23(L).

Wolfe, Linda. "One Tough Hombre." *New York Magazine* (8 January 1990): 42–48.

———. "The Toughest Judges." *New York Magazine* (14 January 1991): 41.

LEE TREVIÑO

(1939–   )

Mexican American Golfer, Philanthropist

One of Lee Treviño's favorite stories is about his first encounter with golf pro Ray Floyd in 1967. Hotshot golfer Floyd pulled up to El Paso's Horizon Hill Country Club in an impressive long white Cadillac, and Treviño, a $30-a-week golf pro and general factotum at the club, took Floyd's bag and led him to the locker room. As he unpacked the bag and cleaned Floyd's shoes, Lee was Mr. Floyd-ing him to a fare-thee-well. Floyd paid him for his services and asked, "Who am I playing tomorrow?" "Me," answered Treviño, and Floyd nearly fell off the bench. The next day Lee Treviño shot a 65. Floyd's score was 67, and he immediately wanted to play nine more holes to get even. He was speechless when Treviño replied, "I can't. I've got to bring in all the carts, clean some shoes, do a lot of stuff." The next day Treviño again bested Floyd; only on the following day did Floyd finally win a round. Back on tour, Floyd reportedly said, "Fellas, there's a little Mexican boy out in El Paso you're going to have to make room for." One year later Lee Treviño won the prestigious U.S. Open with its first-prize money of $30,000. The rivalry has continued. On 17 April 1994 Treviño won his 20th Senior Tour victory by defeating Ray Floyd, among other pros.

Lee Treviño.

Lee Treviño was born on 1 December 1939 in Dallas, Texas, the son of Juanita and José Treviño. He never knew his Mexican father from Monterrey, Nuevo León, and was raised along with two sisters by his Mexican American mother and her father. He grew up in a four-room farmhouse next to a golf course on the outskirts of Dallas. When he was 5 or 6 years old Lee began imitating the golfers he could see from his yard. Using an old cut-down rusty iron and some golf balls he had found, he practiced on a two-hole course he had devised by digging two holes next to the house. He spent whole days hitting balls back and forth from one hole to the other. As he grew older, sometimes at dusk he would climb over the fence to the country club and play a hole or two.

In the eighth grade Lee Treviño was forced to drop out of school in order to contribute to the family's meager income. Lee earned a few dollars caddying and helping the club greenskeeper, and at the day's end he would shoot a practice hole or two. Later he went to work for Hardy Greenwood, who owned a putting and driving range nearby. Ball gatherer, janitor, and handyman, Lee perfected his swing by hitting some 300 balls every day. When he was 15 years old he played his first full 18 holes in a Dallas park tournament. He shot a 77.

In December 1956 Lee Treviño turned 17 and enlisted in the U.S. Marines. After boot training in San Diego he was classified as a machine gunner. However, a year later he borrowed a set of clubs and tried out for the Third Marine Division golf team; during the remainder of his four years in the peacetime Marine Corps he represented the Corps in golf tournaments. He also began to take his game seriously and to consider the possibility of becoming a pro.

Treviño was given his discharge from the Marines at the end of 1960. After working briefly at a Dallas country club, he went back to work for Greenwood. He supplemented his slender salary by "hustling" golfers, playing them for money using a large, taped Dr. Pepper bottle as a club. He also continued to perfect his game.

As he improved, Lee became increasingly interested in joining the professional golf tour. In 1962 he participated in his first pro tournament, the Dallas Open. He played well until pressured and finished out of the money by a single stroke. He continued to work on improving his game and on obtaining a Class A card, which would admit him to the pro tour. When Hardy Greenwood refused to sign his pro card, Treviño quit his job and began playing in non–Class A tournaments. In 1965, financed by friend Bill Gray, he entered the Texas State Open and won first-prize money, $1,200. Later that year Treviño and Gray drove to Mexico City so Lee could play in the Mexican Open. He finished second. The following February the two, short of the airfare, drove all the way to Panama so Lee could play in the Panama Open. Treviño took fifth-place money.

Staunchly supported by his wife and a few good friends, Lee Treviño became convinced he could succeed on the pro tour, but not from Dallas because of ethnic prejudice and other reasons. Early in 1966 he moved to El Paso, where he quickly got a job as assistant pro at the Horizon Hill Country Club. A year later, having obtained his Class A card, he qualified for the U.S. Open with the lowest score of all entrants. In the Open itself he took fifth place, winning $6,000. Lee now went on tour full-time. He finished in the money in 11 of the 13 Professional Golf Association (PGA) tournaments he entered during 1967 and was named Rookie of the Year.

At the 1968 U.S. Open in Rochester, New York, Treviño won by shooting four below-par rounds, the first golfer in the history of the Open to do so. Winning the Open brought him $30,000 and some endorsement contracts. From Rochester he went on to win the Hawaiian Open and the Amana Open, and then he represented the United States at the World Cup Tournament in Italy. During the next two years he won the Tucson Open twice, the Amana Open again and the National Airlines Open in Miami, and was first in the World Cup in Singapore but finished out of the money in the Colonial National Open and the British Open.

In early spring 1971 Lee Treviño began the winning streak of his golfing career, walking off with the Tallahassee, Danny Thomas, Canadian, U.S., and British National opens between April and July. In August El Paso celebrated his victories with Lee Treviño Day and a parade. Three months later, after recovering from an emergency appendectomy, he and Jack Nicklaus won the World Cup in Florida.

By the end of the year Treviño had been named PGA Player of the Year, *Sports Illustrated* Sportsman of the Year, and BBC International Sports Personality of the Year. During the rest of the 1970s and the 1980s he continued to play spectacular golf, winning the British Open again in 1972 and the Canadian in 1977 and 1979 as well as many other tournaments including the World Series of Golf in 1974. Five times he won the Vardon Trophy for the season's low scoring average; he played on the Ryder Cup team in 1971, 1973, 1975, 1979, and 1981 and was its captain in 1985. Meanwhile he did a stint as an NBC sports announcer.

Recipient of numerous awards and honors, "Super Mex" has been installed in the Texas Hall of Fame, the American Golf Hall of Fame, and the World Golf Hall of Fame. As he approached his 50th birthday, he declared he could hardly wait to start on the Senior PGA tour. He did so in 1990, won seven tournaments his first year, including the U.S. Senior Open, and was named PGA Senior Tour Player of the Year. By April 1994, after four years on the Senior tours, he had chalked up 20 victories. In October 1995 he won the Senior Trans-American Pro Am tournament in California. With his wins in 1996 Treviño's lifetime tour earnings have surpassed $10 million, making him one of three golfers who have reached this level.

Lee Treviño is a colorful, irrepressible extrovert who truly enjoys the game for the game's sake; on the links he often jokes and trades repartee with the press and the gallery—especially with his devoted tournament followers, affectionately known as Lee's Fleas. Although his banter occasionally irritates some players, all concede that he is often the butt of his own humor and is always a fair competitor. He is also a generous person, frequently donating a hefty part of his winnings to charity and often staging impromptu hot dog and soft drink parties for youngsters attending the tournaments. Perhaps more than any other golfer, Lee Treviño has helped make golf a popular spectator sport.

Further Reading

Current Biography, 1971. New York: H. W. Wilson Co., 1972.

Garrity, John. "Down Memory Lane." *Sports Illustrated* 76:14 (13 April 1992): 42, 44.

"Lee Treviño." *Sports Illustrated* 80:16 (25 April 1994): 46–47.

Newlon, Clarke. *Famous Mexican-Americans.* New York: Dodd, Mead, 1972.

Treviño, Lee. *The Snake in the Sand Trap*. New York: Holt, Rinehart & Winston, 1985.
———. *They Call Me Super Mex*. New York: Random House, 1982.

TERESA URREA
(1873–1906)
Mexican American Mystic,
Curandera (Herbalist, Faith Healer)

Teresa Urrea was a complex young woman who, at the beginning of the 1900s, provided medical and psychiatric care to the poor, especially *mexicano* poor who consulted her about family matters and social and business affairs as well as health problems. She apparently employed a combination of herbal medicine, auto-suggestion, and a kind of hypnosis, but never divulged the exact nature of her diagnostic and medical techniques. She had devoted followers from all over the Southwest and the northwestern Mexican border region, but she was also the object of disapproval by many. Some clergymen saw her as a spurious religious mystic.

Teresa Urrea was born on 15 October 1873 on a small *rancho* in northern Sinaloa, the result of a casual union between Tomás Urrea, a hacienda owner with a roving eye, and a 15-year-old Tehueco Indian servant named Cayetana Chávez. Teresa seems to have had a reasonably carefree, if ill-provided, early childhood. Because of his opposition to President Porfirio Díaz's government, in 1880 her politically active father thought it necessary to flee the state of Sinaloa to his ranches in Sonora, about 100 miles south of Guaymas. Seven-year-old Teresa and her mother were among the many retainers who accompanied him.

Because her mother disappeared sometime in the 1880s, Teresa was raised with the children of her mother's sister and was resented because she was much lighter complexioned than they. She is described as a slender, mischievous tomboy who charmed everybody—except her aunt. Her father later took her into the ranch household at Cabora, and she was taught along with her many half-sisters, half-brothers, and cousins—her father's nieces and nephews. She also learned herbal lore and herbal

Teresa Urrea. Photo courtesy of the University of Arizona.

remedies from an old Indian *curandera* to whom she acted as assistant, helping her treat various illnesses and accidents on the ranch.

In her early teens Teresa apparently began to suffer epileptic attacks and later had cataleptic seizures. During one of the latter she remained unconscious for several days and was thought at first to have died. After her slow recovery she came to believe she had a mission to help people. When the old *curandera* died, Teresa took over her work. Making use of folk psychology as well as herbal remedies to help the sick, she quickly acquired a devoted following, especially among the Indians, and a wide reputation, becoming known as Santa Teresita and the Santa de Cabora. During 1891 the influx of patients and the curious reached a flood-tide and began disrupting the Cabora ranch daily routine. By the end of the year the teenaged Teresa was being credited with miracles and Cabora had acquired the carnival trappings of a pilgrimage site—food vendors, merchants, gamblers, and entertainers, including Yaqui dancers.

The Yaqui and Tarahumara Indians sought Teresa's counsel in their continuing resistance to the federal government in Mexico City. President Díaz, greatly concerned about her growing influence, seemingly or possibly political, in mid-1892 had her and her father arrested. They were briefly jailed in Guaymas and then sent into exile to Nogales, Arizona. Here Teresa immediately set up her *curandera* practice and continued to be the center of attention and controversy. The American press pictured her as a victim of the Díaz dictatorship, and she was soon forced to flee the city when attempts, presumably by Mexican government agents, were made to kidnap her. She and her father moved twice within Arizona because of harassment and in 1896, for reasons unknown, moved back to the border at El Paso, where she began treating as many as 200 people a day. By this time Teresa had become the focus of an informal cult, many of whose members believed she possessed preternatural powers.

In August 1896 opponents of the Díaz regime, calling themselves *teresistas*, launched an unsuccessful attack on the Mexican customshouse at Nogales, Mexico. The Mexican government blamed Teresa and made a protest to Washington. At the request of the State Department, Teresa and her father moved away from the border to the copper-mining town of Clifton, Arizona, where she continued her ministrations to sick persons from all over the border region. In Clifton she fell in love with a miner named Guadalupe Rodríguez and married him in June 1900 despite her father's disapproval. The marriage was brief; after the wedding her husband apparently tried to kill her, was seized and jailed, and was declared insane. Teresa filed for divorce.

In Clifton Teresa helped not only poor *mexicanos* but also Anglos. One of the families she helped was that of a local banker, Charles Rosencrans, whose young child she treated. The Rosencranses persuaded Teresa to go to California to help the small daughter of a friend in San Jose, a Mrs. A. C. Fessler.

While in California Teresa was convinced by a group of San Francisco entrepreneurs, attracted by the publicity she was receiving, to join them in forming a medical company that would allow her to tour the United States curing people without charge. Part medicine show, part theatrical pageantry, and part religious revival, the medical company's programs were often characterized by emotional outbursts on the part of both Teresa and her audiences. Starting out in San Francisco in late 1900, after a few months the "crusade" moved to St. Louis. While there she married her interpreter, the young son of an Arizona friend, although her divorce from Rodríguez was not yet final. After several months' stay in St. Louis, the company moved to New York.

In New York Teresa received news of her father's death just a few days before the birth of her first child, a daughter. After a disappointing stay the entourage left New York for Los Angeles in December 1902. By this time a disillusioned Teresa was beginning to seriously question the altruism of her medical promoter partners and sought legal help to end her agreement with them. Having terminated the contract she returned to Arizona, where her second daughter was born in June 1904. Teresa then returned to Clifton, where she built a large house from which to continue her work of healing the physically and mentally unwell. About this time she seems to have undergone a considerable physical and temperamental change, turning preoccupied and moody. Her health rapidly deteriorated and her ability to cure also seemed greatly diminished.

In December 1905, apparently as the result of a long exposure to cold rain and local floodwaters, Teresa Urrea contracted a severe bronchial infection, failed to throw it off, and died in the following month. She was only 32 years old.

Further Reading

Aguirre, Lauro. *La Santa de Cabora.* El Paso: El Progresista, 1902.

Gill, Mario. "Teresa Urrea, la santa de Cabora." *Historia Mexicana* 6 (April–June 1957): 626–644.

Holden, William. *Teresita.* Owings Mills, Md.: Stemmer House, 1978.

Larralde, Carlos. *Mexican American Movements and Leaders.* Los Alamitos, Calif.: Hwong Publishing, 1976.

Putnam, Frank Bishop. "Teresa Urrea, 'The Saint of Cabora.' " *Southern California Quarterly* 45 (September 1963): 245–264.

Rodríguez, Richard, and Gloria Rodríguez. "Teresa Urrea: Her Life as It Affected the Mexican–U.S. Frontier." *El Grito* 5 (Summer 1972): 48–68.

LUIS VALDEZ

(1940–)

Mexican American Producer, Director, Cinematographer, Dramatist, Social Activist

Luis Valdez's production of his play *Zoot Suit* at the Mark Taper Forum, Los Angeles, in April 1978 first brought him to the attention of Americans as both a playwright and director. It also launched his artistic career. He then took *Zoot Suit* to Broadway, where it received a cool reception. However, his theatrical skills were validated nine years later by the success of the film *La Bamba*, which he both wrote and directed. He played a major role in the Chicano literary renaissance; he has often been cited as the father of Chicano theater.

Luis Valdez was born in the small California central valley town of Delano on 26 June 1940, the second oldest among ten children of Armida and Francisco Valdez. His parents, who had moved to California from Arizona in the 1920s, worked their own farm on the outskirts of Delano until the late 1940s, when they lost it because of depressed agricultural prices after World War II. The Valdez family then took to the migrant harvest circuit, and as a child Luis worked in the fields and attended a number of rural schools in California. While in the first grade he became enchanted with a class play, and from then on playacting, puppets, and theater were central to his life.

In the mid-1950s the Valdez family settled out of the migrant circuit in San Jose, California, and Luis attended and graduated from Lick High School there. While in high school he had the opportunity to do a theatrical bit on KNTV–San Jose, and as a result he became a Sunday morning television "regular" with a short bilingual puppet show. In 1960 he entered San Jose State College (today University) on a scholarship. Majoring in English, he was able to indulge his appetite for theater. In 1961 his one-act play *The Theft* won a local contest, and as a junior he wrote a full-length play, *The Shrunken Head of Pancho Villa*, which was produced by the San Jose drama department in 1963.

Upon graduation in the following year, Luis Valdez expanded his theatrical horizons by working in the San Francisco Mime Troupe for a number of months, an experience he would later put to good use as a director. In October 1965 he brought his drama skills to the support of **César Chávez** and the farm workers in the Delano grape strike. Without funds, stage, props, or actors he set about to create what was to become the vigorous and effective Teatro Campesino, the farm workers' theater. Leaning heavily on his mime experience, he created an effective tool for educating both the strikers and the general public. Over the following years he developed more than a dozen *actos*, as the one-act plays he put on were called, to explain the Delano strike. Comedy and satire were major ingredients of the *actos*.

Although he continued his connections with the Delano strikers, in 1967 Valdez broadened his base of operations by establishing a farm workers' cultural center, independent of the Chávez union, in the tiny town of Del Rey, near Fresno. Two years later, in order to enlarge the audience for his presentations he moved the cultural center and *teatro* to Fresno. During the last years of the 1960s he took the Teatro Campesino on several tours of college campuses and also performed at the Newport Folk Festival. While in Fresno he produced a film entitled *I Am Joaquín*, 1969, based on **Corky Gonzales**'s epic poem. It won several awards. He also taught at Fresno State College, where he was important in helping mold a newly formed *raza* studies program. Early in the 1970s he was a visiting professor at the University of California in Berkeley, and from 1971 to 1977 he taught at U.C. Santa Cruz.

Meanwhile, in 1969 Valdez and his *teatro* group performed at an international theater festival in the northern French city of Nancy; during the following decade they toured western Europe three more times. They also performed in many cities and towns of the United States and produced television programs, full-length plays, and a few short films. In 1971, in line with his idea of creating a permanent home for the group, Valdez moved the Teatro Campesino to a site in San Juan Bautista, 80 miles south of San Francisco. Here, with the aid of several grants, he shaped the Teatro into a professional production company. Five years later he was honored by Governor "Jerry" Brown with an appointment to the California Arts Council.

Always something of a romantic, in the 1970s Luis Valdez turned to Aztec and Mayan legends and philosophy for inspiration; this was evident in his third play, *Bernabé*, 1970, and later works such as *El Fin del Mundo*, 1972. During the Vietnam War he wrote and produced *actos* that severely criticized the U.S. involvement as well as the high rate of Chicano deaths. *Soldado raso* and especially *Dark Root of a Scream*, both in the early 1970s, combined anti-war rhetoric with Aztec symbolism.

In 1978 Valdez wrote and produced a play based on the Sleepy Lagoon incident in Los Angeles during World War II. Titled *Zoot Suit* and featuring young **Edward James Olmos** as the narrator, it was an outstanding popular success in Los Angeles and also won high praise from the critics. Valdez took *Zoot Suit* to Broadway briefly and in 1981 made it into a film for Universal Pictures. The play also earned him a Rockefeller Foundation playwright-in-residence award. *Zoot Suit* moved him to a higher plane in theater circles, and the film enabled him to purchase a warehouse-theater in San Juan Bautista.

In the early 1980s Valdez turned to *corridos*, Mexican folk ballads, as a source of dramatic inspiration. His production of *Corridos: Tales of Passion and Revolution*, featuring the popular Mexican American singer **Linda Ronstadt**, was a great success on public television in 1987 and led to several tours. In that same year his film *La Bamba*, based on the life of 1950s rock star Ritchie Valens (Valenzuela), was released by Columbia Pictures. It was a resounding success. The artistic and financial success of his films *Zoot Suit* and *La Bamba*, as well as several television productions, turned him increasingly to the filmic medium in which he could pursue his goal of larger audiences for his message.

In addition to his stage and film work, Valdez is the author of a score of plays and *actos*. His best-known works include *La gran carpa de la familia Rascuachi*, 1971; *I Don't Have to Show You No Stinking Badges*, 1986; and *Bandido*, 1993, the last based on the life of California social bandit Tiburcio Vásquez. In early 1994 he completed a television film on the Cisco Kid and was busily at work preparing to stage *Bandido* in Los

Angeles and writing a screen play on the life of **César Chávez**. He continues to produce plays at San Juan Bautista. Particularly well known are his Christmas season presentations of *La virgen de Tepeyac, Las posadas,* and *Las pastorelas,* which are often put on in the historic mission church there.

Almost singlehandedly Luis Valdez has created a "Chicano theater," a grassroots theatrical movement in which his inspiration and vision established the artistic parameters. He has been the animating spirit behind over 100 *teatros* throughout the United States. For his multiple roles he has been honored with a number of awards. His *teatro* company has toured Europe six times, won three Los Angeles Drama Critics Circle awards, an Emmy (for *Los vendidos*), and an off Broadway Obie. He has been the recipient of half a dozen honorary degrees from colleges and universities, and in 1984 he was named Regents' lecturer at the University of California, Irvine.

Further Reading

Beale, Steve. "Connecting with the American Experience: An Interview with Luis Valdez." *Hispanic Business* 9:7 (July 1987): 10–13.

Díaz, Katherine A. "Luis Valdez: The Making of *Zoot Suit.*" *Caminos* (September 1981).

Hurwin, Robert. "The Evolutionary/Revolutionary Luis Valdez." *Image* (5 January 1986).

Lasley, Paul, and Elizabeth Harryman. "Migrant Workers' Theater Ripens after 20 Years." *Christian Science Monitor* (24 September 1985): 25.

Muñoz, Sergio. "Encuentro con Luis Valdez." *La Opinión* [Sunday Supplement, Los Angeles] (13 December 1981).

Valdez, Luis. "The Tale of La Raza" and "El Teatro Campesino, Its Beginnings." In *The Chicanos: Mexican American Voices*, Ed Ludwig and James Santibáñez, eds. Baltimore: Penguin Books, 1971.

Venant, Elizabeth. "Valdez—A Life in the River of Humanity." *Los Angeles Times Calendar* (2 February 1986).

NYDIA VELÁZQUEZ

(1953–)

Puerto Rican Politician, Educator

In September 1992, just a week after her victory in the Democratic primaries, a very determined young woman, Nydia Velázquez, paid a visit to House of Representatives Speaker Thomas Foley. She wanted to make sure he knew what she wanted when she won her seat in Congress in the general elections: namely, to serve on the powerful House Appropriations Committee, an assignment for which novice House members were typically not considered. In November she won election to the House of Representatives over the well-financed Republican incumbent. At age 39 this fast-speaking, attractive young politician with her lightly accented English became the first Puerto Rican woman to serve in the U.S. Congress and quickly made an impression in Washington, D.C.

Nydia Velázquez was born on 28 March 1953 in Yabucoa, an agricultural center of 37,000 inhabitants tucked into a lush valley in southeastern Puerto Rico. She was one of nine children born into a very poor family. In order to help support the family her mother, Carmen Luisa Serrano, made and sold *pasteles*, a typical island delicacy. Her father, Benito Velázquez, having only a third grade education, cut sugar cane during the *zafra* (harvest) for a living and later operated a cockfight pit. Despite impoverished living conditions, Nydia's family life was alive with a Rican *progresista* spirit, a hopeful expectation of future betterment.

At the dinner table Nydia joined in Velázquez family discussions on topics of current interest to her father, such as the island's political status, workers' rights, and labor organizing. In spite of her father's lack of formal education, he was an unusual man for his position in life in that he had developed considerable political leadership qualities and had a very strong social conscience. He also took an active part in island politics. Passionate about political issues, he often delivered speeches in small rural Puerto Rican towns from the back of a flatbed truck. He believed strongly in promoting learning and in personal integrity, attitudes that young Nydia absorbed and admired greatly in him.

As a very young child Nydia begged her parents to let her begin school. Although age 7 was considered ideal for children to begin first grade, she insisted so early and so strongly that her parents took her to school when she was just 5 years old. In school she was found to be so bright that she was quickly promoted from the first to the third grade, later from the third grade to the fifth grade, and then from the fifth grade to the seventh grade. Many teachers in her elementary school remember her as a very intelligent and extremely inquisitive child, forever eagerly asking them questions about everything.

After becoming the first person in her family to complete high school, at age 16 Nydia entered the University of Puerto Rico, where she majored in political science. She received her bachelor's degree *magna cum laude* in 1974. After a short stint as a teacher she applied for a scholarship at New York University to undertake a master's degree in the same field. Her father opposed this move, concerned that she might leave the island permanently if she gained admission to the university. In spite of her father's unease and lack of approval, she entered the university's master's program because she felt she could not turn down the attractive scholarship with its opportunity for her personal growth.

After completing her M.S. at New York University, Nydia returned to Puerto Rico where she taught political science at the University of Puerto Rico branch in Humacao. In the wake of the 1980 election, won by the pro-statehood New Progressive Party, she felt harassed for her views in favor of independence for the island. After the pro-statehood people took office, she was accused of being a leftist and a communist by some of them. Although today she no longer addresses the passionate and divisive issue of the island's political relations to the United States, she readily acknowledges her past support for Puerto Rican independence. Because of official hostility to her political views, she left Puerto Rico in 1981 to become an adjunct professor in Puerto Rican studies at Hunter College in the City University of New York. She taught at Hunter for two years, during which time she became interested in entering the New York political arena.

Having grown up and reached maturity in Puerto Rico, Velázquez was not familiar with the urban political culture of New York City; however, she managed to carve a political niche for herself. She began her political involvement by promoting voter registration. Later she was employed as a special assistant to Representative Edolphus Towns of Brooklyn, specializing in immigrant rights issues. In 1984 at age 31 she was named to fill a vacancy on the city council, thereby becoming the first Latina to serve on the council. In the 1986 election she lost her seat. She then returned to Puerto Rico as director of the Department of Labor and three years later was appointed by the governor of Puerto Rico to manage the Department of Puerto Rican Community Affairs in the United States. This is a cabinet-level position functioning as a major liaison between Puerto Rico and the U.S. government.

At this point in her relatively short political career, Velázquez decided to run for Congress in the 12th district. In the 1992 election she faced many political challenges and some personal ones as well. She was viewed by some voters as a new arrival to the New York political scene, therefore lacking a seasoned approach to urban politics. In the primary election many voters were put off simply by her accent; unlike most traditional inner-city politicians, she spoke Spanish better than English. To others she seemed too parochial; they felt that she could represent only Puerto Ricans, not all Hispanics in the mixed Latino 12th district. During the bitterly fought primary campaign, some of her political opponents suggested that her links to the Puerto Rican government were so strong that she could not adequately represent the interests of her New York City district. Her political agenda was severely criticized, her loyalties were held suspect, and her character was attacked. Letters mailed to Spanish-language publications called her an Eva Perón caricature of banana republic politicians.

The most telling attack against Velázquez in the November election came from an anonymous fax sent to news organizations just after her primary victory, revealing that she had attempted suicide in September 1991 after a bout of depression resulting from extremely serious family problems. The fax even included her poetic farewell suicide note: "Loneliness eats you like the slow dripping of water. And the moment arrives in which one asks oneself if it is worth it here—or on the other side." (Velázquez later sued the St. Clare's Hospital for $10 million for its failure to maintain the confidentiality of patients' files.) Aided by professional counseling, she had recovered from her mental depression and suicide attempt and had forged a strong determination to become even more compassionate toward all who suffer.

In the general election she conducted a grueling grassroots campaign and defeated both her well-financed Republican rival and independent challengers. She received more than three-fourths of the district's vote. After this election triumph, Velázquez returned to Puerto Rico to celebrate her win in her home town. She met with a joyous welcome from the townspeople. Like her father before her, she rode into Yabucoa in the back of a pickup truck, accompanied by the mayor. In her victory speech there in her home town she dedicated her triumph to all the Puerto Rican women who had given her support during the election, especially her mother.

One of 47 female representatives in the 103rd Congress, Velázquez constantly focused on her district's need for jobs, housing, and education. After her re-election in 1994 she continued to work assiduously and unceasingly to get these for her constituency, some of the poorest people in the United States. In Congress her positive qualities of firm resolve and tenacity are most notable; they are exemplified in a statement she made after her visit to the Speaker of the House in September 1992: "If I do not get something I want today, I will come back tomorrow and tomorrow until they get tired of seeing me." Speaking for the 12th district in the House of Representatives, Velázquez has taken an active role in congressional debate, particularly leading in the fight against anti-immigration legislation. True to her principles and her commitment, early in 1996 she was one of the leaders of the National Puerto Rican Affirmation Day solidarity walk in Washington, D.C. on 29 March. At the end of the two-mile walk from the Vietnam Veterans Memorial to the Capitol she addressed the marchers, estimated to number more than 7,000.

Further Reading

Guadalupe, Patricia. "Boricua First and Foremost," *Hispanic Link Weekly Report* 14:15 (8 April 1996):3.

New York Times (27 September 1992): 33.

New York Times (4 November 1992): B13.

Newsday (October 1992): 13.

"Rep. Velázquez Sues St. Clare's Hospital," *New York Times* 143 (14 May 1994): 24(L).

Telgen, Diane, and Jim Kamp, eds. *Notable Hispanic American Women*. Detroit: Gale Research, 1993.

Torres, Joseph. "Thousands of Boricuas March on Washington," *Hispanic Link Weekly Report* 14:15 (8 April 1996): 2.

USA Today (27 October 1992): 2A.

"Winners." *People Weekly* 38:22 (30 November 1992): 86.

JOSÉ ANTONIO VILLARREAL

(1924–)

Mexican American Novelist, Teacher

In mid-1994 José Antonio Villarreal's first novel, *Pocho*, originally published a third of a century earlier by Doubleday, was reissued by Anchor Books in its first Spanish-language edition. It was a delightful birthday present for the 70-year-old Villarreal and was accompanied by a refurbished issuing of the 1970 English-language paperback edition. That first edition has gone through numerous printings and has sold over 150,000 copies. After **Corky Gonzales**'s *Yo soy Joaquín* it is undoubtedly the most widely known and read work in Chicano literature. *Pocho* tells the story of the experiences of a first-generation Mexican American (a *pocho*) bridging the gap between Mexican and American cultures. It is also historically significant as the first Chicano novel published by a major U.S. publisher.

José Antonio Villarreal was born in Los Angeles, California, on 30 July 1924, one of 17 children, of whom 12 survived to adulthood. His parents, Felícitaz Ramírez and José Heladio Villarreal, had come to the United States only three years before from the Mexican state of Zacatecas, where his father, a hacienda worker, had been a follower of Pancho Villa, the controversial revolutionary leader of 1910. At first the Villarreals, like

José Antonio Villarreal. Photo by Michael Elderman.
Courtesy José Antonio Villarreal.

many other Mexican immigrant families, earned a precarious living as migrant harvest agricultural workers. When José was 6 years old the family settled out of the migrant stream in Santa Clara, California, and he was then enrolled in the first grade.

At home the Villarreal children were not allowed to speak English, but in school José Antonio began to learn English and to experience a culture other than the Mexican campesino ways of his parents. His first grade teacher introduced him to the written word and encouraged his interest in reading. With few books at home he soon became an avid patron of the Santa Clara library, where he found an abundance of adventure stories and other fiction. While still in grade school he began to write, and by the time he was in high school he was creating short stories, which he sent off for possible publication. By this time he was certain that he wanted to be a writer when he grew up. In the middle of his senior year in high school the United States entered World War II in December 1941, and after graduation his father signed the necessary papers to allow the 17-year-old José to enlist in the U.S. navy.

Growing up in Santa Clara during the Great Depression, Villarreal has often said and written, he was not aware of racial or ethnic prejudice against himself. The experiences of his alter ego, Richard Rubio, the protagonist in *Pocho*, suggest otherwise. Villarreal describes Santa Clara in the 1930s as a small town with many immigrant and first-generation families—Portuguese, Italian, Japanese, Slavic, and some Mexican. It was a diverse society in which ethnic nicknames were common, but which he judged to be fairly democratic and in which he did not feel singled out.

During World War II Villarreal spent over three years as a sailor in the Pacific theater. Upon being mustered out of the service he made use of the G.I. Bill to enroll in the University of California at Berkeley. Determined to become a writer, he selected English as his major and in 1950 earned a B.A. in English literature. Soon after graduation he returned to Santa Clara and began to write *Pocho*. Later he undertook graduate studies at Berkeley and also at the University of California in Los Angeles.

In the 1950s José Antonio Villarreal struggled to get *Pocho* published, traveled and worked throughout the United States, married, began a family, and returned to the San Francisco bay area. While continuing his literary endeavors he took a job as translator and editor for the Stanford Research Institute in Palo Alto. Throughout the 1950s he continued to pursue his goal of becoming a novelist and was constantly revising *Pocho* for publication.

In 1959 he finally succeeded, and *Pocho* was issued by Doubleday. Ahead of its time, it aroused only limited interest and ultimately went out of print. A decade later it came into its own with the rise of the Chicano movement. The 1970 edition became the foremost novel of the Chicano literary renaissance. Broadly autobiographical, it is based on Villarreal's youth and maturation in the Santa Clara Valley during the 1930s and reflects attitudes of that time. Because these 30-year-old views did not always agree with those of many militants in the Chicano movements at the beginning of the 1970s, Villarreal sometimes found himself bitterly attacked by student leaders, professors, and other activists.

Meanwhile, from 1960 to 1968, Villarreal worked as senior technical editor for Lockheed Aircraft Corporation, and at the end of the decade he spent three years as supervisor of technical publications for Ball Brothers Research Corporation in Boulder, Colorado. He visited Mexico, began work on a loose tetralogy of which *Pocho* was to form a part, free-lanced short stories and articles, and became a peripatetic professor. His experience as an editor and writer and the recognition from *Pocho* enabled him to obtain teaching positions at various universities: Colorado at Boulder, Texas at El Paso, Santa Clara in California.

An unfaltering individualist and romantic, in the early 1970s Villarreal decided to move to Mexico permanently with his family and subsequently became a Mexican citizen without giving up his American citizenship. In Mexico he taught at the Universidad Nacional Autónoma Mexicana, the University of the Americas, and the Preparatoria Americana but also continued to teach and lecture at various U.S. institutions such as Pan American University in Edinburg, Texas, and California State University at Los Angeles.

In 1974 Villarreal's second volume of the projected tetralogy, *The Fifth Horseman*, was published by Doubleday. This broad historical novel of epic proportions, which leads up to *Pocho* chronologically, found little favor with literary critics and soon went out of print. It was republished by the Bilingual Press in 1984. In that same year the Press also brought out Villarreal's third novel, *Clemente Chacón*. Its theme is the price of immigrant success, although Villarreal has always argued that success in the United States need not be at the cost of one's *mexicanidad*. Meanwhile he has continued to write essays and short stories as well as some poetry; currently he is at work on the final volume of his tetralogy.

In 1992 José Antonio Villarreal brought his family back to the United States, where he encountered an industrialized Santa Clara that was very different from the bucolic small town of his youth. He and his wife settled in the agreeable rural environment of northern California in the shadow of Mount Shasta near the small town of Weed.

Further Reading

Bruce-Novoa, Juan. *Chicano Authors: Inquiry by Interview*. Austin: University of Texas Press, 1980.

Donnelly, Kathleen. "Native Son." *San Jose Mercury News*, "Living" (1 July 1994).

Jiménez, Francisco. "An Interview with José Antonio Villarreal." *Bilingual Review* 3 (Spring 1976): 66–72.

Lomelí, Francisco A., and Carl R. Shirley, eds. *Dictionary of Literary Biography*, vol. 82. Detroit: Gale Research, 1989.

Martínez, Julio A., and Francisco A. Lomelí, eds. *Chicano Literature: A Reference Guide*. Westport, Conn.: Greenwood Press, 1985.

Villarreal, José Antonio. "Chicano Literature: Art and Politics from the Perspective of the Artist." In *The Identification and Analysis of Chicano Literature*, Francisco Jiménez, ed. New York: Bilingual Press/Editorial Bilingüe, 1979.

RAQUEL WELCH

(1940–)

Bolivian American Actress, Writer, Producer

Raquel Welch is a talented producer and actress who still has a great deal of difficulty living down her early image as a voluptuous sex symbol with minimal acting ability. Early in her theatrical career her sensual beauty was cleverly promoted by the artful publicity of her husband at the time, Patrick Curtis, and later by various film producers. In recent years images of this earlier persona have retarded recognition of her greatly improved acting skills, despite favorable reviews of her Broadway appearance replacing Lauren Bacall in the musical *Woman of the Year*, 1982, and the made-for-television dramas *Right to Die* in 1987 and *Scandal in a Small Town* in the following year.

Raquel Tejada was born in Chicago, Illinois, on 5 September 1940. Her father, Armand Tejada, a mechanical engineer, was an immigrant from Bolivia in South America; her mother, Josephine Hall, was born in the United States. When Raquel was 2 or 3 years old the family moved to La Jolla, a small oceanside community on the northern edge of San Diego. Raquel had an undistinguished scholastic record in the La Jolla public schools and took private ballet lessons. In high school she became active in the drama club and also took her extracurricular role as cheerleader quite seriously. Apparently she had already decided that she wanted a career in films. At age 15 the sultry beauty won her first beauty contest, and in later competitions she was named Miss La Jolla, then Miss San Diego, and finally Maid of California.

With further success in beauty contests but none in landing an acting job, Raquel took a position as weather reporter for a San Diego television station and took acting classes at San Diego State College (today University). In mid-1959 she and Jim Welch, high school sweethearts, were married and soon had two children. However, the marriage turned sour and they divorced in 1964. Meanwhile Raquel went to Texas, where she worked as a cocktail lounge receptionist for a while in Dallas and obtained some modeling jobs; she then returned to California and moved to Hollywood with her children. Here she began making the rounds of the studios and succeeded in obtaining bit parts in a couple of films.

In Hollywood Welch became acquainted with public relations expert Pat Curtis, and subsequently they formed Curtwel Productions with the avowed and sole object of marketing Raquel Welch. After secondary parts in two movies she was signed by Twentieth Century Fox for a principal role in a science fiction film, *Fantastic Voyage,* released in 1966. Her performance as a scientist clad in a skin-diving suit in *Fantastic Voyage* and as a silent cavewoman in a fur bikini in the subsequent made-in-England film, *One Million Years B.C.,* firmly established her as a promising young cinema attraction.

As a result of Curtis's promotion of Welch in the European media as a Hollywood star, Raquel's photographs soon began to appear in numerous European magazines. This publicity was then released in the United States, making her an instant celebrity there too. Within a short time her seductive photos had appeared on the covers of more than 90 European magazines and nearly 20 American journals. On St. Valentine's Day, 14 February 1967, she wed Patrick Curtis in Paris. There followed lead parts in a string of low-budget films by Italian and other European producers; the only one remembered today is a picture based on the Faust legend, *Bedazzled,* in which she played Lilian Lust. Although Welch returned to the United States she also continued to make films in Europe. The best known, but hardly most memorable, of her American films up to that point was *Myra Breckenridge,* 1970, based on Gore Vidal's best-selling novel. In that same year she also appeared in her first television special, produced by Curtwel Productions. Later in the year she and Curtis separated and later divorced. She then organized her own company, Raquel Welch Productions.

Welch continued to accept generally campy roles in Hollywood films in the first half of the 1970s; in 1975 her lead role in *The Four Musketeers* won her a Golden Globe Award for best actress. In the second half of the 1970s she took on fewer roles but still appeared in about one film per year. She also developed a spectacular singing and dancing act, which she performed in various prominent nightclubs, especially at places like Las Vegas. The 1980s brought a crisis to her career. She was dismissed by Metro-Goldwyn-Mayer (MGM) from the cast of John Steinbeck's *Cannery Row* on a charge of unprofessional behavior on the set. She replied with a $20 million lawsuit against MGM, initiating a long legal battle that resulted in a $10.8 million award from the court in 1986. However, the award was subsequently overturned, much to her distress.

Meanwhile, Welch's improved acting ability and more assured stage presence became evident when she was asked to replace Lauren Bacall for two weeks in the Broadway musical *Woman of the Year.* Her performance was eye-opening for the critics, and they were lavish in their praise of her performance. It marked a substantial improvement in her theatrical career. As a result, the elated Welch was later given a six-month contract while Bacall took a much-needed longer rest. In the meantime Welch appeared in a strictly dramatic role as an American

Indian woman in the television motion picture *The Legend of Walks Far Woman*, 1982, which hinted at her dramatic development and added to her growing reputation as a serious actress.

Taking advantage of her continuing beauty and vigor at age 40-something, Welch authored *The Raquel Welch Total Beauty and Fitness Program* in the mid-1980s. It was accompanied by a video and was followed by several physical fitness and home exercise videos that emphasized mental attitudes and relaxation techniques as well as diet and exercise. In 1987 her sensitive performance as a terminally ill woman in the television film *Right to Die* brought plaudits for her acting; later that year she toured Europe promoting her debut there as a singer with her record "This Girl Is Back in Town." The record was a moderate success, although one critic did comment that she was "no Barbra Streisand." In the following year her second television film, *Scandal in a Small Town*, met with even greater critical acclaim than her first, finally bringing her the artistic recognition she had long been seeking. Most recently, in late 1995 she agreed to undertake her first venture in a television series, accepting a leading role in a Columbia Broadcasting System (CBS) nighttime soap, *Central Park West*.

In addition to the Golden Globe Award for Best Actress that she had received earlier, in 1990 Raquel Welch was named Woman of the Year by the Los Angeles Hispanic Women's Council.

Further Reading

"Cover Q & A: Raquel Welch." *Los Angeles Magazine* (January 1985): 18.

Current Biography Yearbook, 1971. New York: H. W. Wilson Co., 1971.

Haining, Peter. *Raquel Welch: Sex Symbol to Super Star.* New York: St. Martin's Press, 1984.

Lewis, Richard L. "The Sudden Stardom of Raquel Welch." *Saturday Evening Post* 240 (18 November 1967): 32–35.

"Movies/High Exposure Route to Stardom." *Life* (26 August 1966): 64.

"Raquel Welch Retrospective Exhibition, 1964–1970." *Esquire* 73:5 (May 1970): 123–139.

"Right to Die." *People* (12 October 1987): 9.

Telgen, Diane, and Jim Kamp, eds. *Notable Hispanic American Women.* Detroit: Gale Research, 1993.

Unterburger, Amy, ed., *Who's Who among Hispanic Americans.* Detroit: Gale Research, 1992.

BERNICE ZAMORA

(1938–)

Mexican American Poet, Writer, Teacher

Bernice Zamora's position as a seminal poet in the Chicano movement is based heavily on *Restless Serpents*, a collection of poems she published while still a graduate student. It has since been translated into Italian, German, Dutch, Chinese, and Spanish. Her poetry is included in the well-known D. C. Heath *Anthology of American Literature*, and her poems have been chosen for inclusion in other anthologies as well. She is also widely known for her short stories, critical essays, and reviews. Her writings, which began to appear in Chicano journals and anthologies at a critical time in the *movimiento*, secured her a highly respected literary position. Lorna Dee Cervantes, another outstanding Chicana poet, has characterized Zamora as possibly the leading Chicana poet today. In addition to her poetry, her other writing, and her presentations at conferences, she has encouraged other Mexican American writers to practice their craft and is an inspiration and mentor to many of them.

Bernice Ortiz was born on 20 January 1938 in Aguilar, a small farming community on the Apishapa River in sparsely settled south central Colorado, near the border with New Mexico. She was the first of five children born to Marcella Valdez and Victor Ortiz; her father earned his living as a farmer and as a miner in the Allen Coal Mines near Trinidad. The families of both her parents had settled in the area generations earlier while it was still a part of Spain's empire. When Bernice was 6 years old the family moved from Valdez, Colorado, where she spent her early youth, to Denver, where she lived for the next six years; however, she continued to spend summer vacations with relatives in Aguilar.

Although Bernice spoke Spanish with her grandparents and some older relatives, the language at home was primarily English. A precocious child, she learned to read from cereal boxes and other advertising material before she entered first grade. Her primary education was in the parochial schools: St. Dominic's in Denver and St. Leander's in Pueblo, Colorado, where the family moved when she was 12 years old. Largely because of family finances she attended public, rather than parochial, high school after the primary grades.

Her formal education was almost completely English-based, and Bernice learned to read and write Spanish only later. While growing up, she was forbidden by her father to read at home. As a youth she showed a high level of interest in school and studies. In high school she gave evidence of some artistic ability and demonstrated great interest and skill in writing, winning the $10 first prize in an essay contest. Obliged to go to work while a junior in high school, she got a job with hours from 4 o'clock to midnight and was able to complete four years. After her graduation she married at age 19, went to work in a bank in Pueblo, and continued her education through evening classes and by reading widely and voraciously on her own.

When Bernice Zamora was 28 years old, married and with two daughters, she decided to further broaden her horizons by enrolling in college. She began her undergraduate studies at Southern Colorado State College (now University) in Pueblo, majored in English with a minor in French, and earned her B.A. in three years. Upon graduating in 1969 from Southern Colorado she began graduate studies in French literature and English at Colorado State University in Fort Collins, north of Denver, receiving her M.A. there in 1972. While a graduate student, she won first prize in a short story contest at the university. From Fort Collins she entered a Ph.D. program at Marquette University in Milwaukee as a result of recommendations by one of her professors.

In the early 1970s Zamora's marriage began to falter; after a year at Marquette she temporarily abandoned her studies for the doctorate. A year later she moved to California with her daughters and reinitiated her Ph.D. studies in English and American literature at Stanford University. While a graduate student at Stanford she organized small monthly social gatherings of young Chicano writers and poets at which they read and discussed their works. During this time she also wrote numerous poems, short stories, and essays of literary criticism, which she published in various Chicano journals. She also taught part-time at the University of California in Berkeley, at the University of San Francisco, and at Stanford.

To fill a conspicuous need for texts in Chicano culture and literature classes, in 1976 Zamora joined with José Antonio Burciaga of Stanford to publish *Restless Serpents*, a collection of their poetry. It aroused widespread interest. In the following year she was asked to be guest editor for the summer issue of *El Fuego de Aztlán*, a Chicano literary journal. In December 1979 Zamora again interrupted her doctoral studies, accepted a position as editor of the Chicano journal *De Colores*, and moved to Albuquerque. There she also edited (with José Armas, one of the early Chicano publishers) an anthology of poetry, oral history, and short stories as well as a collection of selected works that had come out of the 1970s Chicano literary festivals called Flor y Canto. The latter compilation, published by Pajarito Publications in 1980, was titled *Flor y Canto IV and V: An Anthology of Chicano Literature*.

After a sojourn in Texas, Zamora returned to California and to Stanford University in 1982. Four years later she received her doctorate; her dissertation was titled "Mythopoeia of Chicano Poetry: An Introduction to Cultural Archetypes." In 1990, having been recruited by **Dr. Francisco Jiménez**, she accepted her current position in the English department of Santa Clara University, where she teaches courses in world literature as well as in Chicano, Native American, and contemporary American literature.

In January 1994 Zamora's latest collection of poems, old and new, was published by the Bilingual Press/Editorial Bilingüe under the title *Releasing Serpents*. In the past few years she also has published various articles in international journals; one of them, "Against Extinction: The Native American and Chicano Literary Discourse," was published in June 1996 by SUNY (State University of New York) Press in a literary collection titled *Cross-Addressing: Resistance Literature and Cultural Borders*, edited by John Hawley. Her current long-term creative writing projects include a play, a novel, and a book on La Malinche, the 16th-century Aztec mistress of Hernán Cortés, conqueror of Mexico.

Influenced by poets ranging from William Shakespeare to Emily Dickinson, from Rubén Darío to Pablo Neruda, Bernice Zamora carefully crafts her poems. In interviews she has said that writing poetry comes easily for her. She has several times stated that she feels urged, even compelled, to write verse. "I strongly need to write poetry.... [O]ne poem a day is the normal pace.... If I don't write a poem I get really restless; ... I write a poem in order to sleep."

Like dramatist **Estela Portillo Trambley** and other Latina feminists, Zamora explores topics such as the influence of Mexican customs and traditions on southwestern culture and describes the experiences of women within that culture. Although she concerns herself with and supports women's issues, she does not consider herself a feminist poet. Basically her concern is for women, but in her poems she expresses indignation and censure at all oppression and exploitation in its varied forms. Her poetry manifests concern, outrage, and protest but is not vociferously political; she is interested both in creating a poetic image and in presenting a social narrative. Thus her poetry provides a useful bridge between Chicano and universal literature.

Further Reading

Binder, Wolfgang, ed. *Partial Autobiographies: Interviews with Twenty Chicano Poets.* Erlangen, West Germany: Verlag Palm & Enke, 1985.

Bruce-Novoa, Juan. "Bernice Zamora and Lorna Dee Cervantes: Una estética feminista." *Revista Iberoamericana* 51 (July–December 1985): 565–573.

———. *Chicano Authors: Inquiry by Interview.* Austin: University of Texas Press, 1980.

Desai, Parul. "Interview with Bernice Zamora, a Chicana Poet." *Imagine* 2:1 (Summer 1985): 26–39.

Magill, Frank N. *Masterpieces of Latino Literature.* New York: HarperCollins, 1994.

Sánchez, Marta E. *Contemporary Chicano Poetry: A Critical Approach to an Emerging Literature.* Berkeley: University of California Press, 1985.

Vogeley, Nancy. "Bernice Zamora." In *Dictionary of Literary Biography*, Chicano Writers: First Series, vol. 82. Detroit: Gale Research, 1989.

CARMEN ZAPATA

(1927–   )

Mexican American Actress, Producer, Director, Social Activist

Probably best known for her role in the PBS bilingual children's program *Villa Alegre*, Carmen Zapata is also important as a co-founder and director of the Bilingual Foundation for the Arts in Los Angeles. During a highly successful artistic career that has spanned almost 50 years, she has been active in nearly every aspect of the acting profession and also found time to teach and to take an active part in the Chicano movement of the 1960s and 1970s.

Carmen Margarita Zapata was born in New York City on 15 July 1927, one of three daughters born to Ramona Roca, an immigrant from Argentina in South America, and Julio Zapata from Mexico. She grew up in Spanish Harlem, where she began her early education. Accustomed only to Spanish, the language of home and family, she found her first days in the English-speaking environment of school traumatic in the extreme. As her trauma subsided she felt driven to speak English as grammatically correct and as fluently as she could. Ultimately this compulsion helped lead to her career in the theater.

Carmen's artistic bent and talents were evident early in her life. As a very young child she learned to play the violin and the piano at home and participated in family musical evenings with her parents and sisters. At school she sang in the choir and took part in class plays. Although her mother had some reservations about a career on the stage for her daughter, she made considerable sacrifices to develop Carmen's artistic talents by providing her with dancing and singing lessons.

After high school Carmen studied at Actors Studio and later worked with the well-known actress and drama coach Uta Hagen. Her first theatrical job was in the (today almost legendary) 1940s Broadway musical *Oklahoma* as a member of the chorus. When *Oklahoma* went on a road tour, she moved up to one of the supporting roles. Returning to New York from the tour, she was fortunate to secure a lead part in the highly successful musical *Stop the World. I Want to Get Off* and subsequently played in many other Broadway productions, including *Bells Are Ringing,* 1956, and *Guys and Dolls,* 1957. Between parts in Broadway plays she developed a singing and comedy act, which she did in East Side nightclubs under the stage name Marge Cameron. After 20 years in Broadway musicals her selection in 1966 as one of the principals in the musical *Pousse-Cafe,* by the famous composer and band leader Duke Ellington, seemed to guarantee her place in the theater. Unfortunately for her, *Pousse-Cafe* folded after only two weeks on Broadway despite Ellington's outstanding musical reputation.

As a result of this Broadway mishap, her mother's death less than a year later, and divorce after five years of marriage, Zapata, having spent two decades on Broadway, decided to try a move to the West Coast. She found roles for Latinas to be less than plentiful in Hollywood and was constantly confronted by the specter of stereotyping. Nevertheless, she obtained parts in various films in the late 1960s and in the 1970s, including *Pete and Tillie* in 1972. Her most recent role, 20 years later, was as one of the nuns in *Sister Act,* starring Whoopi Goldberg. Although she has had a career of more than a quarter of a century in films, generally she has found television to be a more rewarding field for her talents. She appeared in various popular series during the 1960s and 1970s, was a frequent guest on *The Dick Van Dyke Show,* and for three years played the part of Carmen Castillo in the daytime soap *Santa Barbara*. Most important, in her role as Doña Luz she was, for nine years, the heart and soul of the Public Broadcasting System's bilingual program, *Villa Alegre.*

In Los Angeles Zapata became acutely aware of the large Spanish-speaking population as a potential audience. This realization led her to establish her own theater company in 1973, putting on plays in both Spanish and English in addition to continuing her extensive film and television work. The next logical step was her role as co-founder of the Bilingual Foundation of the Arts (BFA) to provide the public of greater Los Angeles with the opportunity to experience Latino culture and theater in both Spanish and English. She subsequently continued to play a leading role in the nonprofit organization as its director and highly acclaimed managing producer. In addition to these diverse artistic endeavors, she took on a labor of love, introducing the outstanding works of Latino dramatists to the students of the Los Angeles school system. For a while she taught drama at East Los Angeles College and despite her busy life has taken courses at the University of California at Los Angeles and New York University.

For five decades Carmen Zapata has had a successful career as actress, lecturer, translator, and producer. She has been acclaimed by reviewers and critics as the first lady of the Latino theater and has also been praised in the Latino community for her active participation and leadership in various Chicano organizations. In addition to the kudos she has received in connection with the BFA, she has been singled out for many prestigious acting and other awards. She has had three Emmy nominations. For her leadership and many achievements she was also one of a select group of greater Los Angeles women honored in 1981 by the Young Women's Christian Association with the Silver Achievement Award. Two years later she was given the Women in Film Humanitarian Award; the Rubén Salazar Award by the National Council of La Raza; and the Achievement in the Arts Award by the Mexican American Legal Defense and Education Fund (MALDEF). In 1985 she was named Woman of the Year by the Hispanic Women's Council and during the next year was recipient of the Best Translation Award from the journal *Dramalogue*. In 1991 she was knighted by King Juan Carlos I of Spain.

Further Reading

"Carmen Zapata." *Nuestro* 2:7 (July 1978): 13–14.

Hadley-García, George. *Hollywood Hispano: Los latinos en el mundo del cine*. Secaucus, N.J.: Carol Publishing Group, 1991.

Kanellos, Nicolás, ed. *The Hispanic American Almanac*. Detroit: Gale Research, 1993.

Peck, Stacey. "Home Q & A: Carmen Zapata." *Los Angeles Times* (18 October 1979).

Ragua, David. *Who's Who in Hollywood, 1900–1976*. New Rochelle, N.Y.: Arlington House, 1976.

Appendix A: Fields of Professional Activity

Professions are listed under the following categories:

Actor

Artist

Business leader

Community leader

Composer/songwriter

Conductor

Dancer

Diplomat

Educational administrator

Educator

Engineer

Essayist

Folk hero

Folklorist

Government administrator

Health professional

Journalist

Labor activist

Lawyer

Literary critic

Military leader

Musician

Novelist

Philanthropist

Playwright

Poet

Political activist

Politician

Producer/director

Religious leader

Scientist

Short story writer

Singer

Social activist

Sports figure

Individuals who excel in more than one field will be listed under each relevant field of endeavor.

ACTOR
Desi Arnaz
Rubén Blades
Imogene Coca
Xavier Cugat
José Ferrer
Rita Hayworth
José Iturbi
Raúl Julia
Ricardo Montalbán
Rita Moreno
Edward James Olmos
Dolores Prida
Anthony Quinn
Chita Rivera
Gilbert Roland
César Romero
Martin Sheen
Luis Valdez
Raquel Welch
Carmen Zapata

ARTIST
Alfredo Arreguín
Oscar de la Renta
Chelo (Consuelo) González Amezcua
Marisol (Escobar)
Nicholasa Mohr
Anthony Quinn
Arnaldo Roche-Rabell

BUSINESS LEADER
Desi Arnaz
Elfego Baca
Romana Acosta Bañuelos
Casimiro Barela
Samuel Betances
Henry Cisneros
Margarita Colmenares
Oscar de la Renta
Luis Ferré
Roberto Goizueta
Jorge Mas Canosa
Esteban Ochoa
Miguel Antonio Otero Jr.
Ileana Ros-Lehtinen
Roberto Suárez
María Elena Toraño-Pantín

COMMUNITY LEADER
Ramona Acosta Bañuelos
Héctor Pérez García
Corky (Rodolfo) Gonzales
Henry Barbosa González
José Angel Gutiérrez
Dolores Huerta
Antonio José Martínez
Jorge Mas Canosa
Gloria Molina
Julian Nava
Esteban Ochoa
Felisa Rincón de Gautier
George I. Sánchez
Juan Seguín
Reies López Tijerina
Nydia Velázquez

COMPOSER/SONGWRITER
Joan Báez
Rubén Blades
Mariah Carey
Pablo Casals
Xavier Cugat
Gloria Estefan

José Feliciano
Lydia Mendoza
Tito Puente

CONDUCTOR
Pablo Casals
Xavier Cugat
Plácido Domingo
José Iturbi
Tito (Ernest Anthony) Puente

DANCER
Fernando Bujones
Rita Hayworth
José Arcadio Limón
Rita Moreno
Chita Rivera

DIPLOMAT
Héctor Pérez García
Marí-Luci Jaramillo
Julian Nava

EDUCATIONAL ADMINISTRATOR
Lauro Cavazos Jr.
Linda Chávez
Margarita Colmenares
Rolando Hinojosa-Smith
Marí-Luci Jaramillo
Francisco Jiménez
Antonio José Martínez
Julian Nava
Eduardo Padrón
Tomás Rivera

EDUCATOR
Samuel Betances
Lydia Cabrera
Arthur León Campa
Carlos Castañeda

Lauro Cavazos Jr.
Jaime Escalante
Ernesto Galarza
Cristina García
Fabiola Cabeza de Baca Gilbert
José Angel Gutiérrez
Rolando Hinojosa-Smith
Marí-Luci Jaramillo
Francisco Jiménez
Harold Medina
Julian Nava
Severo Ochoa
Eduardo Padrón
Américo Paredes
Estela Portillo Trambley
Tomás Rivera
Ileana Ros-Lehtinen
Edward Roybal
George I. Sánchez
Luis Rafael Sánchez
George Santayana
Emma Tenayuca
Nydia Velázquez
José Antonio Villarreal
Bernice Zamora

ENGINEER
Margarita Colmenares
Luis Ferré
Ellen Ochoa

ESSAYIST
Reinaldo Arenas
Lydia Cabrera
Ernesto Galarza
José Martí
Luis Muñoz Marín
Richard Rodríguez
Ileana Ros-Lehtinen

Luis Rafael Sánchez
George Santayana
Piri (John Peter) Thomas

FOLK HERO
Elfego Baca
Gregorio Cortez
Juan Cortina
Joaquín Murieta
Juan Seguín
Teresa Urrea

FOLKLORIST
Lydia Cabrera
Arthur León Campa
Fabiola Cabeza de Baca Gilbert
Américo Paredes

GOVERNMENT ADMINISTRATOR
Herman Badillo
Romana Acosta Bañuelos
Casimiro Barela
Lauro Cavazos Jr.
Linda Chávez
Henry Cisneros
David Glasgow Farragut
José Angel Gutiérrez
Marí-Luci Jaramillo
Gloria Molina
Luis Muñoz Marín
Julian Nava
Antonia Novello
Miguel Antonio Otero Jr.
Felisa Rincón de Gautier
María Elena Toraño-Pantín

HEALTH PROFESSIONAL
Lauro Cavazos Jr.
Héctor Pérez García
Fabiola Cabeza de Baca Gilbert

Antonia Novello
Severo Ochoa
Edward Roybal
Teresa Urrea

JOURNALIST
Julia de Burgos
Cristina García
José Martí
Luis Muñoz Marín
Dolores Prida
Geraldo Rivera
Richard Rodríguez
Rubén Salazar
Roberto Suárez

LABOR ACTIVIST
César Chávez
Ernesto Galarza
Dolores Fernandez Huerta
Emma Tenayuca

LAWYER
Elfego Baca
Herman Badillo
Rubén Blades
Dennis Chávez
Lincoln Díaz-Balart
Vilma Socorro Martínez
Harold Medina
Geraldo Rivera
Edwin Torres

LITERARY CRITIC
Rolando Hinojosa-Smith
Francisco Jiménez
Tomás Rivera

MILITARY LEADER
David Glasgow Farragut

Juan Seguín

MUSICIAN

Desi Arnaz
Rubén Blades
Pablo Casals
Xavier Cugat
José Feliciano
José Iturbi
Lydia Mendoza
Tito (Ernest Anthony) Puente

NOVELIST

Reinaldo Arenas
Sandra Cisneros
Cristina García
Oscar Hijuelos
Rolando Hinojosa-Smith
Nicholasa Mohr
Tomás Rivera
Luis Rafael Sánchez
George Santayana
Piri (John Peter) Thomas
Edwin Torres
José Antonio Villarreal

PHILANTHROPIST

Vikki Carr
Luis Ferré
Chi Chi (Juan) Rodríguez
Lee Treviño

PLAYWRIGHT

Reinaldo Arenas
María Fornés
Estela Portillo Trambley
Dolores Prida
Luis Rafael Sánchez
Luis Valdez

POET

Reinaldo Arenas
Julia de Burgos
Lourdes Casal
Sandra Cisneros
Chelo (Consuelo) González Amezcua
José Martí
Dolores Prida
George Santayana
Piri (John Peter) Thomas
Bernice Zamora

POLITICAL ACTIVIST

Rubén Blades
Julia de Burgos
Lourdes Casal
Lincoln Díaz-Balart
José Angel Gutiérrez
José Martí
Jorge Mas Canosa
Gloria Molina
Julian Nava
Felisa Rincón de Gautier
Reies López Tijerina

POLITICIAN

Herman Badillo
Casimiro Barela
Dennis Chávez
Linda Chávez
Henry Cisneros
Juan Cortina
Lincoln Díaz-Balart
Luis Ferré
Henry Barbosa González
Jorge Mas Canosa
Gloria Molina
Luis Muñoz Marín
Miguel A. Otero Jr.

Felisa Rincón de Gautier
Ileana Ros-Lehtinen
Edward Roybal
Juan Seguín
Nydia Velázquez

PRODUCER/DIRECTOR
Desi Arnaz
Plácido Domingo
José Ferrer
María Fornés
Edward James Olmos
Geraldo Rivera
Luis Valdez
Raquel Welch
Carmen Zapata

RELIGIOUS LEADER
Patrick Flores
Antonio José Martínez

SCIENTIST
Luis W. Alvarez
Margarita Colmenares
Ellen Ochoa
Severo Ochoa

SHORT STORY WRITER
Reinaldo Arenas
Lydia Cabrera
Lourdes Casal
Sandra Cisneros
Oscar Hijuelos
Francisco Jiménez
Tomás Rivera
Luis Rafael Sánchez

SINGER
Desi Arnaz
Joan Báez
Rubén Blades

Mariah Carey
Vikki Carr
Celia Cruz
Justino Díaz
Plácido Domingo
Gloria Estefan
José Feliciano
Lydia Mendoza
Rita Moreno
Tito (Ernest Anthony) Puente
Chita Rivera
Linda Ronstadt

SOCIAL ACTIVIST
Joan Báez
Julia de Burgos
Lourdes Casal
César Chávez
Luis Ferré
Patrick Flores
Ernesto Galarza
Héctor Pérez García
Corky (Rodolfo) Gonzales
José Angel Gutiérrez
Dolores Fernández Huerta
Vilma Socorro Martínez
Gloria Molina
Ricardo Montalbán
Martin Sheen
Emma Tenayuca
Piri (John Peter) Thomas
Reies López Tijerina
María Elena Toraño-Pantín
Luis Valdez
Carmen Zapata

SPORTS FIGURE
José Canseco
Roberto Clemente Walker

Gigi (Beatriz) Fernández

Mary Joe Fernández

Rudy (Valentin Joseph) Galindo

Corky (Rodolfo) Gonzales

Pancho (Richard Alonzo) Gonzales

Nancy López

Chi Chi (Juan) Rodríguez

Lee Treviño

Appendix B: Ethnic Subgroups

CUBAN AMERICANS

Reinaldo Arenas
Desi Arnaz
Fernando Bujones
Lydia Cabrera
José Canseco
Lourdes Casal
Celia Cruz
Lincoln Díaz-Balart
Gloria Estefan
María Fornés
Cristina García
Roberto Goizueta
Oscar Hijuelos
José Martí
Jorge Mas Canosa
Eduardo Padrón
Dolores Prida
César Romero
Ileana Ros-Lehtinen
Roberto Suárez
María Elena Toraño-Pantín

MEXICAN AMERICANS

Alfredo Arreguín
Elfego Baca
Joan Báez
Romana Acosta Bañuelos
Casimiro Barela
Arthur León Campa
Vikki Carr
Carlos Castañeda
Lauro Cavazos Jr.
César Chávez
Dennis Chávez
Linda Chávez
Henry Cisneros
Sandra Cisneros
Margarita Colmenares
Gregorio Cortez
Juan Cortina

Patrick Flores

Ernesto Galarza

Rudy (Valentin Joseph) Galindo

Héctor Pérez García

Fabiola Cabeza de Baca Gilbert

Corky (Roldolfo) Gonzales

Pancho (Richard Alonzo) Gonzales

Henry Barbosa González

Chelo (Consuelo) González Amezcua

José Angel Gutiérrez

Rolando Hinojosa-Smith

Dolores Fernández Huerta

Marí-Luci Jaramillo

Francisco Jiménez

José Arcadio Limón

Nancy López

Antonio José Martínez

Vilma Socorro Martínez

Harold Medina

Lydia Mendoza

Gloria Molina

Ricardo Montalbán

Joaquín Murieta

Julian Nava

Ellen Ochoa

Esteban Ochoa

Edward James Olmos

Miguel Antonio Otero Jr.

Américo Paredes

Estela Portillo Trambley

Anthony Quinn

Tomás Rivera

Richard Rodríguez

Gilbert Roland

Linda Ronstadt

Edward Roybal

Rubén Salazar

George I. Sánchez

Juan Seguín

Emma Tenayuca

Reies López Tijerina

Lee Treviño

Teresa Urrea

Luis Valdez

José Antonio Villarreal

Bernice Zamora

Carmen Zapata

PUERTO RICANS

Herman Badillo

Samuel Betances

Julia de Burgos

Roberto Clemente Walker

Justino Díaz

José Feliciano

Gigi (Béatriz) Fernández

Luis Ferré

José Ferrer

Raúl Julia

Nicholasa Mohr

Rita Moreno

Luis Muñoz Marín

Antonia Novello

Tito Puente

Felisa Rincón de Gautier

Chita Rivera

Geraldo Rivera

Arnaldo Roche-Rabell

Chi Chi (Juan) Rodríguez

Luis Rafael Sánchez

Piri (John Peter) Thomas

Edwin Torres

Nydia Velázquez

OTHER LATINOS

Luis W. Alvarez

Rubén Blades

Mariah Carey

Pablo Casals

Imogene Coca

Xavier Cugat

Oscar de la Renta

Plácido Domingo

Jaime Escalante

David Glasgow Farragut

Mary Joe Fernández

Rita Hayworth

José Iturbi

Marisol (Escobar)

Severo Ochoa

George Santayana

Martin Sheen

Raquel Welch

Index

Page numbers in **bold** refer to main entries.

MATT S. MEIER is Patrick A. Donohoe, S.J. Professor Emeritus at Santa Clara University in California. A pioneer in researching and teaching the history of Mexican Americans, he is author of *Mexican American Biographies* (Greenwood, 1988), the update of Carey McWilliams's *North from Mexico* (1990), and *Bibliography of Mexican American History* (Greenwood, 1984), and coauthor with F. Rivera of *Dictionary of Mexican American History* (Greenwood, 1981; an ALA Outstanding Reference Book of 1982), *Mexican Americans/American Mexicans* (1993), *Readings on La Raza* (1974), and *Chicanos: A History of Mexican Americans* (1972). In 1985 he received Santa Clara University's Ethnic Studies Distinguished Service Award.

CONCHITA FRANCO SERRI, J.D., is director of Affirmative Action at Santa Clara University. Born in San Juan, she earned her undergraduate degree in psychology at the University of Puerto Rico. She then came to the mainland to obtain her M.A. in education at Harvard University and for her law degree went to Boston College, where she wrote for the *Uniform Commercial Code Reporter-Digest* and was editor of the law school's *Third World Law Journal*. She is actively involved in children's education and research.

RICHARD A. GARCIA is Professor of Ethnic Studies at California State University, Hayward. He is an American cultural and intellectual historian who specializes in ethnic and cultural studies. He is author of *Rise of the Mexican American Middle Class: San Antonio, 1929–1941* (1991) and coauthor with Richard Griswold del Castillo of *César Chávez: A Triumph of Spirit* (1995).